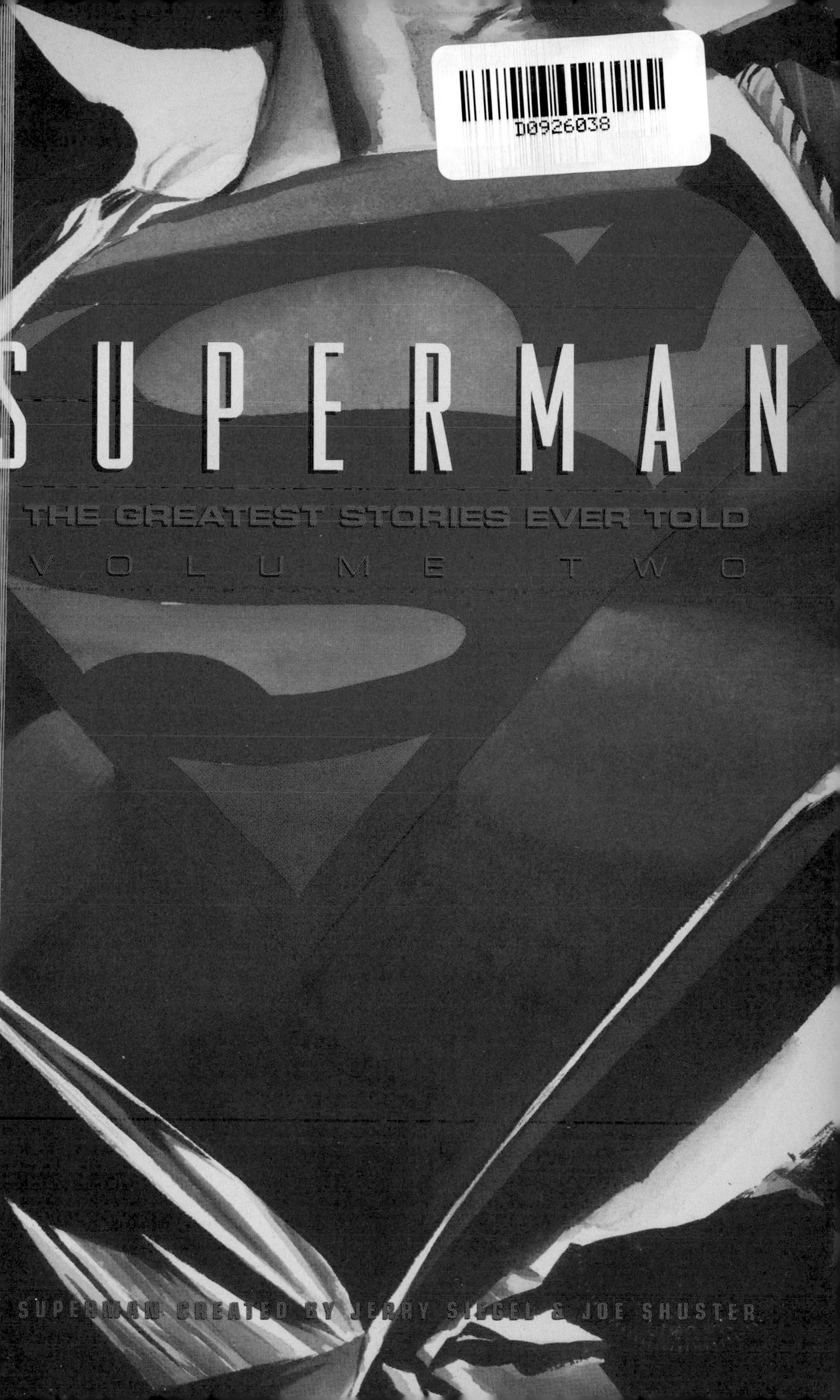

SUPERMAN

THE GREATEST STORIES EVER TOLD

VOLUME TWO

SUPERMAN CREATED BY JERRY SIEGEL & JOE SHUSTER

Dan DiDio   Senior VP-Executive Editor

Anton Kawasaki   Editor-collected edition

Robbin Brosterman   Senior Art Director

Paul Levitz   President & Publisher

Georg Brewer   VP-Design & DC Direct Creative

Richard Bruning   Senior VP-Creative Director

Patrick Caldon   Executive VP-Finance & Operations

Chris Caramalis   VP-Finance

John Cunningham   VP-Marketing

Terri Cunningham   VP-Managing Editor

Stephanie Fierman   Senior VP-Sales & Marketing

Alison Gill   VP-Manufacturing

Hank Kanalz   VP-General Manager, WildStorm

Jim Lee   Editorial Director-WildStorm

Paula Lowitt   Senior VP-Business & Legal Affairs

MaryEllen McLaughlin   VP-Advertising & Custom Publishing

John Nee   VP-Business Development

Gregory Noveck   Senior VP-Creative Affairs

Cheryl Rubin   Senior VP-Brand Management

Jeff Trojan   VP-Business Development, DC Direct

Bob Wayne   VP-Sales

1/2007 Genfund 20⁰⁰

SUPERMAN: THE GREATEST STORIES EVER TOLD
VOLUME TWO. Published by DC Comics. Cover, compilation
and introduction copyright © 2006 DC Comics. All Rights
Reserved. Originally published in single magazine form in
SUPERMAN (first series) #30, 132, 141, 167, 233, 400,
SUPERMAN (second series) #2, and ADVENTURES OF
SUPERMAN #500, 638. Copyright 1944, © 1959, 1960, 1964,
1971, 1984, 1987, 1993, 2005 DC Comics. All Rights
Reserved. All characters, their distinctive likenesses and
related elements featured in this publication are trademarks
of DC Comics. The stories, characters and incidents featured in
this publication are entirely fictional. DC Comics does not
read or accept unsolicited submissions of ideas, stories
or artwork.

DC Comics, 1700 Broadway, New York, NY 10019.
A Warner Bros. Entertainment Company.
Printed in Canada. First Printing.
ISBN: 1-4012-0956-4. ISBN 13: 978-1-4012-0956-8.
Interior color reconstruction by Jamison.
Cover by Alex Ross

CONTENTS

INTRODUCTION

BY ROBERT GREENBERGER

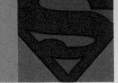

When Jerry Siegel and Joe Shuster created him, Superman was a character that existed to fill a void in their lives. It was during the Depression and the two teenagers were your typical ostracized kids. They didn't interact well with others, preferring the escape offered by the pulp magazines and comic strips. Both wanted something better for themselves and for the people they cared about.

Their earliest Superman exploits showed a costumed social worker taking on the common, everyday problems of the working man. He traveled in and about Metropolis coming to the aid of construction workers and abused wives, cracking wise and taking no guff from the oppressors.

People responded to his exploits because he was exactly what they needed when they needed him most.

Times changed and as World War II began to wind down, Superman's stories shucked the Depression-era feel and saboteurs had become old hat. He needed new challenges to match his ever-expanding array of powers and abilities that set him apart from mortal man.

Editor Jack Schiff recognized the need to vary the stories, and one day he bought a story from Siegel that featured an imp. He had a name that was nearly impossible to pronounce (Mix-yizt-pulk), and his size belied the great powers he wielded. This was something new for the Metropolis Marvel, and readers seemed to delight in it since the Fifth Dimension's best-known citizen returned throughout the 1940s to bedevil Superman and his friends.

It should be noted that an earlier comic strip storyline featured a similar story by Whitney Ellsworth and Siegel-shop artist Wayne Boring. Siegel claimed all along that his story purchased first but scheduled to run later.

The magical menace remained a staple ever since, and writers continue to delight in his shenanigans as witness the last story in this collection, "Narrative Interruptus Tertiarius."

America continued to change, and that change occurred rapidly as the country moved quickly from war to peace and amazing prosperity. As a result, expectations for children's entertainment, to which comic books had been quickly consigned, altered so the stories could no longer overly thrill them. Superman's challenges became tricks and clever traps; each eight-page story in SUPERMAN, ACTION COMICS and WORLD'S FINEST COMICS meant that Superman used his mighty mind to outthink and get one up over crooks, evil scientists and Mother Nature herself.

The 1950s also gave America *The Adventures of Superman* TV show which prevented the comic books from altering the status quo so as not to alienate viewers who turned to the comic books between episodes. Once the show went off the air, Mort Weisinger was no longer so constrained, and the late 1950s marked an incredibly fertile period for Superman and his expanding cast of characters. New and powerful villains were introduced, from Brainiac to the Parasite. Stories now continued from month to month or took over the entire issue.

And then there were the imaginary stories.

Weisinger began a series of "what if" tales that showed the road not taken. It brought out some of the best in the writers, notably science fiction master Otto Binder. His story

"Superman's Other Life" is one of the early explorations of an adult Kal-El still living on a Krypton that did not explode. A year later, Siegel outdid him with the emotional "Superman's Return to Krypton."

As the 1950s gave way to the 1960s, much of the Superman mythos had been set and it was time to see what variations could be brought to the mix. If Luthor or Brainiac could pose a deadly challenge, what might happen if they teamed up against the Man of Tomorrow? Edmond Hamilton's "The Team of Luthor and Brainiac" showed that first combination, but credit should be given to then-fan Cary Bates who deluged editors with cover sketches along with his fan letters. Weisinger bought the cover sketch that inspired the story.

America endured something of an identity crisis in the late 1960s, reeling from President Kennedy's assassination and the disillusionment of the Vietnam war. And Superman seemed at a bit of a loss, too. Weisinger retired and Julius Schwartz, then seen as DC's fixit editor, was given the Man of Steel to modernize. Gone was Kryptonite, the blue business suit and the Daily Planet as Schwartz tried to find ways to freshen the character. The Superman of writer Denny O'Neil, who lasted just a year on the character, reflected the Vietnam-era United States,

cocky and seemingly invincible at the start but weaker and humbled in the end.

Those changes merited media attention, but the fans were appalled and sales did not reward the fresh approach. Schwartz slowly restored the Weisinger status quo until 1986.

To celebrate DC Comics' 50th anniversary, and recognizing that the fans were jaded concerning the icon that served as the template for all costumed crimefighters, the company undertook to recreate Superman. Under the creative direction of writer/artist John Byrne, aided and abetted by Marv Wolfman and Jerry Ordway, the legend was pared back to the essential elements. This time, Superman struggled against powerful foes, his cape regularly shredded to show the effort expended. "The Secret Revealed" shows new depths of depravity for Luthor, now a ruthless but brilliant scientist turned business tycoon. His torture of Lana Lang and refusal to accept a computer's analysis that Superman masqueraded as Clark Kent clearly demonstrated his mindset for a new audience.

This version has essentially remained the guiding one that has passed from one set of creative hands to another. To shake things up and demonstrate his importance to the world, Superman was killed and removed from the world

stage in 1992. Certainly, he was going to get better, but it was the journey back that had readers engaged. "Life After Death" was a turning pointing of that particular saga, exemplifying the enduring bond between father and son.

But not every Superman tale reflects the era; some are just variations on the super-hero theme which provide broad opportunities for interpretation and reflection as seen in "Legend of Earth Prime."

As long as there are readers, there will be storytellers. And as long as people need stories, there will remain larger-than-life characters to fulfill that thirst for entertainment and enlightenment. Superman, the premier American folk hero, will therefore continue his never-ending battle for truth and justice. We need that. If you think you don't, just turn the page.

Robert Greenberger
2006

Robert Greenberger is a former DC Comics editor and administrator now serving as Production Manager at *Weekly World News*. He continues to write about comics history.

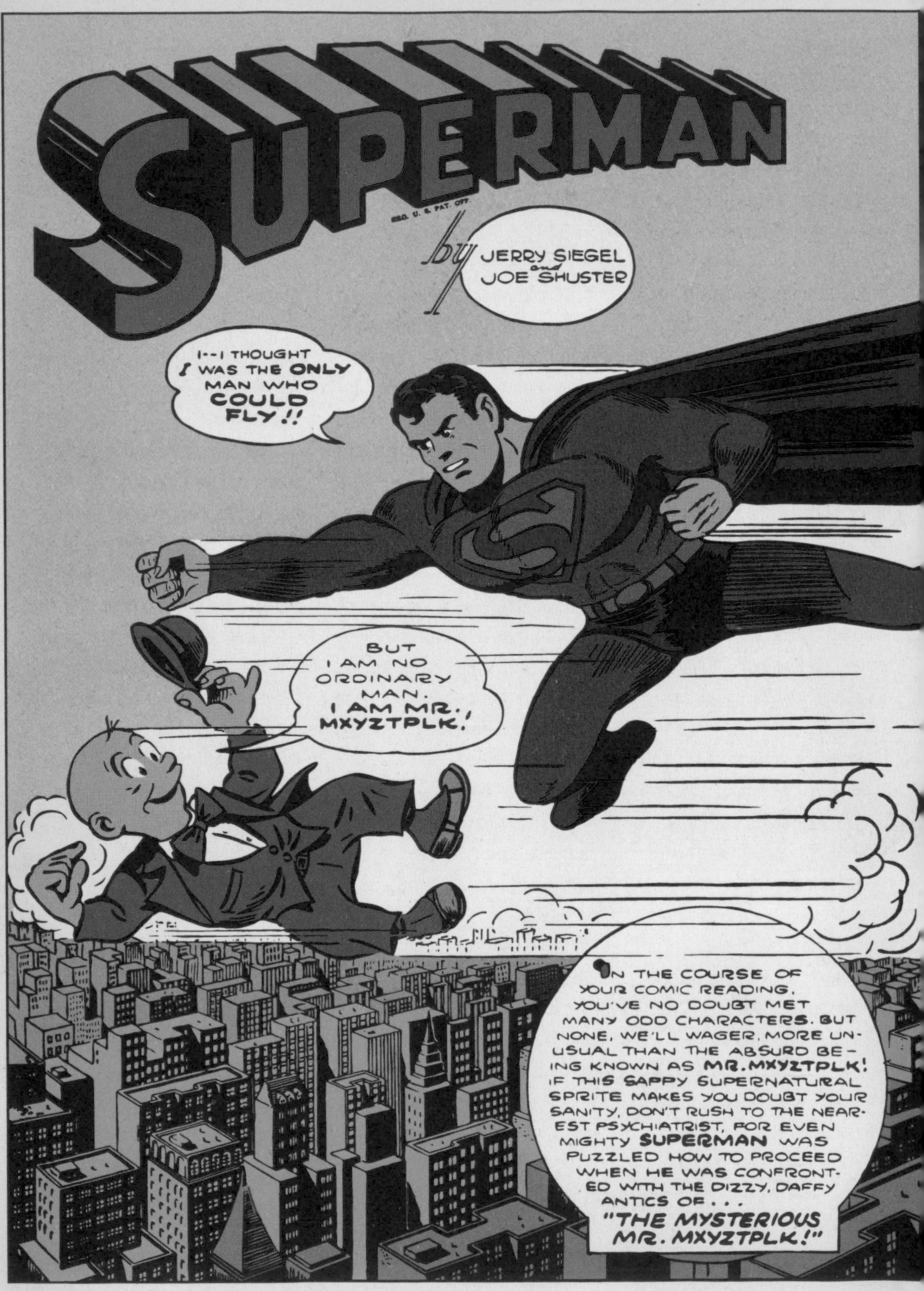
SUPERMAN
REG. U. S. PAT. OFF.
by JERRY SIEGEL and JOE SHUSTER
I--I THOUGHT I WAS THE ONLY MAN WHO COULD FLY!!
BUT I AM NO ORDINARY MAN. I AM MR. MXYZTPLK!
IN THE COURSE OF YOUR COMIC READING, YOU'VE NO DOUBT MET MANY ODD CHARACTERS. BUT NONE, WE'LL WAGER, MORE UNUSUAL THAN THE ABSURD BEING KNOWN AS MR. MXYZTPLK! IF THIS SAPPY SUPERNATURAL SPRITE MAKES YOU DOUBT YOUR SANITY, DON'T RUSH TO THE NEAREST PSYCHIATRIST, FOR EVEN MIGHTY SUPERMAN WAS PUZZLED HOW TO PROCEED WHEN HE WAS CONFRONTED WITH THE DIZZY, DAFFY ANTICS OF . . .
"THE MYSTERIOUS MR. MXYZTPLK!"

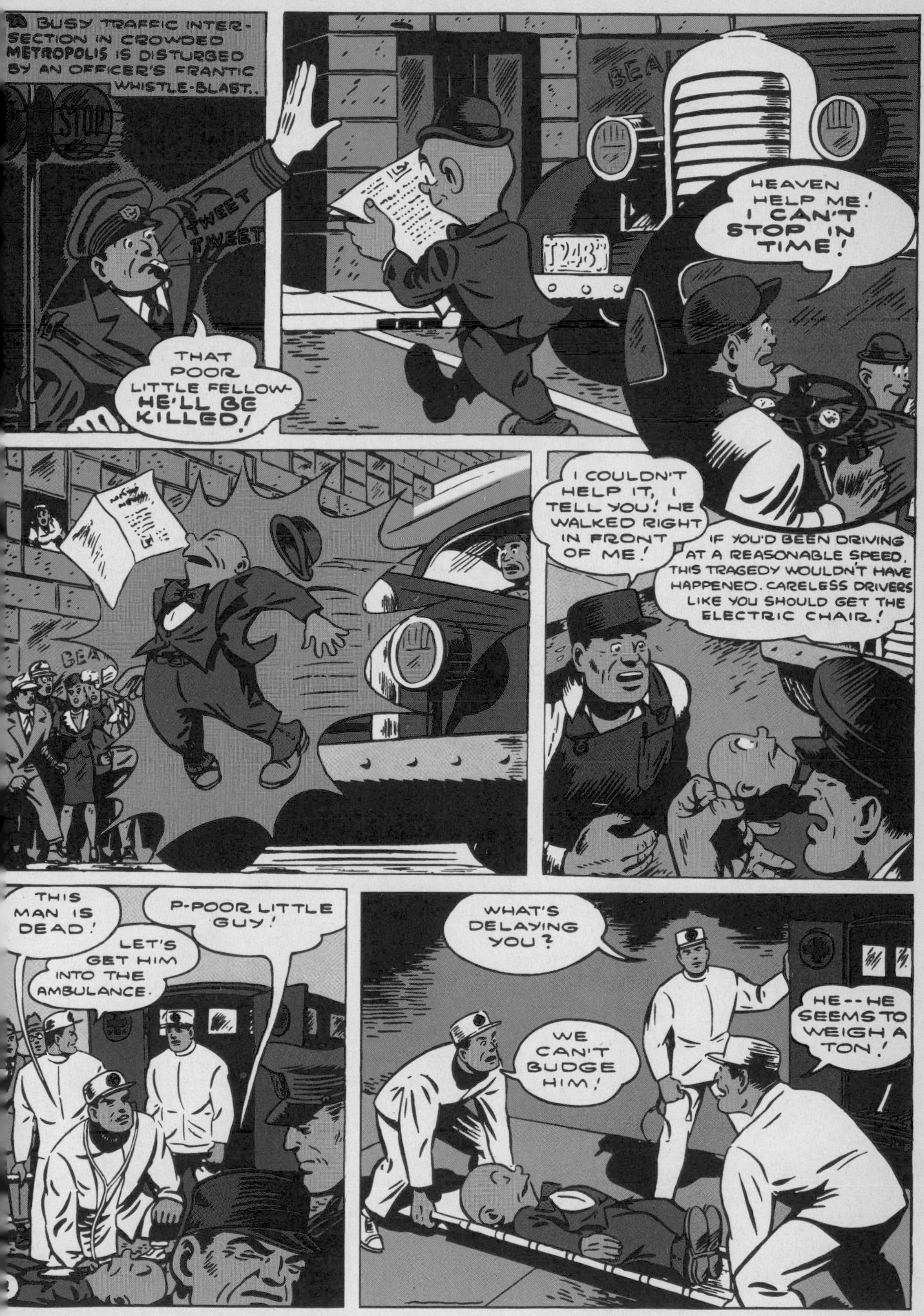
A BUSY TRAFFIC INTER-SECTION IN CROWDED METROPOLIS IS DISTURBED BY AN OFFICER'S FRANTIC WHISTLE-BLAST..
STOP
TWEET
TWEET
THAT POOR LITTLE FELLOW-- HE'LL BE KILLED!
HEAVEN HELP ME! I CAN'T STOP IN TIME!
T2437
I COULDN'T HELP IT, I TELL YOU! HE WALKED RIGHT IN FRONT OF ME!
IF YOU'D BEEN DRIVING AT A REASONABLE SPEED, THIS TRAGEDY WOULDN'T HAVE HAPPENED. CARELESS DRIVERS LIKE YOU SHOULD GET THE ELECTRIC CHAIR!
THIS MAN IS DEAD!
P-POOR LITTLE GUY!
LET'S GET HIM INTO THE AMBULANCE.
WHAT'S DELAYING YOU?
WE CAN'T BUDGE HIM!
HE--HE SEEMS TO WEIGH A TON!

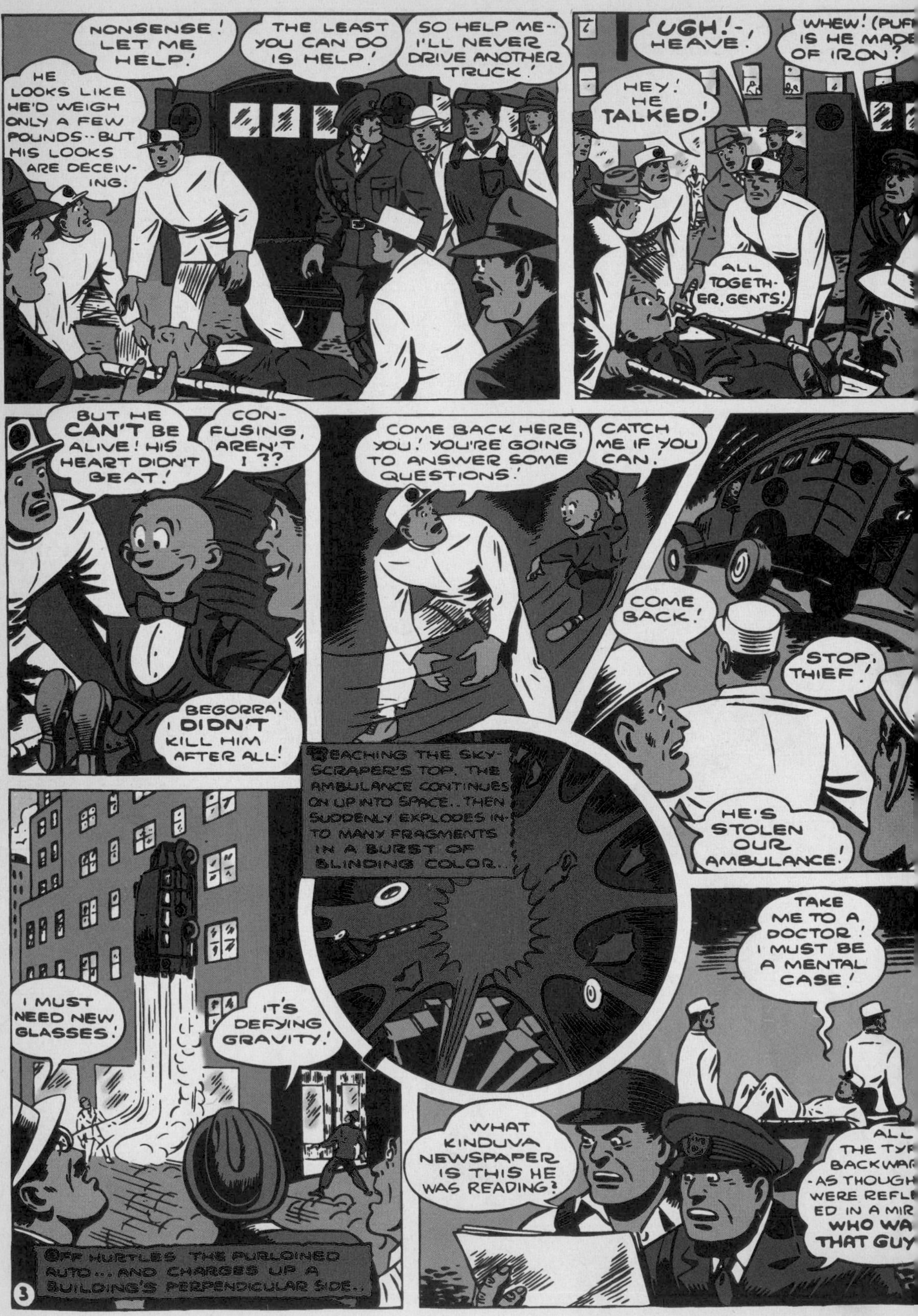
NONSENSE! LET ME HELP!
HE LOOKS LIKE HE'D WEIGH ONLY A FEW POUNDS--BUT HIS LOOKS ARE DECEIV-ING.
THE LEAST YOU CAN DO IS HELP!
SO HELP ME-- I'LL NEVER DRIVE ANOTHER TRUCK!
UGH!-, HEAVE!
WHEW! (PUF IS HE MADE OF IRON?
HEY! HE TALKED!
ALL TOGETH-ER, GENTS!
BUT HE CAN'T BE ALIVE! HIS HEART DIDN'T BEAT!
CON-FUSING, AREN'T I ??
BEGORRA! I DIDN'T KILL HIM AFTER ALL!
COME BACK HERE, YOU! YOU'RE GOING TO ANSWER SOME QUESTIONS!
CATCH ME IF YOU CAN!
COME BACK!
STOP, THIEF!
HE'S STOLEN OUR AMBULANCE!
OFF HURTLES THE PURLOINED AUTO... AND CHARGES UP A BUILDING'S PERPENDICULAR SIDE...
I MUST NEED NEW GLASSES!
IT'S DEFYING GRAVITY!
REACHING THE SKY-SCRAPER'S TOP, THE AMBULANCE CONTINUES ON UP INTO SPACE.. THEN SUDDENLY EXPLODES IN-TO MANY FRAGMENTS IN A BURST OF BLINDING COLOR..
TAKE ME TO A DOCTOR! I MUST BE A MENTAL CASE!
WHAT KINDUVA NEWSPAPER IS THIS HE WAS READING?
ALL THE TYP BACKWAR -AS THOUGH WERE REFL ED IN A MIR WHO WA THAT GUY
3

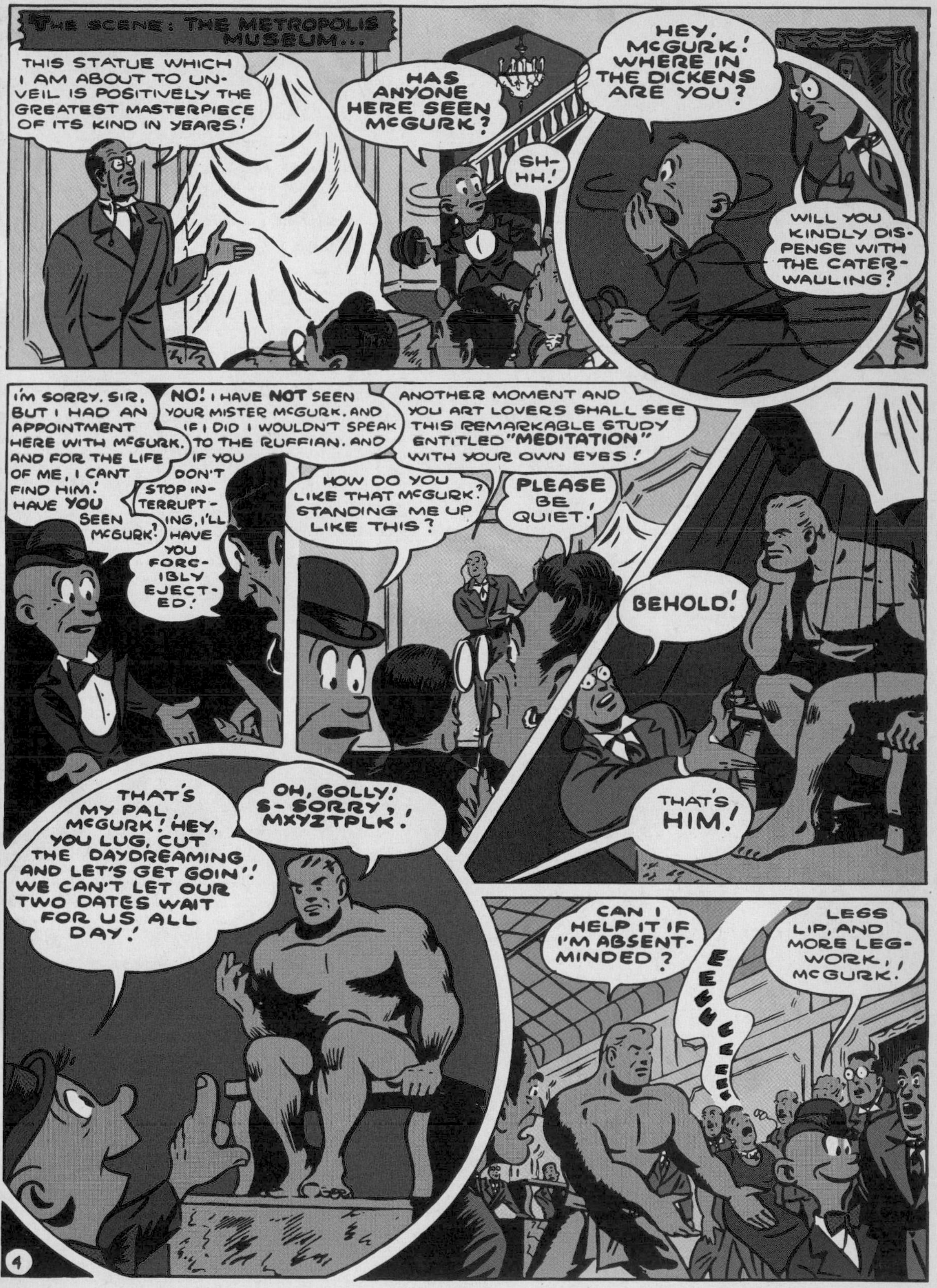
THE SCENE: THE METROPOLIS MUSEUM...
THIS STATUE WHICH I AM ABOUT TO UNVEIL IS POSITIVELY THE GREATEST MASTERPIECE OF ITS KIND IN YEARS!
HAS ANYONE HERE SEEN McGURK?
SH-HH!
HEY, McGURK! WHERE IN THE DICKENS ARE YOU?
WILL YOU KINDLY DISPENSE WITH THE CATERWAULING?
I'M SORRY, SIR, BUT I HAD AN APPOINTMENT HERE WITH McGURK, AND FOR THE LIFE OF ME, I CANT FIND HIM! HAVE YOU SEEN McGURK?
NO! I HAVE NOT SEEN YOUR MISTER McGURK, AND IF I DID I WOULDN'T SPEAK TO THE RUFFIAN. AND IF YOU DON'T STOP INTERRUPTING, I'LL HAVE YOU FORCIBLY EJECTED!
ANOTHER MOMENT AND YOU ART LOVERS SHALL SEE THIS REMARKABLE STUDY ENTITLED "MEDITATION" WITH YOUR OWN EYES!
HOW DO YOU LIKE THAT McGURK? STANDING ME UP LIKE THIS?
PLEASE BE QUIET!
BEHOLD!
THAT'S HIM!
THAT'S MY PAL, McGURK! HEY, YOU LUG, CUT THE DAYDREAMING AND LET'S GET GOIN'! WE CAN'T LET OUR TWO DATES WAIT FOR US ALL DAY!
OH, GOLLY! S-SORRY, MXYZTPLK!
CAN I HELP IT IF I'M ABSENT-MINDED?
EEEEEEEE
LESS LIP, AND MORE LEGWORK, McGURK!
4

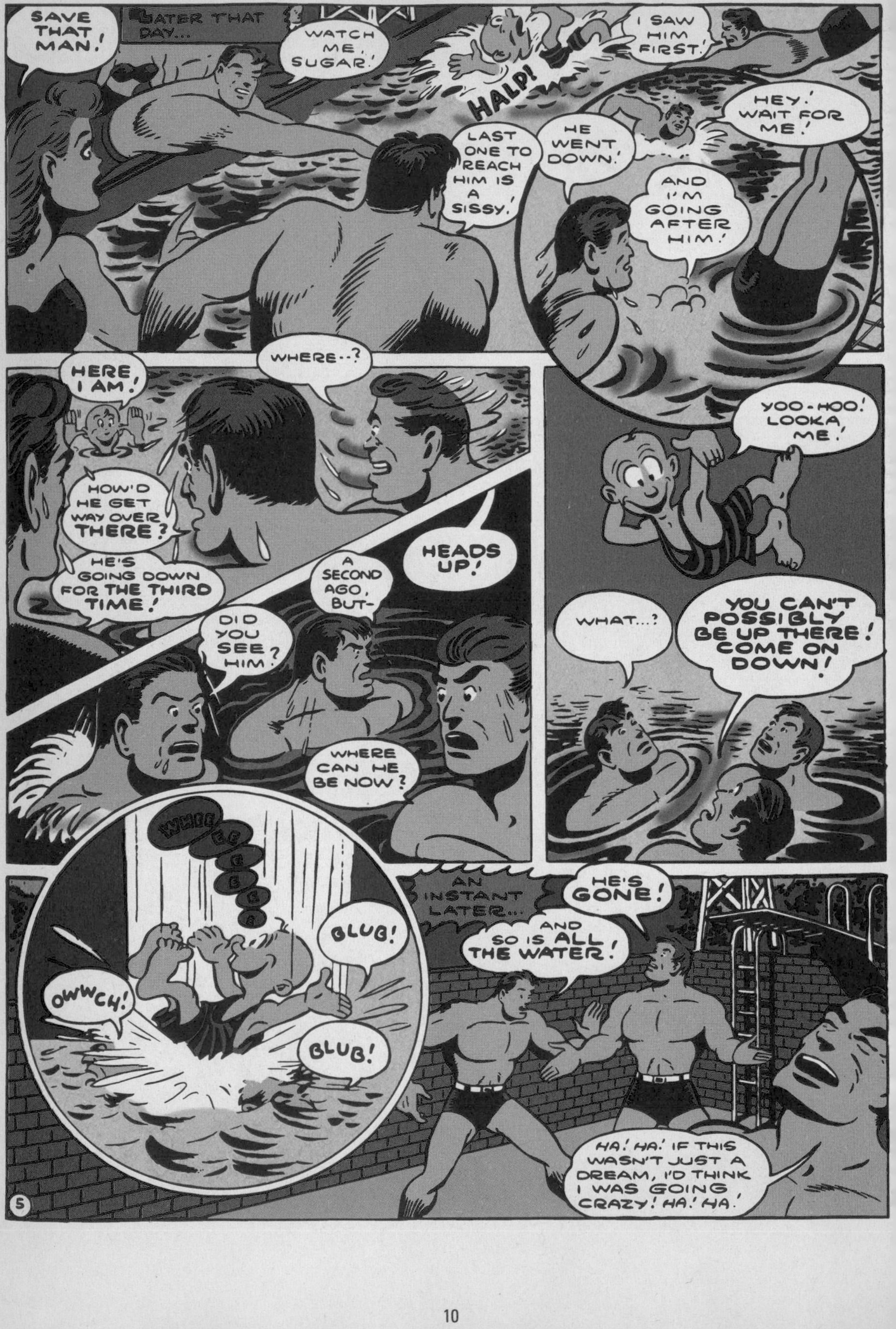
LATER THAT DAY...
SAVE THAT MAN!
WATCH ME, SUGAR!
HALP!
I SAW HIM FIRST!
LAST ONE TO REACH HIM IS A SISSY!
HE WENT DOWN!
HEY! WAIT FOR ME!
AND I'M GOING AFTER HIM!
HERE I AM!
WHERE--?
HOW'D HE GET WAY OVER THERE?
HE'S GOING DOWN FOR THE THIRD TIME!
A SECOND AGO, BUT-
HEADS UP!
DID YOU SEE HIM?
WHERE CAN HE BE NOW?
YOO-HOO! LOOKA ME!
WHAT...?
YOU CAN'T POSSIBLY BE UP THERE! COME ON DOWN!
OWWCH!
BLUB!
BLUB!
AN INSTANT LATER...
HE'S GONE!
AND SO IS ALL THE WATER!
HA! HA! IF THIS WASN'T JUST A DREAM, I'D THINK I WAS GOING CRAZY! HA! HA!
5

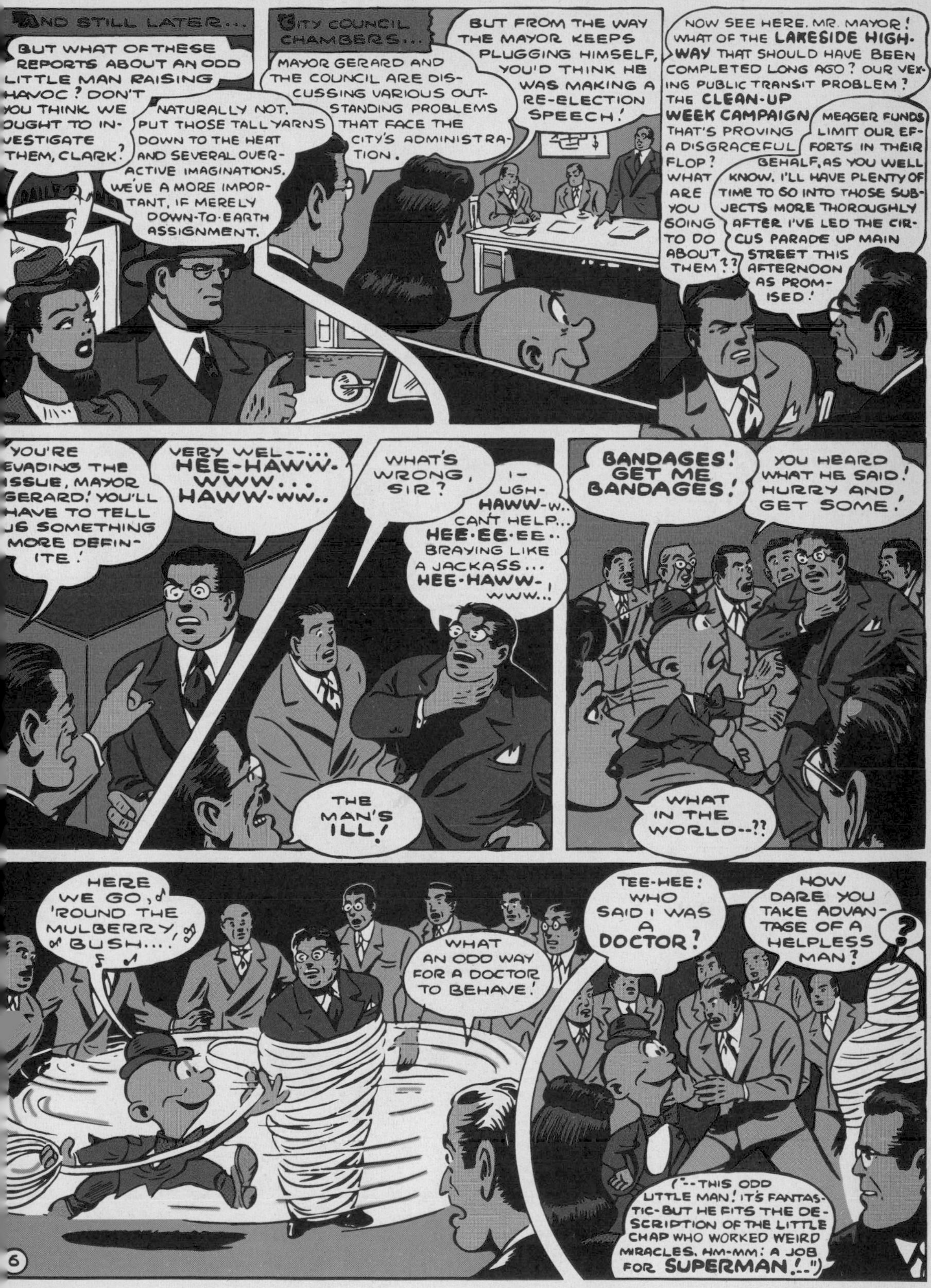
AND STILL LATER...
BUT WHAT OF THESE REPORTS ABOUT AN ODD LITTLE MAN RAISING HAVOC? DON'T YOU THINK WE OUGHT TO INVESTIGATE THEM, CLARK?
NATURALLY NOT. PUT THOSE TALL YARNS DOWN TO THE HEAT AND SEVERAL OVER-ACTIVE IMAGINATIONS. WE'VE A MORE IMPORTANT, IF MERELY DOWN-TO-EARTH ASSIGNMENT.
CITY COUNCIL CHAMBERS...
MAYOR GERARD AND THE COUNCIL ARE DISCUSSING VARIOUS OUTSTANDING PROBLEMS THAT FACE THE CITY'S ADMINISTRATION.
BUT FROM THE WAY THE MAYOR KEEPS PLUGGING HIMSELF, YOU'D THINK HE WAS MAKING A RE-ELECTION SPEECH!
NOW SEE HERE, MR. MAYOR! WHAT OF THE LAKESIDE HIGHWAY THAT SHOULD HAVE BEEN COMPLETED LONG AGO? OUR VEXING PUBLIC TRANSIT PROBLEM? THE CLEAN-UP WEEK CAMPAIGN THAT'S PROVING A DISGRACEFUL FLOP? WHAT ARE YOU GOING TO DO ABOUT THEM??
MEAGER FUNDS LIMIT OUR EFFORTS IN THEIR BEHALF, AS YOU WELL KNOW. I'LL HAVE PLENTY OF TIME TO GO INTO THOSE SUBJECTS MORE THOROUGHLY AFTER I'VE LED THE CIRCUS PARADE UP MAIN STREET THIS AFTERNOON AS PROMISED!
YOU'RE EVADING THE ISSUE, MAYOR GERARD! YOU'LL HAVE TO TELL US SOMETHING MORE DEFINITE!
VERY WEL--... HEE-HAWW-WWW... HAWW-WW..
WHAT'S WRONG, SIR?
I- UGH- HAWW-W.. CAN'T HELP... HEE-EE-EE- BRAYING LIKE A JACKASS... HEE-HAWW-WWW..!
THE MAN'S ILL!
BANDAGES! GET ME BANDAGES!
YOU HEARD WHAT HE SAID! HURRY AND GET SOME!
WHAT IN THE WORLD--??
HERE WE GO, 'ROUND THE MULBERRY BUSH...
WHAT AN ODD WAY FOR A DOCTOR TO BEHAVE!
TEE-HEE! WHO SAID I WAS A DOCTOR?
HOW DARE YOU TAKE ADVANTAGE OF A HELPLESS MAN?
?
("--THIS ODD LITTLE MAN! IT'S FANTASTIC-BUT HE FITS THE DESCRIPTION OF THE LITTLE CHAP WHO WORKED WEIRD MIRACLES. HM-MM! A JOB FOR SUPERMAN!--")
6

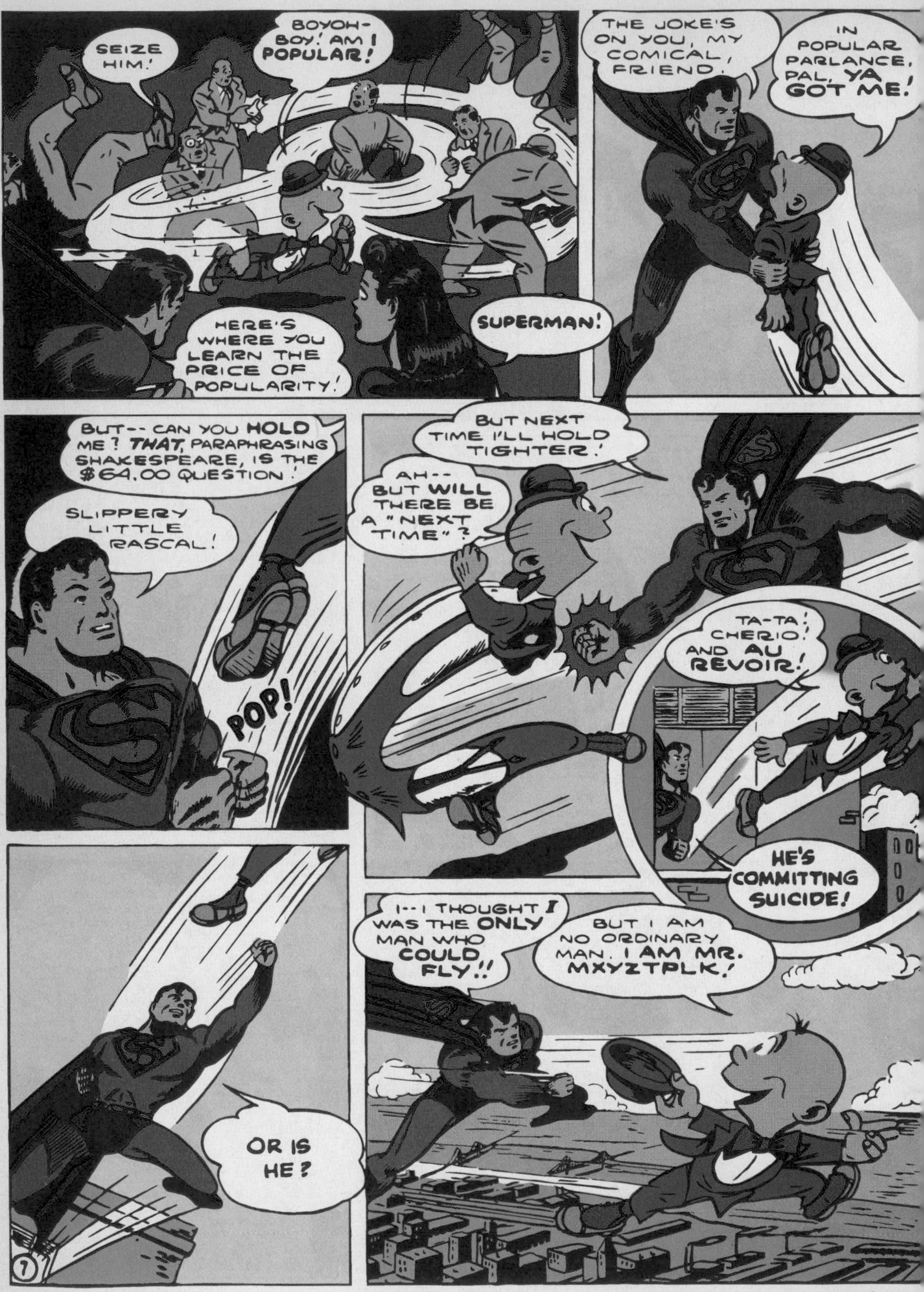
SEIZE HIM!
BOYOH-BOY! AM I POPULAR!
HERE'S WHERE YOU LEARN THE PRICE OF POPULARITY!
SUPERMAN!
THE JOKE'S ON YOU, MY COMICAL FRIEND.
IN POPULAR PARLANCE, PAL, YA GOT ME!
BUT-- CAN YOU HOLD ME? THAT, PARAPHRASING SHAKESPEARE, IS THE $64.00 QUESTION!
SLIPPERY LITTLE RASCAL!
POP!
BUT NEXT TIME I'LL HOLD TIGHTER!
AH-- BUT WILL THERE BE A "NEXT TIME"?
TA-TA! CHERIO! AND AU REVOIR!
HE'S COMMITTING SUICIDE!
OR IS HE?
I-- I THOUGHT I WAS THE ONLY MAN WHO COULD FLY!!
BUT I AM NO ORDINARY MAN. I AM MR. MXYZTPLK!
7

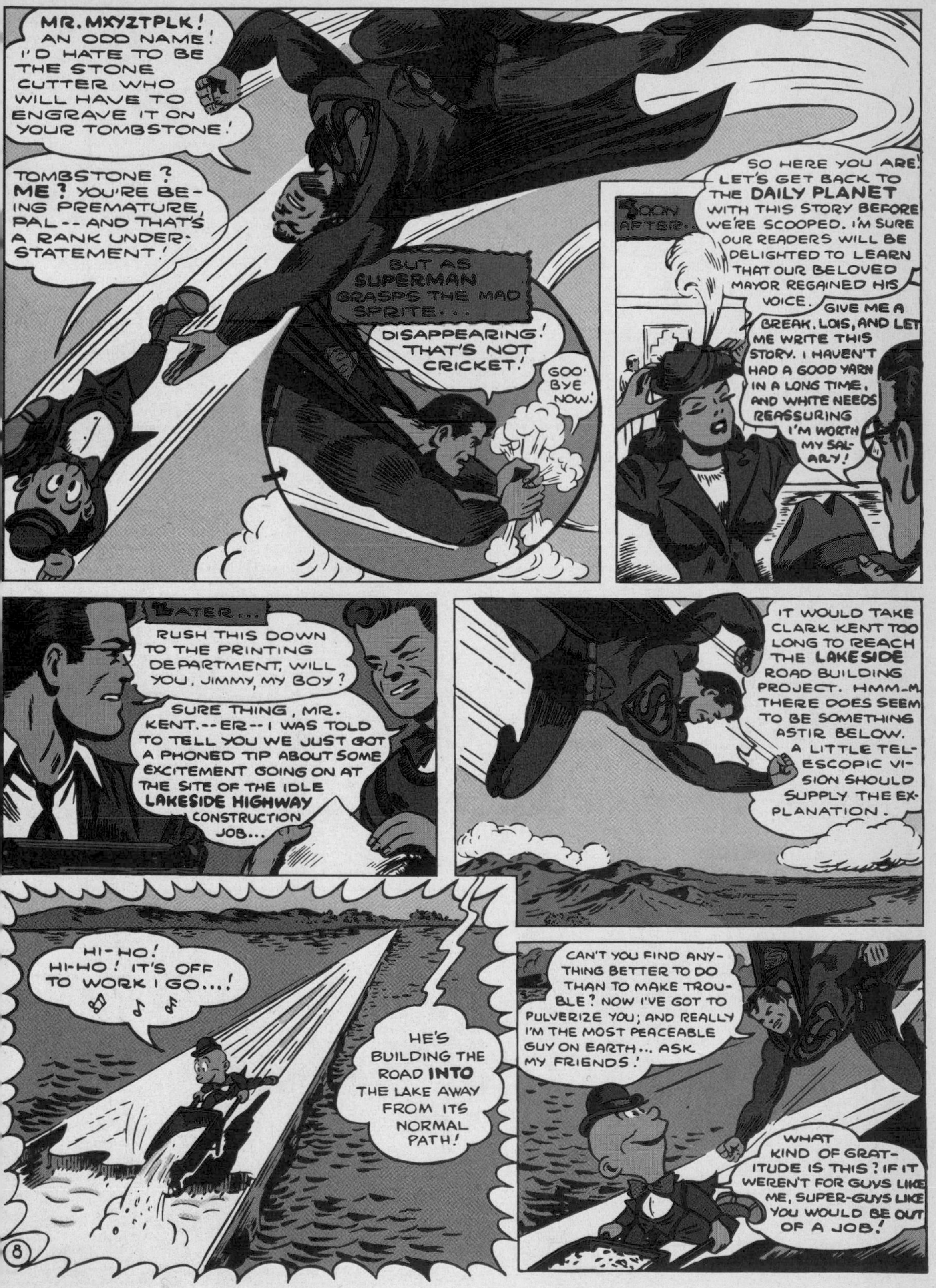
MR. MXYZTPLK! AN ODD NAME! I'D HATE TO BE THE STONE CUTTER WHO WILL HAVE TO ENGRAVE IT ON YOUR TOMBSTONE!
TOMBSTONE? ME? YOU'RE BEING PREMATURE, PAL -- AND THAT'S A RANK UNDERSTATEMENT!
BUT AS SUPERMAN GRASPS THE MAD SPRITE...
DISAPPEARING! THAT'S NOT CRICKET!
GOO'BYE NOW!
SOON AFTER...
SO HERE YOU ARE! LET'S GET BACK TO THE DAILY PLANET WITH THIS STORY BEFORE WE'RE SCOOPED. I'M SURE OUR READERS WILL BE DELIGHTED TO LEARN THAT OUR BELOVED MAYOR REGAINED HIS VOICE.
GIVE ME A BREAK, LOIS, AND LET ME WRITE THIS STORY. I HAVEN'T HAD A GOOD YARN IN A LONG TIME, AND WHITE NEEDS REASSURING I'M WORTH MY SALARY!
LATER...
RUSH THIS DOWN TO THE PRINTING DEPARTMENT, WILL YOU, JIMMY, MY BOY?
SURE THING, MR. KENT. -- ER -- I WAS TOLD TO TELL YOU WE JUST GOT A PHONED TIP ABOUT SOME EXCITEMENT GOING ON AT THE SITE OF THE IDLE LAKESIDE HIGHWAY CONSTRUCTION JOB...
IT WOULD TAKE CLARK KENT TOO LONG TO REACH THE LAKESIDE ROAD BUILDING PROJECT. HMM-M, THERE DOES SEEM TO BE SOMETHING ASTIR BELOW. A LITTLE TELESCOPIC VISION SHOULD SUPPLY THE EXPLANATION.
HI-HO! HI-HO! IT'S OFF TO WORK I GO...!
HE'S BUILDING THE ROAD INTO THE LAKE AWAY FROM ITS NORMAL PATH!
CAN'T YOU FIND ANYTHING BETTER TO DO THAN TO MAKE TROUBLE? NOW I'VE GOT TO PULVERIZE YOU; AND REALLY I'M THE MOST PEACEABLE GUY ON EARTH... ASK MY FRIENDS!
WHAT KIND OF GRATITUDE IS THIS? IF IT WEREN'T FOR GUYS LIKE ME, SUPER-GUYS LIKE YOU WOULD BE OUT OF A JOB!
8

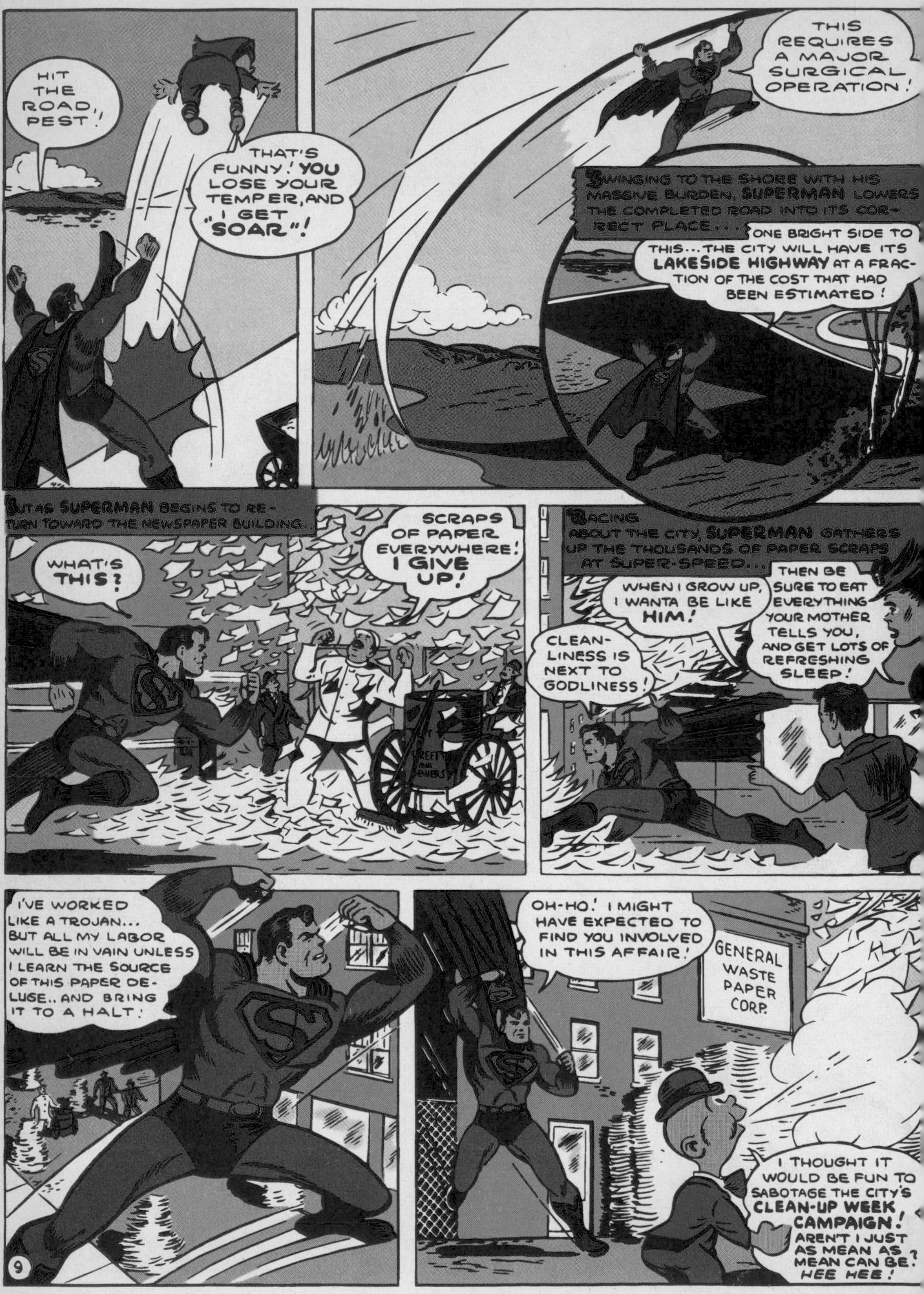
HIT THE ROAD, PEST!
THAT'S FUNNY! YOU LOSE YOUR TEMPER, AND I GET "SOAR"!
THIS REQUIRES A MAJOR SURGICAL OPERATION!
SWINGING TO THE SHORE WITH HIS MASSIVE BURDEN, SUPERMAN LOWERS THE COMPLETED ROAD INTO ITS CORRECT PLACE...
ONE BRIGHT SIDE TO THIS... THE CITY WILL HAVE ITS LAKESIDE HIGHWAY AT A FRACTION OF THE COST THAT HAD BEEN ESTIMATED!
BUT AS SUPERMAN BEGINS TO RETURN TOWARD THE NEWSPAPER BUILDING...
WHAT'S THIS?
SCRAPS OF PAPER EVERYWHERE! I GIVE UP!
RACING ABOUT THE CITY, SUPERMAN GATHERS UP THE THOUSANDS OF PAPER SCRAPS AT SUPER-SPEED...
WHEN I GROW UP, I WANTA BE LIKE HIM!
THEN BE SURE TO EAT EVERYTHING YOUR MOTHER TELLS YOU, AND GET LOTS OF REFRESHING SLEEP!
CLEANLINESS IS NEXT TO GODLINESS!
I'VE WORKED LIKE A TROJAN... BUT ALL MY LABOR WILL BE IN VAIN UNLESS I LEARN THE SOURCE OF THIS PAPER DELUSE.. AND BRING IT TO A HALT!
9
OH-HO! I MIGHT HAVE EXPECTED TO FIND YOU INVOLVED IN THIS AFFAIR!
GENERAL WASTE PAPER CORP.
I THOUGHT IT WOULD BE FUN TO SABOTAGE THE CITY'S CLEAN-UP WEEK CAMPAIGN! AREN'T I JUST AS MEAN AS MEAN CAN BE? HEE HEE!

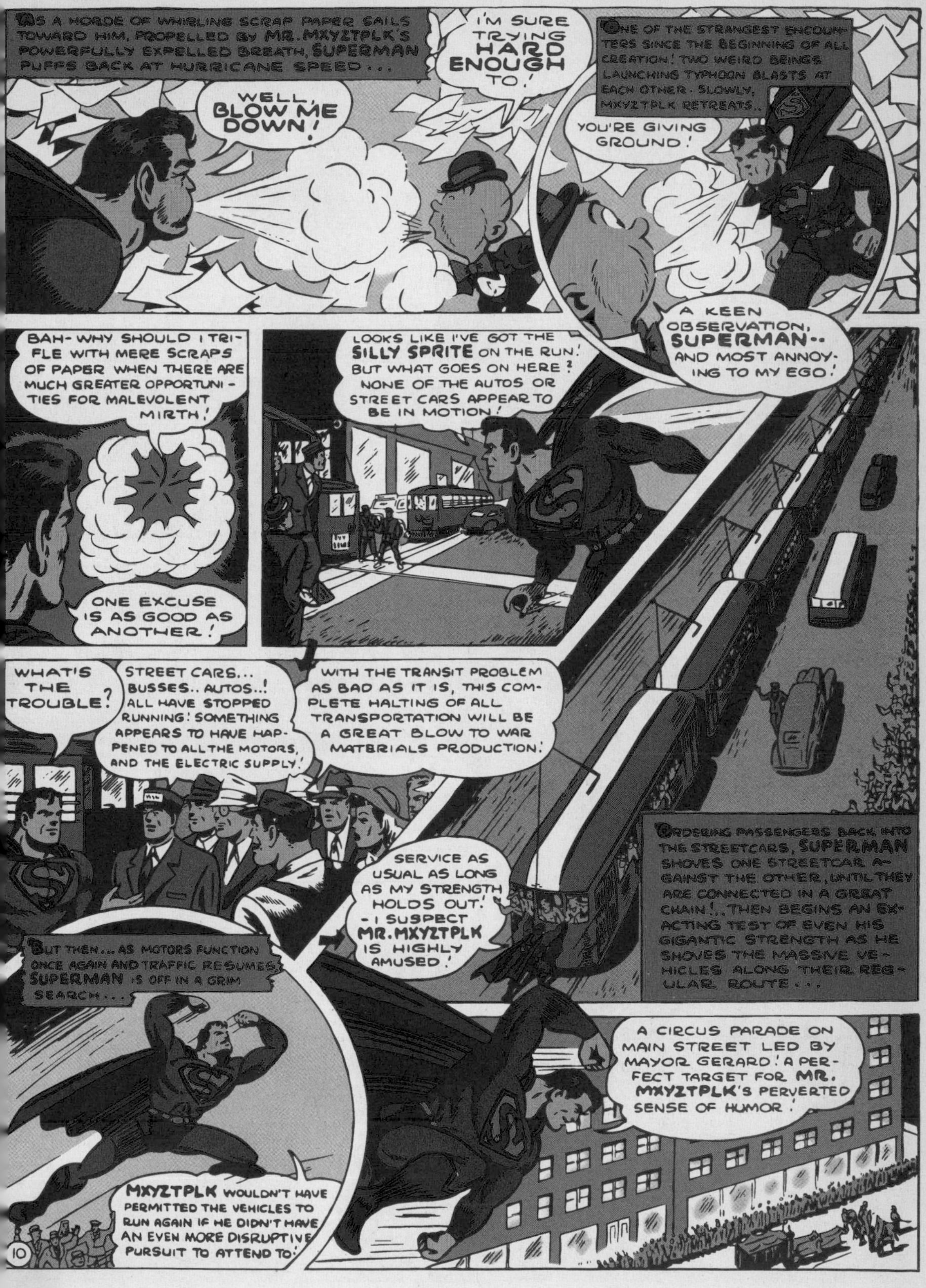
AS A HORDE OF WHIRLING SCRAP PAPER SAILS TOWARD HIM, PROPELLED BY MR. MXYZTPLK'S POWERFULLY EXPELLED BREATH, SUPERMAN PUFFS BACK AT HURRICANE SPEED . . .
WELL, BLOW ME DOWN!
I'M SURE TRYING HARD ENOUGH TO!
ONE OF THE STRANGEST ENCOUNTERS SINCE THE BEGINNING OF ALL CREATION! TWO WEIRD BEINGS LAUNCHING TYPHOON BLASTS AT EACH OTHER. SLOWLY, MXYZTPLK RETREATS..
YOU'RE GIVING GROUND!
A KEEN OBSERVATION, SUPERMAN -- AND MOST ANNOYING TO MY EGO!
BAH- WHY SHOULD I TRIFLE WITH MERE SCRAPS OF PAPER WHEN THERE ARE MUCH GREATER OPPORTUNITIES FOR MALEVOLENT MIRTH!
ONE EXCUSE IS AS GOOD AS ANOTHER!
LOOKS LIKE I'VE GOT THE SILLY SPRITE ON THE RUN! BUT WHAT GOES ON HERE? NONE OF THE AUTOS OR STREET CARS APPEAR TO BE IN MOTION!
WHAT'S THE TROUBLE?
STREET CARS... BUSSES.. AUTOS..! ALL HAVE STOPPED RUNNING! SOMETHING APPEARS TO HAVE HAPPENED TO ALL THE MOTORS, AND THE ELECTRIC SUPPLY!
WITH THE TRANSIT PROBLEM AS BAD AS IT IS, THIS COMPLETE HALTING OF ALL TRANSPORTATION WILL BE A GREAT BLOW TO WAR MATERIALS PRODUCTION!
ORDERING PASSENGERS BACK INTO THE STREETCARS, SUPERMAN SHOVES ONE STREETCAR AGAINST THE OTHER, UNTIL THEY ARE CONNECTED IN A GREAT CHAIN!.. THEN BEGINS AN EXACTING TEST OF EVEN HIS GIGANTIC STRENGTH AS HE SHOVES THE MASSIVE VEHICLES ALONG THEIR REGULAR ROUTE . . .
SERVICE AS USUAL AS LONG AS MY STRENGTH HOLDS OUT! - I SUSPECT MR. MXYZTPLK IS HIGHLY AMUSED!
BUT THEN... AS MOTORS FUNCTION ONCE AGAIN AND TRAFFIC RESUMES, SUPERMAN IS OFF IN A GRIM SEARCH . . .
MXYZTPLK WOULDN'T HAVE PERMITTED THE VEHICLES TO RUN AGAIN IF HE DIDN'T HAVE AN EVEN MORE DISRUPTIVE PURSUIT TO ATTEND TO!
A CIRCUS PARADE ON MAIN STREET LED BY MAYOR GERARD! A PERFECT TARGET FOR MR. MXYZTPLK'S PERVERTED SENSE OF HUMOR!
10

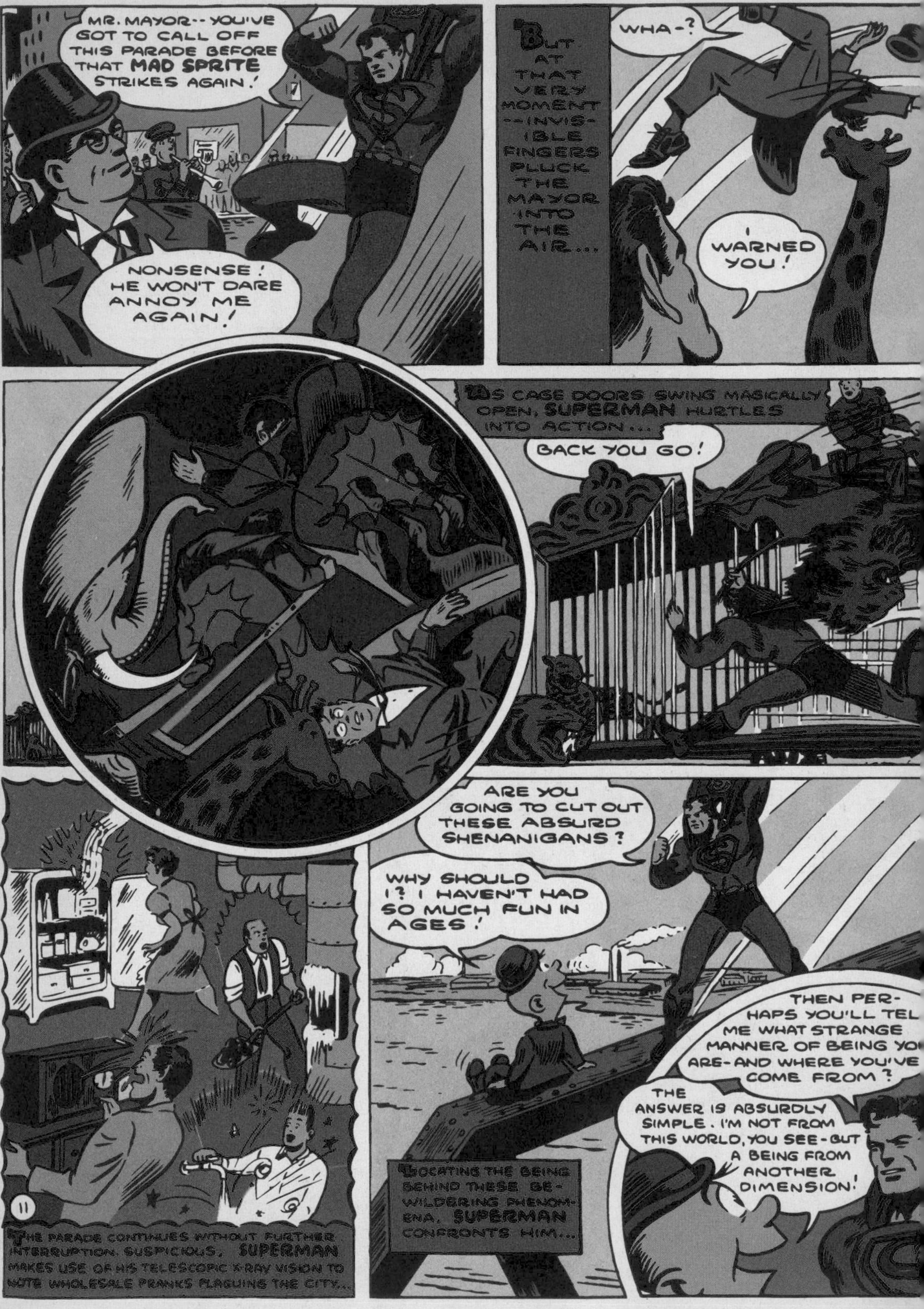
MR. MAYOR-- YOU'VE GOT TO CALL OFF THIS PARADE BEFORE THAT MAD SPRITE STRIKES AGAIN!
NONSENSE! HE WON'T DARE ANNOY ME AGAIN!
BUT AT THAT VERY MOMENT --INVISIBLE FINGERS PLUCK THE MAYOR INTO THE AIR...
WHA-?
I WARNED YOU!
AS CAGE DOORS SWING MAGICALLY OPEN, SUPERMAN HURTLES INTO ACTION...
BACK YOU GO!
11
THE PARADE CONTINUES WITHOUT FURTHER INTERRUPTION. SUSPICIOUS, SUPERMAN MAKES USE OF HIS TELESCOPIC X-RAY VISION TO NOTE WHOLESALE PRANKS PLAGUING THE CITY...
LOCATING THE BEING BEHIND THESE BEWILDERING PHENOMENA, SUPERMAN CONFRONTS HIM...
ARE YOU GOING TO CUT OUT THESE ABSURD SHENANIGANS?
WHY SHOULD I? I HAVEN'T HAD SO MUCH FUN IN AGES!
THEN PERHAPS YOU'LL TEL ME WHAT STRANGE MANNER OF BEING YO ARE- AND WHERE YOU'VE COME FROM?
THE ANSWER IS ABSURDLY SIMPLE. I'M NOT FROM THIS WORLD, YOU SEE- BUT A BEING FROM ANOTHER DIMENSION!

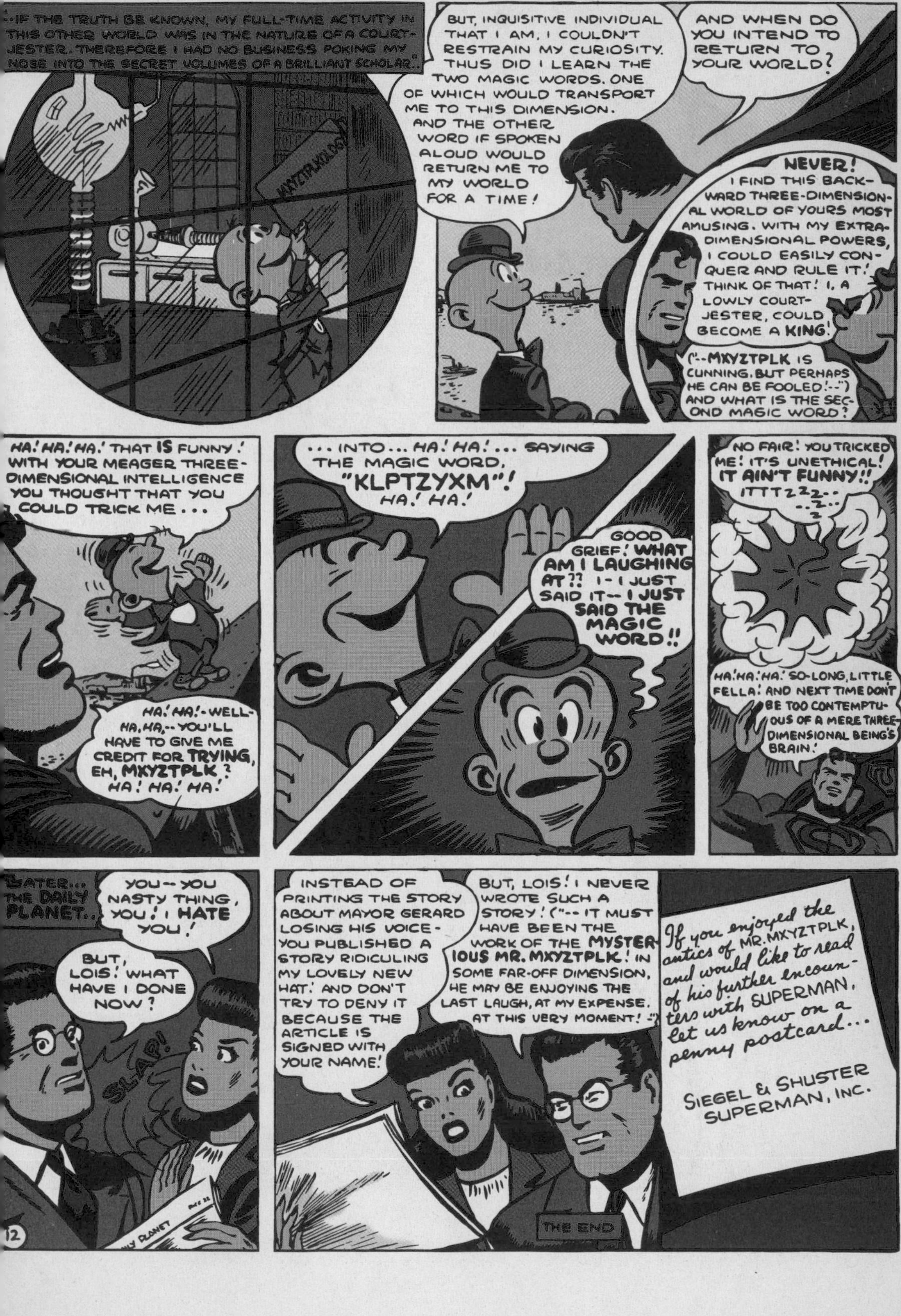

--IF THE TRUTH BE KNOWN, MY FULL-TIME ACTIVITY IN THIS OTHER WORLD WAS IN THE NATURE OF A COURT-JESTER. THEREFORE I HAD NO BUSINESS POKING MY NOSE INTO THE SECRET VOLUMES OF A BRILLIANT SCHOLAR".
MXYZTPLK-KLPTZYXM
BUT, INQUISITIVE INDIVIDUAL THAT I AM, I COULDN'T RESTRAIN MY CURIOSITY. THUS DID I LEARN THE TWO MAGIC WORDS. ONE OF WHICH WOULD TRANSPORT ME TO THIS DIMENSION. AND THE OTHER WORD IF SPOKEN ALOUD WOULD RETURN ME TO MY WORLD FOR A TIME!
AND WHEN DO YOU INTEND TO RETURN TO YOUR WORLD?
NEVER! I FIND THIS BACKWARD THREE-DIMENSIONAL WORLD OF YOURS MOST AMUSING. WITH MY EXTRA-DIMENSIONAL POWERS, I COULD EASILY CONQUER AND RULE IT! THINK OF THAT! I, A LOWLY COURT-JESTER, COULD BECOME A KING!
("--MXYZTPLK IS CUNNING, BUT PERHAPS HE CAN BE FOOLED!--") AND WHAT IS THE SECOND MAGIC WORD?
HA! HA! HA! THAT IS FUNNY! WITH YOUR MEAGER THREE-DIMENSIONAL INTELLIGENCE YOU THOUGHT THAT YOU COULD TRICK ME...
HA! HA!-WELL-HA, HA,--YOU'LL HAVE TO GIVE ME CREDIT FOR TRYING, EH, MXYZTPLK? HA! HA! HA!
...INTO...HA! HA!... SAYING THE MAGIC WORD, "KLPTZYXM"! HA! HA!
GOOD GRIEF! WHAT AM I LAUGHING AT?? I-I JUST SAID IT-- I JUST SAID THE MAGIC WORD!!
NO FAIR! YOU TRICKED ME! IT'S UNETHICAL! IT AIN'T FUNNY!! ITTTZZZ...
HA! HA! HA! SO-LONG, LITTLE FELLA! AND NEXT TIME DON'T BE TOO CONTEMPTUOUS OF A MERE THREE-DIMENSIONAL BEING'S BRAIN!
LATER... THE DAILY PLANET...
YOU--YOU NASTY THING, YOU! I HATE YOU!
BUT, LOIS! WHAT HAVE I DONE NOW?
SLAP!
12
INSTEAD OF PRINTING THE STORY ABOUT MAYOR GERARD LOSING HIS VOICE-YOU PUBLISHED A STORY RIDICULING MY LOVELY NEW HAT! AND DON'T TRY TO DENY IT BECAUSE THE ARTICLE IS SIGNED WITH YOUR NAME!
BUT, LOIS! I NEVER WROTE SUCH A STORY! ("--IT MUST HAVE BEEN THE WORK OF THE MYSTERIOUS MR. MXYZTPLK! IN SOME FAR-OFF DIMENSION, HE MAY BE ENJOYING THE LAST LAUGH, AT MY EXPENSE, AT THIS VERY MOMENT!--")
If you enjoyed the antics of MR. MXYZTPLK, and would like to read of his further encounters with SUPERMAN, let us know on a penny postcard...
SIEGEL & SHUSTER SUPERMAN, INC.
THE END

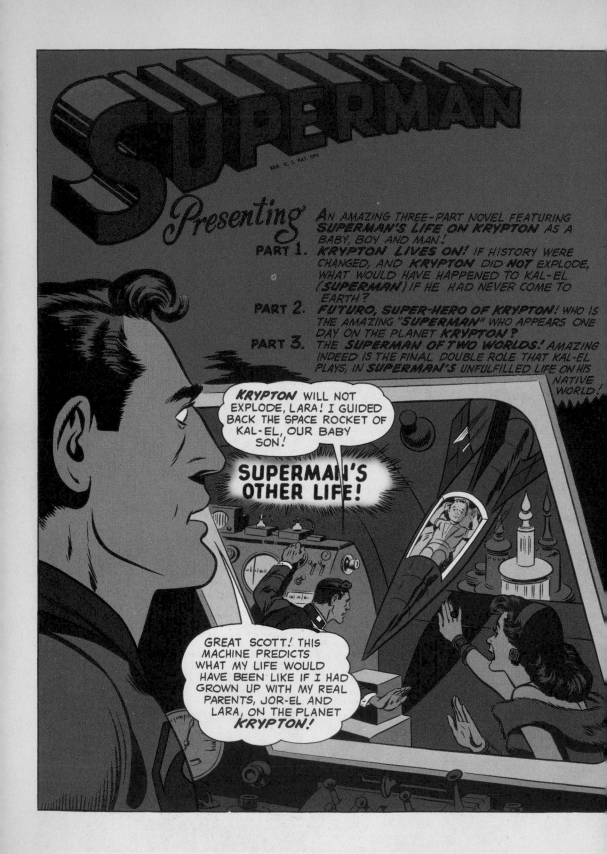

SUPERMAN

REG. U. S. PAT. OFF.

Presenting AN AMAZING THREE-PART NOVEL FEATURING *SUPERMAN'S LIFE ON KRYPTON* AS A BABY, BOY AND MAN!

PART 1. *KRYPTON LIVES ON!* IF HISTORY WERE CHANGED, AND *KRYPTON* DID *NOT* EXPLODE, WHAT WOULD HAVE HAPPENED TO KAL-EL *(SUPERMAN)* IF HE HAD NEVER COME TO EARTH?

PART 2. *FUTURO, SUPER-HERO OF KRYPTON!* WHO IS THE AMAZING "SUPERMAN" WHO APPEARS ONE DAY ON THE PLANET *KRYPTON?*

PART 3. THE *SUPERMAN OF TWO WORLDS!* AMAZING INDEED IS THE FINAL DOUBLE ROLE THAT KAL-EL PLAYS, IN *SUPERMAN'S* UNFULFILLED LIFE ON HIS NATIVE WORLD!

KRYPTON WILL NOT EXPLODE, LARA! I GUIDED BACK THE SPACE ROCKET OF KAL-EL, OUR BABY SON!

SUPERMAN'S OTHER LIFE!

GREAT SCOTT! THIS MACHINE PREDICTS WHAT MY LIFE WOULD HAVE BEEN LIKE IF I HAD GROWN UP WITH MY REAL PARENTS, JOR-EL AND LARA, ON THE PLANET *KRYPTON!*

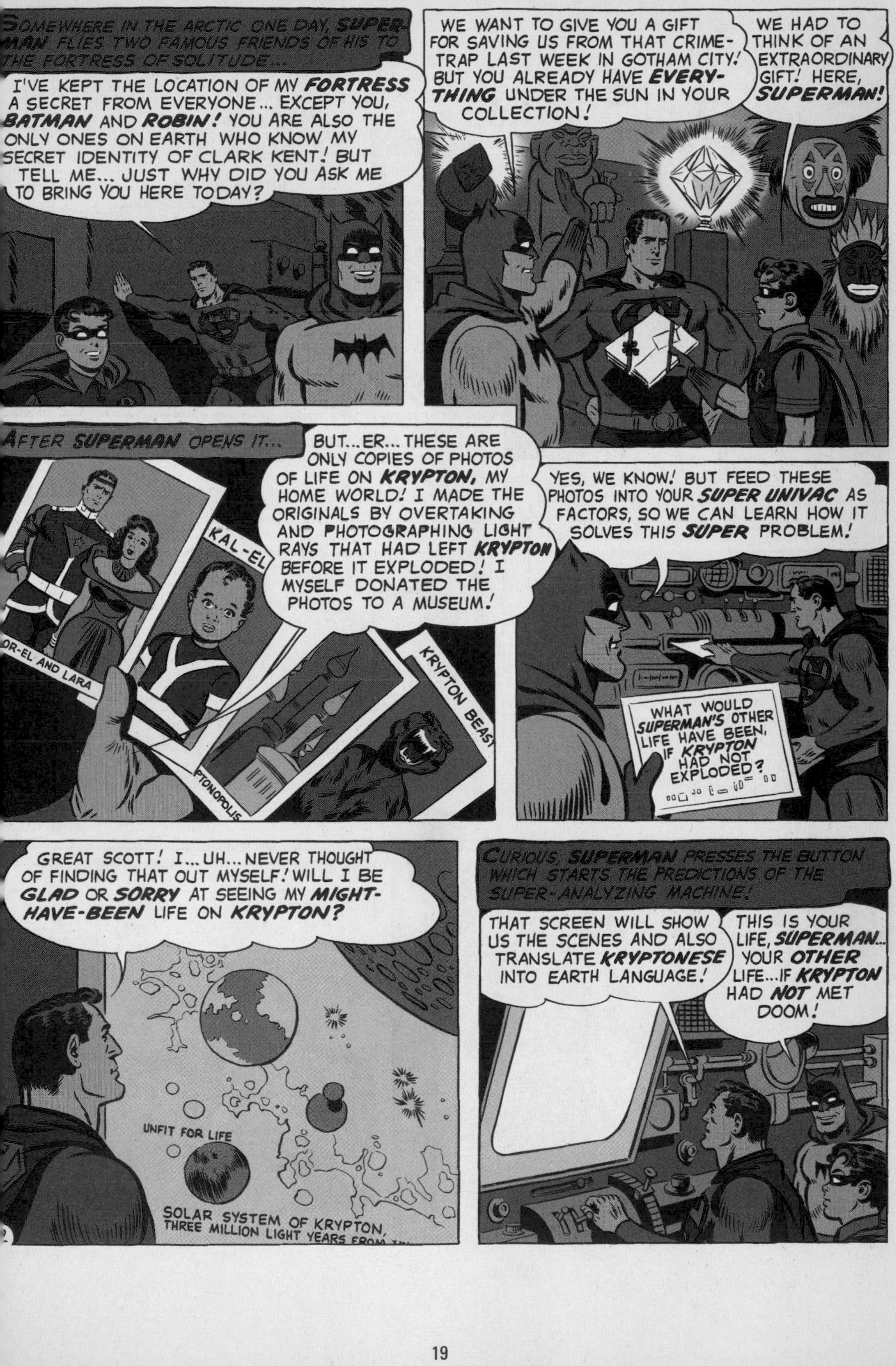
SOMEWHERE IN THE ARCTIC ONE DAY, SUPERMAN FLIES TWO FAMOUS FRIENDS OF HIS TO THE FORTRESS OF SOLITUDE...
I'VE KEPT THE LOCATION OF MY FORTRESS A SECRET FROM EVERYONE... EXCEPT YOU, BATMAN AND ROBIN! YOU ARE ALSO THE ONLY ONES ON EARTH WHO KNOW MY SECRET IDENTITY OF CLARK KENT! BUT TELL ME... JUST WHY DID YOU ASK ME TO BRING YOU HERE TODAY?
WE WANT TO GIVE YOU A GIFT FOR SAVING US FROM THAT CRIME-TRAP LAST WEEK IN GOTHAM CITY! BUT YOU ALREADY HAVE EVERYTHING UNDER THE SUN IN YOUR COLLECTION!
WE HAD TO THINK OF AN EXTRAORDINARY GIFT! HERE, SUPERMAN!
AFTER SUPERMAN OPENS IT...
BUT...ER...THESE ARE ONLY COPIES OF PHOTOS OF LIFE ON KRYPTON, MY HOME WORLD! I MADE THE ORIGINALS BY OVERTAKING AND PHOTOGRAPHING LIGHT RAYS THAT HAD LEFT KRYPTON BEFORE IT EXPLODED! I MYSELF DONATED THE PHOTOS TO A MUSEUM!
KAL-EL
OR-EL AND LARA
KRYPTON BEAST
PTONOPOLIS
YES, WE KNOW! BUT FEED THESE PHOTOS INTO YOUR SUPER UNIVAC AS FACTORS, SO WE CAN LEARN HOW IT SOLVES THIS SUPER PROBLEM!
WHAT WOULD SUPERMAN'S OTHER LIFE HAVE BEEN, IF KRYPTON HAD NOT EXPLODED?
GREAT SCOTT! I...UH...NEVER THOUGHT OF FINDING THAT OUT MYSELF! WILL I BE GLAD OR SORRY AT SEEING MY MIGHT-HAVE-BEEN LIFE ON KRYPTON?
UNFIT FOR LIFE
SOLAR SYSTEM OF KRYPTON, THREE MILLION LIGHT YEARS FROM
CURIOUS, SUPERMAN PRESSES THE BUTTON WHICH STARTS THE PREDICTIONS OF THE SUPER-ANALYZING MACHINE!
THAT SCREEN WILL SHOW US THE SCENES AND ALSO TRANSLATE KRYPTONESE INTO EARTH LANGUAGE!
THIS IS YOUR LIFE, SUPERMAN... YOUR OTHER LIFE...IF KRYPTON HAD NOT MET DOOM!

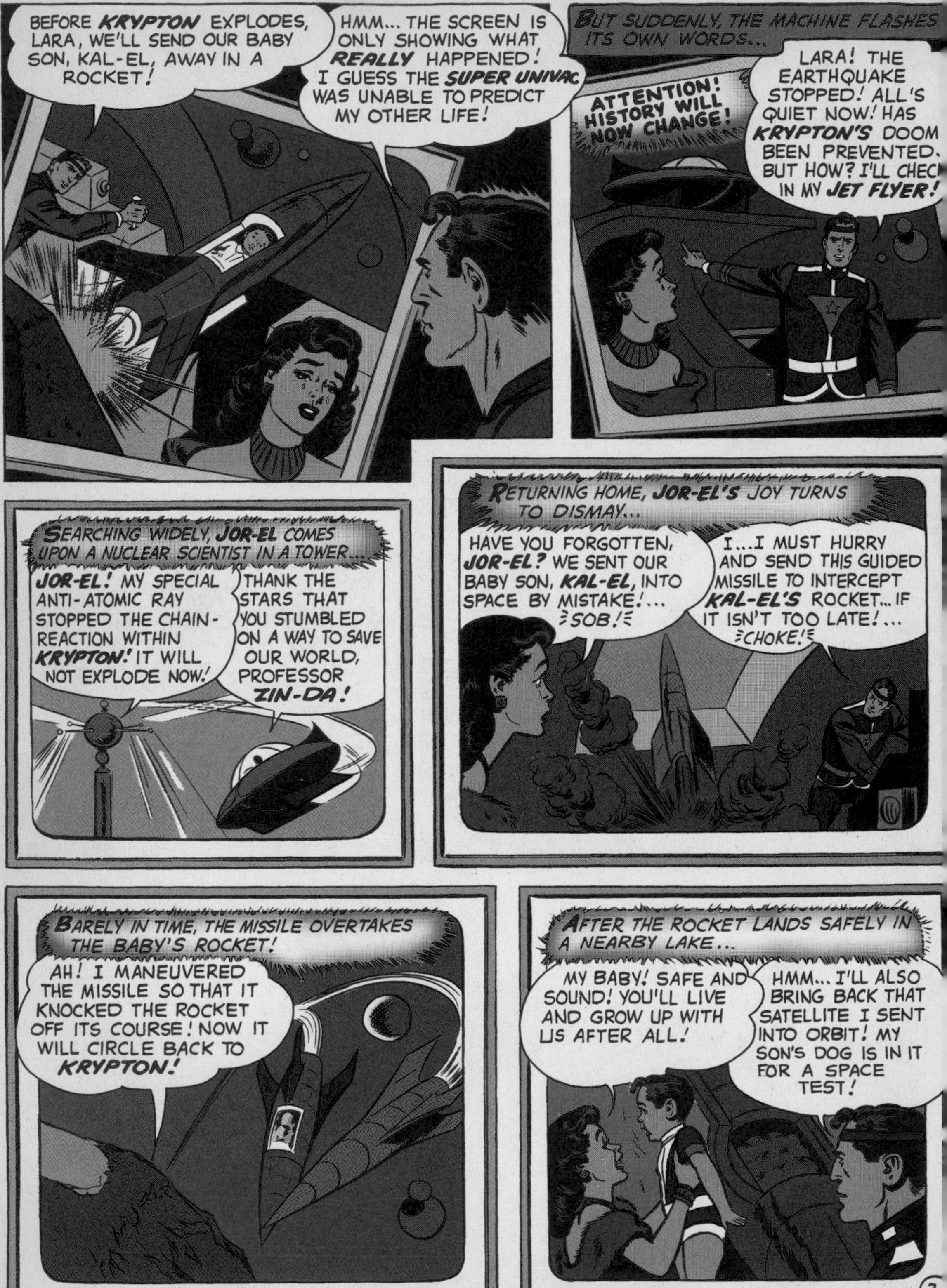
BEFORE KRYPTON EXPLODES, LARA, WE'LL SEND OUR BABY SON, KAL-EL, AWAY IN A ROCKET!
HMM... THE SCREEN IS ONLY SHOWING WHAT REALLY HAPPENED! I GUESS THE SUPER UNIVAC WAS UNABLE TO PREDICT MY OTHER LIFE!
BUT SUDDENLY, THE MACHINE FLASHES ITS OWN WORDS...
ATTENTION! HISTORY WILL NOW CHANGE!
LARA! THE EARTHQUAKE STOPPED! ALL'S QUIET NOW! HAS KRYPTON'S DOOM BEEN PREVENTED. BUT HOW? I'LL CHEC IN MY JET FLYER!
SEARCHING WIDELY, JOR-EL COMES UPON A NUCLEAR SCIENTIST IN A TOWER...
JOR-EL! MY SPECIAL ANTI-ATOMIC RAY STOPPED THE CHAIN-REACTION WITHIN KRYPTON! IT WILL NOT EXPLODE NOW!
THANK THE STARS THAT YOU STUMBLED ON A WAY TO SAVE OUR WORLD, PROFESSOR ZIN-DA!
RETURNING HOME, JOR-EL'S JOY TURNS TO DISMAY...
HAVE YOU FORGOTTEN, JOR-EL? WE SENT OUR BABY SON, KAL-EL, INTO SPACE BY MISTAKE!... SOB!
I...I MUST HURRY AND SEND THIS GUIDED MISSILE TO INTERCEPT KAL-EL'S ROCKET... IF IT ISN'T TOO LATE!... CHOKE!
BARELY IN TIME, THE MISSILE OVERTAKES THE BABY'S ROCKET!
AH! I MANEUVERED THE MISSILE SO THAT IT KNOCKED THE ROCKET OFF ITS COURSE! NOW IT WILL CIRCLE BACK TO KRYPTON!
AFTER THE ROCKET LANDS SAFELY IN A NEARBY LAKE...
MY BABY! SAFE AND SOUND! YOU'LL LIVE AND GROW UP WITH US AFTER ALL!
HMM... I'LL ALSO BRING BACK THAT SATELLITE I SENT INTO ORBIT! MY SON'S DOG IS IN IT FOR A SPACE TEST!
3

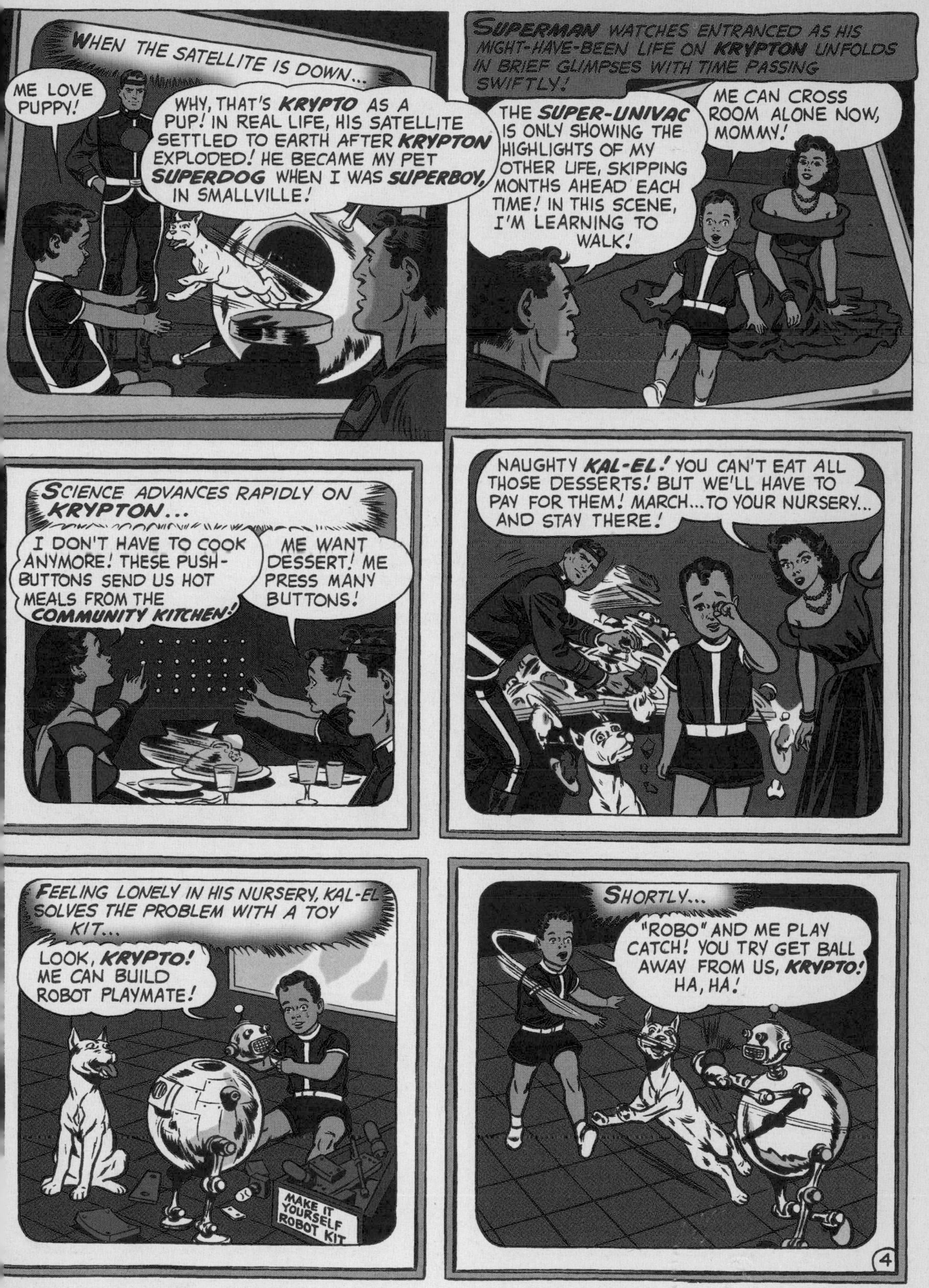
WHEN THE SATELLITE IS DOWN...
ME LOVE PUPPY!
WHY, THAT'S KRYPTO AS A PUP! IN REAL LIFE, HIS SATELLITE SETTLED TO EARTH AFTER KRYPTON EXPLODED! HE BECAME MY PET SUPERDOG WHEN I WAS SUPERBOY, IN SMALLVILLE!
SUPERMAN WATCHES ENTRANCED AS HIS MIGHT-HAVE-BEEN LIFE ON KRYPTON UNFOLDS IN BRIEF GLIMPSES WITH TIME PASSING SWIFTLY!
THE SUPER-UNIVAC IS ONLY SHOWING THE HIGHLIGHTS OF MY OTHER LIFE, SKIPPING MONTHS AHEAD EACH TIME! IN THIS SCENE, I'M LEARNING TO WALK!
ME CAN CROSS ROOM ALONE NOW, MOMMY!
SCIENCE ADVANCES RAPIDLY ON KRYPTON...
I DON'T HAVE TO COOK ANYMORE! THESE PUSH-BUTTONS SEND US HOT MEALS FROM THE COMMUNITY KITCHEN!
ME WANT DESSERT! ME PRESS MANY BUTTONS!
NAUGHTY KAL-EL! YOU CAN'T EAT ALL THOSE DESSERTS! BUT WE'LL HAVE TO PAY FOR THEM! MARCH...TO YOUR NURSERY... AND STAY THERE!
FEELING LONELY IN HIS NURSERY, KAL-EL SOLVES THE PROBLEM WITH A TOY KIT...
LOOK, KRYPTO! ME CAN BUILD ROBOT PLAYMATE!
MAKE IT YOURSELF ROBOT KIT
SHORTLY...
"ROBO" AND ME PLAY CATCH! YOU TRY GET BALL AWAY FROM US, KRYPTO! HA, HA!
4

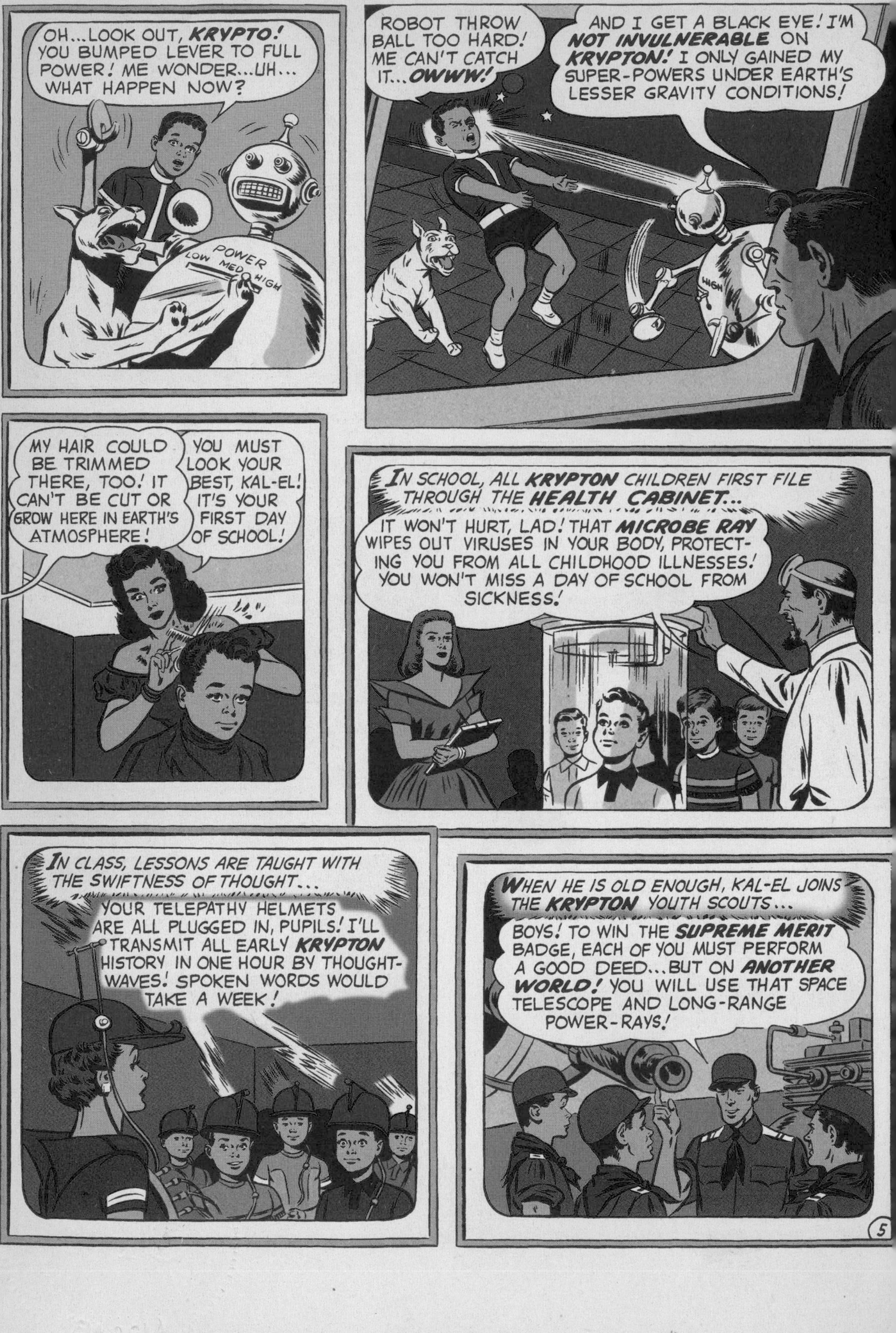
OH...LOOK OUT, KRYPTO! YOU BUMPED LEVER TO FULL POWER! ME WONDER...UH... WHAT HAPPEN NOW?
POWER
LOW MED HIGH
ROBOT THROW BALL TOO HARD! ME CAN'T CATCH IT...OWWW!
AND I GET A BLACK EYE! I'M NOT INVULNERABLE ON KRYPTON! I ONLY GAINED MY SUPER-POWERS UNDER EARTH'S LESSER GRAVITY CONDITIONS!
MY HAIR COULD BE TRIMMED THERE, TOO! IT CAN'T BE CUT OR GROW HERE IN EARTH'S ATMOSPHERE!
YOU MUST LOOK YOUR BEST, KAL-EL! IT'S YOUR FIRST DAY OF SCHOOL!
IN SCHOOL, ALL KRYPTON CHILDREN FIRST FILE THROUGH THE HEALTH CABINET...
IT WON'T HURT, LAD! THAT MICROBE RAY WIPES OUT VIRUSES IN YOUR BODY, PROTECTING YOU FROM ALL CHILDHOOD ILLNESSES! YOU WON'T MISS A DAY OF SCHOOL FROM SICKNESS!
IN CLASS, LESSONS ARE TAUGHT WITH THE SWIFTNESS OF THOUGHT...
YOUR TELEPATHY HELMETS ARE ALL PLUGGED IN, PUPILS! I'LL TRANSMIT ALL EARLY KRYPTON HISTORY IN ONE HOUR BY THOUGHT-WAVES! SPOKEN WORDS WOULD TAKE A WEEK!
WHEN HE IS OLD ENOUGH, KAL-EL JOINS THE KRYPTON YOUTH SCOUTS...
BOYS! TO WIN THE SUPREME MERIT BADGE, EACH OF YOU MUST PERFORM A GOOD DEED...BUT ON ANOTHER WORLD! YOU WILL USE THAT SPACE TELESCOPE AND LONG-RANGE POWER-RAYS!
5

WHEN *KAL-EL'S* TURN COMES...

OUR ASTRONOMERS HAVE FOUND LIFE ON THOSE DISTANT WORLDS! CHOOSE ANY ONE YOU WISH FOR YOUR GOOD DEED, *KAL-EL!*

HMM... I'LL TAKE *EARTH!*

EARTH

BLUE PLANET

ZORNIA

DYON II

AFTER SCANNING EARTH WITH THE SUPER-TELE-SCOPE...

THAT EARTHLY VEHICLE WENT OUT OF CONTROL!

HELP! WE'LL PLUNGE INTO THAT LAKE AND DROWN!

SWIFTLY, KAL-EL USES THE PUSHBUTTONS FOR THE POWER RAYS AND...

I'LL SEND THE *HEAT RAY* TO EARTH, INSTANTLY DRYING UP THAT LAKE!

GOOD HEAVENS! IS... IS THE WATER VANISHING?

SOME MIRACLE SAVED US, MARTHA!

GREAT GUNS! BY SHEER CHANCE, *KAL-EL* SAVED *MOM AND DAD KENT!* IN REAL LIFE, THEY WERE MY FOSTER PARENTS! THEY RAISED ME IN SMALLVILLE WHEN I WAS *SUPERBOY!*

THEY WERE ON THEIR WAY TO AN ORPHANAGE! SINCE I NEVER REACHED EARTH TO BECOME THEIR ADOPTED *SUPERBABY,* THEY'RE ADOPTING ANOTHER CHILD! IT'S A *GIRL!* WHAT A STRANGE TWIST OF FATE!

HAPPY VALLEY ORPHANAGE

BUT OBSERVING HIS MIGHT-HAVE-BEEN LIFE, *SUPER-MAN* AND *BATMAN* ARE EVEN MORE STARTLED AT WHAT *JOR-EL* AND *LARA* ONE DAY SHOW *KAL-EL,* PROUDLY...

SEE, *KAL-EL?* *ZAL-EL* LOOKS LIKE YOU!

LOOK, *SUPER-MAN!* IF YOU HAD LIVED ON *KRYPTON,* YOU WOULD HAVE HAD A BABY *BROTHER!*

6

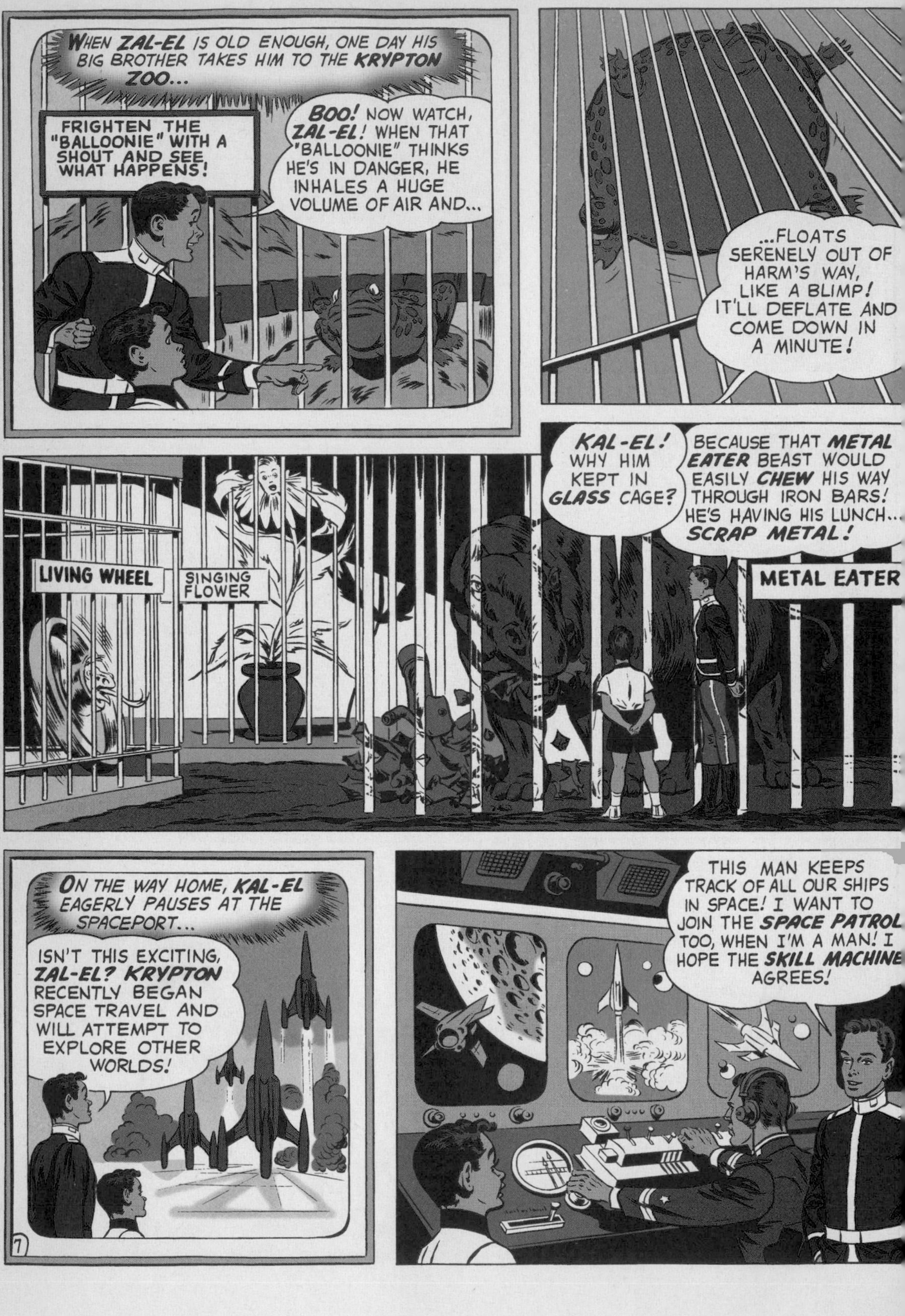
WHEN ZAL-EL IS OLD ENOUGH, ONE DAY HIS BIG BROTHER TAKES HIM TO THE KRYPTON ZOO...
FRIGHTEN THE "BALLOONIE" WITH A SHOUT AND SEE WHAT HAPPENS!
BOO! NOW WATCH, ZAL-EL! WHEN THAT "BALLOONIE" THINKS HE'S IN DANGER, HE INHALES A HUGE VOLUME OF AIR AND...
...FLOATS SERENELY OUT OF HARM'S WAY, LIKE A BLIMP! IT'LL DEFLATE AND COME DOWN IN A MINUTE!
KAL-EL! WHY HIM KEPT IN GLASS CAGE?
BECAUSE THAT METAL EATER BEAST WOULD EASILY CHEW HIS WAY THROUGH IRON BARS! HE'S HAVING HIS LUNCH... SCRAP METAL!
LIVING WHEEL
SINGING FLOWER
METAL EATER
ON THE WAY HOME, KAL-EL EAGERLY PAUSES AT THE SPACEPORT...
ISN'T THIS EXCITING, ZAL-EL? KRYPTON RECENTLY BEGAN SPACE TRAVEL AND WILL ATTEMPT TO EXPLORE OTHER WORLDS!
7
THIS MAN KEEPS TRACK OF ALL OUR SHIPS IN SPACE! I WANT TO JOIN THE SPACE PATROL TOO, WHEN I'M A MAN! I HOPE THE SKILL MACHINE AGREES!

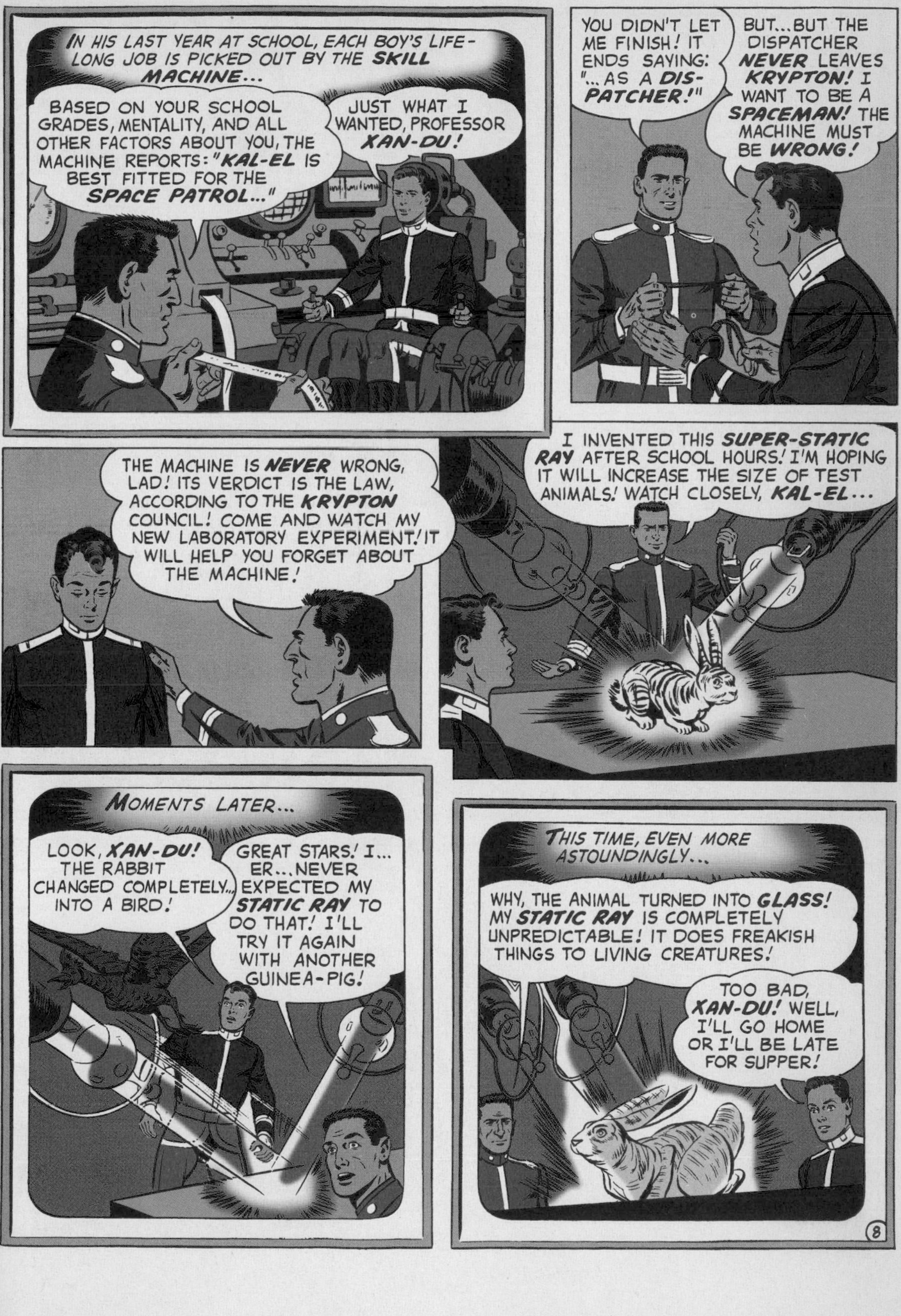
IN HIS LAST YEAR AT SCHOOL, EACH BOY'S LIFE-LONG JOB IS PICKED OUT BY THE SKILL MACHINE...
BASED ON YOUR SCHOOL GRADES, MENTALITY, AND ALL OTHER FACTORS ABOUT YOU, THE MACHINE REPORTS: "KAL-EL IS BEST FITTED FOR THE SPACE PATROL..."
JUST WHAT I WANTED, PROFESSOR XAN-DU!
YOU DIDN'T LET ME FINISH! IT ENDS SAYING: "...AS A DIS-PATCHER!"
BUT...BUT THE DISPATCHER NEVER LEAVES KRYPTON! I WANT TO BE A SPACEMAN! THE MACHINE MUST BE WRONG!
THE MACHINE IS NEVER WRONG, LAD! ITS VERDICT IS THE LAW, ACCORDING TO THE KRYPTON COUNCIL! COME AND WATCH MY NEW LABORATORY EXPERIMENT! IT WILL HELP YOU FORGET ABOUT THE MACHINE!
I INVENTED THIS SUPER-STATIC RAY AFTER SCHOOL HOURS! I'M HOPING IT WILL INCREASE THE SIZE OF TEST ANIMALS! WATCH CLOSELY, KAL-EL...
MOMENTS LATER...
LOOK, XAN-DU! THE RABBIT CHANGED COMPLETELY... INTO A BIRD!
GREAT STARS! I... ER...NEVER EXPECTED MY STATIC RAY TO DO THAT! I'LL TRY IT AGAIN WITH ANOTHER GUINEA-PIG!
THIS TIME, EVEN MORE ASTOUNDINGLY...
WHY, THE ANIMAL TURNED INTO GLASS! MY STATIC RAY IS COMPLETELY UNPREDICTABLE! IT DOES FREAKISH THINGS TO LIVING CREATURES!
TOO BAD, XAN-DU! WELL, I'LL GO HOME OR I'LL BE LATE FOR SUPPER!
8

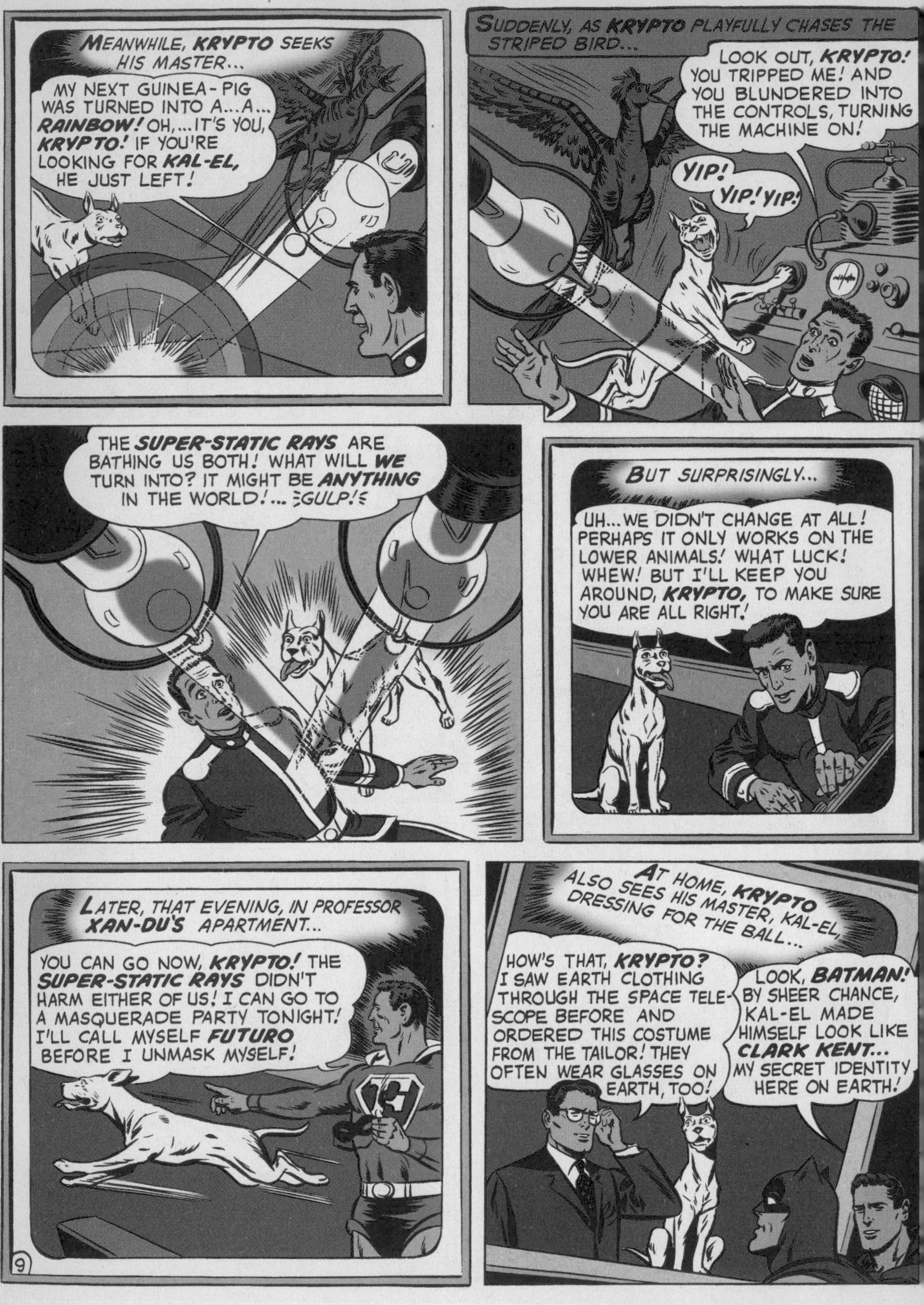
MEANWHILE, KRYPTO SEEKS HIS MASTER...
MY NEXT GUINEA-PIG WAS TURNED INTO A...A... RAINBOW! OH,...IT'S YOU, KRYPTO! IF YOU'RE LOOKING FOR KAL-EL, HE JUST LEFT!
SUDDENLY, AS KRYPTO PLAYFULLY CHASES THE STRIPED BIRD...
LOOK OUT, KRYPTO! YOU TRIPPED ME! AND YOU BLUNDERED INTO THE CONTROLS, TURNING THE MACHINE ON!
YIP!
YIP! YIP!
THE SUPER-STATIC RAYS ARE BATHING US BOTH! WHAT WILL WE TURN INTO? IT MIGHT BE ANYTHING IN THE WORLD!... GULP!
BUT SURPRISINGLY...
UH...WE DIDN'T CHANGE AT ALL! PERHAPS IT ONLY WORKS ON THE LOWER ANIMALS! WHAT LUCK! WHEW! BUT I'LL KEEP YOU AROUND, KRYPTO, TO MAKE SURE YOU ARE ALL RIGHT!
LATER, THAT EVENING, IN PROFESSOR XAN-DU'S APARTMENT...
YOU CAN GO NOW, KRYPTO! THE SUPER-STATIC RAYS DIDN'T HARM EITHER OF US! I CAN GO TO A MASQUERADE PARTY TONIGHT! I'LL CALL MYSELF FUTURO BEFORE I UNMASK MYSELF!
9
AT HOME, KRYPTO ALSO SEES HIS MASTER, KAL-EL, DRESSING FOR THE BALL...
HOW'S THAT, KRYPTO? I SAW EARTH CLOTHING THROUGH THE SPACE TELE-SCOPE BEFORE AND ORDERED THIS COSTUME FROM THE TAILOR! THEY OFTEN WEAR GLASSES ON EARTH, TOO!
LOOK, BATMAN! BY SHEER CHANCE, KAL-EL MADE HIMSELF LOOK LIKE CLARK KENT... MY SECRET IDENTITY HERE ON EARTH!

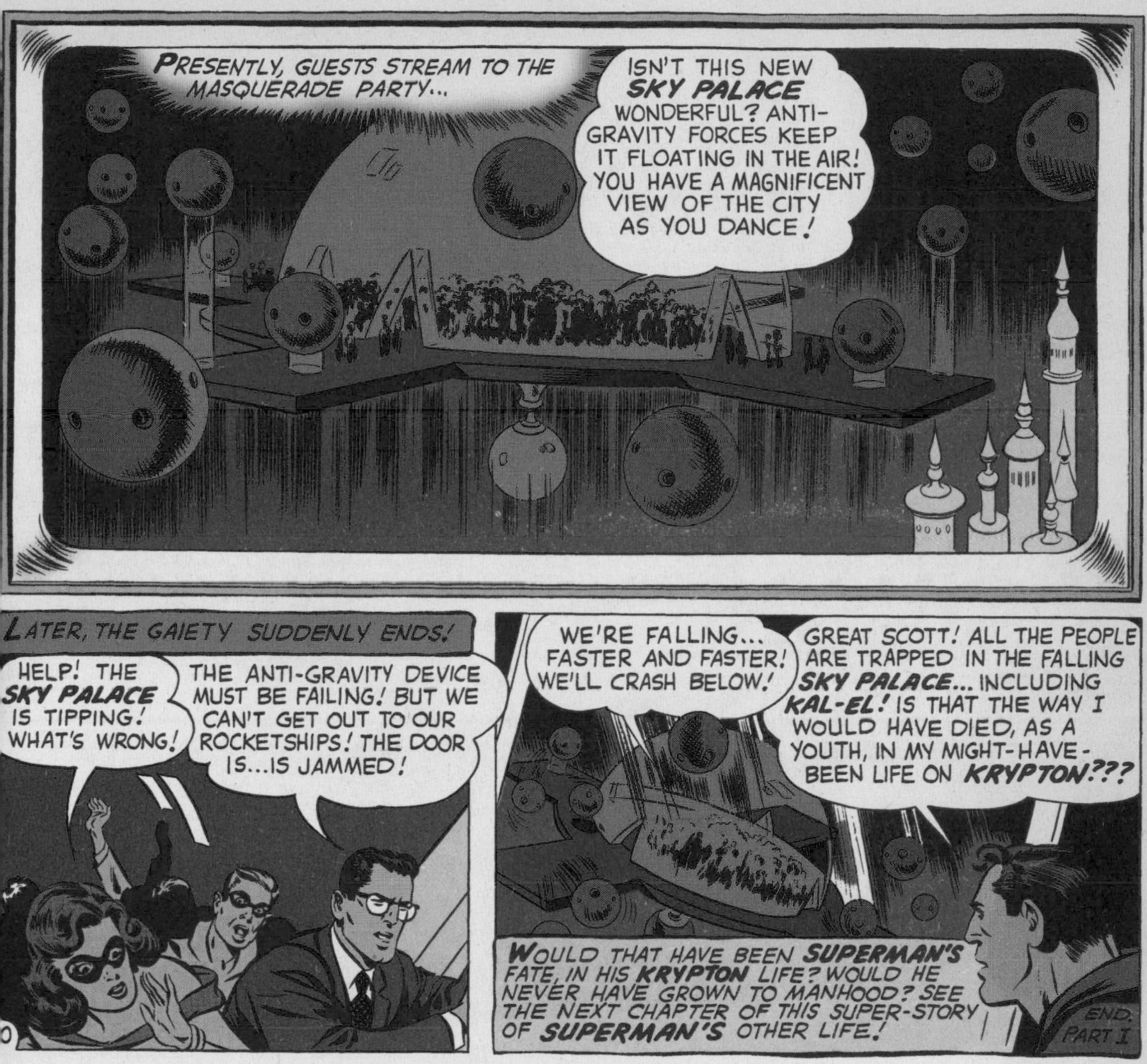
PRESENTLY, GUESTS STREAM TO THE MASQUERADE PARTY...
ISN'T THIS NEW SKY PALACE WONDERFUL? ANTI-GRAVITY FORCES KEEP IT FLOATING IN THE AIR! YOU HAVE A MAGNIFICENT VIEW OF THE CITY AS YOU DANCE!
LATER, THE GAIETY SUDDENLY ENDS!
HELP! THE SKY PALACE IS TIPPING! WHAT'S WRONG!
THE ANTI-GRAVITY DEVICE MUST BE FAILING! BUT WE CAN'T GET OUT TO OUR ROCKETSHIPS! THE DOOR IS...IS JAMMED!
WE'RE FALLING... FASTER AND FASTER! WE'LL CRASH BELOW!
GREAT SCOTT! ALL THE PEOPLE ARE TRAPPED IN THE FALLING SKY PALACE... INCLUDING KAL-EL! IS THAT THE WAY I WOULD HAVE DIED, AS A YOUTH, IN MY MIGHT-HAVE-BEEN LIFE ON KRYPTON???
WOULD THAT HAVE BEEN SUPERMAN'S FATE, IN HIS KRYPTON LIFE? WOULD HE NEVER HAVE GROWN TO MANHOOD? SEE THE NEXT CHAPTER OF THIS SUPER-STORY OF SUPERMAN'S OTHER LIFE!
END. PART I

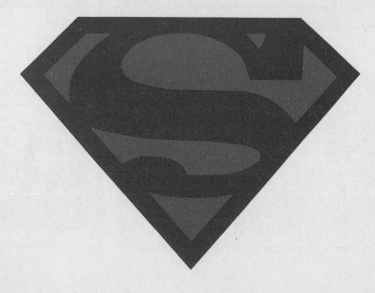

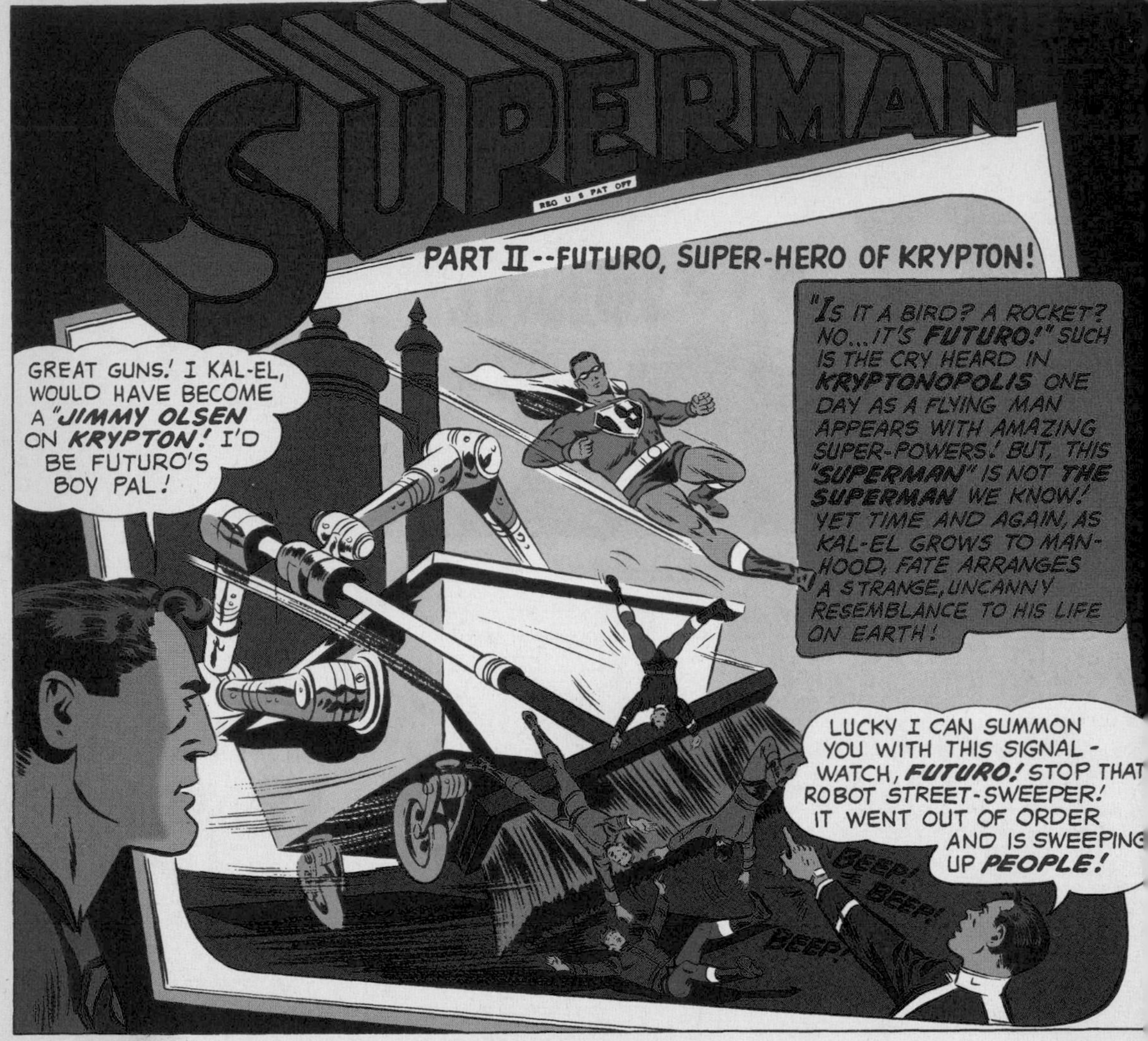
SUPERMAN
REG U S PAT OFF
PART II--FUTURO, SUPER-HERO OF KRYPTON!
"IS IT A BIRD? A ROCKET? NO...IT'S FUTURO!" SUCH IS THE CRY HEARD IN KRYPTONOPOLIS ONE DAY AS A FLYING MAN APPEARS WITH AMAZING SUPER-POWERS! BUT, THIS "SUPERMAN" IS NOT THE SUPERMAN WE KNOW! YET TIME AND AGAIN, AS KAL-EL GROWS TO MANHOOD, FATE ARRANGES A STRANGE, UNCANNY RESEMBLANCE TO HIS LIFE ON EARTH!
GREAT GUNS! I KAL-EL, WOULD HAVE BECOME A "JIMMY OLSEN ON KRYPTON! I'D BE FUTURO'S BOY PAL!
LUCKY I CAN SUMMON YOU WITH THIS SIGNAL-WATCH, FUTURO! STOP THAT ROBOT STREET-SWEEPER! IT WENT OUT OF ORDER AND IS SWEEPING UP PEOPLE!
BEEP! BEEP! BEEP!

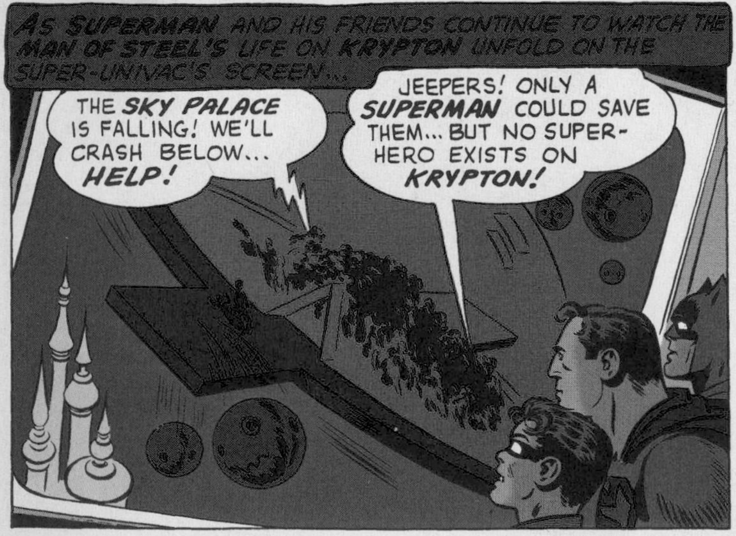
AS SUPERMAN AND HIS FRIENDS CONTINUE TO WATCH THE MAN OF STEEL'S LIFE ON KRYPTON UNFOLD ON THE SUPER-UNIVAC'S SCREEN...
THE SKY PALACE IS FALLING! WE'LL CRASH BELOW... HELP!
JEEPERS! ONLY A SUPERMAN COULD SAVE THEM... BUT NO SUPER-HERO EXISTS ON KRYPTON!

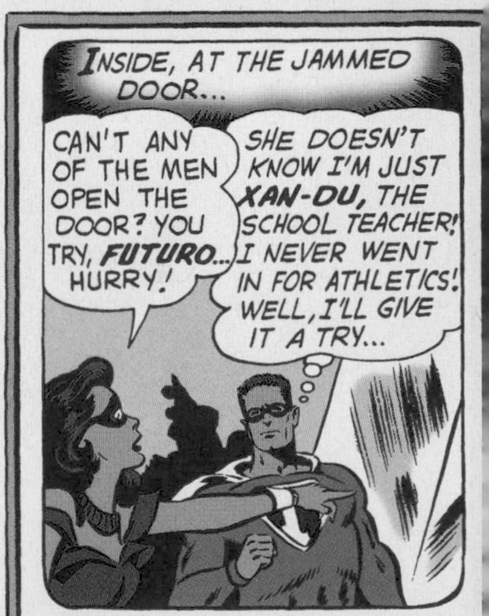
INSIDE, AT THE JAMMED DOOR...
CAN'T ANY OF THE MEN OPEN THE DOOR? YOU TRY, FUTURO...HURRY!
SHE DOESN'T KNOW I'M JUST XAN-DU, THE SCHOOL TEACHER! I NEVER WENT IN FOR ATHLETICS! WELL, I'LL GIVE IT A TRY...

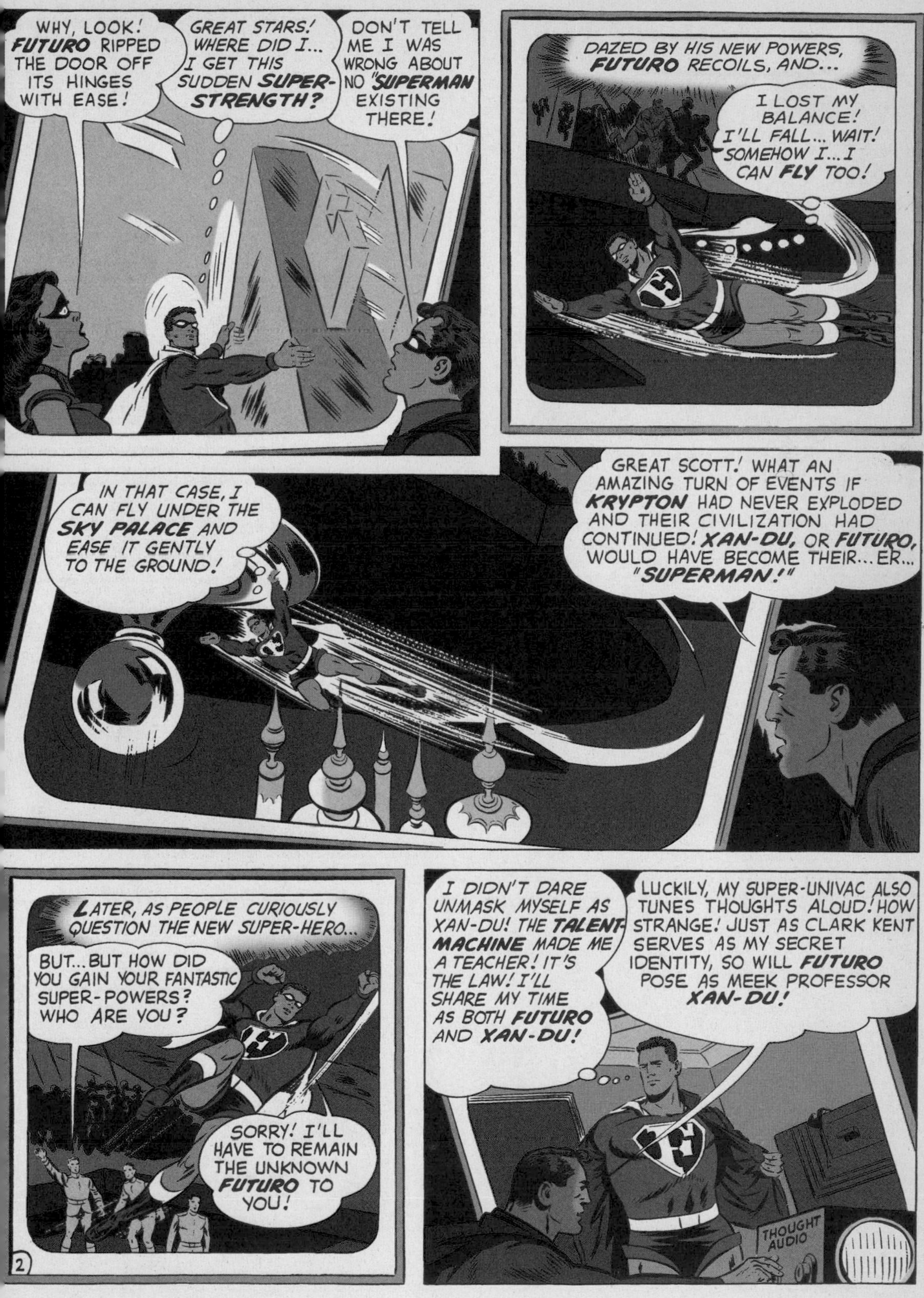
WHY, LOOK! FUTURO RIPPED THE DOOR OFF ITS HINGES WITH EASE!
GREAT STARS! WHERE DID I... I GET THIS SUDDEN SUPER-STRENGTH?
DON'T TELL ME I WAS WRONG ABOUT NO "SUPERMAN" EXISTING THERE!
DAZED BY HIS NEW POWERS, FUTURO RECOILS, AND...
I LOST MY BALANCE! I'LL FALL... WAIT! SOMEHOW I...I CAN FLY TOO!
IN THAT CASE, I CAN FLY UNDER THE SKY PALACE AND EASE IT GENTLY TO THE GROUND!
GREAT SCOTT! WHAT AN AMAZING TURN OF EVENTS IF KRYPTON HAD NEVER EXPLODED AND THEIR CIVILIZATION HAD CONTINUED! XAN-DU, OR FUTURO, WOULD HAVE BECOME THEIR... ER... "SUPERMAN!"
LATER, AS PEOPLE CURIOUSLY QUESTION THE NEW SUPER-HERO...
BUT... BUT HOW DID YOU GAIN YOUR FANTASTIC SUPER-POWERS? WHO ARE YOU?
SORRY! I'LL HAVE TO REMAIN THE UNKNOWN FUTURO TO YOU!
2
I DIDN'T DARE UNMASK MYSELF AS XAN-DU! THE TALENT-MACHINE MADE ME A TEACHER! IT'S THE LAW! I'LL SHARE MY TIME AS BOTH FUTURO AND XAN-DU!
LUCKILY, MY SUPER-UNIVAC ALSO TUNES THOUGHTS ALOUD! HOW STRANGE! JUST AS CLARK KENT SERVES AS MY SECRET IDENTITY, SO WILL FUTURO POSE AS MEEK PROFESSOR XAN-DU!
THOUGHT AUDIO

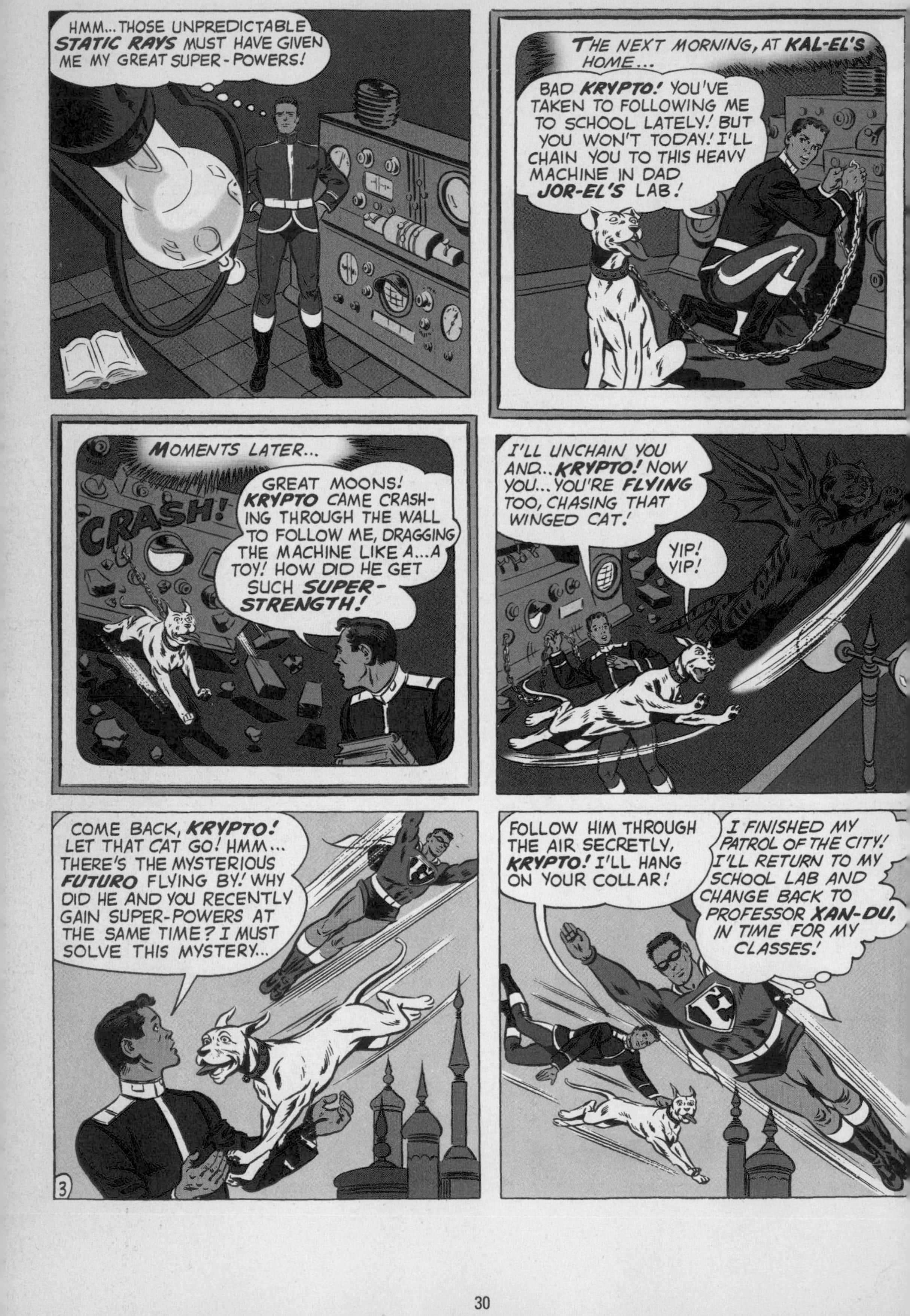
HMM...THOSE UNPREDICTABLE STATIC RAYS MUST HAVE GIVEN ME MY GREAT SUPER-POWERS!
THE NEXT MORNING, AT KAL-EL'S HOME...
BAD KRYPTO! YOU'VE TAKEN TO FOLLOWING ME TO SCHOOL LATELY! BUT YOU WON'T TODAY! I'LL CHAIN YOU TO THIS HEAVY MACHINE IN DAD JOR-EL'S LAB!
MOMENTS LATER...
CRASH!
GREAT MOONS! KRYPTO CAME CRASHING THROUGH THE WALL TO FOLLOW ME, DRAGGING THE MACHINE LIKE A...A TOY! HOW DID HE GET SUCH SUPER-STRENGTH!
I'LL UNCHAIN YOU AND...KRYPTO! NOW YOU...YOU'RE FLYING TOO, CHASING THAT WINGED CAT!
YIP! YIP!
COME BACK, KRYPTO! LET THAT CAT GO! HMM... THERE'S THE MYSTERIOUS FUTURO FLYING BY! WHY DID HE AND YOU RECENTLY GAIN SUPER-POWERS AT THE SAME TIME? I MUST SOLVE THIS MYSTERY...
3
FOLLOW HIM THROUGH THE AIR SECRETLY, KRYPTO! I'LL HANG ON YOUR COLLAR!
I FINISHED MY PATROL OF THE CITY! I'LL RETURN TO MY SCHOOL LAB AND CHANGE BACK TO PROFESSOR XAN-DU, IN TIME FOR MY CLASSES!

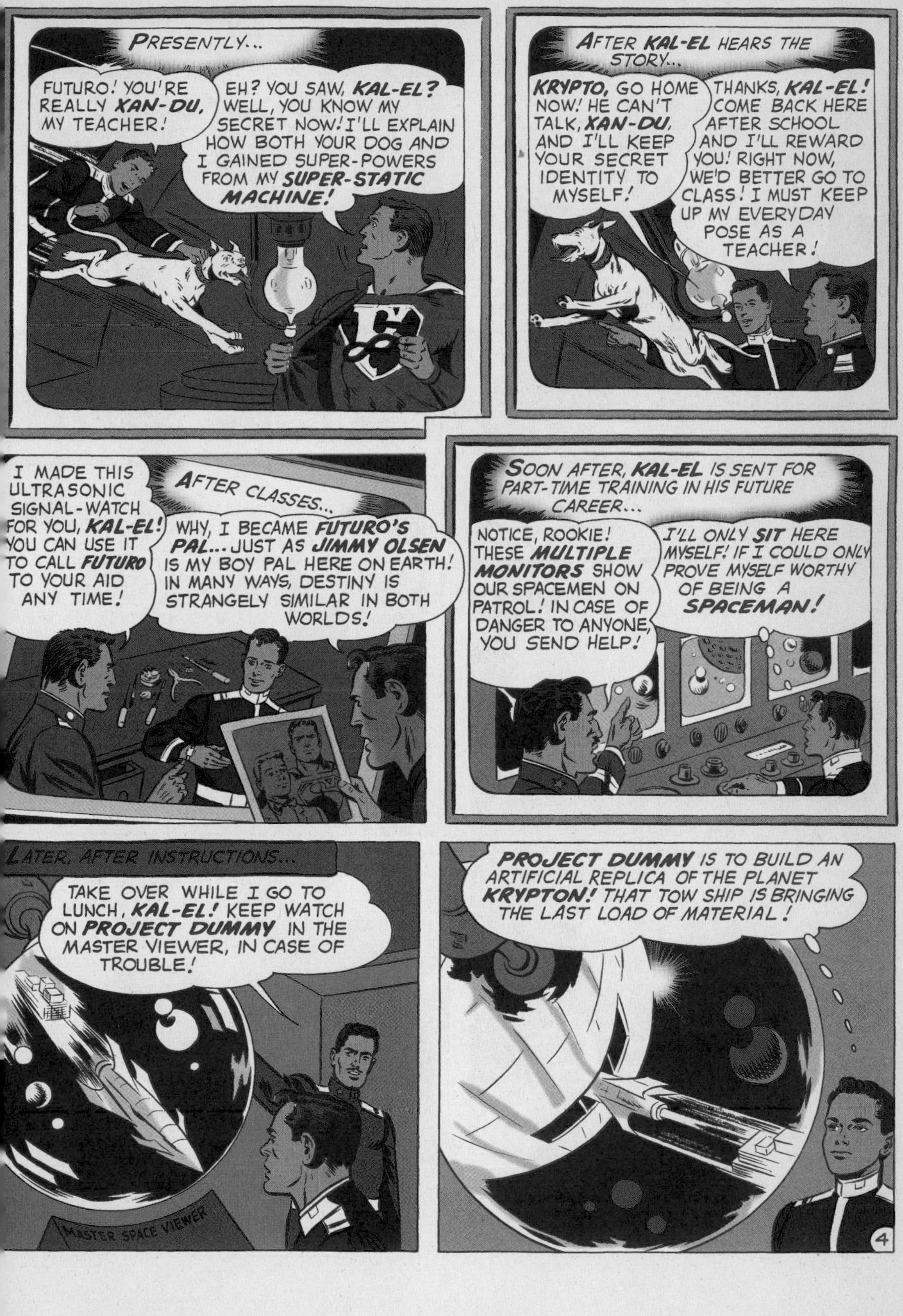
PRESENTLY...
FUTURO! YOU'RE REALLY XAN-DU, MY TEACHER!
EH? YOU SAW, KAL-EL? WELL, YOU KNOW MY SECRET NOW! I'LL EXPLAIN HOW BOTH YOUR DOG AND I GAINED SUPER-POWERS FROM MY SUPER-STATIC MACHINE!
AFTER KAL-EL HEARS THE STORY...
KRYPTO, GO HOME NOW! HE CAN'T TALK, XAN-DU, AND I'LL KEEP YOUR SECRET IDENTITY TO MYSELF!
THANKS, KAL-EL! COME BACK HERE AFTER SCHOOL AND I'LL REWARD YOU! RIGHT NOW, WE'D BETTER GO TO CLASS! I MUST KEEP UP MY EVERYDAY POSE AS A TEACHER!
AFTER CLASSES...
I MADE THIS ULTRASONIC SIGNAL-WATCH FOR YOU, KAL-EL! YOU CAN USE IT TO CALL FUTURO TO YOUR AID ANY TIME!
WHY, I BECAME FUTURO'S PAL... JUST AS JIMMY OLSEN IS MY BOY PAL HERE ON EARTH! IN MANY WAYS, DESTINY IS STRANGELY SIMILAR IN BOTH WORLDS!
SOON AFTER, KAL-EL IS SENT FOR PART-TIME TRAINING IN HIS FUTURE CAREER...
NOTICE, ROOKIE! THESE MULTIPLE MONITORS SHOW OUR SPACEMEN ON PATROL! IN CASE OF DANGER TO ANYONE, YOU SEND HELP!
I'LL ONLY SIT HERE MYSELF! IF I COULD ONLY PROVE MYSELF WORTHY OF BEING A SPACEMAN!
LATER, AFTER INSTRUCTIONS...
TAKE OVER WHILE I GO TO LUNCH, KAL-EL! KEEP WATCH ON PROJECT DUMMY IN THE MASTER VIEWER, IN CASE OF TROUBLE!
MASTER SPACE VIEWER
PROJECT DUMMY IS TO BUILD AN ARTIFICIAL REPLICA OF THE PLANET KRYPTON! THAT TOW SHIP IS BRINGING THE LAST LOAD OF MATERIAL!
4

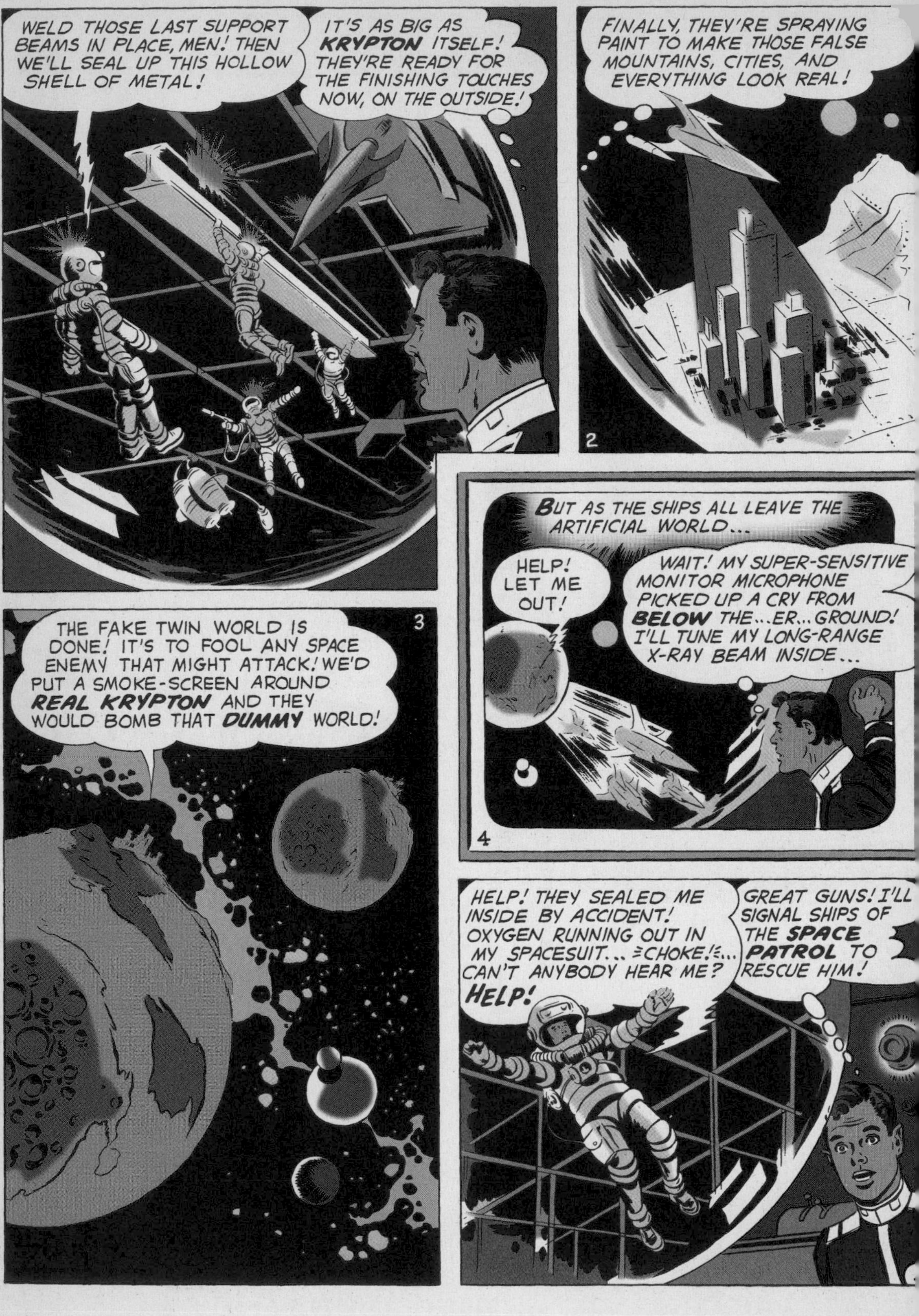
WELD THOSE LAST SUPPORT BEAMS IN PLACE, MEN! THEN WE'LL SEAL UP THIS HOLLOW SHELL OF METAL!
IT'S AS BIG AS KRYPTON ITSELF! THEY'RE READY FOR THE FINISHING TOUCHES NOW, ON THE OUTSIDE!
FINALLY, THEY'RE SPRAYING PAINT TO MAKE THOSE FALSE MOUNTAINS, CITIES, AND EVERYTHING LOOK REAL!
THE FAKE TWIN WORLD IS DONE! IT'S TO FOOL ANY SPACE ENEMY THAT MIGHT ATTACK! WE'D PUT A SMOKE-SCREEN AROUND REAL KRYPTON AND THEY WOULD BOMB THAT DUMMY WORLD!
BUT AS THE SHIPS ALL LEAVE THE ARTIFICIAL WORLD...
HELP! LET ME OUT!
WAIT! MY SUPER-SENSITIVE MONITOR MICROPHONE PICKED UP A CRY FROM BELOW THE...ER...GROUND! I'LL TUNE MY LONG-RANGE X-RAY BEAM INSIDE...
HELP! THEY SEALED ME INSIDE BY ACCIDENT! OXYGEN RUNNING OUT IN MY SPACESUIT... CHOKE!... CAN'T ANYBODY HEAR ME? HELP!
GREAT GUNS! I'LL SIGNAL SHIPS OF THE SPACE PATROL TO RESCUE HIM!

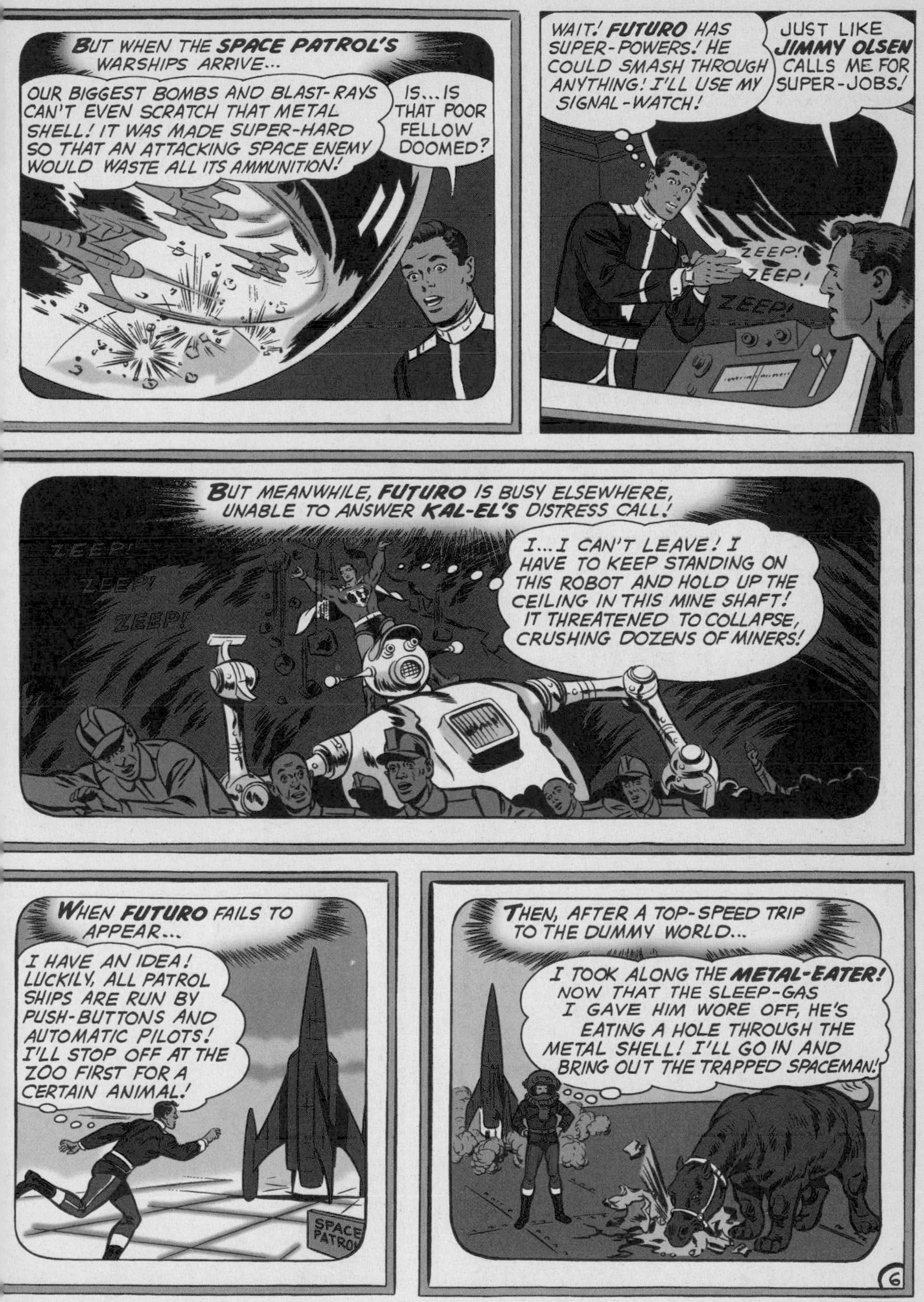
BUT WHEN THE SPACE PATROL'S WARSHIPS ARRIVE...
OUR BIGGEST BOMBS AND BLAST-RAYS CAN'T EVEN SCRATCH THAT METAL SHELL! IT WAS MADE SUPER-HARD SO THAT AN ATTACKING SPACE ENEMY WOULD WASTE ALL ITS AMMUNITION!
IS...IS THAT POOR FELLOW DOOMED?
WAIT! FUTURO HAS SUPER-POWERS! HE COULD SMASH THROUGH ANYTHING! I'LL USE MY SIGNAL-WATCH!
JUST LIKE JIMMY OLSEN CALLS ME FOR SUPER-JOBS!
ZEEP! ZEEP! ZEEP!
BUT MEANWHILE, FUTURO IS BUSY ELSEWHERE, UNABLE TO ANSWER KAL-EL'S DISTRESS CALL!
ZEEP! ZEEP! ZEEP!
I...I CAN'T LEAVE! I HAVE TO KEEP STANDING ON THIS ROBOT AND HOLD UP THE CEILING IN THIS MINE SHAFT! IT THREATENED TO COLLAPSE, CRUSHING DOZENS OF MINERS!
WHEN FUTURO FAILS TO APPEAR...
I HAVE AN IDEA! LUCKILY, ALL PATROL SHIPS ARE RUN BY PUSH-BUTTONS AND AUTOMATIC PILOTS! I'LL STOP OFF AT THE ZOO FIRST FOR A CERTAIN ANIMAL!
SPACE PATROL
THEN, AFTER A TOP-SPEED TRIP TO THE DUMMY WORLD...
I TOOK ALONG THE METAL-EATER! NOW THAT THE SLEEP-GAS I GAVE HIM WORE OFF, HE'S EATING A HOLE THROUGH THE METAL SHELL! I'LL GO IN AND BRING OUT THE TRAPPED SPACEMAN!
6

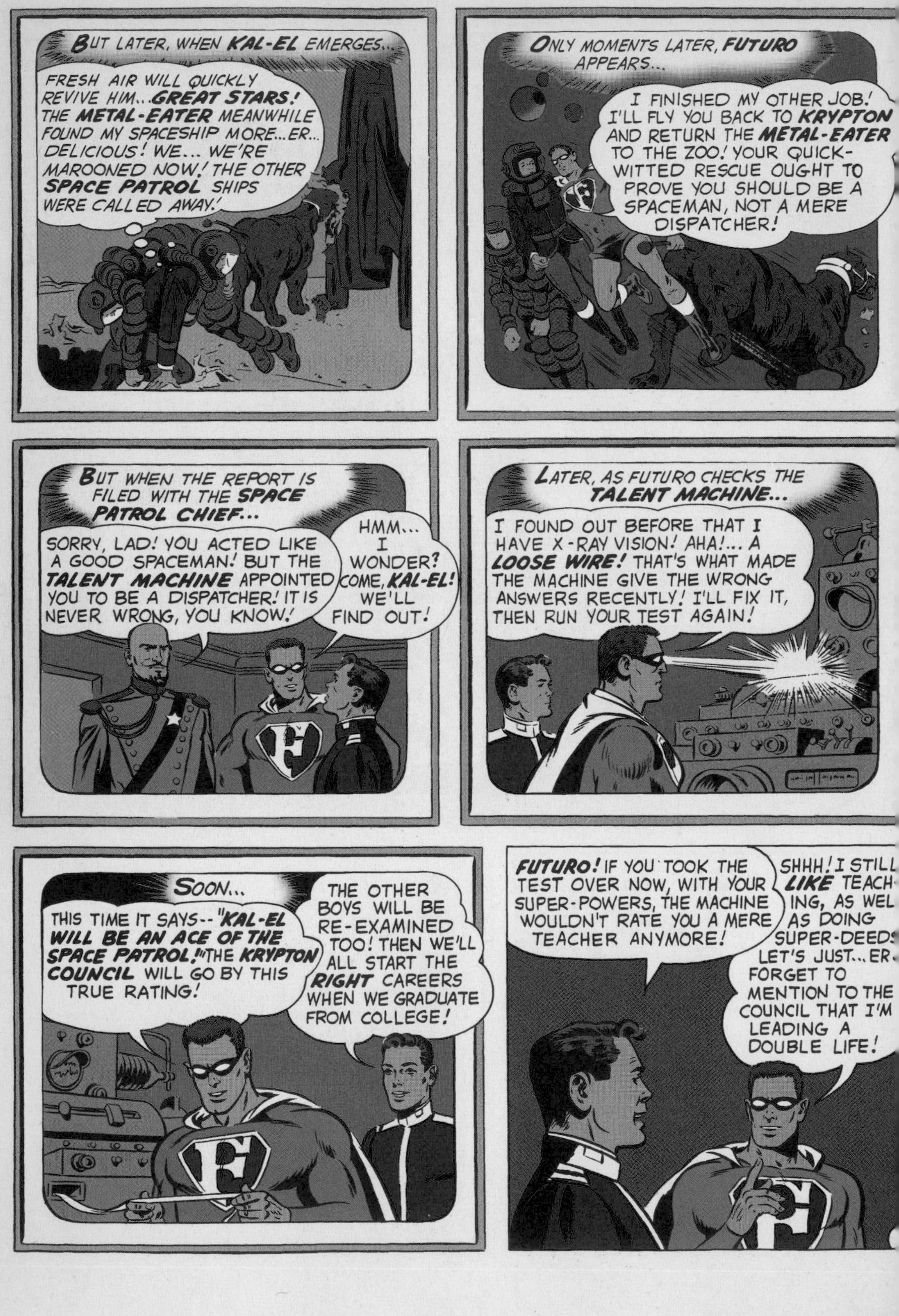
BUT LATER, WHEN KAL-EL EMERGES...
FRESH AIR WILL QUICKLY REVIVE HIM... GREAT STARS! THE METAL-EATER MEANWHILE FOUND MY SPACESHIP MORE... ER... DELICIOUS! WE... WE'RE MAROONED NOW! THE OTHER SPACE PATROL SHIPS WERE CALLED AWAY!
ONLY MOMENTS LATER, FUTURO APPEARS...
I FINISHED MY OTHER JOB! I'LL FLY YOU BACK TO KRYPTON AND RETURN THE METAL-EATER TO THE ZOO! YOUR QUICK-WITTED RESCUE OUGHT TO PROVE YOU SHOULD BE A SPACEMAN, NOT A MERE DISPATCHER!
BUT WHEN THE REPORT IS FILED WITH THE SPACE PATROL CHIEF...
SORRY, LAD! YOU ACTED LIKE A GOOD SPACEMAN! BUT THE TALENT MACHINE APPOINTED YOU TO BE A DISPATCHER! IT IS NEVER WRONG, YOU KNOW!
HMM... I WONDER? COME, KAL-EL! WE'LL FIND OUT!
LATER, AS FUTURO CHECKS THE TALENT MACHINE...
I FOUND OUT BEFORE THAT I HAVE X-RAY VISION! AHA!... A LOOSE WIRE! THAT'S WHAT MADE THE MACHINE GIVE THE WRONG ANSWERS RECENTLY! I'LL FIX IT, THEN RUN YOUR TEST AGAIN!
SOON...
THIS TIME IT SAYS--"KAL-EL WILL BE AN ACE OF THE SPACE PATROL!" THE KRYPTON COUNCIL WILL GO BY THIS TRUE RATING!
THE OTHER BOYS WILL BE RE-EXAMINED TOO! THEN WE'LL ALL START THE RIGHT CAREERS WHEN WE GRADUATE FROM COLLEGE!
FUTURO! IF YOU TOOK THE TEST OVER NOW, WITH YOUR SUPER-POWERS, THE MACHINE WOULDN'T RATE YOU A MERE TEACHER ANYMORE!
SHHH! I STILL LIKE TEACH-ING, AS WEL AS DOING SUPER-DEED LET'S JUST... ER. FORGET TO MENTION TO THE COUNCIL THAT I'M LEADING A DOUBLE LIFE!

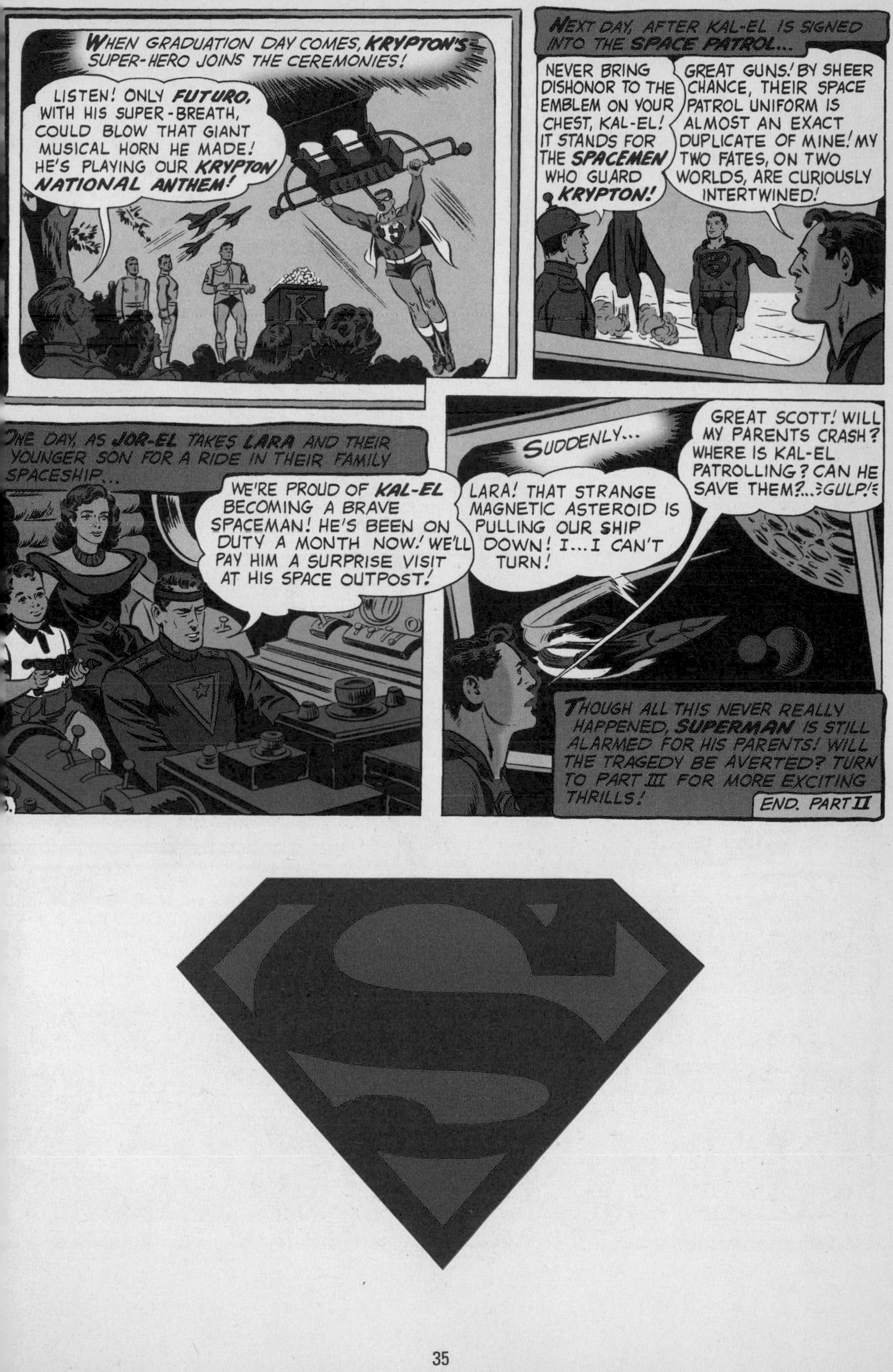
WHEN GRADUATION DAY COMES, KRYPTON'S SUPER-HERO JOINS THE CEREMONIES!
LISTEN! ONLY FUTURO, WITH HIS SUPER-BREATH, COULD BLOW THAT GIANT MUSICAL HORN HE MADE! HE'S PLAYING OUR KRYPTON NATIONAL ANTHEM!
NEXT DAY, AFTER KAL-EL IS SIGNED INTO THE SPACE PATROL...
NEVER BRING DISHONOR TO THE EMBLEM ON YOUR CHEST, KAL-EL! IT STANDS FOR THE SPACEMEN WHO GUARD KRYPTON!
GREAT GUNS! BY SHEER CHANCE, THEIR SPACE PATROL UNIFORM IS ALMOST AN EXACT DUPLICATE OF MINE! MY TWO FATES, ON TWO WORLDS, ARE CURIOUSLY INTERTWINED!
ONE DAY, AS JOR-EL TAKES LARA AND THEIR YOUNGER SON FOR A RIDE IN THEIR FAMILY SPACESHIP...
WE'RE PROUD OF KAL-EL BECOMING A BRAVE SPACEMAN! HE'S BEEN ON DUTY A MONTH NOW! WE'LL PAY HIM A SURPRISE VISIT AT HIS SPACE OUTPOST!
SUDDENLY...
LARA! THAT STRANGE MAGNETIC ASTEROID IS PULLING OUR SHIP DOWN! I...I CAN'T TURN!
GREAT SCOTT! WILL MY PARENTS CRASH? WHERE IS KAL-EL PATROLLING? CAN HE SAVE THEM?...GULP!
THOUGH ALL THIS NEVER REALLY HAPPENED, SUPERMAN IS STILL ALARMED FOR HIS PARENTS! WILL THE TRAGEDY BE AVERTED? TURN TO PART III FOR MORE EXCITING THRILLS!
END. PART II

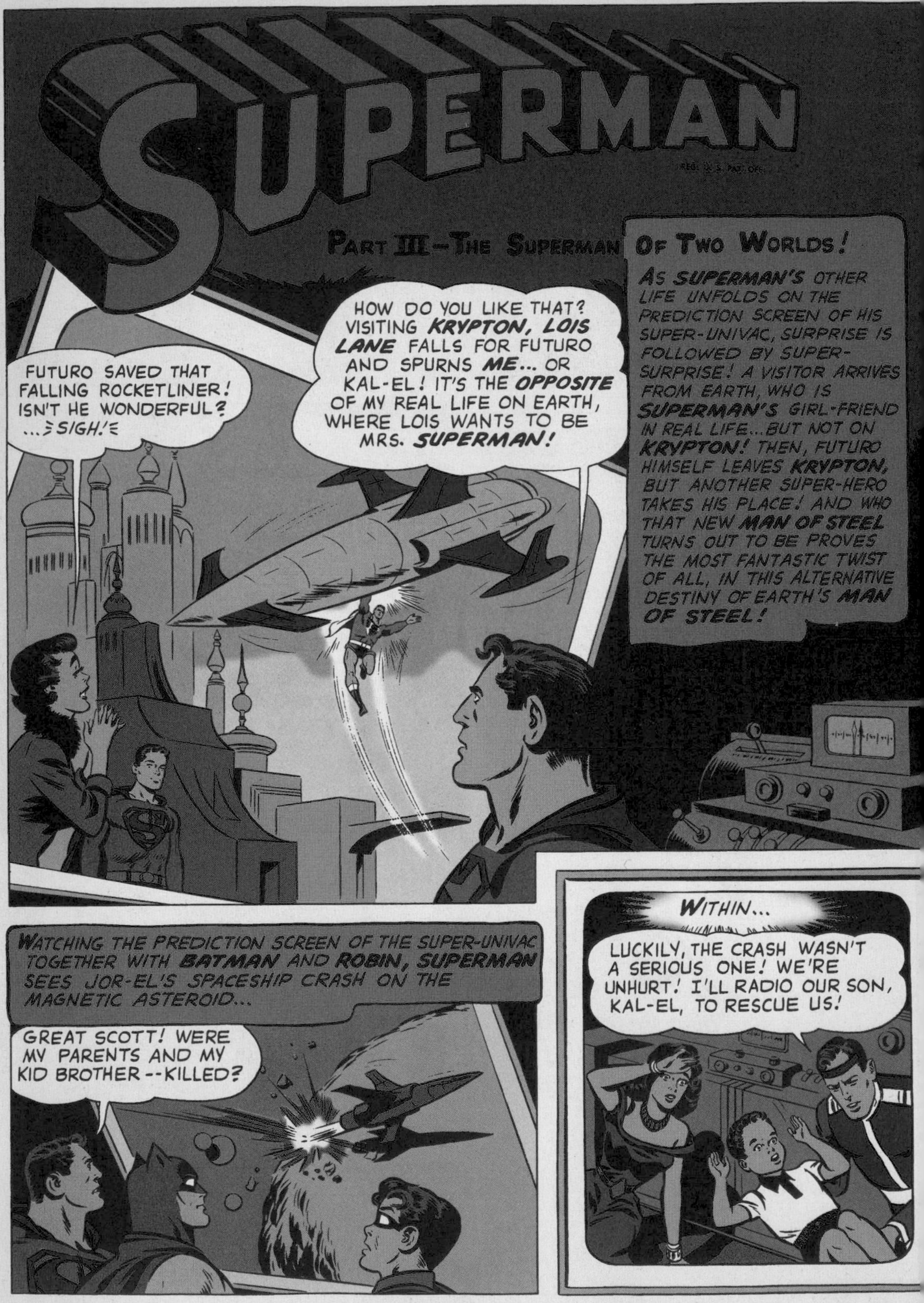
SUPERMAN
REG. U.S. PAT. OFF.
PART III—THE SUPERMAN OF TWO WORLDS!
AS SUPERMAN'S OTHER LIFE UNFOLDS ON THE PREDICTION SCREEN OF HIS SUPER-UNIVAC, SURPRISE IS FOLLOWED BY SUPER-SURPRISE! A VISITOR ARRIVES FROM EARTH, WHO IS SUPERMAN'S GIRL-FRIEND IN REAL LIFE...BUT NOT ON KRYPTON! THEN, FUTURO HIMSELF LEAVES KRYPTON, BUT ANOTHER SUPER-HERO TAKES HIS PLACE! AND WHO THAT NEW MAN OF STEEL TURNS OUT TO BE PROVES THE MOST FANTASTIC TWIST OF ALL, IN THIS ALTERNATIVE DESTINY OF EARTH'S MAN OF STEEL!
FUTURO SAVED THAT FALLING ROCKETLINER! ISN'T HE WONDERFUL? ...SIGH!
HOW DO YOU LIKE THAT? VISITING KRYPTON, LOIS LANE FALLS FOR FUTURO AND SPURNS ME... OR KAL-EL! IT'S THE OPPOSITE OF MY REAL LIFE ON EARTH, WHERE LOIS WANTS TO BE MRS. SUPERMAN!
WATCHING THE PREDICTION SCREEN OF THE SUPER-UNIVAC TOGETHER WITH BATMAN AND ROBIN, SUPERMAN SEES JOR-EL'S SPACESHIP CRASH ON THE MAGNETIC ASTEROID...
GREAT SCOTT! WERE MY PARENTS AND MY KID BROTHER--KILLED?
WITHIN...
LUCKILY, THE CRASH WASN'T A SERIOUS ONE! WE'RE UNHURT! I'LL RADIO OUR SON, KAL-EL, TO RESCUE US!

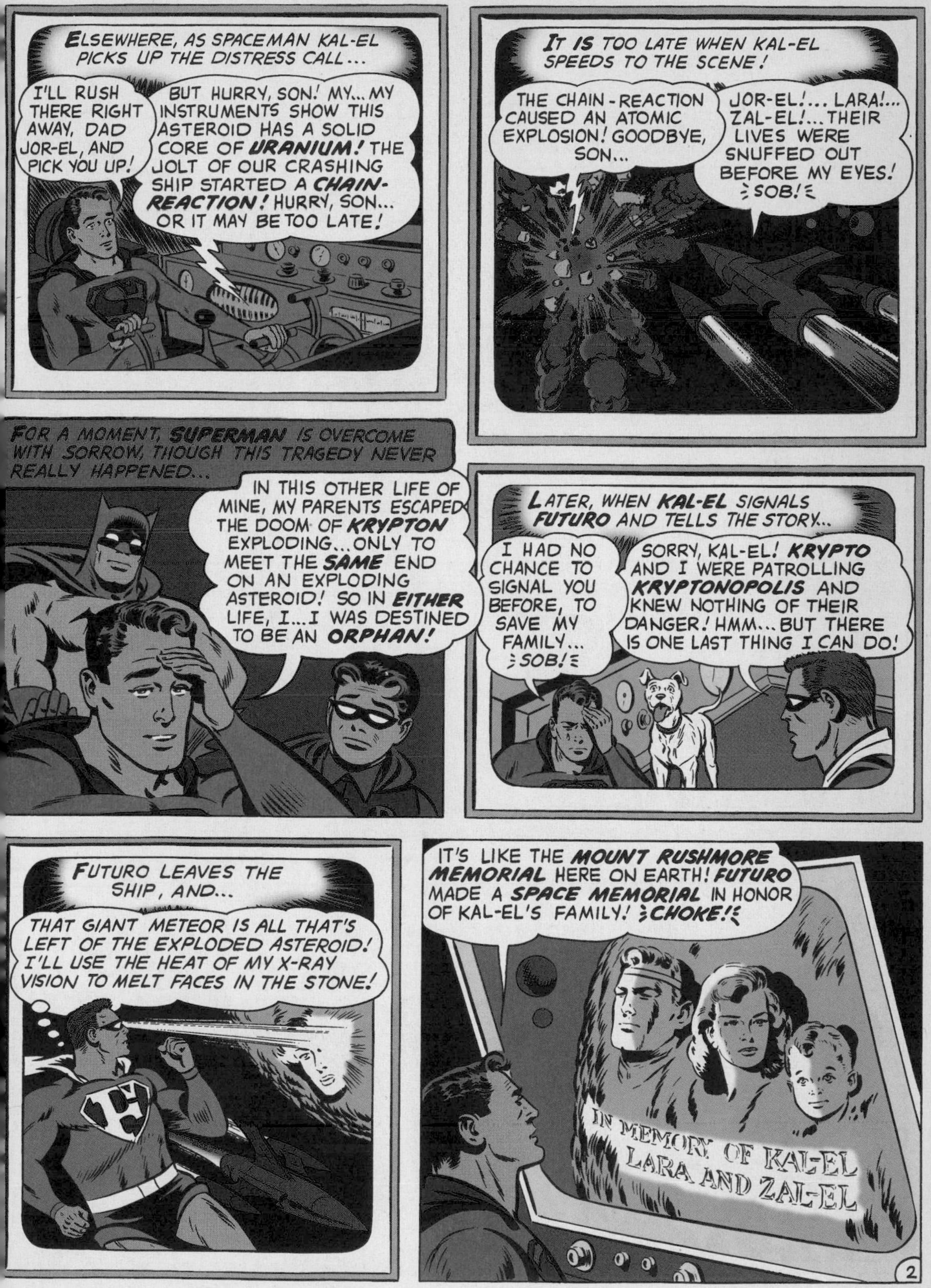
ELSEWHERE, AS SPACEMAN KAL-EL PICKS UP THE DISTRESS CALL...
I'LL RUSH THERE RIGHT AWAY, DAD JOR-EL, AND PICK YOU UP!
BUT HURRY, SON! MY... MY INSTRUMENTS SHOW THIS ASTEROID HAS A SOLID CORE OF URANIUM! THE JOLT OF OUR CRASHING SHIP STARTED A CHAIN-REACTION! HURRY, SON... OR IT MAY BE TOO LATE!
IT IS TOO LATE WHEN KAL-EL SPEEDS TO THE SCENE!
THE CHAIN-REACTION CAUSED AN ATOMIC EXPLOSION! GOODBYE, SON...
JOR-EL!... LARA!... ZAL-EL!... THEIR LIVES WERE SNUFFED OUT BEFORE MY EYES! SOB!
FOR A MOMENT, SUPERMAN IS OVERCOME WITH SORROW, THOUGH THIS TRAGEDY NEVER REALLY HAPPENED...
IN THIS OTHER LIFE OF MINE, MY PARENTS ESCAPED THE DOOM OF KRYPTON EXPLODING... ONLY TO MEET THE SAME END ON AN EXPLODING ASTEROID! SO IN EITHER LIFE, I... I WAS DESTINED TO BE AN ORPHAN!
LATER, WHEN KAL-EL SIGNALS FUTURO AND TELLS THE STORY...
I HAD NO CHANCE TO SIGNAL YOU BEFORE, TO SAVE MY FAMILY... SOB!
SORRY, KAL-EL! KRYPTO AND I WERE PATROLLING KRYPTONOPOLIS AND KNEW NOTHING OF THEIR DANGER! HMM... BUT THERE IS ONE LAST THING I CAN DO!
FUTURO LEAVES THE SHIP, AND...
THAT GIANT METEOR IS ALL THAT'S LEFT OF THE EXPLODED ASTEROID! I'LL USE THE HEAT OF MY X-RAY VISION TO MELT FACES IN THE STONE!
IT'S LIKE THE MOUNT RUSHMORE MEMORIAL HERE ON EARTH! FUTURO MADE A SPACE MEMORIAL IN HONOR OF KAL-EL'S FAMILY! CHOKE!
IN MEMORY OF KAL-EL LARA AND ZAL-EL
2

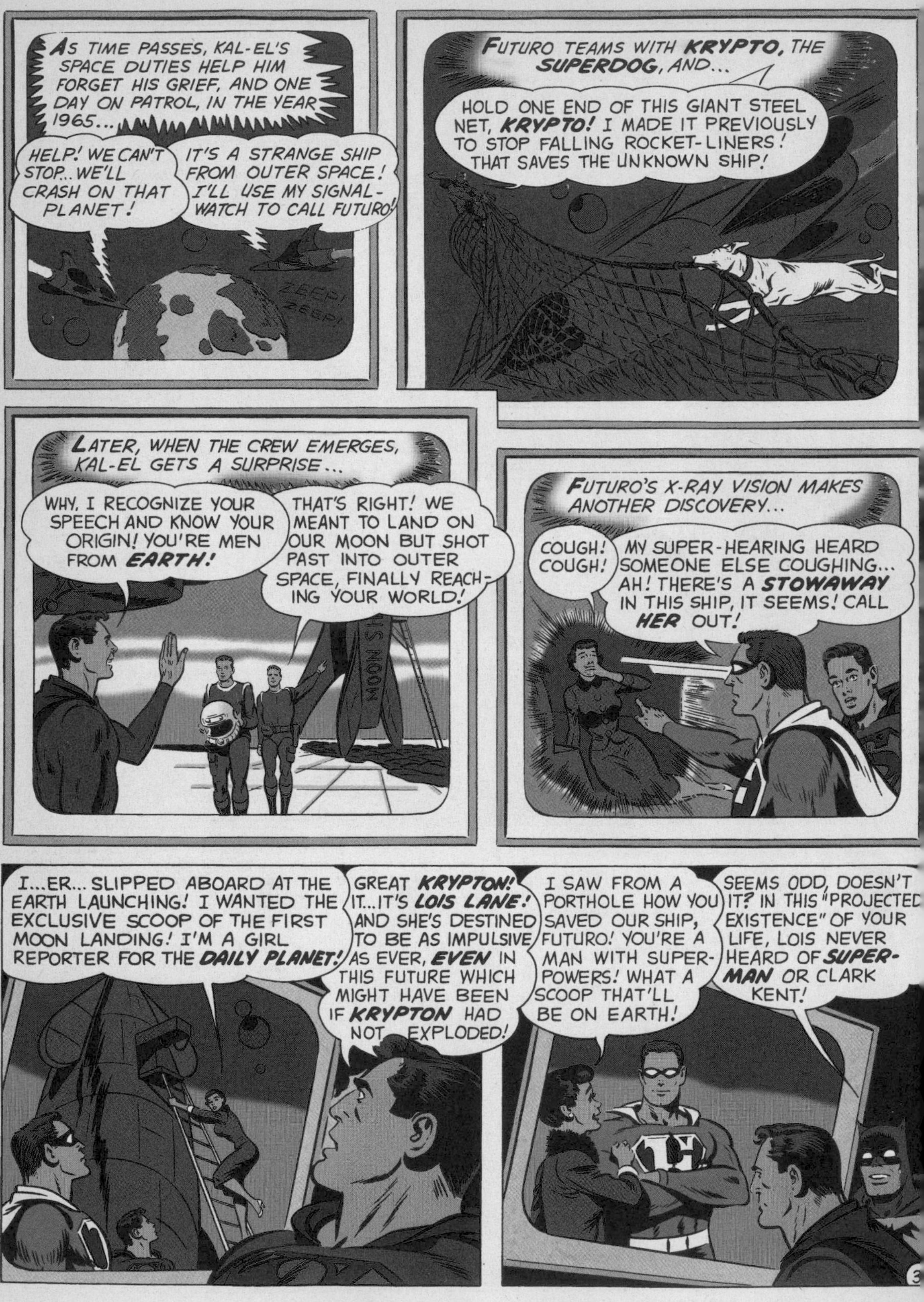
AS TIME PASSES, KAL-EL'S SPACE DUTIES HELP HIM FORGET HIS GRIEF, AND ONE DAY ON PATROL, IN THE YEAR 1965...
HELP! WE CAN'T STOP...WE'LL CRASH ON THAT PLANET!
IT'S A STRANGE SHIP FROM OUTER SPACE! I'LL USE MY SIGNAL-WATCH TO CALL FUTURO!
ZEEP! ZEEP!
FUTURO TEAMS WITH KRYPTO, THE SUPERDOG, AND...
HOLD ONE END OF THIS GIANT STEEL NET, KRYPTO! I MADE IT PREVIOUSLY TO STOP FALLING ROCKET-LINERS! THAT SAVES THE UNKNOWN SHIP!
LATER, WHEN THE CREW EMERGES, KAL-EL GETS A SURPRISE...
WHY, I RECOGNIZE YOUR SPEECH AND KNOW YOUR ORIGIN! YOU'RE MEN FROM EARTH!
THAT'S RIGHT! WE MEANT TO LAND ON OUR MOON BUT SHOT PAST INTO OUTER SPACE, FINALLY REACHING YOUR WORLD!
MOON SHIP
FUTURO'S X-RAY VISION MAKES ANOTHER DISCOVERY...
COUGH! COUGH!
MY SUPER-HEARING HEARD SOMEONE ELSE COUGHING... AH! THERE'S A STOWAWAY IN THIS SHIP, IT SEEMS! CALL HER OUT!
I...ER... SLIPPED ABOARD AT THE EARTH LAUNCHING! I WANTED THE EXCLUSIVE SCOOP OF THE FIRST MOON LANDING! I'M A GIRL REPORTER FOR THE DAILY PLANET!
GREAT KRYPTON! IT...IT'S LOIS LANE! AND SHE'S DESTINED TO BE AS IMPULSIVE AS EVER, EVEN IN THIS FUTURE WHICH MIGHT HAVE BEEN IF KRYPTON HAD NOT EXPLODED!
I SAW FROM A PORTHOLE HOW YOU SAVED OUR SHIP, FUTURO! YOU'RE A MAN WITH SUPER-POWERS! WHAT A SCOOP THAT'LL BE ON EARTH!
SEEMS ODD, DOESN'T IT? IN THIS "PROJECTED EXISTENCE" OF YOUR LIFE, LOIS NEVER HEARD OF SUPERMAN OR CLARK KENT!
3

PRESENTLY, WHEN KAL-EL'S CHIEF ARRIVES TO GREET THE VISITORS FROM EARTH...

THE TWO EARTH PILOTS AND I WILL COMPARE NOTES ON SPACE TRAVEL! KAL-EL, YOU ESCORT MISS LANE AROUND TOWN AND SHOW HER THE SIGHTS!

WITH PLEASURE, SIR!

KRYPTON'S SCIENTIFIC WONDERS ARE SHOWN TO THE EARTHGIRL!

WHEN A BLIZZARD STARTS, WE TURN ON OUR ARTIFICIAL SUN TO MELT THE SNOW BEFORE IT FALLS!

GOODNESS! YOU CONTROL YOUR OWN WEATHER!

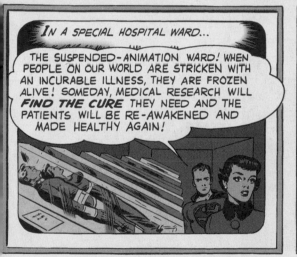

IN A SPECIAL HOSPITAL WARD...

THE SUSPENDED-ANIMATION WARD! WHEN PEOPLE ON OUR WORLD ARE STRICKEN WITH AN INCURABLE ILLNESS, THEY ARE FROZEN ALIVE! SOMEDAY, MEDICAL RESEARCH WILL FIND THE CURE THEY NEED AND THE PATIENTS WILL BE RE-AWAKENED AND MADE HEALTHY AGAIN!

LATER, TAKING LOIS IN A PASSENGER ROCKET TO THE DESERT...

WAR IS OBSOLETE ON KRYPTON, MISS LANE! FORMER WEAPONS ARE ON EXHIBIT IN THAT MUSEUM AS CURIOSITIES! THEY HAVEN'T BEEN USED FOR CENTURIES!

HMM... IS THAT A SUBMARINE LIKE WE HAVE ON EARTH?

NO! THAT'S THE SUBSURFACER! IT COULD DRILL THROUGH ROCK AND CRUISE UNDERGROUND! IT WOULD TORPEDO CITIES FROM BELOW!

4

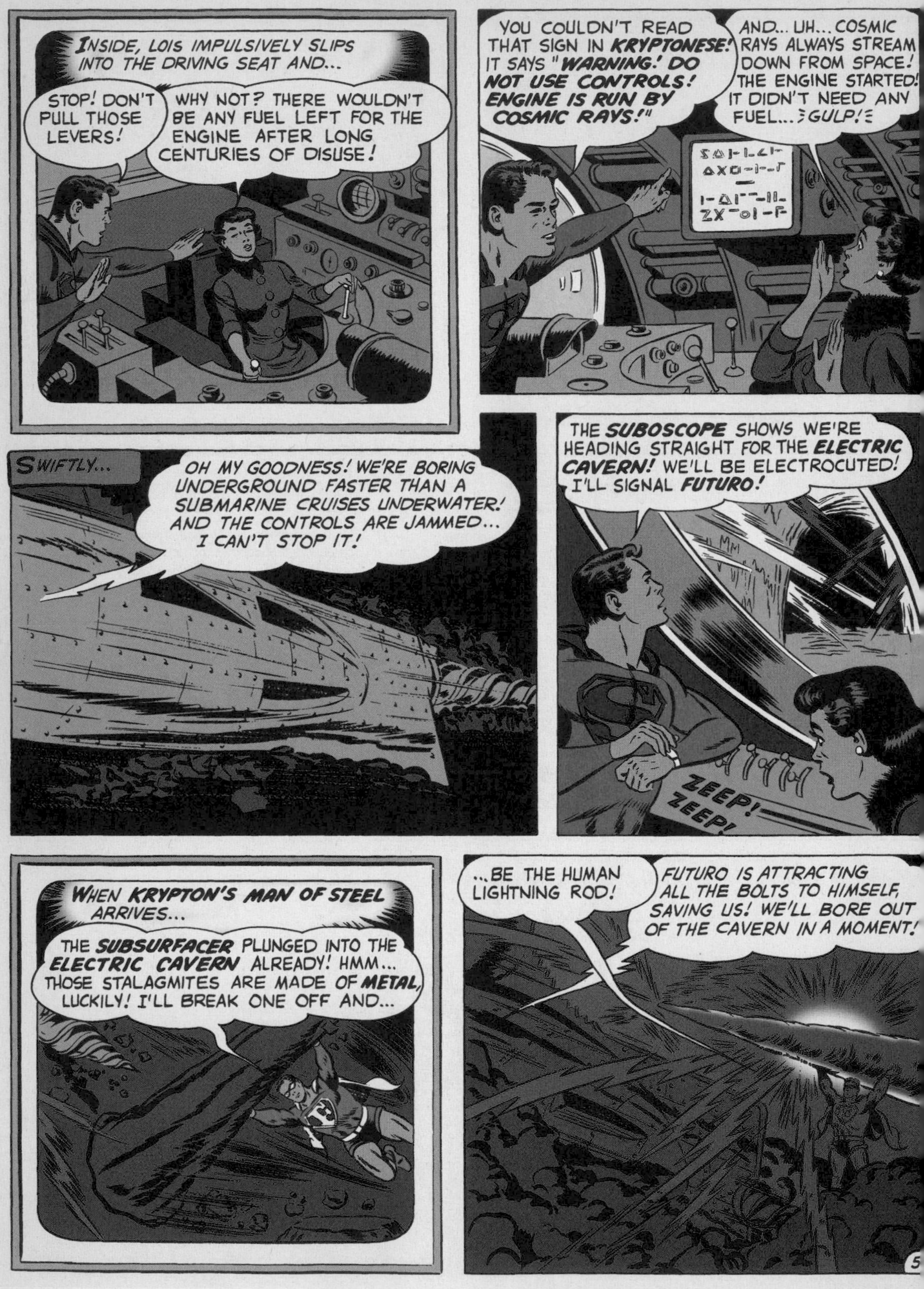
INSIDE, LOIS IMPULSIVELY SLIPS INTO THE DRIVING SEAT AND...
STOP! DON'T PULL THOSE LEVERS!
WHY NOT? THERE WOULDN'T BE ANY FUEL LEFT FOR THE ENGINE AFTER LONG CENTURIES OF DISUSE!
YOU COULDN'T READ THAT SIGN IN KRYPTONESE! IT SAYS "WARNING! DO NOT USE CONTROLS! ENGINE IS RUN BY COSMIC RAYS!"
AND... UH... COSMIC RAYS ALWAYS STREAM DOWN FROM SPACE! THE ENGINE STARTED! IT DIDN'T NEED ANY FUEL... GULP!
SWIFTLY...
OH MY GOODNESS! WE'RE BORING UNDERGROUND FASTER THAN A SUBMARINE CRUISES UNDERWATER! AND THE CONTROLS ARE JAMMED... I CAN'T STOP IT!
THE SUBOSCOPE SHOWS WE'RE HEADING STRAIGHT FOR THE ELECTRIC CAVERN! WE'LL BE ELECTROCUTED! I'LL SIGNAL FUTURO!
ZEEP! ZEEP!
WHEN KRYPTON'S MAN OF STEEL ARRIVES...
THE SUBSURFACER PLUNGED INTO THE ELECTRIC CAVERN ALREADY! HMM... THOSE STALAGMITES ARE MADE OF METAL, LUCKILY! I'LL BREAK ONE OFF AND...
...BE THE HUMAN LIGHTNING ROD!
FUTURO IS ATTRACTING ALL THE BOLTS TO HIMSELF, SAVING US! WE'LL BORE OUT OF THE CAVERN IN A MOMENT!
5

AFTER KAL-EL MANAGES TO TURN THE CRAFT UPWARD TO THE SURFACE...

BUT THE CORKSCREW IS STILL WHIRLING! I'LL LET IT HIT MY INVULNERABLE BODY AND BURST APART! THIS DANGEROUS CRAFT SHOULD BE DESTROYED ANYWAY!

WHEN LOIS AND KAL-EL COME OUT...

YOU'RE SO WONDERFUL, FUTURO! WHOEVER BECOMES MRS. FUTURO WOULD BE THE LUCKIEST GIRL ALIVE!...SIGH!

SAME OLD LOIS, EH, SUPERMAN? SHE FELL FOR YOU ON EARTH...AND SHE'S FALLING FOR THAT OTHER "SUPERMAN" ON KRYPTON!

BUT LOOK! THERE'S A NEW TWIST! SUPERMAN NEVER FELL FOR LOIS...BUT FUTURO DID!

I...ER...LIKED YOU AT FIRST SIGHT, EARTHGIRL! I...UH...WELL, WHY WASTE TIME? WILL YOU MARRY ME?

OH, YES...YES, FUTURO DARLING! BUT I WANT TO HAVE A HOME ON MY OWN WORLD, NOT HERE!

HMM...I WOULD STILL HAVE SUPER-POWERS ON EARTH, SO WE'LL SETTLE DOWN THERE! ANYTHING TO MAKE YOU HAPPY, MY DEAR!

BUT...BUT FUTURO! IF YOU MOVE TO EARTH, YOU'LL BE LEAVING YOUR OWN NATIVE WORLD WITHOUT A SUPER-HERO!

NO, KAL-EL! COME WITH ME TO MY LAB!

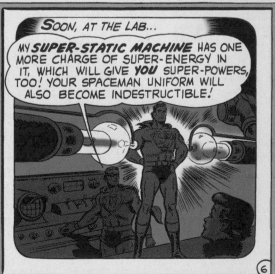

SOON, AT THE LAB...

MY SUPER-STATIC MACHINE HAS ONE MORE CHARGE OF SUPER-ENERGY IN IT, WHICH WILL GIVE YOU SUPER-POWERS, TOO! YOUR SPACEMAN UNIFORM WILL ALSO BECOME INDESTRUCTIBLE!

6

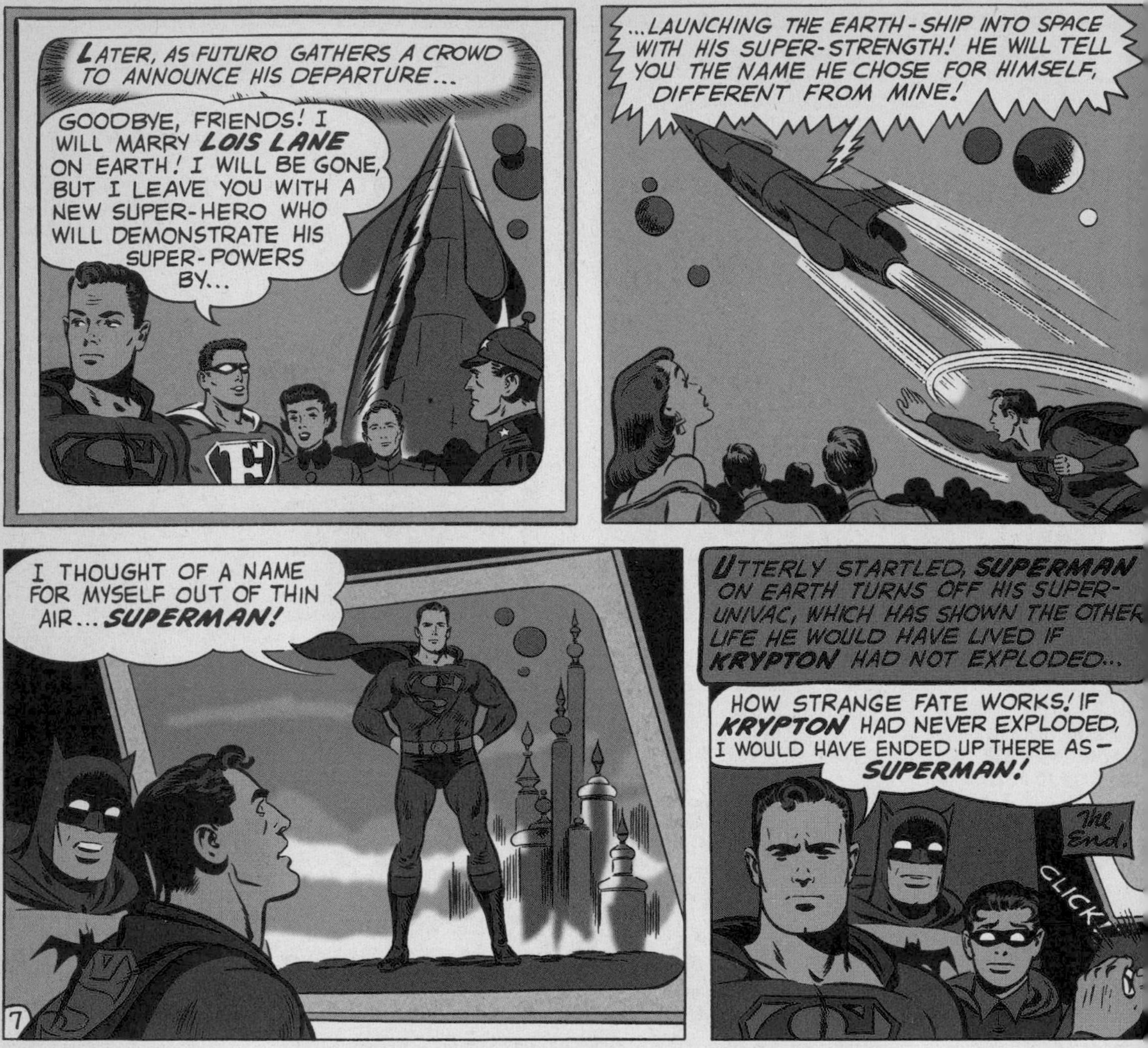
LATER, AS FUTURO GATHERS A CROWD TO ANNOUNCE HIS DEPARTURE...
GOODBYE, FRIENDS! I WILL MARRY LOIS LANE ON EARTH! I WILL BE GONE, BUT I LEAVE YOU WITH A NEW SUPER-HERO WHO WILL DEMONSTRATE HIS SUPER-POWERS BY...
...LAUNCHING THE EARTH-SHIP INTO SPACE WITH HIS SUPER-STRENGTH! HE WILL TELL YOU THE NAME HE CHOSE FOR HIMSELF, DIFFERENT FROM MINE!
I THOUGHT OF A NAME FOR MYSELF OUT OF THIN AIR... SUPERMAN!
7
UTTERLY STARTLED, SUPERMAN ON EARTH TURNS OFF HIS SUPER-UNIVAC, WHICH HAS SHOWN THE OTHER LIFE HE WOULD HAVE LIVED IF KRYPTON HAD NOT EXPLODED...
HOW STRANGE FATE WORKS! IF KRYPTON HAD NEVER EXPLODED, I WOULD HAVE ENDED UP THERE AS—SUPERMAN!
The End.
CLICK!

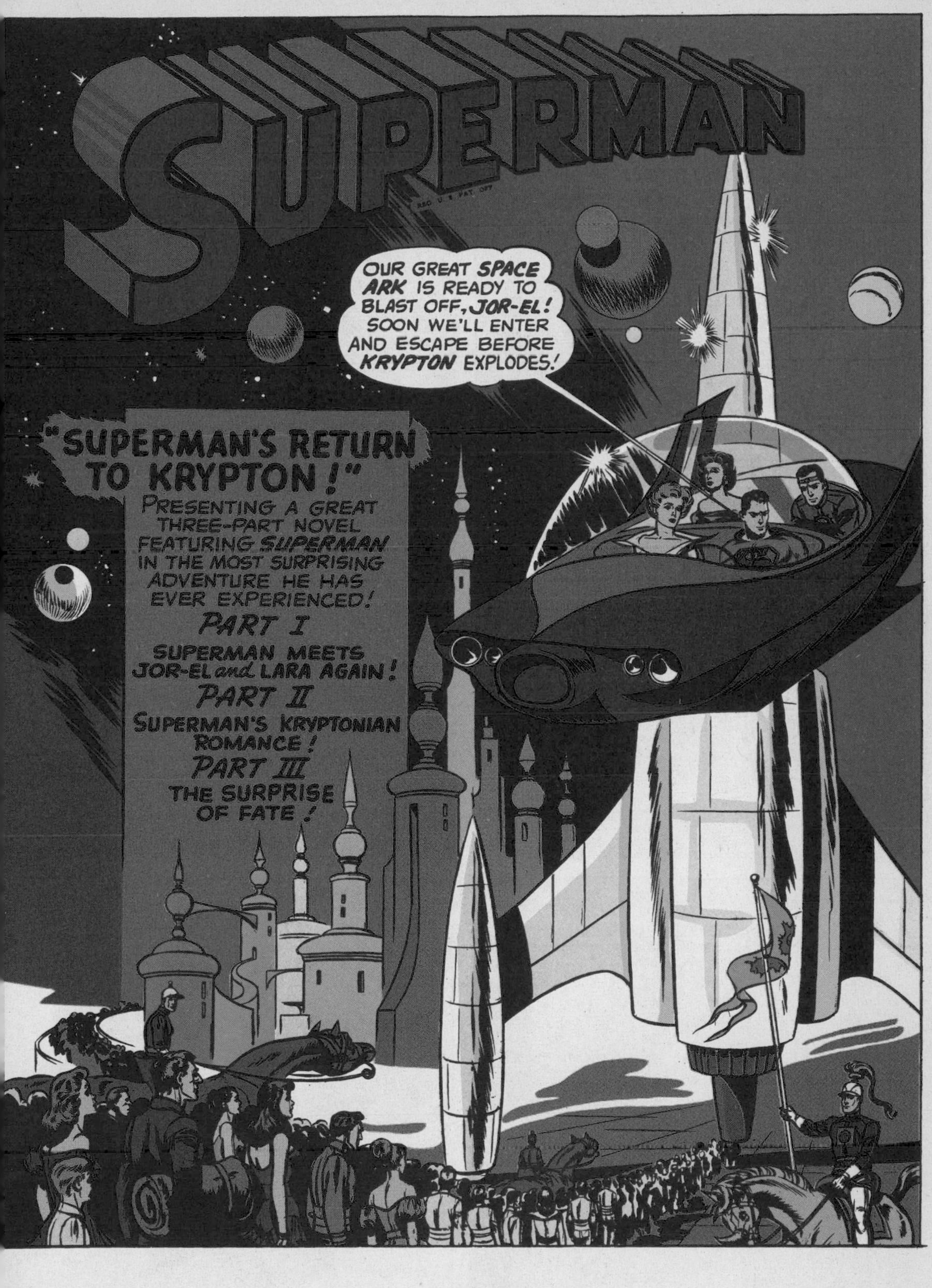
SUPERMAN
REG. U.S. PAT. OFF.
OUR GREAT SPACE ARK IS READY TO BLAST OFF, JOR-EL! SOON WE'LL ENTER AND ESCAPE BEFORE KRYPTON EXPLODES!
"SUPERMAN'S RETURN TO KRYPTON!"
PRESENTING A GREAT THREE-PART NOVEL FEATURING SUPERMAN IN THE MOST SURPRISING ADVENTURE HE HAS EVER EXPERIENCED!
PART I
SUPERMAN MEETS JOR-EL and LARA AGAIN!
PART II
SUPERMAN'S KRYPTONIAN ROMANCE!
PART III
THE SURPRISE OF FATE!

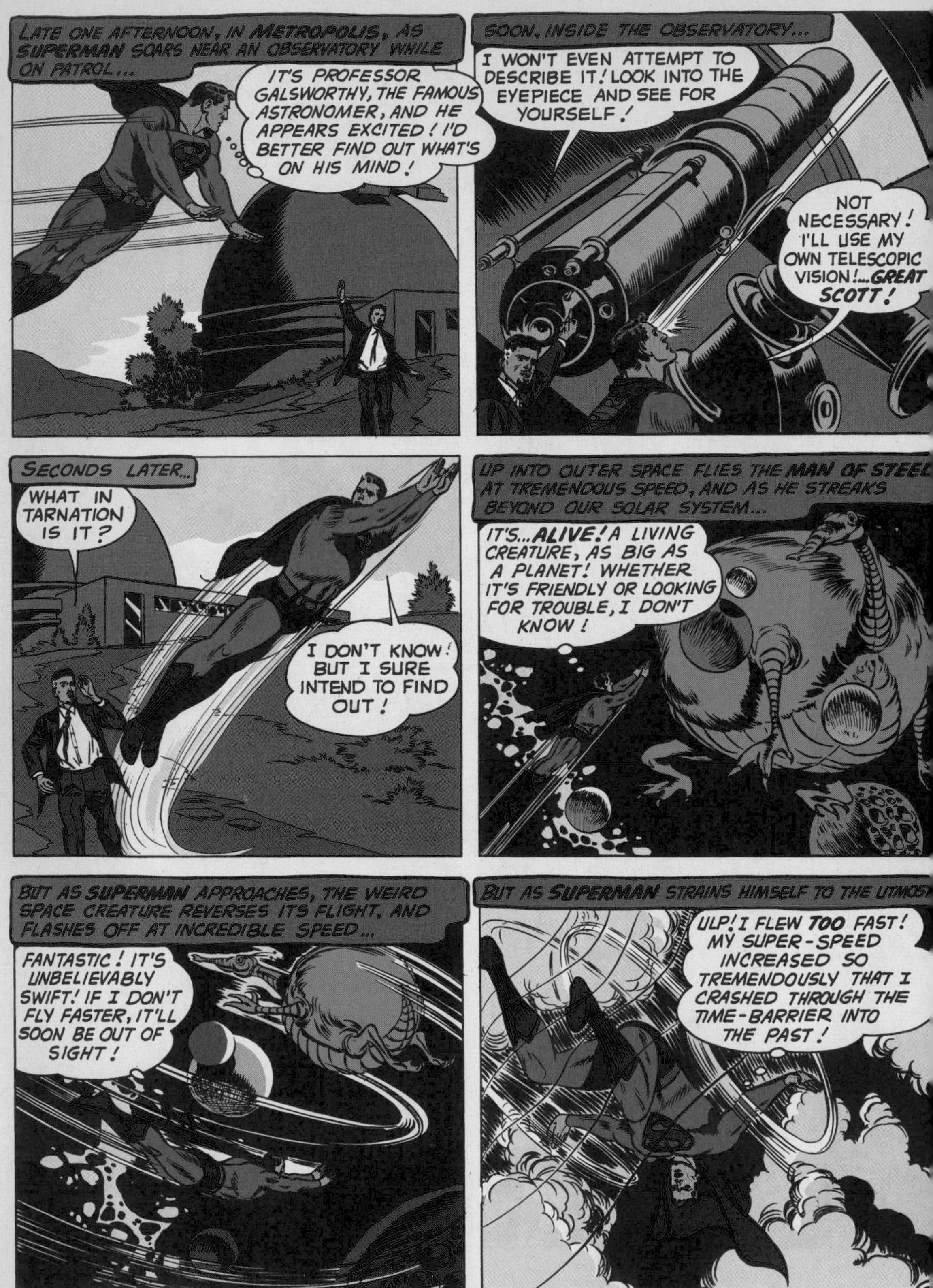
LATE ONE AFTERNOON, IN METROPOLIS, AS SUPERMAN SOARS NEAR AN OBSERVATORY WHILE ON PATROL...
IT'S PROFESSOR GALSWORTHY, THE FAMOUS ASTRONOMER, AND HE APPEARS EXCITED! I'D BETTER FIND OUT WHAT'S ON HIS MIND!
SOON, INSIDE THE OBSERVATORY...
I WON'T EVEN ATTEMPT TO DESCRIBE IT! LOOK INTO THE EYEPIECE AND SEE FOR YOURSELF!
NOT NECESSARY! I'LL USE MY OWN TELESCOPIC VISION!...GREAT SCOTT!
SECONDS LATER...
WHAT IN TARNATION IS IT?
I DON'T KNOW! BUT I SURE INTEND TO FIND OUT!
UP INTO OUTER SPACE FLIES THE MAN OF STEEL AT TREMENDOUS SPEED, AND AS HE STREAKS BEYOND OUR SOLAR SYSTEM...
IT'S...ALIVE! A LIVING CREATURE, AS BIG AS A PLANET! WHETHER IT'S FRIENDLY OR LOOKING FOR TROUBLE, I DON'T KNOW!
BUT AS SUPERMAN APPROACHES, THE WEIRD SPACE CREATURE REVERSES ITS FLIGHT, AND FLASHES OFF AT INCREDIBLE SPEED...
FANTASTIC! IT'S UNBELIEVABLY SWIFT! IF I DON'T FLY FASTER, IT'LL SOON BE OUT OF SIGHT!
BUT AS SUPERMAN STRAINS HIMSELF TO THE UTMOST
ULP! I FLEW TOO FAST! MY SUPER-SPEED INCREASED SO TREMENDOUSLY THAT I CRASHED THROUGH THE TIME-BARRIER INTO THE PAST!

AND AS *SUPERMAN* MATERIALIZES IN A TIME ERA OF YESTERYEAR...

GREAT GUNS! THAT PLANET... AND ITS *RED* SUN! I RECOGNIZE THEM BECAUSE OF REBOUNDING LIGHT-RAYS I ONCE OVERTOOK AND STUDIED! THE PLANET IS *KRYPTON,* THE WORLD WHERE I WAS BORN...IT BLEW UP JUST AFTER I WAS ROCKETED TO EARTH!

DOWN TOWARD *KRYPTON'S* SURFACE FLASHES EARTH'S MIGHTIEST MORTAL...

I'VE ACCIDENTALLY RETURNED TO A PERIOD IN THE PAST, WHEN *KRYPTON* STILL EXISTED! BECAUSE OF THAT *RED* SUN, I MUST LAND IMMEDIATELY OR I'M DOOMED!

A FRACTION OF AN INSTANT LATER...

I MADE IT...AND BARELY IN TIME! IN ANOTHER SPLIT SECOND, I'LL LOSE MY SUPER-POWERS!

TESTING HIMSELF, *SUPERMAN* LIFTS A ROCK, AND AS HE ATTEMPTS TO CRUSH IT IN HIS FIST...

NO CAN DO! I'M AN ORDINARY KRYPTONIAN AGAIN! YEARS AGO, WHEN MY PARENTS *JOR-EL* AND *LARA* LAUNCHED ME TOWARD EARTH IN A MODEL ROCKET SHIP SECONDS BEFORE *KRYPTON* EXPLODED, I HAD NO SUPER-POWERS AT ALL...

"WHAT GAVE ME SUPER-POWERS ON EARTH WAS EARTH'S LESSER GRAVITY AND THE FACT THAT, UNLIKE *KRYPTON'S* RED SUN, EARTH'S SOLAR SYSTEM HAS A *YELLOW* SUN..."

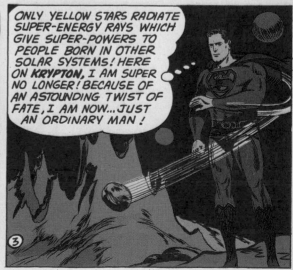

ONLY YELLOW STARS RADIATE SUPER-ENERGY RAYS WHICH GIVE SUPER-POWERS TO PEOPLE BORN IN OTHER SOLAR SYSTEMS! HERE ON *KRYPTON,* I AM SUPER NO LONGER! BECAUSE OF AN ASTOUNDING TWIST OF FATE, I AM NOW...JUST AN ORDINARY MAN!

③

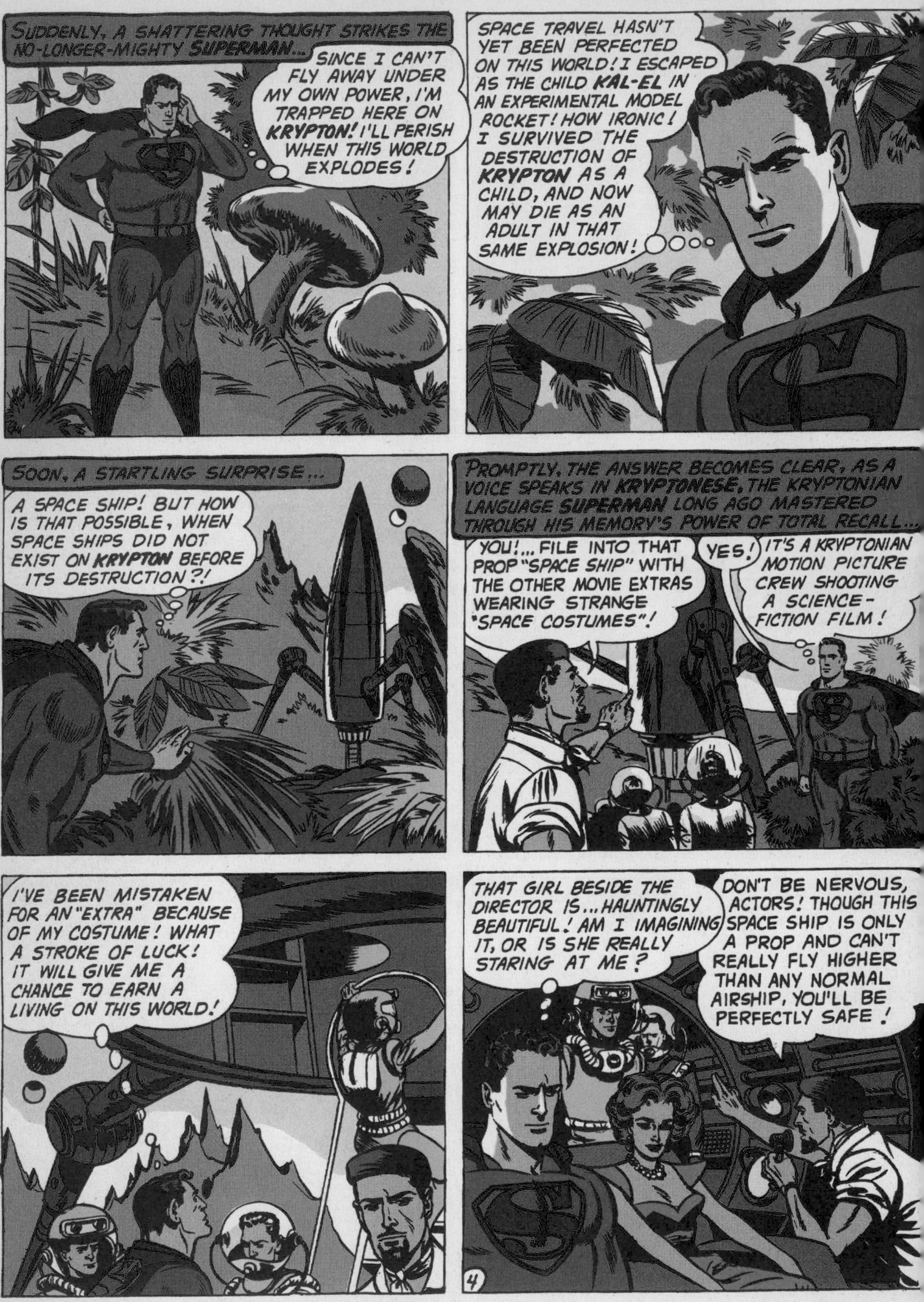
SUDDENLY, A SHATTERING THOUGHT STRIKES THE NO-LONGER-MIGHTY SUPERMAN...
SINCE I CAN'T FLY AWAY UNDER MY OWN POWER, I'M TRAPPED HERE ON KRYPTON! I'LL PERISH WHEN THIS WORLD EXPLODES!
SPACE TRAVEL HASN'T YET BEEN PERFECTED ON THIS WORLD! I ESCAPED AS THE CHILD KAL-EL IN AN EXPERIMENTAL MODEL ROCKET! HOW IRONIC! I SURVIVED THE DESTRUCTION OF KRYPTON AS A CHILD, AND NOW MAY DIE AS AN ADULT IN THAT SAME EXPLOSION!
SOON, A STARTLING SURPRISE...
A SPACE SHIP! BUT HOW IS THAT POSSIBLE, WHEN SPACE SHIPS DID NOT EXIST ON KRYPTON BEFORE ITS DESTRUCTION?!
PROMPTLY, THE ANSWER BECOMES CLEAR, AS A VOICE SPEAKS IN KRYPTONESE, THE KRYPTONIAN LANGUAGE SUPERMAN LONG AGO MASTERED THROUGH HIS MEMORY'S POWER OF TOTAL RECALL...
YOU!... FILE INTO THAT PROP "SPACE SHIP" WITH THE OTHER MOVIE EXTRAS WEARING STRANGE "SPACE COSTUMES"!
YES! IT'S A KRYPTONIAN MOTION PICTURE CREW SHOOTING A SCIENCE-FICTION FILM!
I'VE BEEN MISTAKEN FOR AN "EXTRA" BECAUSE OF MY COSTUME! WHAT A STROKE OF LUCK! IT WILL GIVE ME A CHANCE TO EARN A LIVING ON THIS WORLD!
THAT GIRL BESIDE THE DIRECTOR IS... HAUNTINGLY BEAUTIFUL! AM I IMAGINING IT, OR IS SHE REALLY STARING AT ME?
DON'T BE NERVOUS, ACTORS! THOUGH THIS SPACE SHIP IS ONLY A PROP AND CAN'T REALLY FLY HIGHER THAN ANY NORMAL AIRSHIP, YOU'LL BE PERFECTLY SAFE!
4

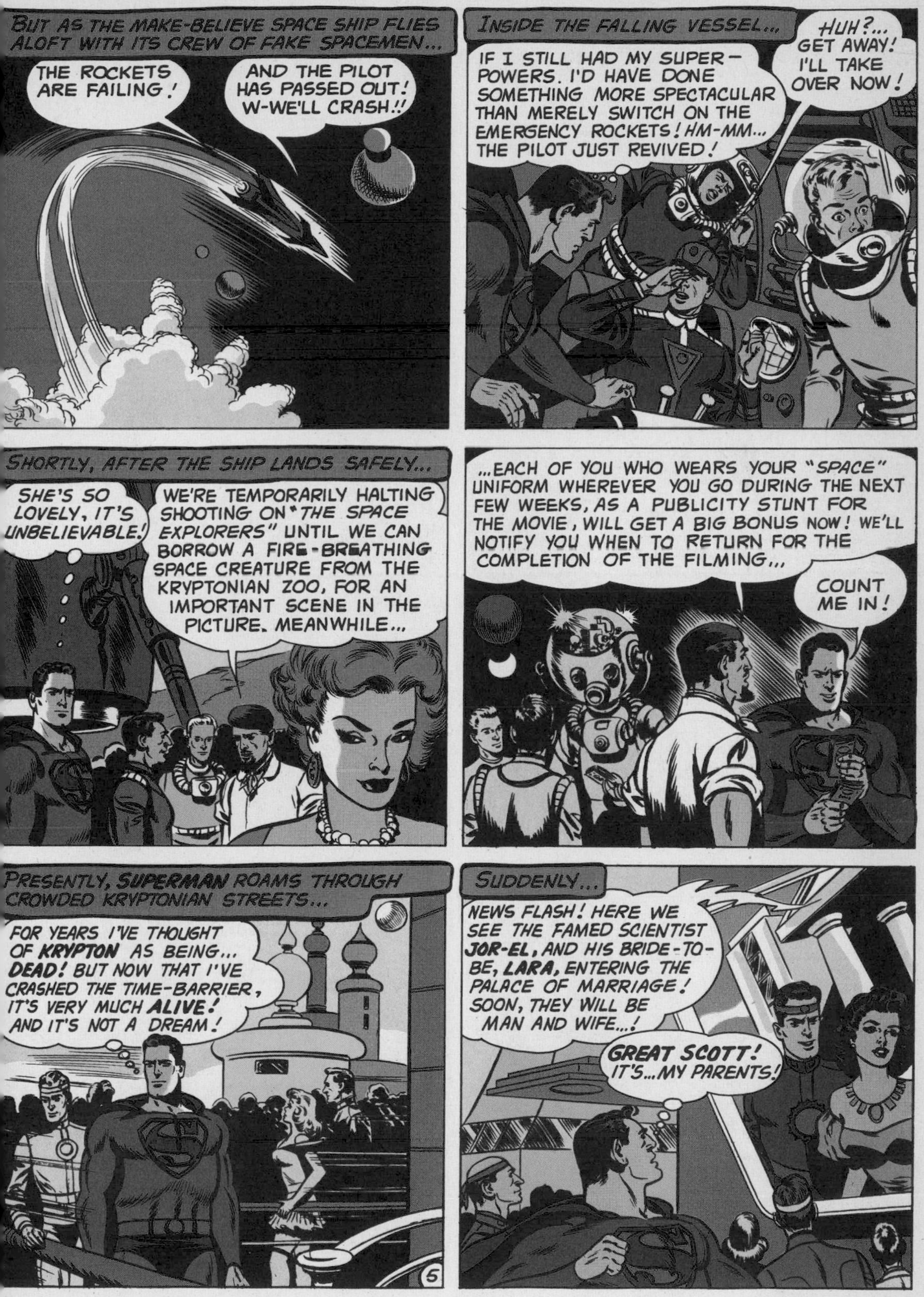

BUT AS THE MAKE-BELIEVE SPACE SHIP FLIES ALOFT WITH ITS CREW OF FAKE SPACEMEN...
THE ROCKETS ARE FAILING!
AND THE PILOT HAS PASSED OUT! W-WE'LL CRASH!!
INSIDE THE FALLING VESSEL...
IF I STILL HAD MY SUPER-POWERS, I'D HAVE DONE SOMETHING MORE SPECTACULAR THAN MERELY SWITCH ON THE EMERGENCY ROCKETS! HM-MM... THE PILOT JUST REVIVED!
HUH?... GET AWAY! I'LL TAKE OVER NOW!
SHORTLY, AFTER THE SHIP LANDS SAFELY...
SHE'S SO LOVELY, IT'S UNBELIEVABLE!
WE'RE TEMPORARILY HALTING SHOOTING ON "THE SPACE EXPLORERS" UNTIL WE CAN BORROW A FIRE-BREATHING SPACE CREATURE FROM THE KRYPTONIAN ZOO, FOR AN IMPORTANT SCENE IN THE PICTURE. MEANWHILE...
...EACH OF YOU WHO WEARS YOUR "SPACE" UNIFORM WHEREVER YOU GO DURING THE NEXT FEW WEEKS, AS A PUBLICITY STUNT FOR THE MOVIE, WILL GET A BIG BONUS NOW! WE'LL NOTIFY YOU WHEN TO RETURN FOR THE COMPLETION OF THE FILMING...
COUNT ME IN!
PRESENTLY, SUPERMAN ROAMS THROUGH CROWDED KRYPTONIAN STREETS...
FOR YEARS I'VE THOUGHT OF KRYPTON AS BEING... DEAD! BUT NOW THAT I'VE CRASHED THE TIME-BARRIER, IT'S VERY MUCH ALIVE! AND IT'S NOT A DREAM!
5
SUDDENLY...
NEWS FLASH! HERE WE SEE THE FAMED SCIENTIST JOR-EL, AND HIS BRIDE-TO-BE, LARA, ENTERING THE PALACE OF MARRIAGE! SOON, THEY WILL BE MAN AND WIFE...!
GREAT SCOTT! IT'S... MY PARENTS!

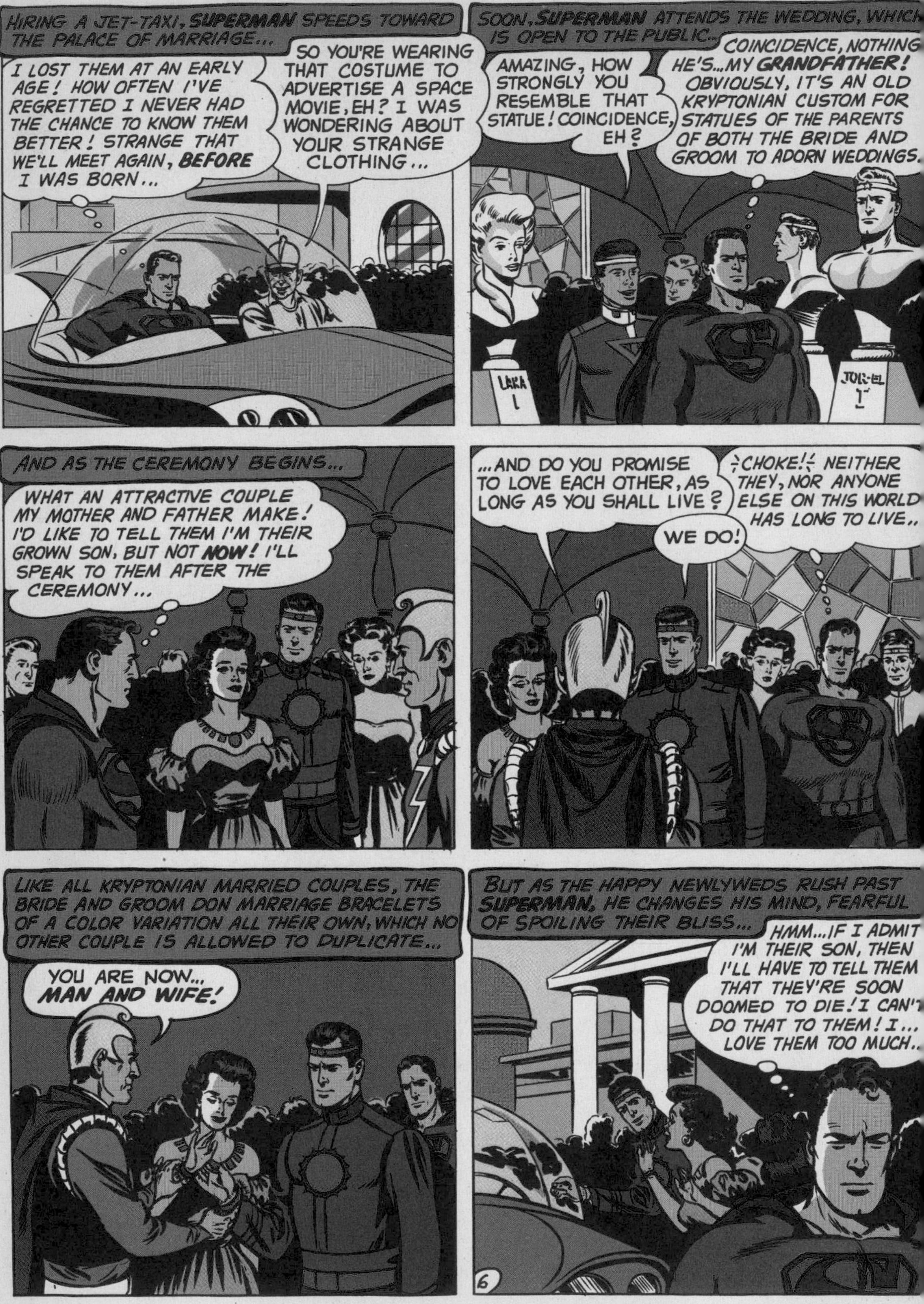
HIRING A JET-TAXI, SUPERMAN SPEEDS TOWARD THE PALACE OF MARRIAGE...
I LOST THEM AT AN EARLY AGE! HOW OFTEN I'VE REGRETTED I NEVER HAD THE CHANCE TO KNOW THEM BETTER! STRANGE THAT WE'LL MEET AGAIN, BEFORE I WAS BORN...
SO YOU'RE WEARING THAT COSTUME TO ADVERTISE A SPACE MOVIE, EH? I WAS WONDERING ABOUT YOUR STRANGE CLOTHING...
SOON, SUPERMAN ATTENDS THE WEDDING, WHICH IS OPEN TO THE PUBLIC...
AMAZING, HOW STRONGLY YOU RESEMBLE THAT STATUE! COINCIDENCE, EH?
COINCIDENCE, NOTHING! HE'S...MY GRANDFATHER! OBVIOUSLY, IT'S AN OLD KRYPTONIAN CUSTOM FOR STATUES OF THE PARENTS OF BOTH THE BRIDE AND GROOM TO ADORN WEDDINGS.
LARA
JOR-EL
AND AS THE CEREMONY BEGINS...
WHAT AN ATTRACTIVE COUPLE MY MOTHER AND FATHER MAKE! I'D LIKE TO TELL THEM I'M THEIR GROWN SON, BUT NOT NOW! I'LL SPEAK TO THEM AFTER THE CEREMONY...
...AND DO YOU PROMISE TO LOVE EACH OTHER, AS LONG AS YOU SHALL LIVE?
WE DO!
CHOKE! NEITHER THEY, NOR ANYONE ELSE ON THIS WORLD HAS LONG TO LIVE...
LIKE ALL KRYPTONIAN MARRIED COUPLES, THE BRIDE AND GROOM DON MARRIAGE BRACELETS OF A COLOR VARIATION ALL THEIR OWN, WHICH NO OTHER COUPLE IS ALLOWED TO DUPLICATE...
YOU ARE NOW... MAN AND WIFE!
BUT AS THE HAPPY NEWLYWEDS RUSH PAST SUPERMAN, HE CHANGES HIS MIND, FEARFUL OF SPOILING THEIR BLISS...
HMM...IF I ADMIT I'M THEIR SON, THEN I'LL HAVE TO TELL THEM THAT THEY'RE SOON DOOMED TO DIE! I CAN'T DO THAT TO THEM! I... LOVE THEM TOO MUCH...
6

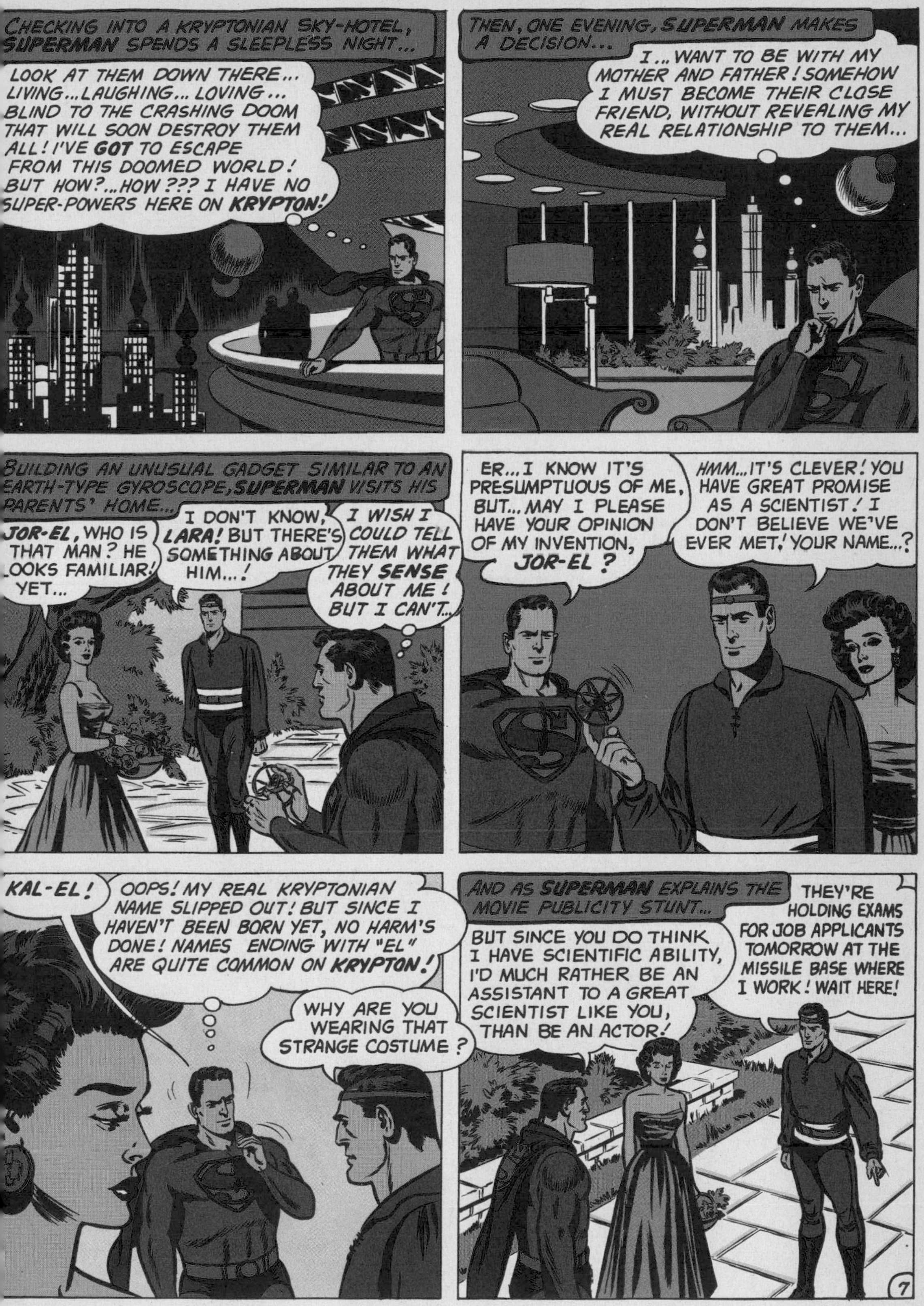
CHECKING INTO A KRYPTONIAN SKY-HOTEL, SUPERMAN SPENDS A SLEEPLESS NIGHT...
LOOK AT THEM DOWN THERE... LIVING...LAUGHING... LOVING... BLIND TO THE CRASHING DOOM THAT WILL SOON DESTROY THEM ALL! I'VE GOT TO ESCAPE FROM THIS DOOMED WORLD! BUT HOW?...HOW??? I HAVE NO SUPER-POWERS HERE ON KRYPTON!
THEN, ONE EVENING, SUPERMAN MAKES A DECISION...
I...WANT TO BE WITH MY MOTHER AND FATHER! SOMEHOW I MUST BECOME THEIR CLOSE FRIEND, WITHOUT REVEALING MY REAL RELATIONSHIP TO THEM...
BUILDING AN UNUSUAL GADGET SIMILAR TO AN EARTH-TYPE GYROSCOPE, SUPERMAN VISITS HIS PARENTS' HOME...
JOR-EL, WHO IS THAT MAN? HE LOOKS FAMILIAR! YET...
I DON'T KNOW, LARA! BUT THERE'S SOMETHING ABOUT HIM...!
I WISH I COULD TELL THEM WHAT THEY SENSE ABOUT ME! BUT I CAN'T...
ER...I KNOW IT'S PRESUMPTUOUS OF ME, BUT...MAY I PLEASE HAVE YOUR OPINION OF MY INVENTION, JOR-EL?
HMM...IT'S CLEVER! YOU HAVE GREAT PROMISE AS A SCIENTIST! I DON'T BELIEVE WE'VE EVER MET! YOUR NAME...?
KAL-EL!
OOPS! MY REAL KRYPTONIAN NAME SLIPPED OUT! BUT SINCE I HAVEN'T BEEN BORN YET, NO HARM'S DONE! NAMES ENDING WITH "EL" ARE QUITE COMMON ON KRYPTON!
WHY ARE YOU WEARING THAT STRANGE COSTUME?
AND AS SUPERMAN EXPLAINS THE MOVIE PUBLICITY STUNT...
BUT SINCE YOU DO THINK I HAVE SCIENTIFIC ABILITY, I'D MUCH RATHER BE AN ASSISTANT TO A GREAT SCIENTIST LIKE YOU, THAN BE AN ACTOR!
THEY'RE HOLDING EXAMS FOR JOB APPLICANTS TOMORROW AT THE MISSILE BASE WHERE I WORK! WAIT HERE!
7

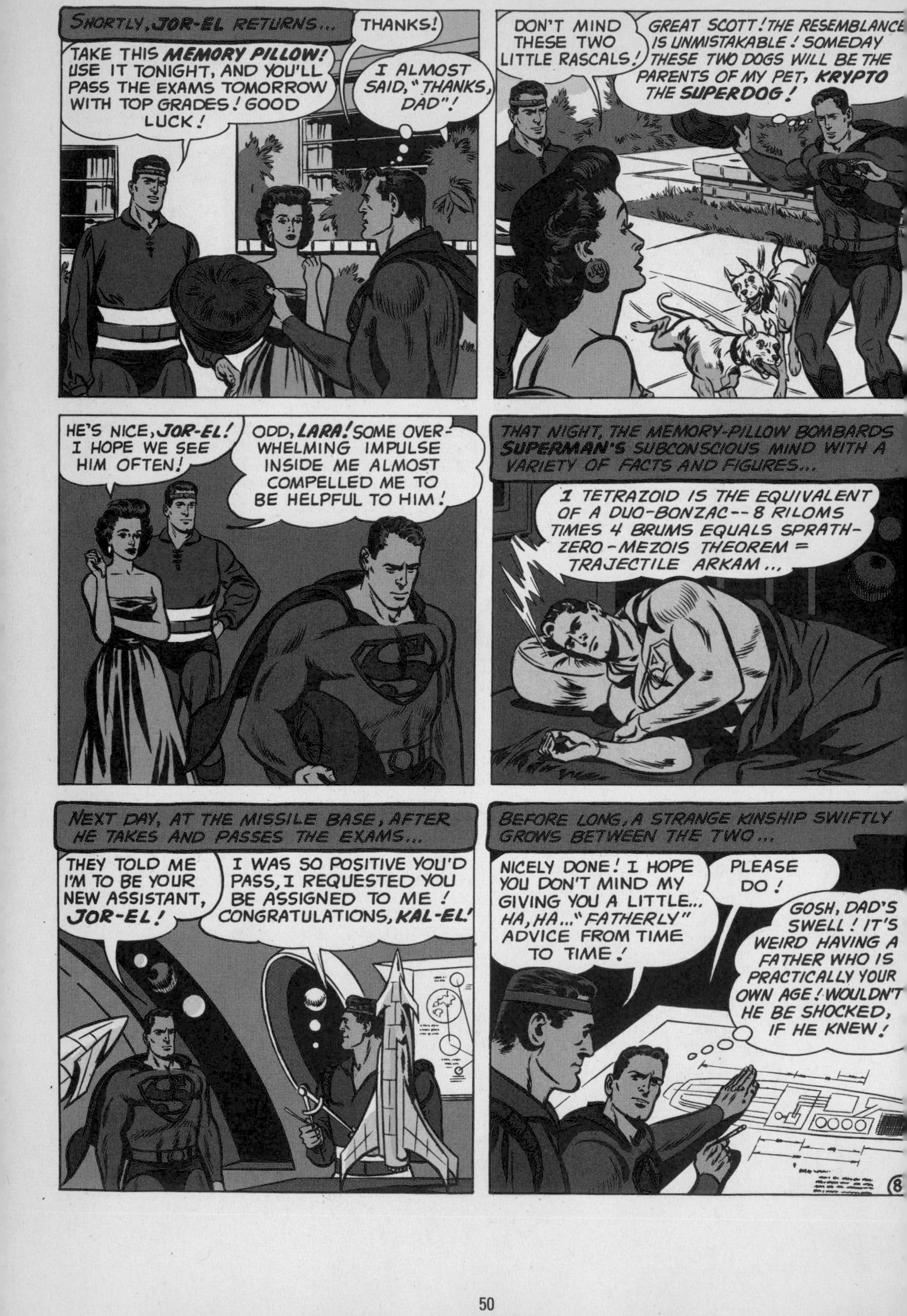
SHORTLY, JOR-EL RETURNS...
TAKE THIS MEMORY PILLOW! USE IT TONIGHT, AND YOU'LL PASS THE EXAMS TOMORROW WITH TOP GRADES! GOOD LUCK!
THANKS!
I ALMOST SAID, "THANKS, DAD"!
DON'T MIND THESE TWO LITTLE RASCALS!
GREAT SCOTT! THE RESEMBLANCE IS UNMISTAKABLE! SOMEDAY THESE TWO DOGS WILL BE THE PARENTS OF MY PET, KRYPTO THE SUPERDOG!
HE'S NICE, JOR-EL! I HOPE WE SEE HIM OFTEN!
ODD, LARA! SOME OVER-WHELMING IMPULSE INSIDE ME ALMOST COMPELLED ME TO BE HELPFUL TO HIM!
THAT NIGHT, THE MEMORY-PILLOW BOMBARDS SUPERMAN'S SUBCONSCIOUS MIND WITH A VARIETY OF FACTS AND FIGURES...
1 TETRAZOID IS THE EQUIVALENT OF A DUO-BONZAC--8 RILOMS TIMES 4 BRUMS EQUALS SPRATH-ZERO-MEZOIS THEOREM = TRAJECTILE ARKAM...
NEXT DAY, AT THE MISSILE BASE, AFTER HE TAKES AND PASSES THE EXAMS...
THEY TOLD ME I'M TO BE YOUR NEW ASSISTANT, JOR-EL!
I WAS SO POSITIVE YOU'D PASS, I REQUESTED YOU BE ASSIGNED TO ME! CONGRATULATIONS, KAL-EL!
BEFORE LONG, A STRANGE KINSHIP SWIFTLY GROWS BETWEEN THE TWO...
NICELY DONE! I HOPE YOU DON'T MIND MY GIVING YOU A LITTLE... HA, HA... "FATHERLY" ADVICE FROM TIME TO TIME!
PLEASE DO!
GOSH, DAD'S SWELL! IT'S WEIRD HAVING A FATHER WHO IS PRACTICALLY YOUR OWN AGE! WOULDN'T HE BE SHOCKED, IF HE KNEW!
8

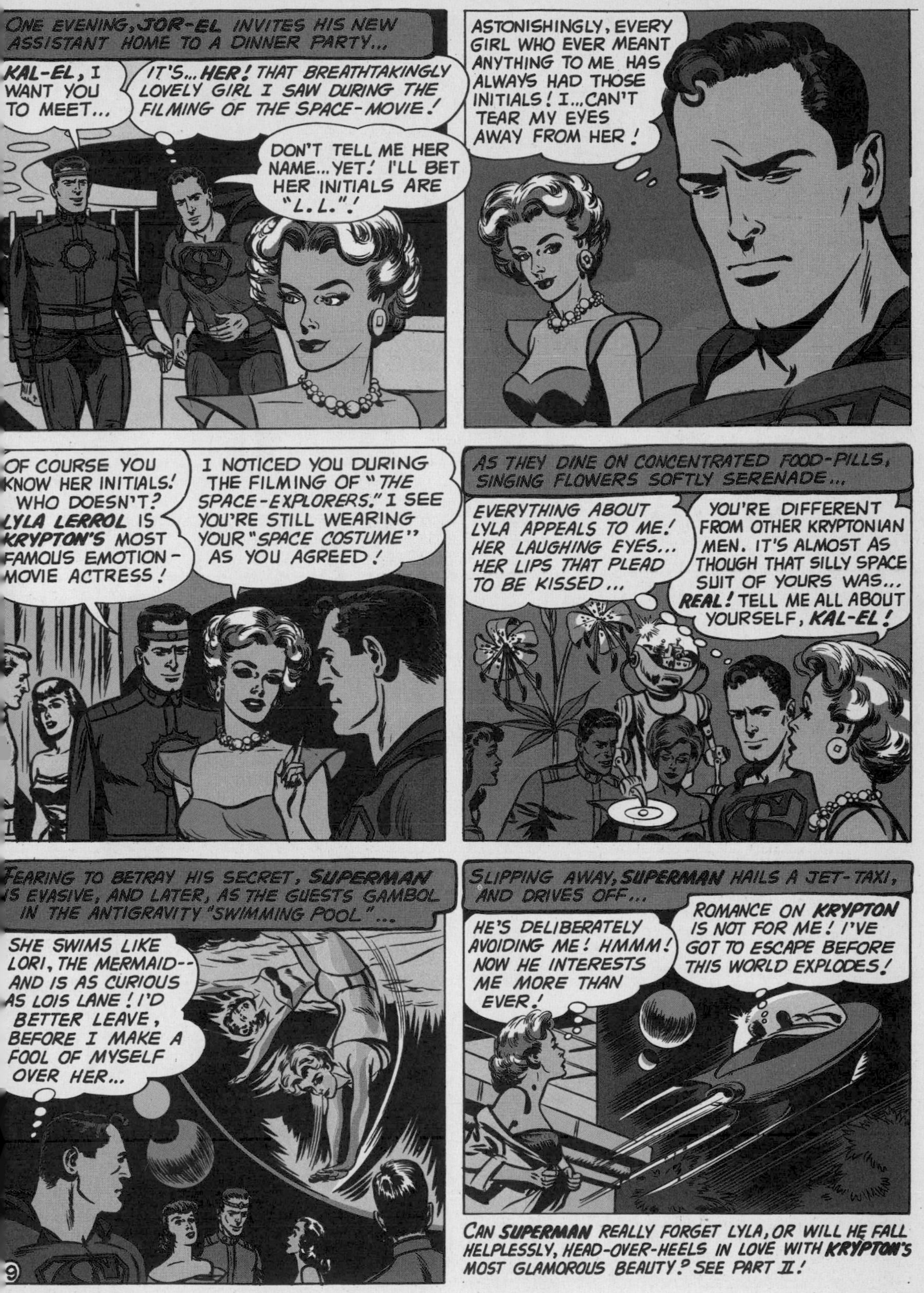
ONE EVENING, JOR-EL INVITES HIS NEW ASSISTANT HOME TO A DINNER PARTY...
KAL-EL, I WANT YOU TO MEET...
IT'S... HER! THAT BREATHTAKINGLY LOVELY GIRL I SAW DURING THE FILMING OF THE SPACE-MOVIE!
DON'T TELL ME HER NAME... YET! I'LL BET HER INITIALS ARE "L. L."!
ASTONISHINGLY, EVERY GIRL WHO EVER MEANT ANYTHING TO ME HAS ALWAYS HAD THOSE INITIALS! I... CAN'T TEAR MY EYES AWAY FROM HER!
OF COURSE YOU KNOW HER INITIALS! WHO DOESN'T? LYLA LERROL IS KRYPTON'S MOST FAMOUS EMOTION-MOVIE ACTRESS!
I NOTICED YOU DURING THE FILMING OF "THE SPACE-EXPLORERS." I SEE YOU'RE STILL WEARING YOUR "SPACE COSTUME" AS YOU AGREED!
AS THEY DINE ON CONCENTRATED FOOD-PILLS, SINGING FLOWERS SOFTLY SERENADE...
EVERYTHING ABOUT LYLA APPEALS TO ME! HER LAUGHING EYES... HER LIPS THAT PLEAD TO BE KISSED...
YOU'RE DIFFERENT FROM OTHER KRYPTONIAN MEN. IT'S ALMOST AS THOUGH THAT SILLY SPACE SUIT OF YOURS WAS... REAL! TELL ME ALL ABOUT YOURSELF, KAL-EL!
FEARING TO BETRAY HIS SECRET, SUPERMAN IS EVASIVE, AND LATER, AS THE GUESTS GAMBOL IN THE ANTIGRAVITY "SWIMMING POOL"...
SHE SWIMS LIKE LORI, THE MERMAID-- AND IS AS CURIOUS AS LOIS LANE! I'D BETTER LEAVE, BEFORE I MAKE A FOOL OF MYSELF OVER HER...
9
SLIPPING AWAY, SUPERMAN HAILS A JET-TAXI, AND DRIVES OFF...
HE'S DELIBERATELY AVOIDING ME! HMMM! NOW HE INTERESTS ME MORE THAN EVER!
ROMANCE ON KRYPTON IS NOT FOR ME! I'VE GOT TO ESCAPE BEFORE THIS WORLD EXPLODES!

CAN SUPERMAN REALLY FORGET LYLA, OR WILL HE FALL HELPLESSLY, HEAD-OVER-HEELS IN LOVE WITH KRYPTON'S MOST GLAMOROUS BEAUTY? SEE PART II!

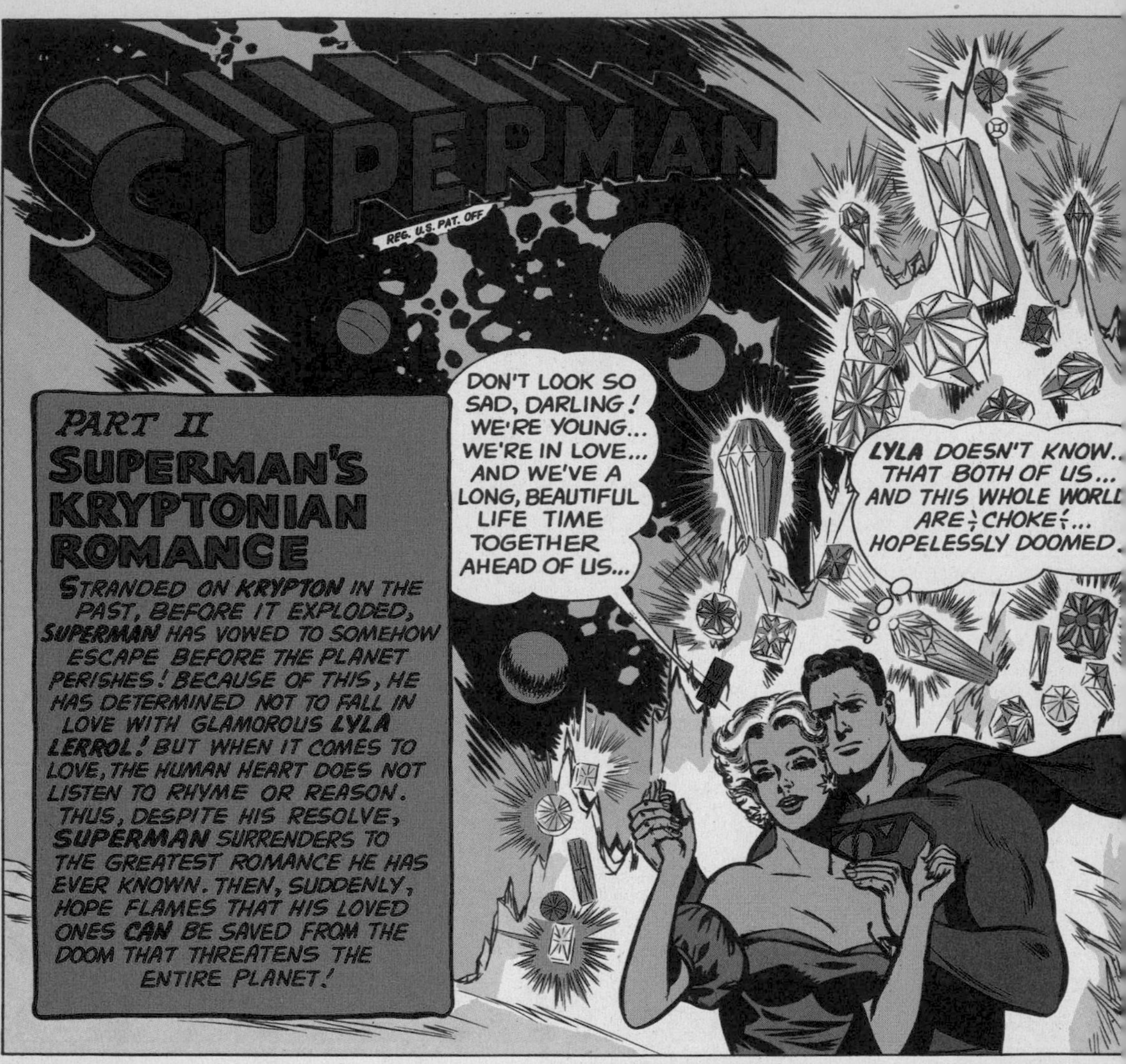
SUPERMAN
REG. U.S. PAT. OFF.
PART II
SUPERMAN'S KRYPTONIAN ROMANCE
STRANDED ON KRYPTON IN THE PAST, BEFORE IT EXPLODED, SUPERMAN HAS VOWED TO SOMEHOW ESCAPE BEFORE THE PLANET PERISHES! BECAUSE OF THIS, HE HAS DETERMINED NOT TO FALL IN LOVE WITH GLAMOROUS LYLA LERROL! BUT WHEN IT COMES TO LOVE, THE HUMAN HEART DOES NOT LISTEN TO RHYME OR REASON. THUS, DESPITE HIS RESOLVE, SUPERMAN SURRENDERS TO THE GREATEST ROMANCE HE HAS EVER KNOWN. THEN, SUDDENLY, HOPE FLAMES THAT HIS LOVED ONES CAN BE SAVED FROM THE DOOM THAT THREATENS THE ENTIRE PLANET!
DON'T LOOK SO SAD, DARLING! WE'RE YOUNG... WE'RE IN LOVE... AND WE'VE A LONG, BEAUTIFUL LIFE TIME TOGETHER AHEAD OF US...
LYLA DOESN'T KNOW... THAT BOTH OF US... AND THIS WHOLE WORLD ARE ÷CHOKE÷... HOPELESSLY DOOMED...

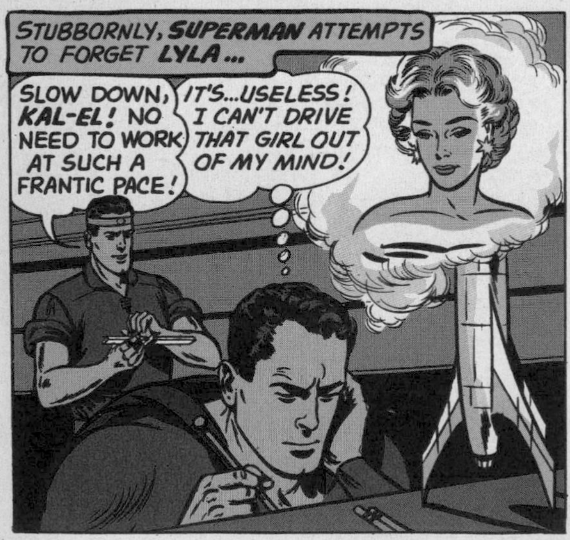
STUBBORNLY, SUPERMAN ATTEMPTS TO FORGET LYLA...
SLOW DOWN, KAL-EL! NO NEED TO WORK AT SUCH A FRANTIC PACE!
IT'S...USELESS! I CAN'T DRIVE THAT GIRL OUT OF MY MIND!

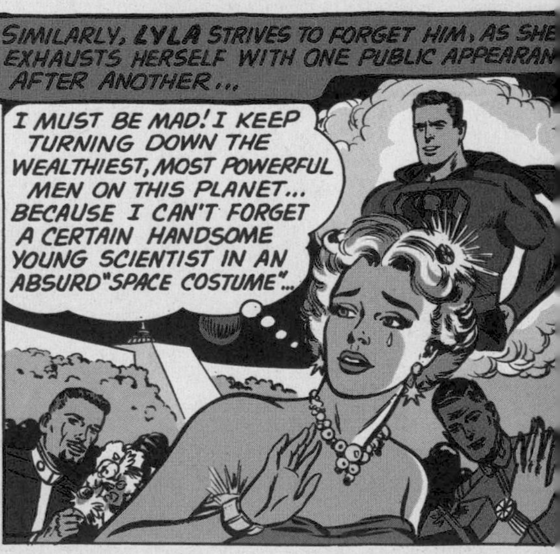
SIMILARLY, LYLA STRIVES TO FORGET HIM, AS SHE EXHAUSTS HERSELF WITH ONE PUBLIC APPEARAN AFTER ANOTHER...
I MUST BE MAD! I KEEP TURNING DOWN THE WEALTHIEST, MOST POWERFUL MEN ON THIS PLANET... BECAUSE I CAN'T FORGET A CERTAIN HANDSOME YOUNG SCIENTIST IN AN ABSURD "SPACE COSTUME"...

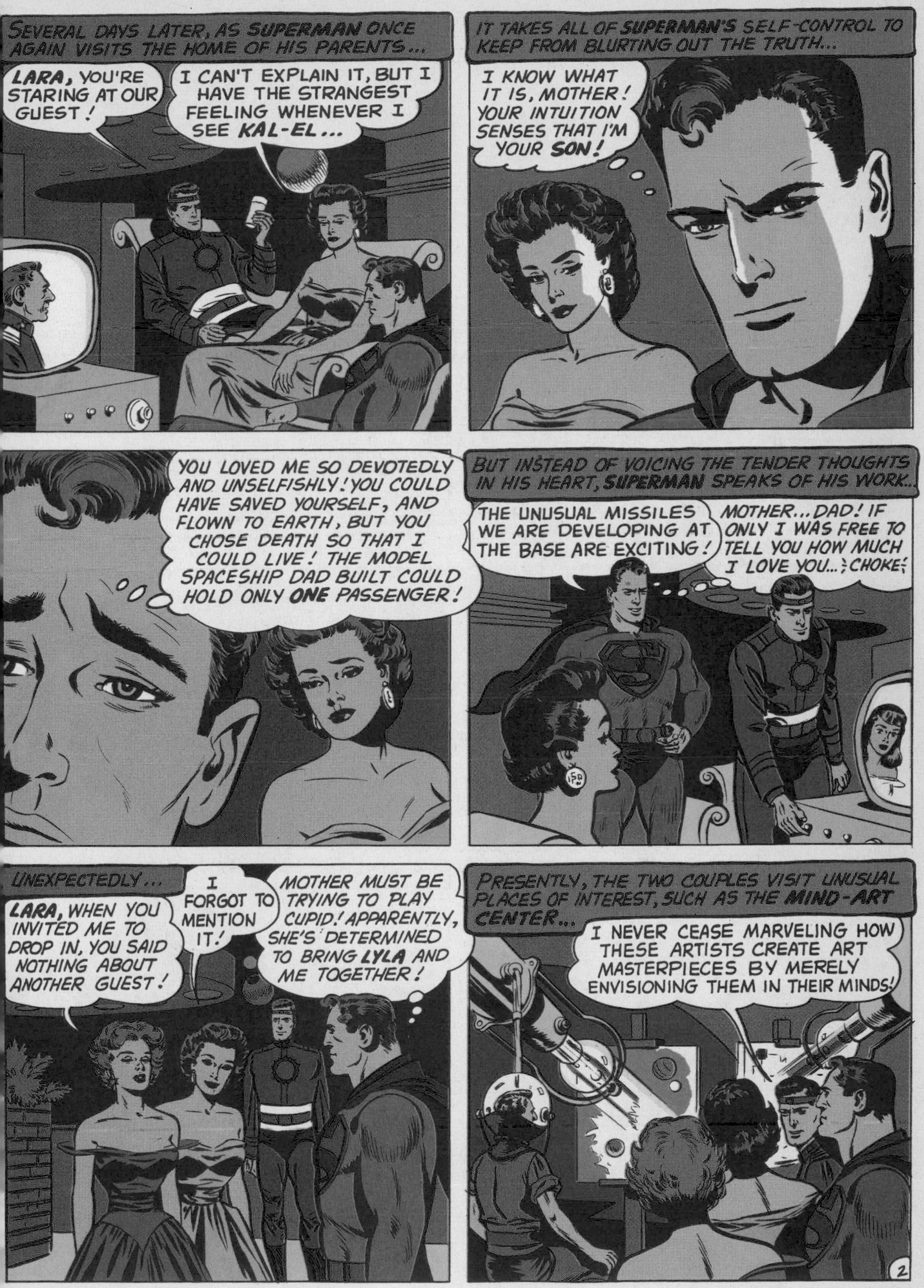
SEVERAL DAYS LATER, AS SUPERMAN ONCE AGAIN VISITS THE HOME OF HIS PARENTS...
LARA, YOU'RE STARING AT OUR GUEST!
I CAN'T EXPLAIN IT, BUT I HAVE THE STRANGEST FEELING WHENEVER I SEE KAL-EL...
IT TAKES ALL OF SUPERMAN'S SELF-CONTROL TO KEEP FROM BLURTING OUT THE TRUTH...
I KNOW WHAT IT IS, MOTHER! YOUR INTUITION SENSES THAT I'M YOUR SON!
YOU LOVED ME SO DEVOTEDLY AND UNSELFISHLY! YOU COULD HAVE SAVED YOURSELF, AND FLOWN TO EARTH, BUT YOU CHOSE DEATH SO THAT I COULD LIVE! THE MODEL SPACESHIP DAD BUILT COULD HOLD ONLY ONE PASSENGER!
BUT INSTEAD OF VOICING THE TENDER THOUGHTS IN HIS HEART, SUPERMAN SPEAKS OF HIS WORK..
THE UNUSUAL MISSILES WE ARE DEVELOPING AT THE BASE ARE EXCITING!
MOTHER...DAD! IF ONLY I WAS FREE TO TELL YOU HOW MUCH I LOVE YOU...;CHOKE;
UNEXPECTEDLY...
LARA, WHEN YOU INVITED ME TO DROP IN, YOU SAID NOTHING ABOUT ANOTHER GUEST!
I FORGOT TO MENTION IT!
MOTHER MUST BE TRYING TO PLAY CUPID! APPARENTLY, SHE'S DETERMINED TO BRING LYLA AND ME TOGETHER!
PRESENTLY, THE TWO COUPLES VISIT UNUSUAL PLACES OF INTEREST, SUCH AS THE MIND-ART CENTER...
I NEVER CEASE MARVELING HOW THESE ARTISTS CREATE ART MASTERPIECES BY MERELY ENVISIONING THEM IN THEIR MINDS!
2

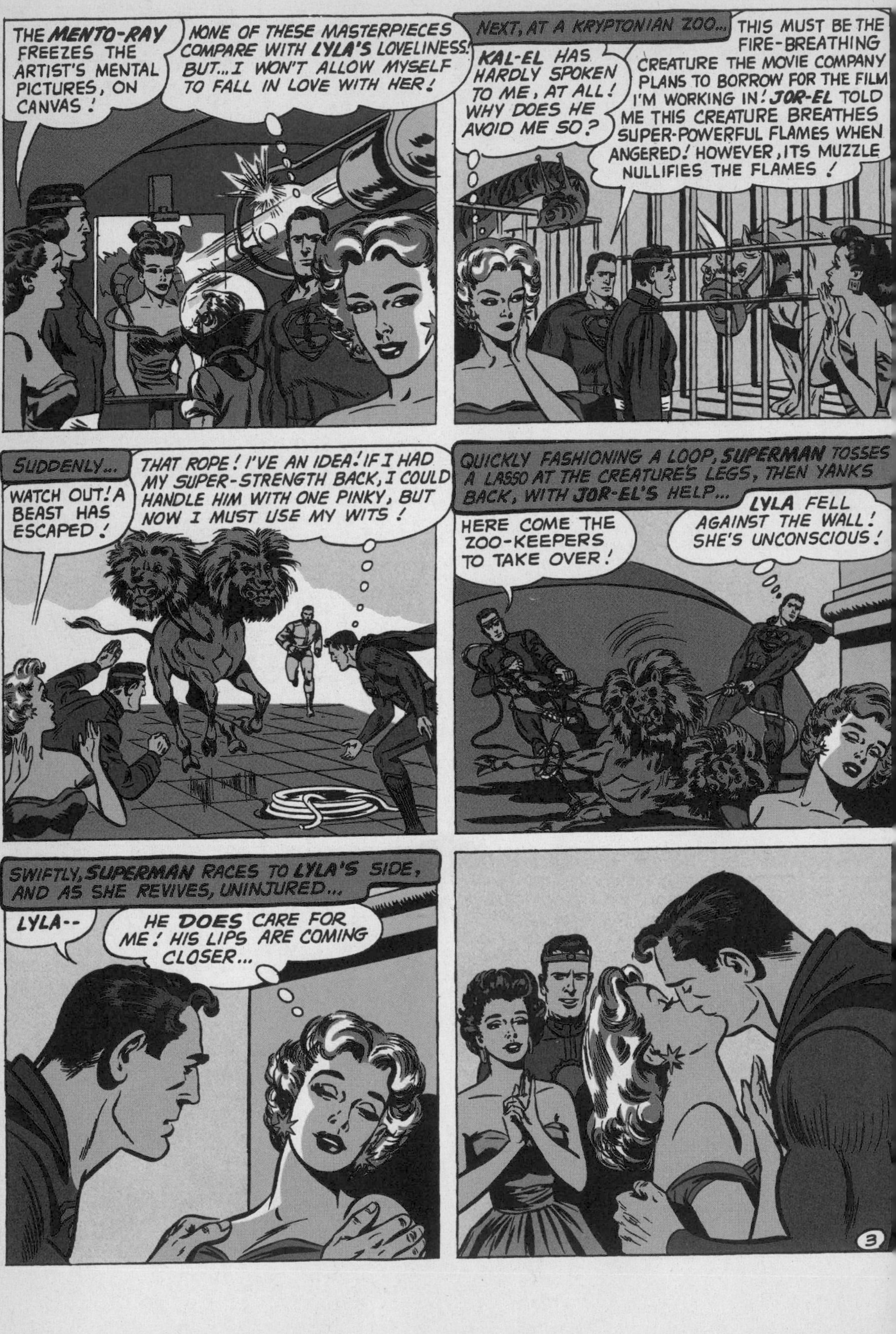
THE MENTO-RAY FREEZES THE ARTIST'S MENTAL PICTURES, ON CANVAS!
NONE OF THESE MASTERPIECES COMPARE WITH LYLA'S LOVELINESS! BUT...I WON'T ALLOW MYSELF TO FALL IN LOVE WITH HER!
NEXT, AT A KRYPTONIAN ZOO...
KAL-EL HAS HARDLY SPOKEN TO ME, AT ALL! WHY DOES HE AVOID ME SO?
THIS MUST BE THE FIRE-BREATHING CREATURE THE MOVIE COMPANY PLANS TO BORROW FOR THE FILM I'M WORKING IN! JOR-EL TOLD ME THIS CREATURE BREATHES SUPER-POWERFUL FLAMES WHEN ANGERED! HOWEVER, ITS MUZZLE NULLIFIES THE FLAMES!
SUDDENLY...
WATCH OUT! A BEAST HAS ESCAPED!
THAT ROPE! I'VE AN IDEA! IF I HAD MY SUPER-STRENGTH BACK, I COULD HANDLE HIM WITH ONE PINKY, BUT NOW I MUST USE MY WITS!
QUICKLY FASHIONING A LOOP, SUPERMAN TOSSES A LASSO AT THE CREATURE'S LEGS, THEN YANKS BACK, WITH JOR-EL'S HELP...
HERE COME THE ZOO-KEEPERS TO TAKE OVER!
LYLA FELL AGAINST THE WALL! SHE'S UNCONSCIOUS!
SWIFTLY, SUPERMAN RACES TO LYLA'S SIDE, AND AS SHE REVIVES, UNINJURED...
LYLA--
HE DOES CARE FOR ME! HIS LIPS ARE COMING CLOSER...
3

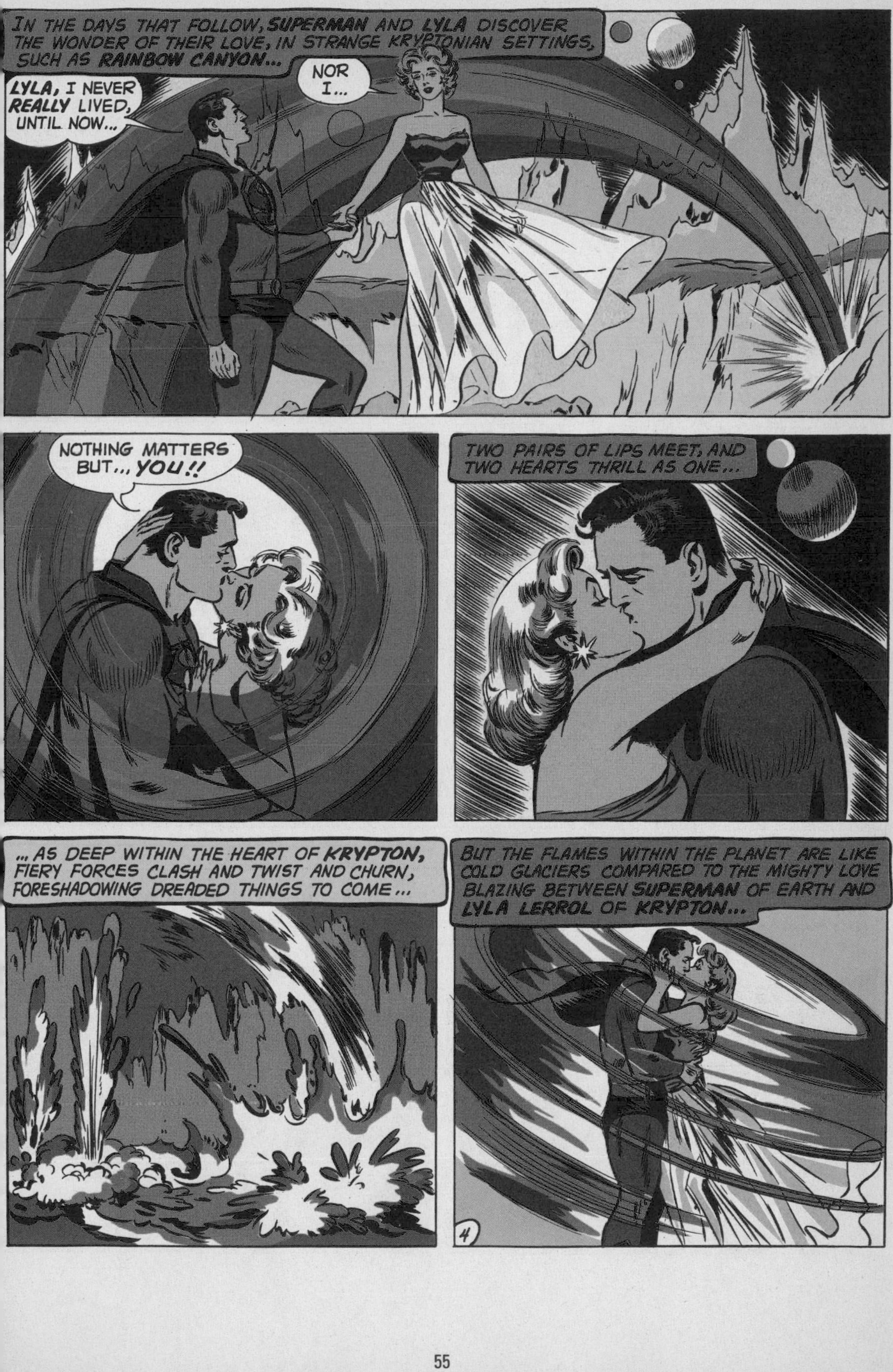
IN THE DAYS THAT FOLLOW, SUPERMAN AND LYLA DISCOVER THE WONDER OF THEIR LOVE, IN STRANGE KRYPTONIAN SETTINGS, SUCH AS RAINBOW CANYON...
LYLA, I NEVER REALLY LIVED, UNTIL NOW...
NOR I...
NOTHING MATTERS BUT... YOU!!
TWO PAIRS OF LIPS MEET, AND TWO HEARTS THRILL AS ONE...
...AS DEEP WITHIN THE HEART OF KRYPTON, FIERY FORCES CLASH AND TWIST AND CHURN, FORESHADOWING DREADED THINGS TO COME...
BUT THE FLAMES WITHIN THE PLANET ARE LIKE COLD GLACIERS COMPARED TO THE MIGHTY LOVE BLAZING BETWEEN SUPERMAN OF EARTH AND LYLA LERROL OF KRYPTON...
4

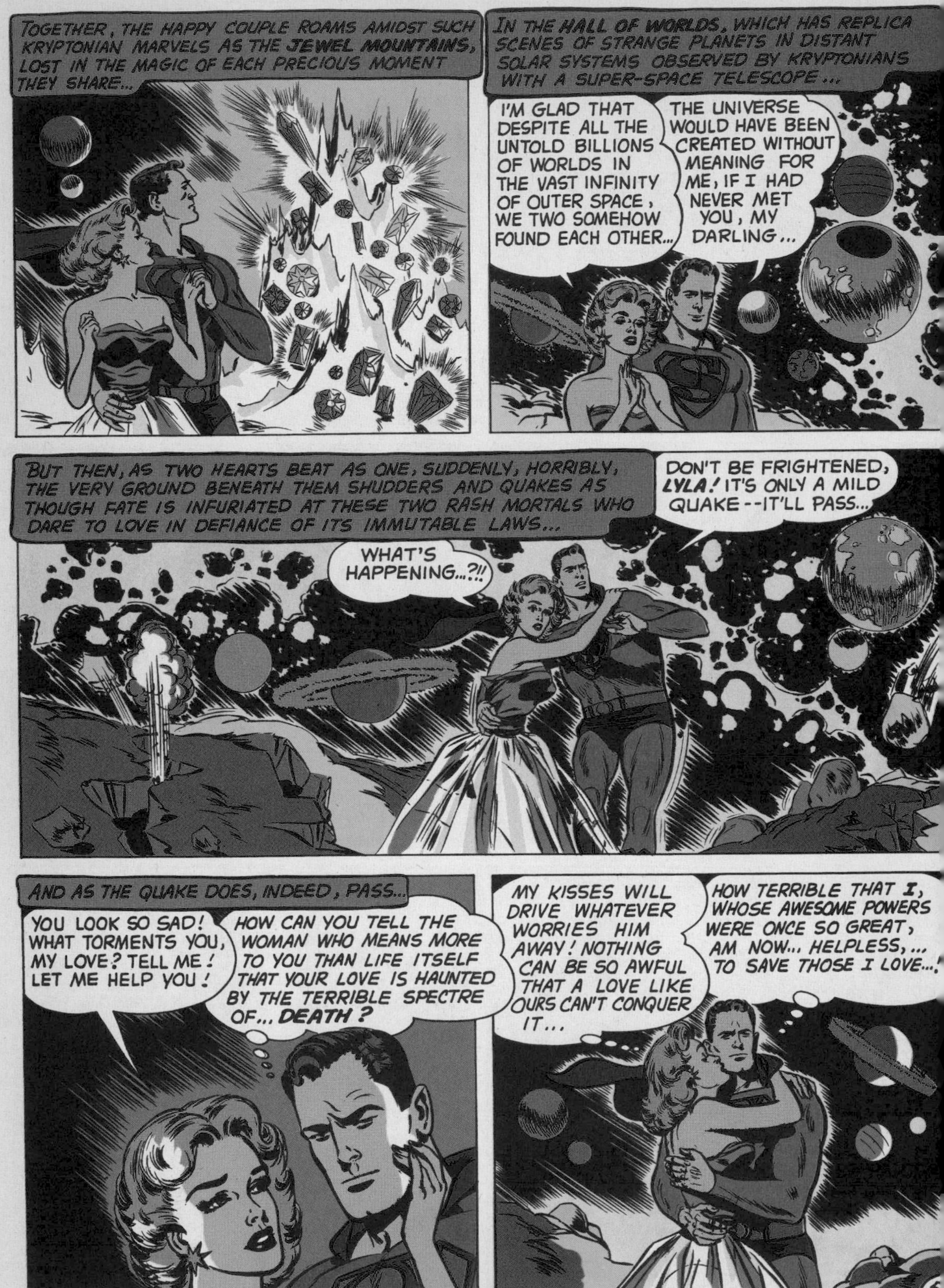
TOGETHER, THE HAPPY COUPLE ROAMS AMIDST SUCH KRYPTONIAN MARVELS AS THE JEWEL MOUNTAINS, LOST IN THE MAGIC OF EACH PRECIOUS MOMENT THEY SHARE...
IN THE HALL OF WORLDS, WHICH HAS REPLICA SCENES OF STRANGE PLANETS IN DISTANT SOLAR SYSTEMS OBSERVED BY KRYPTONIANS WITH A SUPER-SPACE TELESCOPE...
I'M GLAD THAT DESPITE ALL THE UNTOLD BILLIONS OF WORLDS IN THE VAST INFINITY OF OUTER SPACE, WE TWO SOMEHOW FOUND EACH OTHER...
THE UNIVERSE WOULD HAVE BEEN CREATED WITHOUT MEANING FOR ME, IF I HAD NEVER MET YOU, MY DARLING...
BUT THEN, AS TWO HEARTS BEAT AS ONE, SUDDENLY, HORRIBLY, THE VERY GROUND BENEATH THEM SHUDDERS AND QUAKES AS THOUGH FATE IS INFURIATED AT THESE TWO RASH MORTALS WHO DARE TO LOVE IN DEFIANCE OF ITS IMMUTABLE LAWS...
DON'T BE FRIGHTENED, LYLA! IT'S ONLY A MILD QUAKE--IT'LL PASS...
WHAT'S HAPPENING...?!!
AND AS THE QUAKE DOES, INDEED, PASS...
YOU LOOK SO SAD! WHAT TORMENTS YOU, MY LOVE? TELL ME! LET ME HELP YOU!
HOW CAN YOU TELL THE WOMAN WHO MEANS MORE TO YOU THAN LIFE ITSELF THAT YOUR LOVE IS HAUNTED BY THE TERRIBLE SPECTRE OF... DEATH?
MY KISSES WILL DRIVE WHATEVER WORRIES HIM AWAY! NOTHING CAN BE SO AWFUL THAT A LOVE LIKE OURS CAN'T CONQUER IT...
HOW TERRIBLE THAT I, WHOSE AWESOME POWERS WERE ONCE SO GREAT, AM NOW... HELPLESS, ... TO SAVE THOSE I LOVE...!

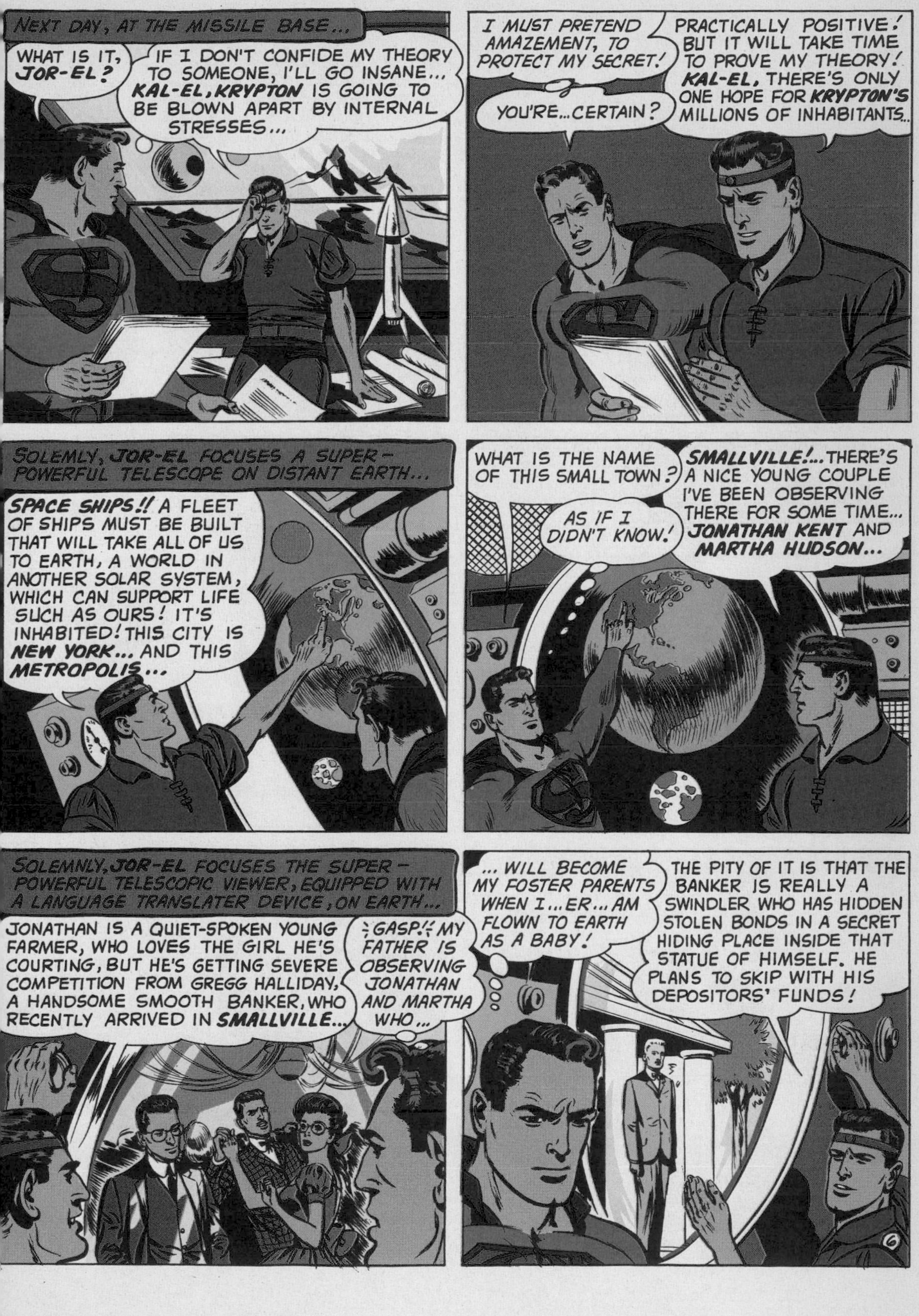

NEXT DAY, AT THE MISSILE BASE...
WHAT IS IT, JOR-EL?
IF I DON'T CONFIDE MY THEORY TO SOMEONE, I'LL GO INSANE... KAL-EL, KRYPTON IS GOING TO BE BLOWN APART BY INTERNAL STRESSES...
I MUST PRETEND AMAZEMENT, TO PROTECT MY SECRET!
YOU'RE...CERTAIN?
PRACTICALLY POSITIVE! BUT IT WILL TAKE TIME TO PROVE MY THEORY! KAL-EL, THERE'S ONLY ONE HOPE FOR KRYPTON'S MILLIONS OF INHABITANTS...
SOLEMLY, JOR-EL FOCUSES A SUPER-POWERFUL TELESCOPE ON DISTANT EARTH...
SPACE SHIPS!! A FLEET OF SHIPS MUST BE BUILT THAT WILL TAKE ALL OF US TO EARTH, A WORLD IN ANOTHER SOLAR SYSTEM, WHICH CAN SUPPORT LIFE SUCH AS OURS! IT'S INHABITED! THIS CITY IS NEW YORK... AND THIS METROPOLIS...
WHAT IS THE NAME OF THIS SMALL TOWN?
AS IF I DIDN'T KNOW!
SMALLVILLE!... THERE'S A NICE YOUNG COUPLE I'VE BEEN OBSERVING THERE FOR SOME TIME... JONATHAN KENT AND MARTHA HUDSON...
SOLEMNLY, JOR-EL FOCUSES THE SUPER-POWERFUL TELESCOPIC VIEWER, EQUIPPED WITH A LANGUAGE TRANSLATER DEVICE, ON EARTH...
JONATHAN IS A QUIET-SPOKEN YOUNG FARMER, WHO LOVES THE GIRL HE'S COURTING, BUT HE'S GETTING SEVERE COMPETITION FROM GREGG HALLIDAY, A HANDSOME SMOOTH BANKER, WHO RECENTLY ARRIVED IN SMALLVILLE...
GASP! MY FATHER IS OBSERVING JONATHAN AND MARTHA WHO...
... WILL BECOME MY FOSTER PARENTS WHEN I... ER... AM FLOWN TO EARTH AS A BABY!
THE PITY OF IT IS THAT THE BANKER IS REALLY A SWINDLER WHO HAS HIDDEN STOLEN BONDS IN A SECRET HIDING PLACE INSIDE THAT STATUE OF HIMSELF. HE PLANS TO SKIP WITH HIS DEPOSITORS' FUNDS!
6

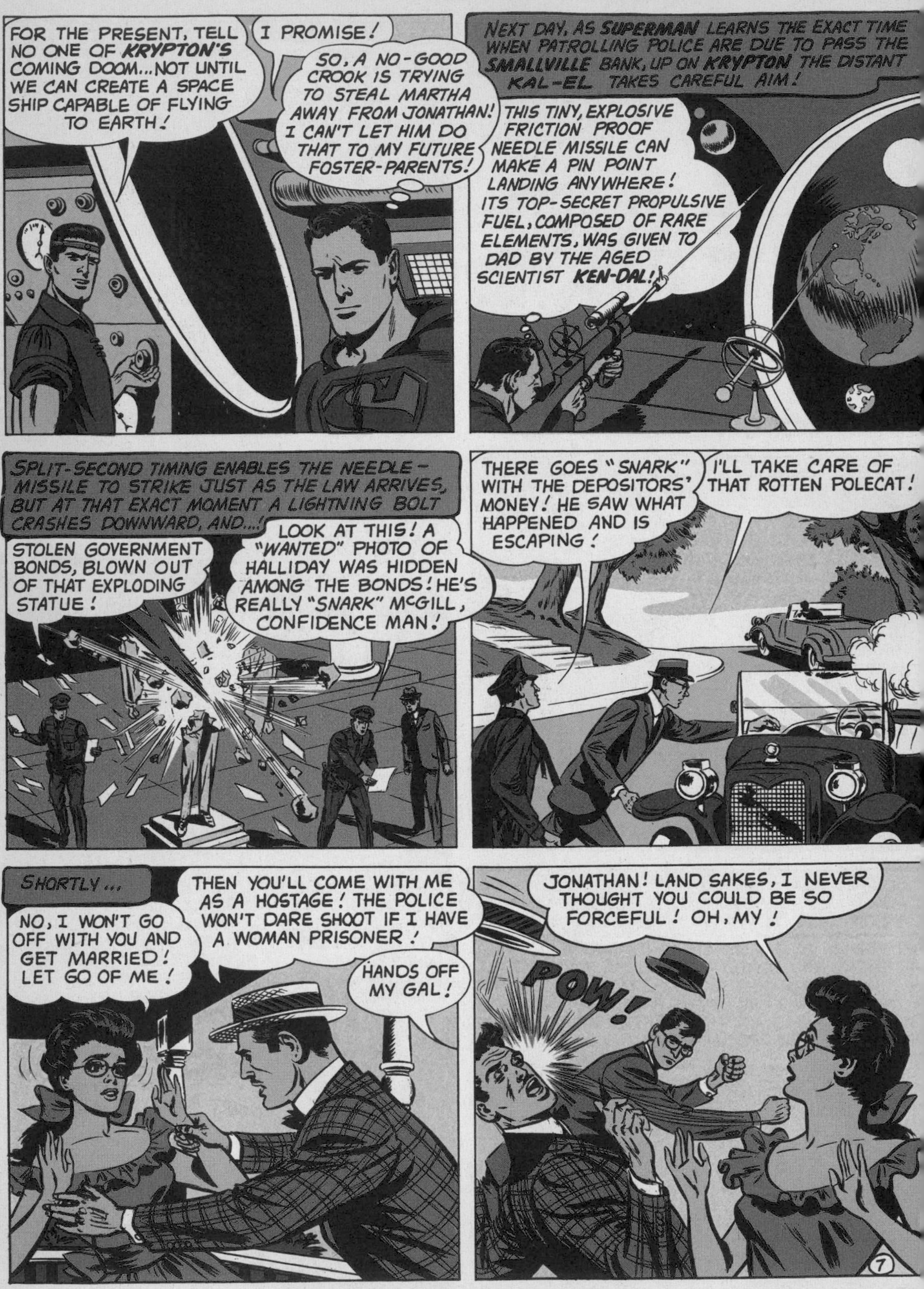
FOR THE PRESENT, TELL NO ONE OF KRYPTON'S COMING DOOM...NOT UNTIL WE CAN CREATE A SPACE SHIP CAPABLE OF FLYING TO EARTH!
I PROMISE!
SO, A NO-GOOD CROOK IS TRYING TO STEAL MARTHA AWAY FROM JONATHAN! I CAN'T LET HIM DO THAT TO MY FUTURE FOSTER-PARENTS!
NEXT DAY, AS SUPERMAN LEARNS THE EXACT TIME WHEN PATROLLING POLICE ARE DUE TO PASS THE SMALLVILLE BANK, UP ON KRYPTON THE DISTANT KAL-EL TAKES CAREFUL AIM!
THIS TINY, EXPLOSIVE FRICTION PROOF NEEDLE MISSILE CAN MAKE A PIN POINT LANDING ANYWHERE! ITS TOP-SECRET PROPULSIVE FUEL, COMPOSED OF RARE ELEMENTS, WAS GIVEN TO DAD BY THE AGED SCIENTIST KEN-DAL!
SPLIT-SECOND TIMING ENABLES THE NEEDLE-MISSILE TO STRIKE JUST AS THE LAW ARRIVES, BUT AT THAT EXACT MOMENT A LIGHTNING BOLT CRASHES DOWNWARD, AND...!
STOLEN GOVERNMENT BONDS, BLOWN OUT OF THAT EXPLODING STATUE!
LOOK AT THIS! A "WANTED" PHOTO OF HALLIDAY WAS HIDDEN AMONG THE BONDS! HE'S REALLY "SNARK" McGILL, CONFIDENCE MAN!
THERE GOES "SNARK" WITH THE DEPOSITORS' MONEY! HE SAW WHAT HAPPENED AND IS ESCAPING!
I'LL TAKE CARE OF THAT ROTTEN POLECAT!
SHORTLY...
NO, I WON'T GO OFF WITH YOU AND GET MARRIED! LET GO OF ME!
THEN YOU'LL COME WITH ME AS A HOSTAGE! THE POLICE WON'T DARE SHOOT IF I HAVE A WOMAN PRISONER!
HANDS OFF MY GAL!
JONATHAN! LAND SAKES, I NEVER THOUGHT YOU COULD BE SO FORCEFUL! OH, MY!
POW!
7

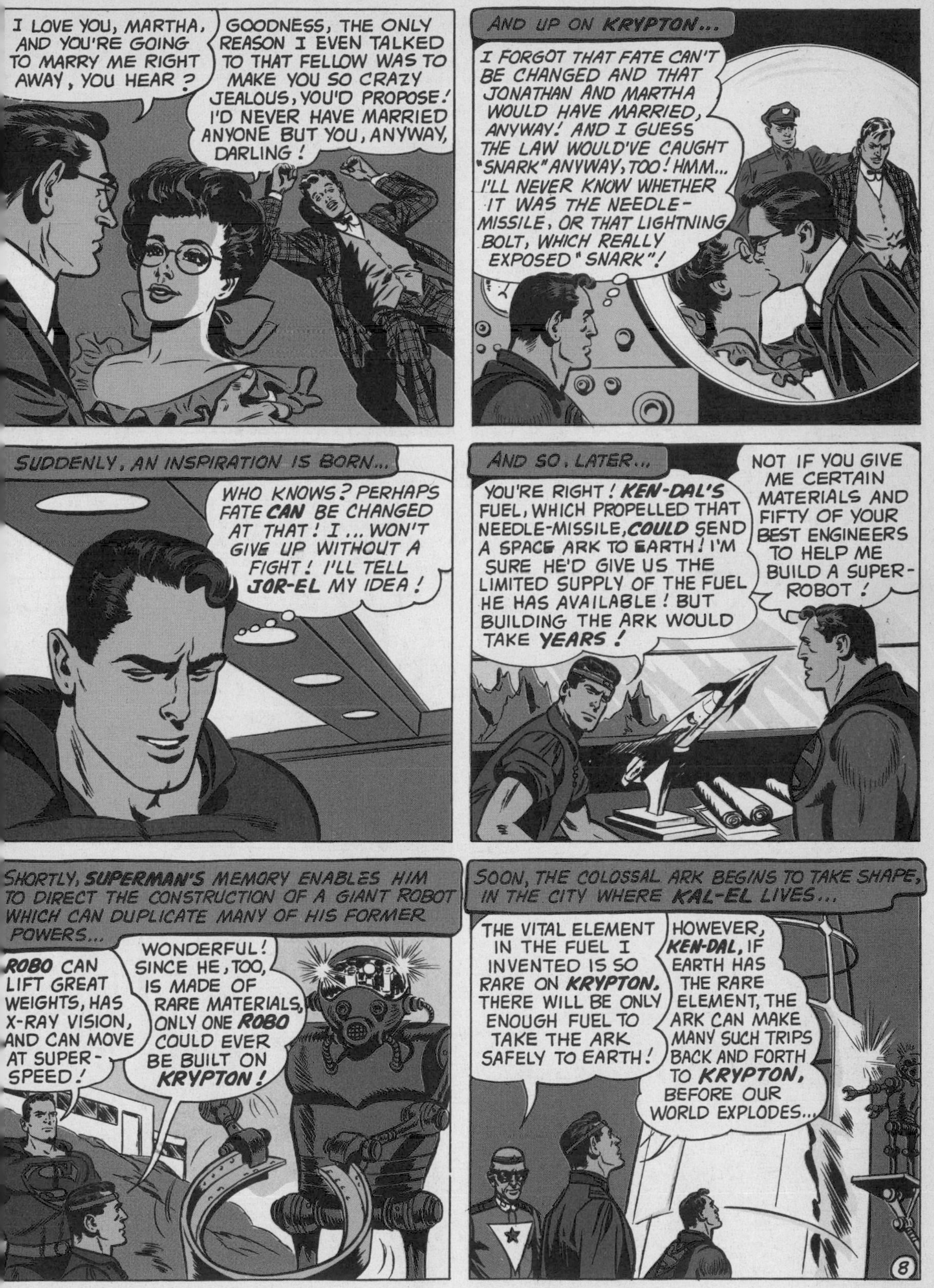
I LOVE YOU, MARTHA, AND YOU'RE GOING TO MARRY ME RIGHT AWAY, YOU HEAR?
GOODNESS, THE ONLY REASON I EVEN TALKED TO THAT FELLOW WAS TO MAKE YOU SO CRAZY JEALOUS, YOU'D PROPOSE! I'D NEVER HAVE MARRIED ANYONE BUT YOU, ANYWAY, DARLING!
AND UP ON KRYPTON...
I FORGOT THAT FATE CAN'T BE CHANGED AND THAT JONATHAN AND MARTHA WOULD HAVE MARRIED, ANYWAY! AND I GUESS THE LAW WOULD'VE CAUGHT "SNARK" ANYWAY, TOO! HMM... I'LL NEVER KNOW WHETHER IT WAS THE NEEDLE-MISSILE, OR THAT LIGHTNING BOLT, WHICH REALLY EXPOSED "SNARK"!
SUDDENLY, AN INSPIRATION IS BORN...
WHO KNOWS? PERHAPS FATE CAN BE CHANGED AT THAT! I ... WON'T GIVE UP WITHOUT A FIGHT! I'LL TELL JOR-EL MY IDEA!
AND SO, LATER...
YOU'RE RIGHT! KEN-DAL'S FUEL, WHICH PROPELLED THAT NEEDLE-MISSILE, COULD SEND A SPACE ARK TO EARTH! I'M SURE HE'D GIVE US THE LIMITED SUPPLY OF THE FUEL HE HAS AVAILABLE! BUT BUILDING THE ARK WOULD TAKE YEARS!
NOT IF YOU GIVE ME CERTAIN MATERIALS AND FIFTY OF YOUR BEST ENGINEERS TO HELP ME BUILD A SUPER-ROBOT!
SHORTLY, SUPERMAN'S MEMORY ENABLES HIM TO DIRECT THE CONSTRUCTION OF A GIANT ROBOT WHICH CAN DUPLICATE MANY OF HIS FORMER POWERS...
ROBO CAN LIFT GREAT WEIGHTS, HAS X-RAY VISION, AND CAN MOVE AT SUPER-SPEED!
WONDERFUL! SINCE HE, TOO, IS MADE OF RARE MATERIALS, ONLY ONE ROBO COULD EVER BE BUILT ON KRYPTON!
SOON, THE COLOSSAL ARK BEGINS TO TAKE SHAPE, IN THE CITY WHERE KAL-EL LIVES...
THE VITAL ELEMENT IN THE FUEL I INVENTED IS SO RARE ON KRYPTON. THERE WILL BE ONLY ENOUGH FUEL TO TAKE THE ARK SAFELY TO EARTH!
HOWEVER, KEN-DAL, IF EARTH HAS THE RARE ELEMENT, THE ARK CAN MAKE MANY SUCH TRIPS BACK AND FORTH TO KRYPTON, BEFORE OUR WORLD EXPLODES...
8

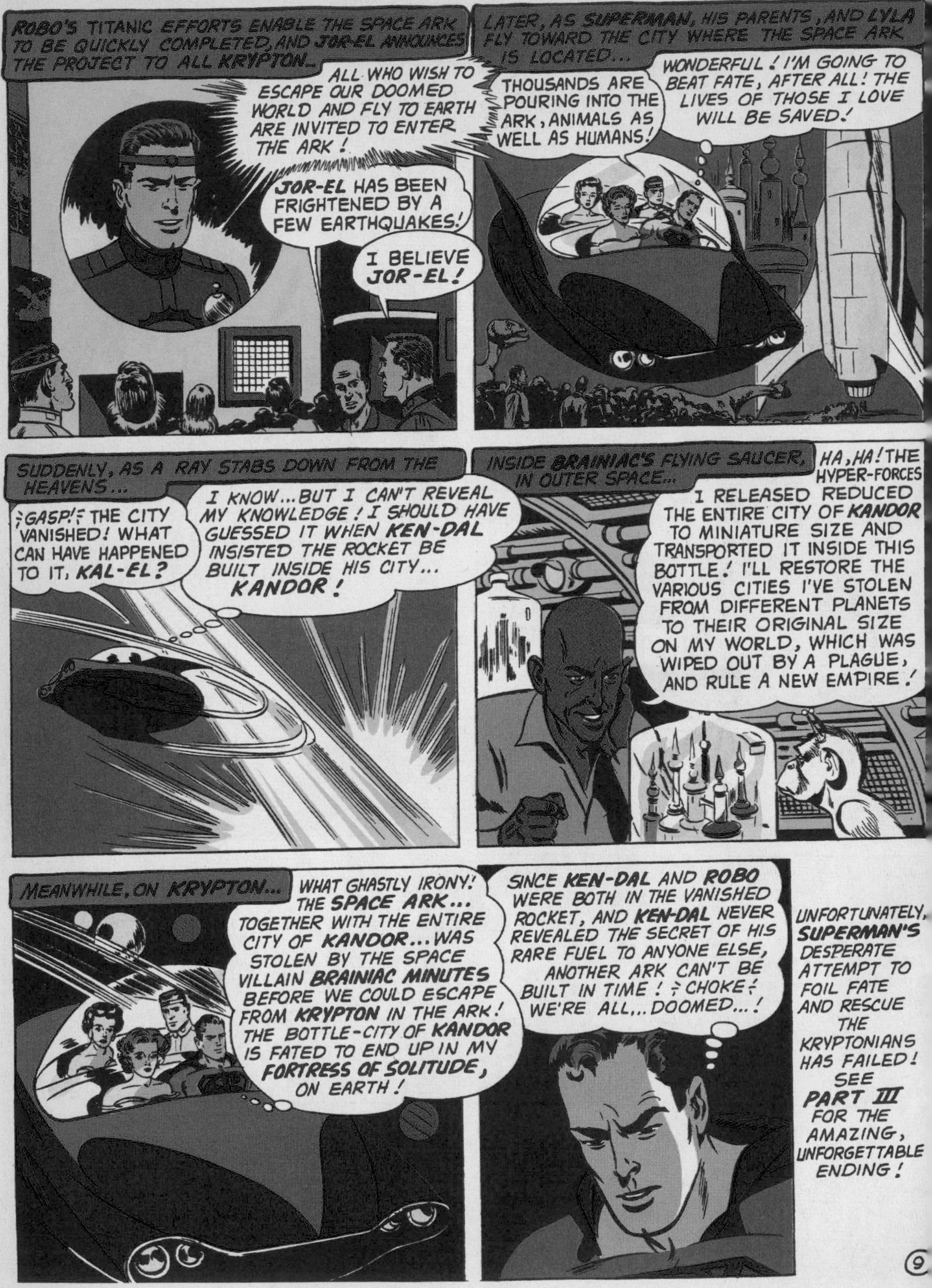
ROBO'S TITANIC EFFORTS ENABLE THE SPACE ARK TO BE QUICKLY COMPLETED, AND JOR-EL ANNOUNCES THE PROJECT TO ALL KRYPTON...
ALL WHO WISH TO ESCAPE OUR DOOMED WORLD AND FLY TO EARTH ARE INVITED TO ENTER THE ARK!
JOR-EL HAS BEEN FRIGHTENED BY A FEW EARTHQUAKES!
I BELIEVE JOR-EL!
LATER, AS SUPERMAN, HIS PARENTS, AND LYLA FLY TOWARD THE CITY WHERE THE SPACE ARK IS LOCATED...
THOUSANDS ARE POURING INTO THE ARK, ANIMALS AS WELL AS HUMANS!
WONDERFUL! I'M GOING TO BEAT FATE, AFTER ALL! THE LIVES OF THOSE I LOVE WILL BE SAVED!
SUDDENLY, AS A RAY STABS DOWN FROM THE HEAVENS...
-GASP!- THE CITY VANISHED! WHAT CAN HAVE HAPPENED TO IT, KAL-EL?
I KNOW... BUT I CAN'T REVEAL MY KNOWLEDGE! I SHOULD HAVE GUESSED IT WHEN KEN-DAL INSISTED THE ROCKET BE BUILT INSIDE HIS CITY... KANDOR!
INSIDE BRAINIAC'S FLYING SAUCER, IN OUTER SPACE...
HA, HA! THE HYPER-FORCES I RELEASED REDUCED THE ENTIRE CITY OF KANDOR TO MINIATURE SIZE AND TRANSPORTED IT INSIDE THIS BOTTLE! I'LL RESTORE THE VARIOUS CITIES I'VE STOLEN FROM DIFFERENT PLANETS TO THEIR ORIGINAL SIZE ON MY WORLD, WHICH WAS WIPED OUT BY A PLAGUE, AND RULE A NEW EMPIRE!
MEANWHILE, ON KRYPTON...
WHAT GHASTLY IRONY! THE SPACE ARK... TOGETHER WITH THE ENTIRE CITY OF KANDOR... WAS STOLEN BY THE SPACE VILLAIN BRAINIAC MINUTES BEFORE WE COULD ESCAPE FROM KRYPTON IN THE ARK! THE BOTTLE-CITY OF KANDOR IS FATED TO END UP IN MY FORTRESS OF SOLITUDE, ON EARTH!
SINCE KEN-DAL AND ROBO WERE BOTH IN THE VANISHED ROCKET, AND KEN-DAL NEVER REVEALED THE SECRET OF HIS RARE FUEL TO ANYONE ELSE, ANOTHER ARK CAN'T BE BUILT IN TIME! -CHOKE- WE'RE ALL... DOOMED...!
UNFORTUNATELY, SUPERMAN'S DESPERATE ATTEMPT TO FOIL FATE AND RESCUE THE KRYPTONIANS HAS FAILED! SEE PART III FOR THE AMAZING, UNFORGETTABLE ENDING!
9

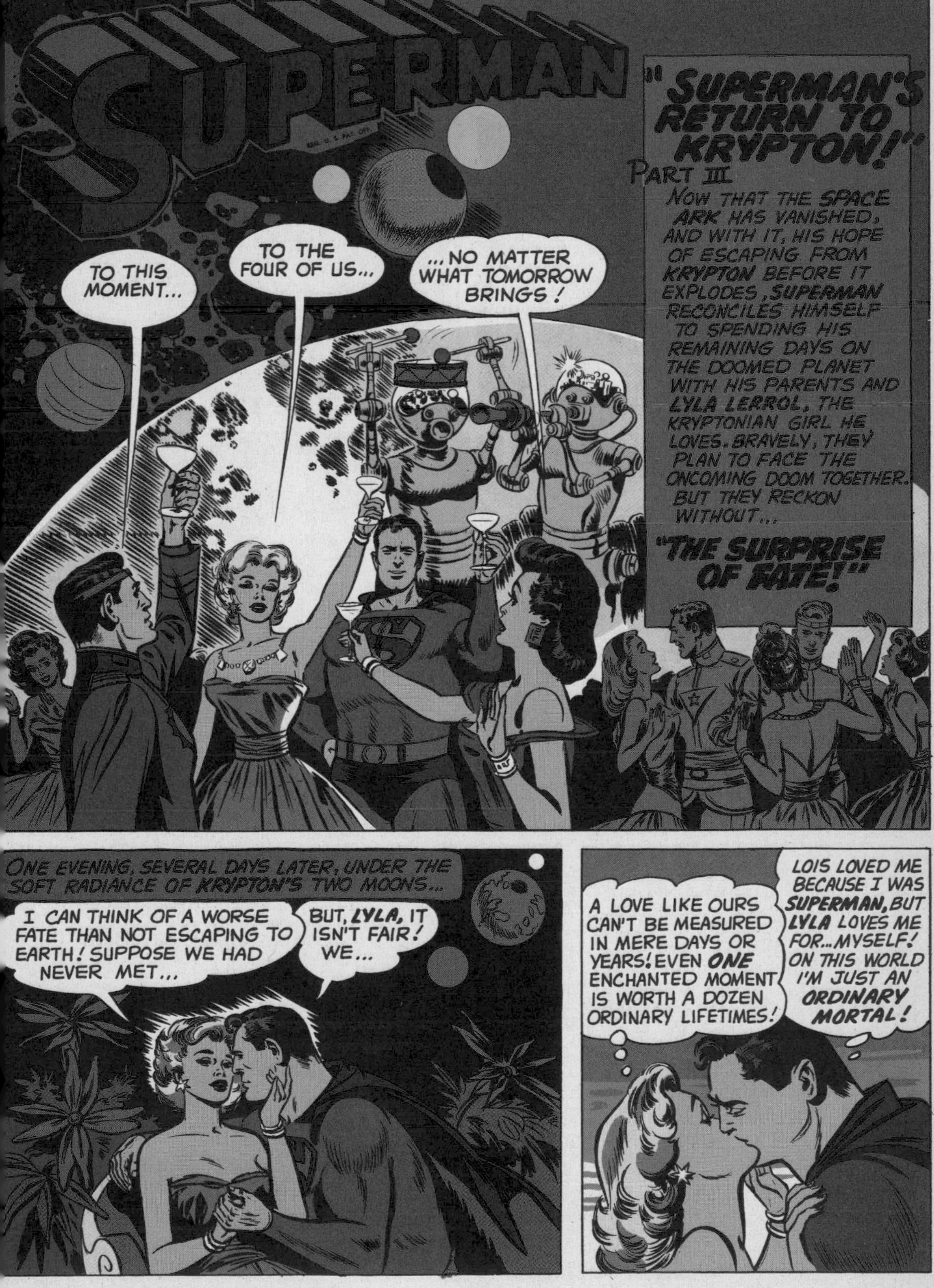
SUPERMAN
"SUPERMAN'S RETURN TO KRYPTON!"
PART III
NOW THAT THE SPACE ARK HAS VANISHED, AND WITH IT, HIS HOPE OF ESCAPING FROM KRYPTON BEFORE IT EXPLODES, SUPERMAN RECONCILES HIMSELF TO SPENDING HIS REMAINING DAYS ON THE DOOMED PLANET WITH HIS PARENTS AND LYLA LERROL, THE KRYPTONIAN GIRL HE LOVES. BRAVELY, THEY PLAN TO FACE THE ONCOMING DOOM TOGETHER. BUT THEY RECKON WITHOUT...
"THE SURPRISE OF FATE!"
TO THIS MOMENT...
TO THE FOUR OF US...
...NO MATTER WHAT TOMORROW BRINGS!
ONE EVENING, SEVERAL DAYS LATER, UNDER THE SOFT RADIANCE OF KRYPTON'S TWO MOONS...
I CAN THINK OF A WORSE FATE THAN NOT ESCAPING TO EARTH! SUPPOSE WE HAD NEVER MET...
BUT, LYLA, IT ISN'T FAIR! WE...
A LOVE LIKE OURS CAN'T BE MEASURED IN MERE DAYS OR YEARS! EVEN ONE ENCHANTED MOMENT IS WORTH A DOZEN ORDINARY LIFETIMES!
LOIS LOVED ME BECAUSE I WAS SUPERMAN, BUT LYLA LOVES ME FOR...MYSELF! ON THIS WORLD I'M JUST AN ORDINARY MORTAL!

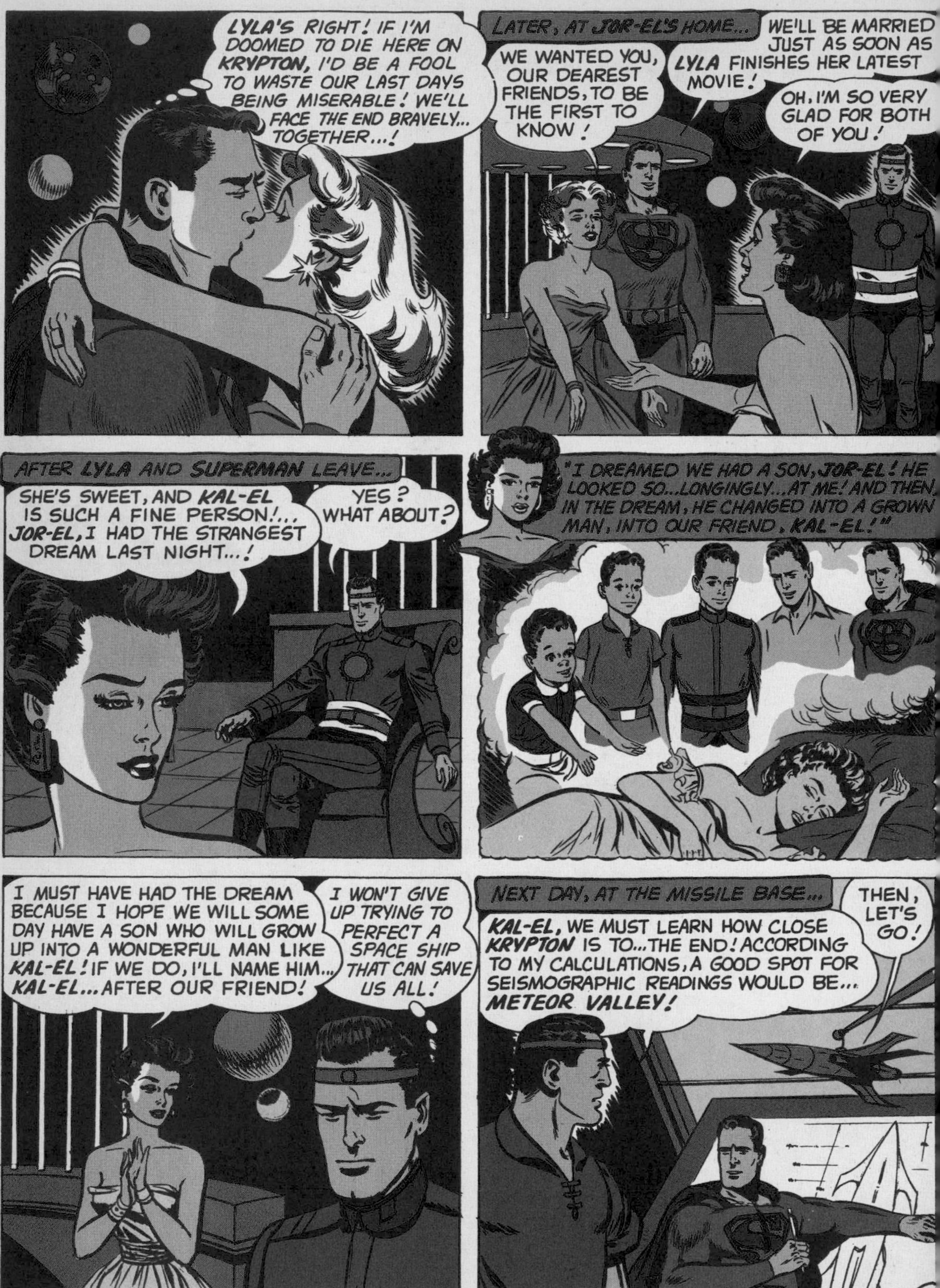
LYLA'S RIGHT! IF I'M DOOMED TO DIE HERE ON KRYPTON, I'D BE A FOOL TO WASTE OUR LAST DAYS BEING MISERABLE! WE'LL FACE THE END BRAVELY... TOGETHER...!
LATER, AT JOR-EL'S HOME...
WE WANTED YOU, OUR DEAREST FRIENDS, TO BE THE FIRST TO KNOW!
WE'LL BE MARRIED JUST AS SOON AS LYLA FINISHES HER LATEST MOVIE!
OH, I'M SO VERY GLAD FOR BOTH OF YOU!
AFTER LYLA AND SUPERMAN LEAVE...
SHE'S SWEET, AND KAL-EL IS SUCH A FINE PERSON!... JOR-EL, I HAD THE STRANGEST DREAM LAST NIGHT...!
YES? WHAT ABOUT?
"I DREAMED WE HAD A SON, JOR-EL! HE LOOKED SO...LONGINGLY...AT ME! AND THEN, IN THE DREAM, HE CHANGED INTO A GROWN MAN, INTO OUR FRIEND, KAL-EL!"
I MUST HAVE HAD THE DREAM BECAUSE I HOPE WE WILL SOME DAY HAVE A SON WHO WILL GROW UP INTO A WONDERFUL MAN LIKE KAL-EL! IF WE DO, I'LL NAME HIM... KAL-EL... AFTER OUR FRIEND!
I WON'T GIVE UP TRYING TO PERFECT A SPACE SHIP THAT CAN SAVE US ALL!
NEXT DAY, AT THE MISSILE BASE...
KAL-EL, WE MUST LEARN HOW CLOSE KRYPTON IS TO...THE END! ACCORDING TO MY CALCULATIONS, A GOOD SPOT FOR SEISMOGRAPHIC READINGS WOULD BE... METEOR VALLEY!
THEN, LET'S GO!
2

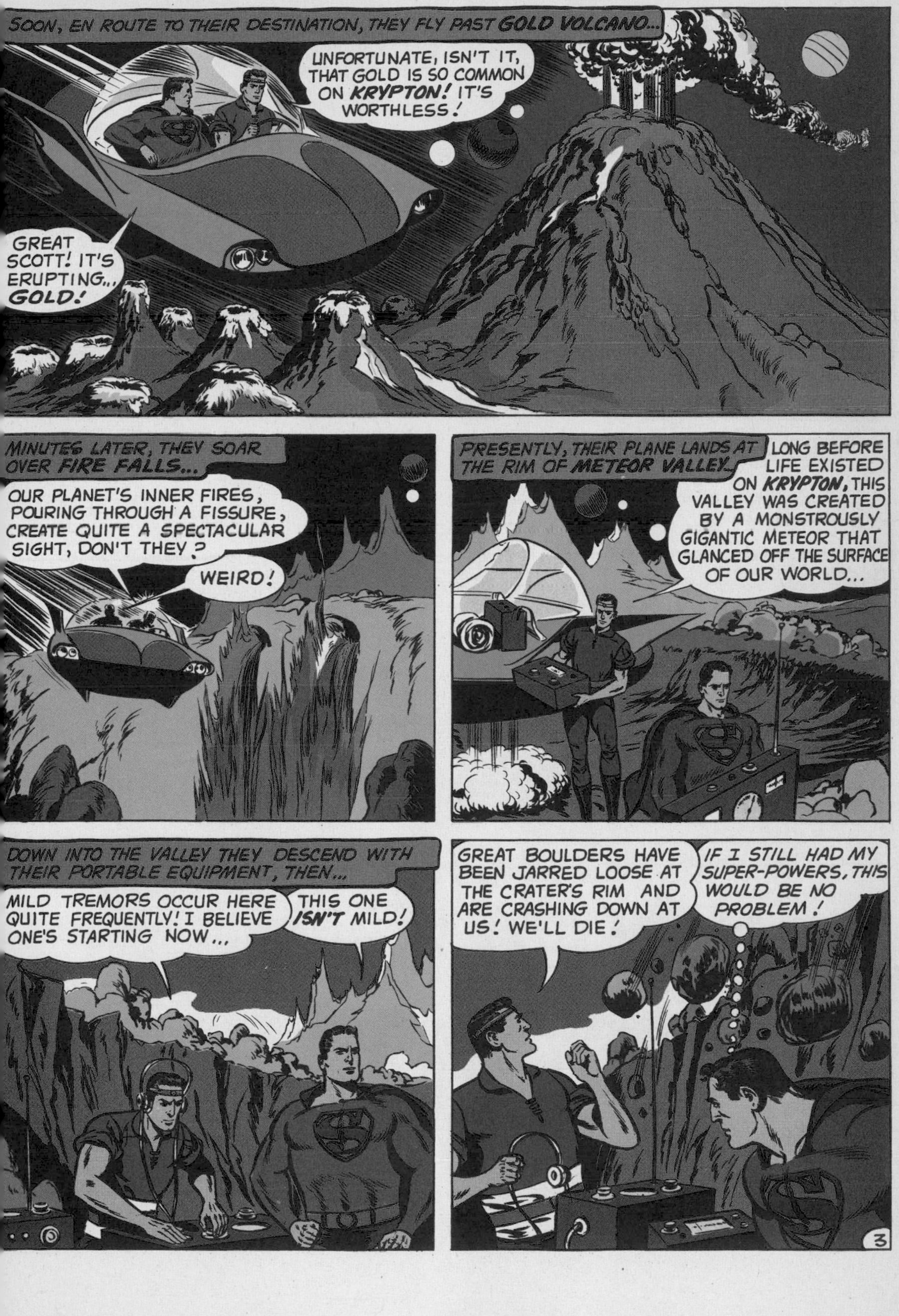
SOON, EN ROUTE TO THEIR DESTINATION, THEY FLY PAST GOLD VOLCANO...
UNFORTUNATE, ISN'T IT, THAT GOLD IS SO COMMON ON KRYPTON! IT'S WORTHLESS!
GREAT SCOTT! IT'S ERUPTING... GOLD!
MINUTES LATER, THEY SOAR OVER FIRE FALLS...
OUR PLANET'S INNER FIRES, POURING THROUGH A FISSURE, CREATE QUITE A SPECTACULAR SIGHT, DON'T THEY?
WEIRD!
PRESENTLY, THEIR PLANE LANDS AT THE RIM OF METEOR VALLEY...
LONG BEFORE LIFE EXISTED ON KRYPTON, THIS VALLEY WAS CREATED BY A MONSTROUSLY GIGANTIC METEOR THAT GLANCED OFF THE SURFACE OF OUR WORLD...
DOWN INTO THE VALLEY THEY DESCEND WITH THEIR PORTABLE EQUIPMENT, THEN...
MILD TREMORS OCCUR HERE QUITE FREQUENTLY! I BELIEVE ONE'S STARTING NOW...
THIS ONE ISN'T MILD!
GREAT BOULDERS HAVE BEEN JARRED LOOSE AT THE CRATER'S RIM AND ARE CRASHING DOWN AT US! WE'LL DIE!
IF I STILL HAD MY SUPER-POWERS, THIS WOULD BE NO PROBLEM!
3

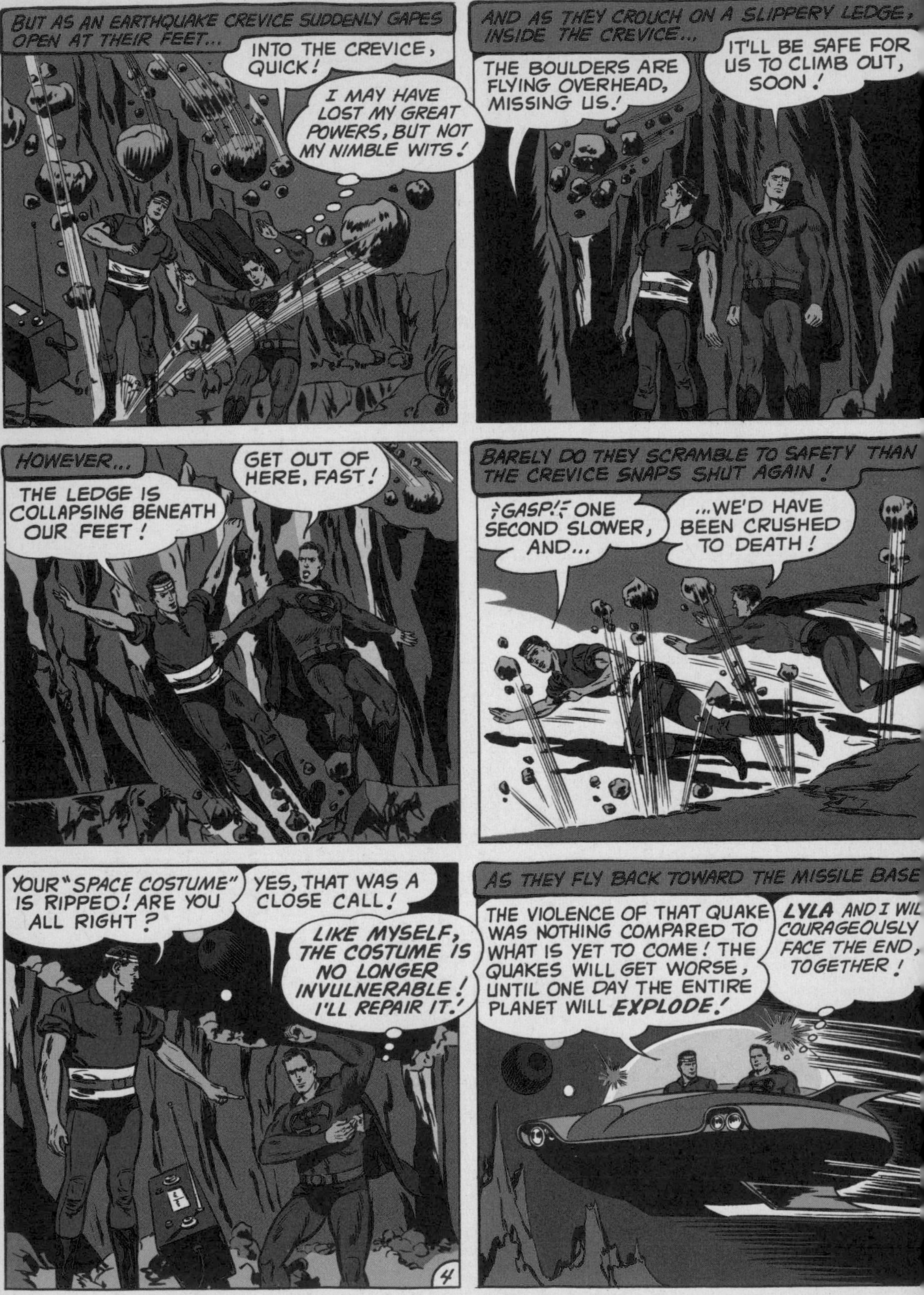
BUT AS AN EARTHQUAKE CREVICE SUDDENLY GAPES OPEN AT THEIR FEET...
INTO THE CREVICE, QUICK!
I MAY HAVE LOST MY GREAT POWERS, BUT NOT MY NIMBLE WITS!
AND AS THEY CROUCH ON A SLIPPERY LEDGE, INSIDE THE CREVICE...
THE BOULDERS ARE FLYING OVERHEAD, MISSING US!
IT'LL BE SAFE FOR US TO CLIMB OUT, SOON!
HOWEVER...
THE LEDGE IS COLLAPSING BENEATH OUR FEET!
GET OUT OF HERE, FAST!
BARELY DO THEY SCRAMBLE TO SAFETY THAN THE CREVICE SNAPS SHUT AGAIN!
GASP! ONE SECOND SLOWER, AND...
...WE'D HAVE BEEN CRUSHED TO DEATH!
YOUR "SPACE COSTUME" IS RIPPED! ARE YOU ALL RIGHT?
YES, THAT WAS A CLOSE CALL!
LIKE MYSELF, THE COSTUME IS NO LONGER INVULNERABLE! I'LL REPAIR IT.
4
AS THEY FLY BACK TOWARD THE MISSILE BASE
THE VIOLENCE OF THAT QUAKE WAS NOTHING COMPARED TO WHAT IS YET TO COME! THE QUAKES WILL GET WORSE, UNTIL ONE DAY THE ENTIRE PLANET WILL EXPLODE!
LYLA AND I WIL COURAGEOUSLY FACE THE END, TOGETHER!

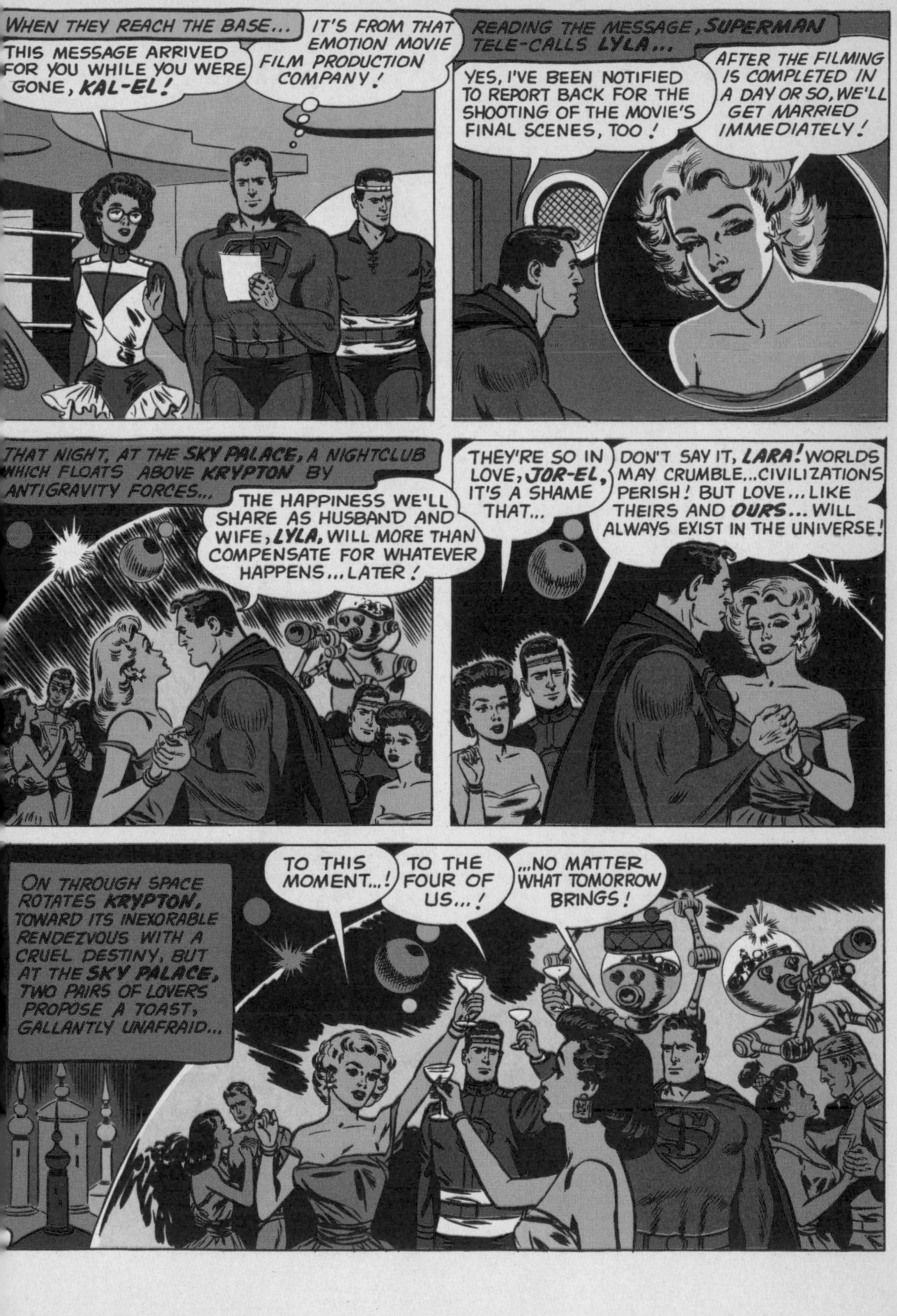
WHEN THEY REACH THE BASE...
THIS MESSAGE ARRIVED FOR YOU WHILE YOU WERE GONE, KAL-EL!
IT'S FROM THAT EMOTION MOVIE FILM PRODUCTION COMPANY!
READING THE MESSAGE, SUPERMAN TELE-CALLS LYLA...
YES, I'VE BEEN NOTIFIED TO REPORT BACK FOR THE SHOOTING OF THE MOVIE'S FINAL SCENES, TOO!
AFTER THE FILMING IS COMPLETED IN A DAY OR SO, WE'LL GET MARRIED IMMEDIATELY!
THAT NIGHT, AT THE SKY PALACE, A NIGHTCLUB WHICH FLOATS ABOVE KRYPTON BY ANTIGRAVITY FORCES...
THE HAPPINESS WE'LL SHARE AS HUSBAND AND WIFE, LYLA, WILL MORE THAN COMPENSATE FOR WHATEVER HAPPENS...LATER!
THEY'RE SO IN LOVE, JOR-EL, IT'S A SHAME THAT...
DON'T SAY IT, LARA! WORLDS MAY CRUMBLE...CIVILIZATIONS PERISH! BUT LOVE...LIKE THEIRS AND OURS...WILL ALWAYS EXIST IN THE UNIVERSE!
ON THROUGH SPACE ROTATES KRYPTON, TOWARD ITS INEXORABLE RENDEZVOUS WITH A CRUEL DESTINY. BUT AT THE SKY PALACE, TWO PAIRS OF LOVERS PROPOSE A TOAST, GALLANTLY UNAFRAID...
TO THIS MOMENT...!
TO THE FOUR OF US...!
...NO MATTER WHAT TOMORROW BRINGS!

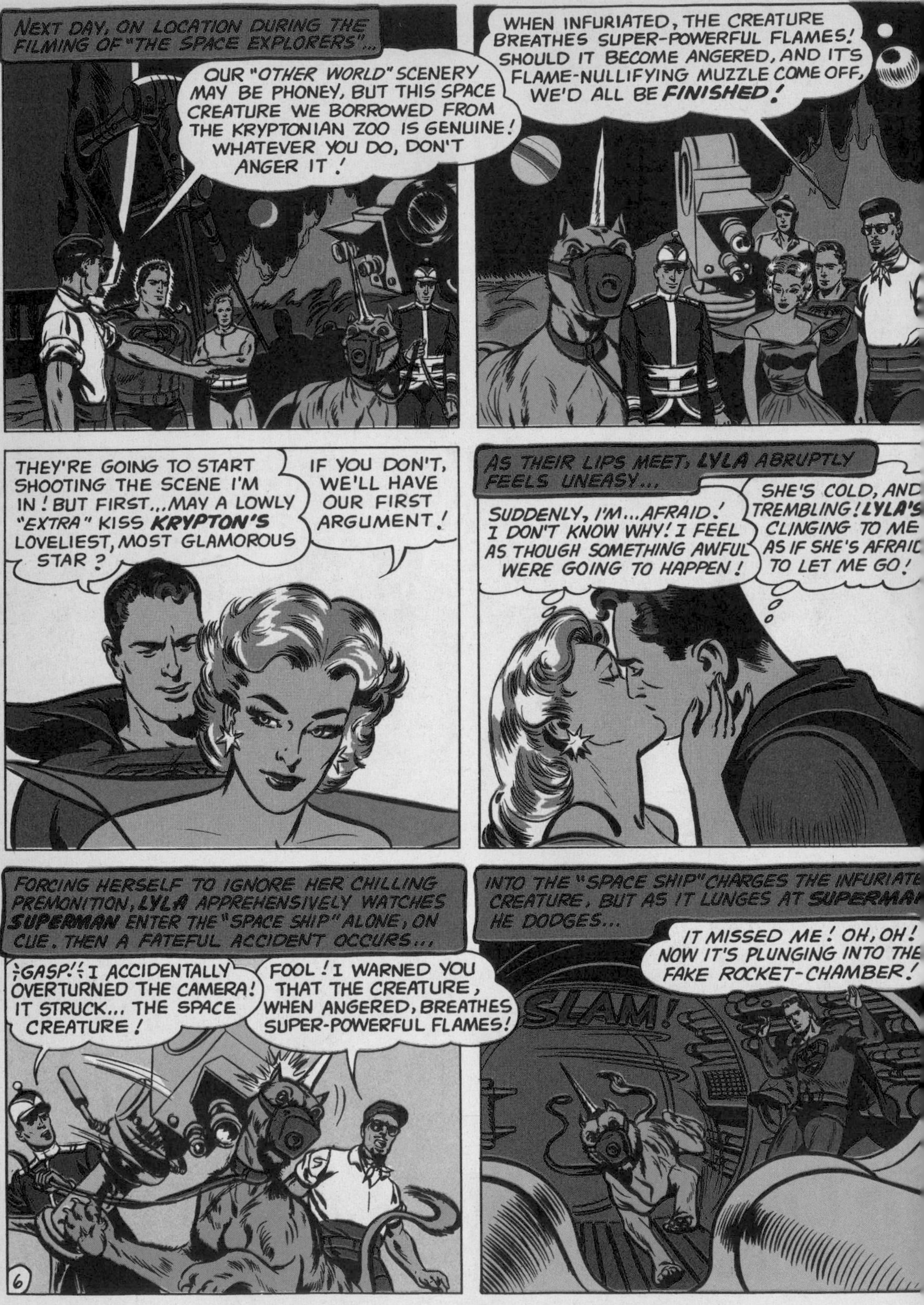
NEXT DAY, ON LOCATION DURING THE FILMING OF "THE SPACE EXPLORERS"...
OUR "OTHER WORLD" SCENERY MAY BE PHONEY, BUT THIS SPACE CREATURE WE BORROWED FROM THE KRYPTONIAN ZOO IS GENUINE! WHATEVER YOU DO, DON'T ANGER IT!
WHEN INFURIATED, THE CREATURE BREATHES SUPER-POWERFUL FLAMES! SHOULD IT BECOME ANGERED, AND IT'S FLAME-NULLIFYING MUZZLE COME OFF, WE'D ALL BE FINISHED!
THEY'RE GOING TO START SHOOTING THE SCENE I'M IN! BUT FIRST... MAY A LOWLY "EXTRA" KISS KRYPTON'S LOVELIEST, MOST GLAMOROUS STAR?
IF YOU DON'T, WE'LL HAVE OUR FIRST ARGUMENT!
AS THEIR LIPS MEET, LYLA ABRUPTLY FEELS UNEASY...
SUDDENLY, I'M... AFRAID! I DON'T KNOW WHY! I FEEL AS THOUGH SOMETHING AWFUL WERE GOING TO HAPPEN!
SHE'S COLD, AND TREMBLING! LYLA'S CLINGING TO ME AS IF SHE'S AFRAID TO LET ME GO!
FORCING HERSELF TO IGNORE HER CHILLING PREMONITION, LYLA APPREHENSIVELY WATCHES SUPERMAN ENTER THE "SPACE SHIP" ALONE, ON CUE. THEN A FATEFUL ACCIDENT OCCURS...
-GASP!- I ACCIDENTALLY OVERTURNED THE CAMERA! IT STRUCK... THE SPACE CREATURE!
FOOL! I WARNED YOU THAT THE CREATURE, WHEN ANGERED, BREATHES SUPER-POWERFUL FLAMES!
6
INTO THE "SPACE SHIP" CHARGES THE INFURIATE CREATURE, BUT AS IT LUNGES AT SUPERMAN HE DODGES...
IT MISSED ME! OH, OH! NOW IT'S PLUNGING INTO THE FAKE ROCKET-CHAMBER!
SLAM!

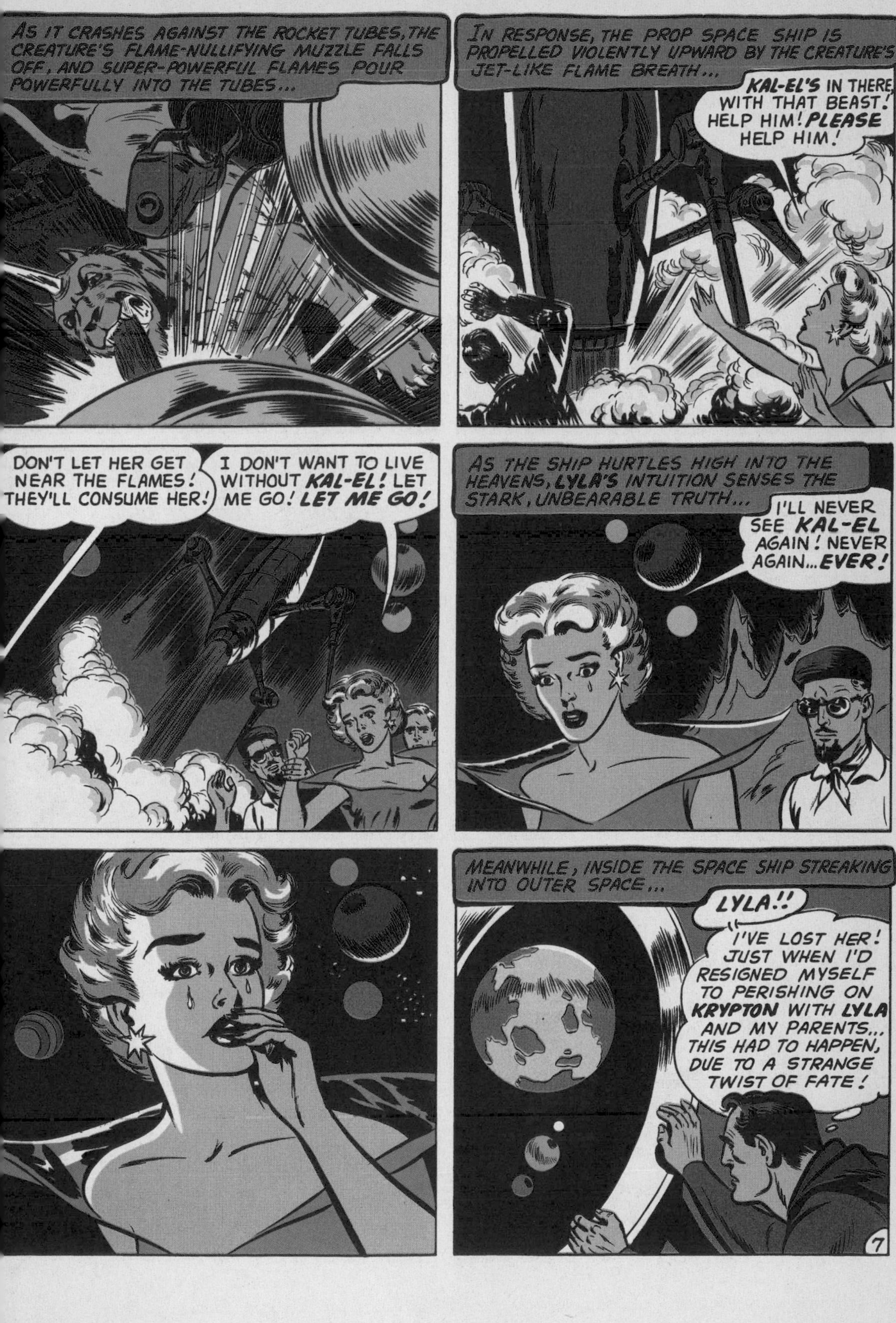
AS IT CRASHES AGAINST THE ROCKET TUBES, THE CREATURE'S FLAME-NULLIFYING MUZZLE FALLS OFF, AND SUPER-POWERFUL FLAMES POUR POWERFULLY INTO THE TUBES...
IN RESPONSE, THE PROP SPACE SHIP IS PROPELLED VIOLENTLY UPWARD BY THE CREATURE'S JET-LIKE FLAME BREATH...
KAL-EL'S IN THERE, WITH THAT BEAST! HELP HIM! PLEASE HELP HIM!
DON'T LET HER GET NEAR THE FLAMES! THEY'LL CONSUME HER!
I DON'T WANT TO LIVE WITHOUT KAL-EL! LET ME GO! LET ME GO!
AS THE SHIP HURTLES HIGH INTO THE HEAVENS, LYLA'S INTUITION SENSES THE STARK, UNBEARABLE TRUTH...
I'LL NEVER SEE KAL-EL AGAIN! NEVER AGAIN...EVER!
MEANWHILE, INSIDE THE SPACE SHIP STREAKING INTO OUTER SPACE...
LYLA!!
I'VE LOST HER! JUST WHEN I'D RESIGNED MYSELF TO PERISHING ON KRYPTON WITH LYLA AND MY PARENTS... THIS HAD TO HAPPEN, DUE TO A STRANGE TWIST OF FATE!
7

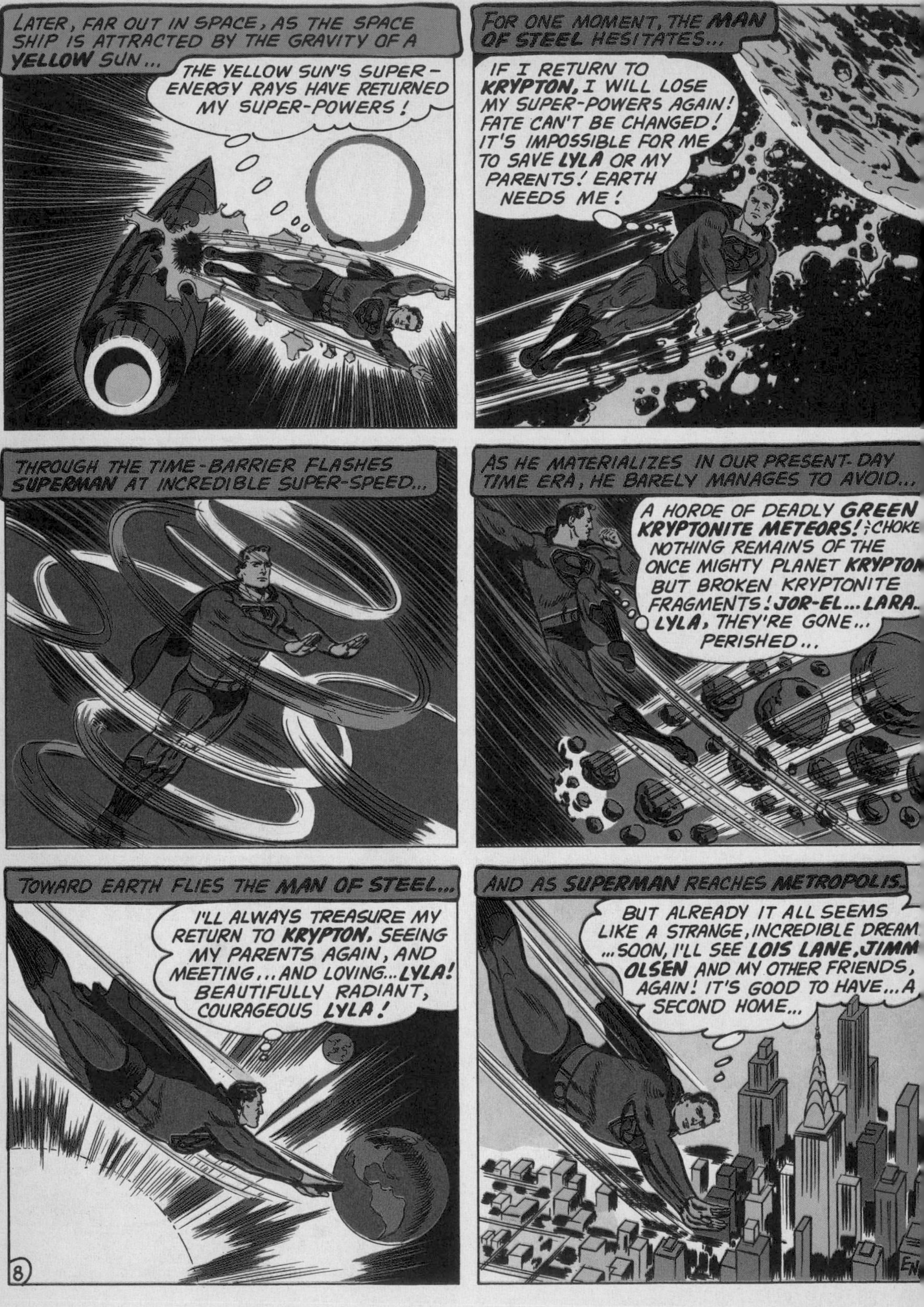
LATER, FAR OUT IN SPACE, AS THE SPACE SHIP IS ATTRACTED BY THE GRAVITY OF A YELLOW SUN...
THE YELLOW SUN'S SUPER-ENERGY RAYS HAVE RETURNED MY SUPER-POWERS!
FOR ONE MOMENT, THE MAN OF STEEL HESITATES...
IF I RETURN TO KRYPTON, I WILL LOSE MY SUPER-POWERS AGAIN! FATE CAN'T BE CHANGED! IT'S IMPOSSIBLE FOR ME TO SAVE LYLA OR MY PARENTS! EARTH NEEDS ME!
THROUGH THE TIME-BARRIER FLASHES SUPERMAN AT INCREDIBLE SUPER-SPEED...
AS HE MATERIALIZES IN OUR PRESENT-DAY TIME ERA, HE BARELY MANAGES TO AVOID...
A HORDE OF DEADLY GREEN KRYPTONITE METEORS! ;CHOKE NOTHING REMAINS OF THE ONCE MIGHTY PLANET KRYPTON BUT BROKEN KRYPTONITE FRAGMENTS! JOR-EL... LARA... LYLA, THEY'RE GONE... PERISHED...
TOWARD EARTH FLIES THE MAN OF STEEL...
I'LL ALWAYS TREASURE MY RETURN TO KRYPTON. SEEING MY PARENTS AGAIN, AND MEETING... AND LOVING... LYLA! BEAUTIFULLY RADIANT, COURAGEOUS LYLA!
8
AND AS SUPERMAN REACHES METROPOLIS...
BUT ALREADY IT ALL SEEMS LIKE A STRANGE, INCREDIBLE DREAM ...SOON, I'LL SEE LOIS LANE, JIMMY OLSEN AND MY OTHER FRIENDS, AGAIN! IT'S GOOD TO HAVE... A SECOND HOME...

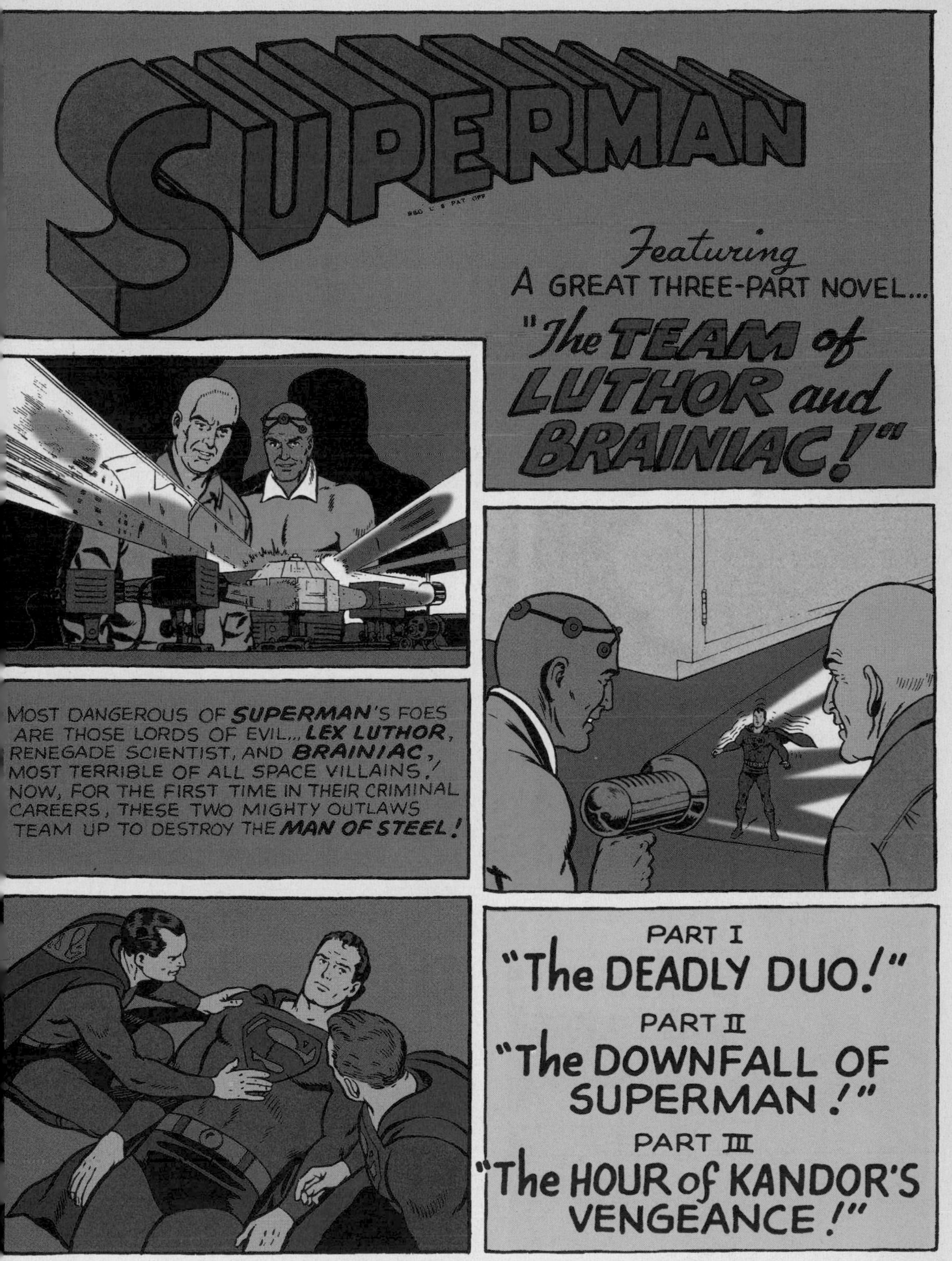
SUPERMAN
Featuring A GREAT THREE-PART NOVEL...
"The TEAM of LUTHOR and BRAINIAC!"
MOST DANGEROUS OF SUPERMAN'S FOES ARE THOSE LORDS OF EVIL... LEX LUTHOR, RENEGADE SCIENTIST, AND BRAINIAC, MOST TERRIBLE OF ALL SPACE VILLAINS! NOW, FOR THE FIRST TIME IN THEIR CRIMINAL CAREERS, THESE TWO MIGHTY OUTLAWS TEAM UP TO DESTROY THE MAN OF STEEL!
PART I
"The DEADLY DUO!"
PART II
"The DOWNFALL OF SUPERMAN!"
PART III
"The HOUR of KANDOR'S VENGEANCE!"

STORY: *EDMOND HAMILTON* PENCILS: *CURT SWAN* INKS: *GEORGE KLEIN*

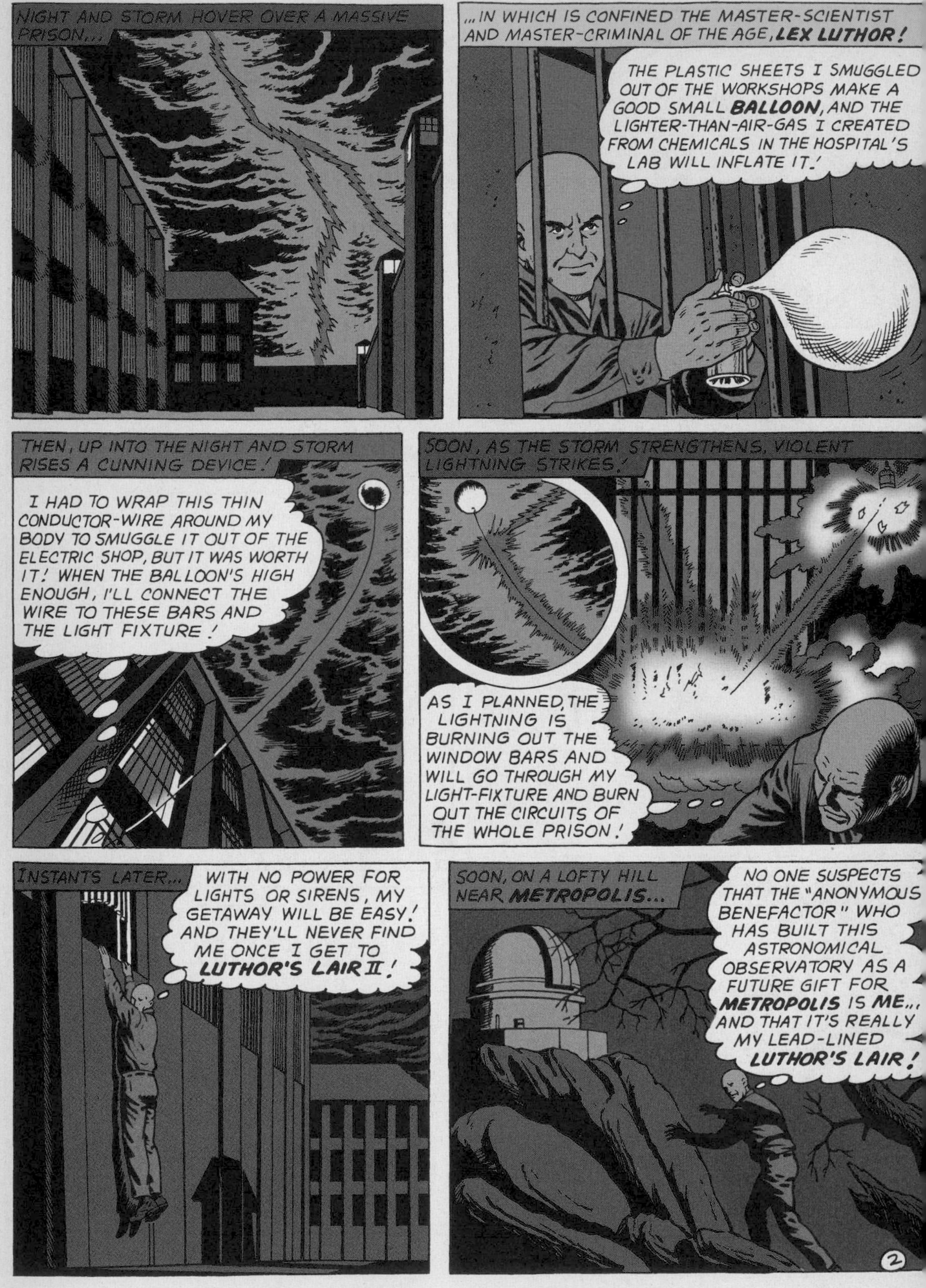
NIGHT AND STORM HOVER OVER A MASSIVE PRISON...
...IN WHICH IS CONFINED THE MASTER-SCIENTIST AND MASTER-CRIMINAL OF THE AGE, LEX LUTHOR!
THE PLASTIC SHEETS I SMUGGLED OUT OF THE WORKSHOPS MAKE A GOOD SMALL BALLOON, AND THE LIGHTER-THAN-AIR-GAS I CREATED FROM CHEMICALS IN THE HOSPITAL'S LAB WILL INFLATE IT.'
THEN, UP INTO THE NIGHT AND STORM RISES A CUNNING DEVICE!
I HAD TO WRAP THIS THIN CONDUCTOR-WIRE AROUND MY BODY TO SMUGGLE IT OUT OF THE ELECTRIC SHOP, BUT IT WAS WORTH IT! WHEN THE BALLOON'S HIGH ENOUGH, I'LL CONNECT THE WIRE TO THESE BARS AND THE LIGHT FIXTURE!
SOON, AS THE STORM STRENGTHENS, VIOLENT LIGHTNING STRIKES!
AS I PLANNED, THE LIGHTNING IS BURNING OUT THE WINDOW BARS AND WILL GO THROUGH MY LIGHT-FIXTURE AND BURN OUT THE CIRCUITS OF THE WHOLE PRISON!
INSTANTS LATER...
WITH NO POWER FOR LIGHTS OR SIRENS, MY GETAWAY WILL BE EASY! AND THEY'LL NEVER FIND ME ONCE I GET TO LUTHOR'S LAIR II!
SOON, ON A LOFTY HILL NEAR METROPOLIS...
NO ONE SUSPECTS THAT THE "ANONYMOUS BENEFACTOR" WHO HAS BUILT THIS ASTRONOMICAL OBSERVATORY AS A FUTURE GIFT FOR METROPOLIS IS ME... AND THAT IT'S REALLY MY LEAD-LINED LUTHOR'S LAIR!
2

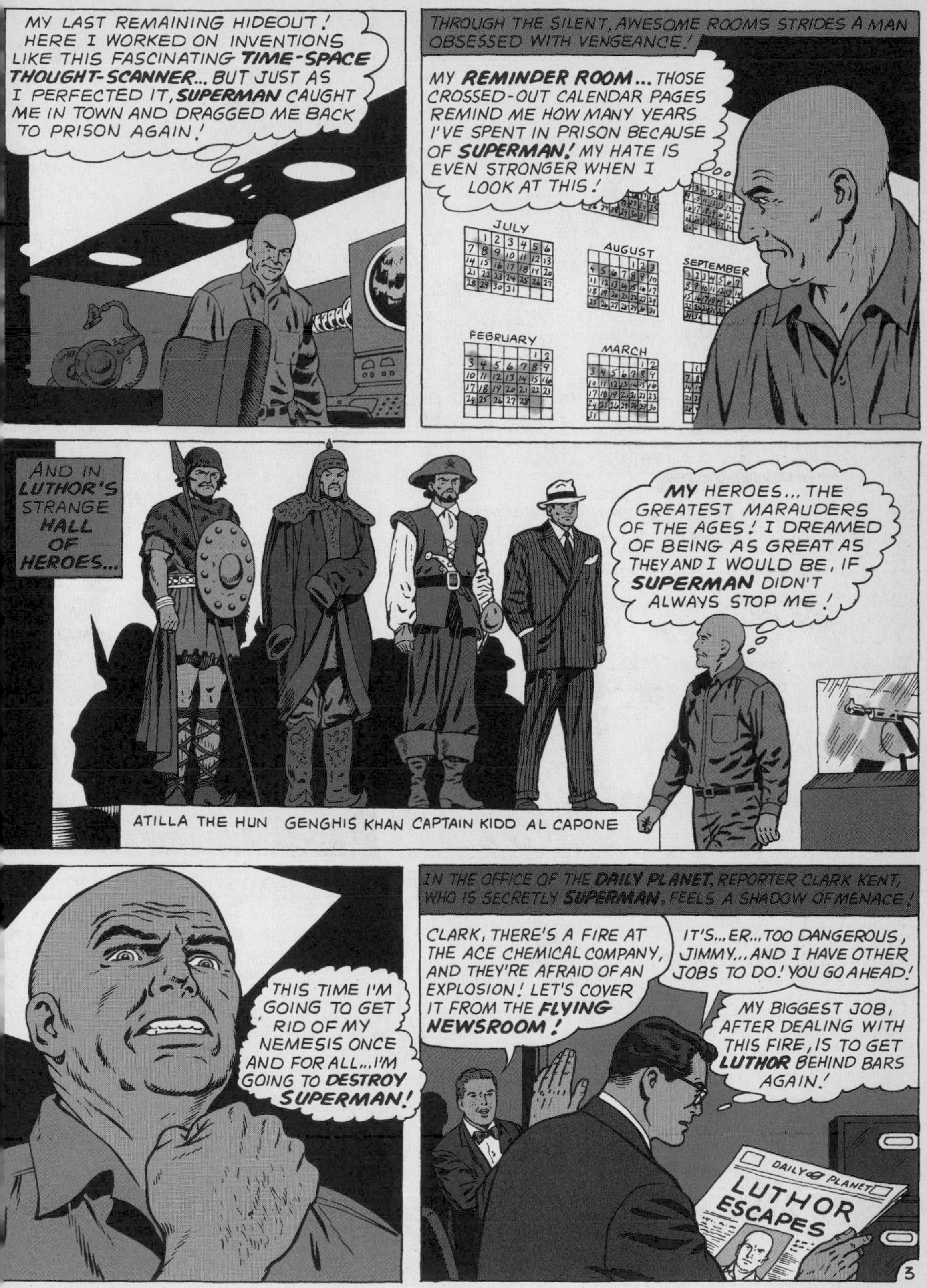

MY LAST REMAINING HIDEOUT! HERE I WORKED ON INVENTIONS LIKE THIS FASCINATING TIME-SPACE THOUGHT-SCANNER... BUT JUST AS I PERFECTED IT, SUPERMAN CAUGHT ME IN TOWN AND DRAGGED ME BACK TO PRISON AGAIN!
THROUGH THE SILENT, AWESOME ROOMS STRIDES A MAN OBSESSED WITH VENGEANCE!
MY REMINDER ROOM... THOSE CROSSED-OUT CALENDAR PAGES REMIND ME HOW MANY YEARS I'VE SPENT IN PRISON BECAUSE OF SUPERMAN! MY HATE IS EVEN STRONGER WHEN I LOOK AT THIS!
JULY
AUGUST
SEPTEMBER
FEBRUARY
MARCH
AND IN LUTHOR'S STRANGE HALL OF HEROES...
MY HEROES... THE GREATEST MARAUDERS OF THE AGES! I DREAMED OF BEING AS GREAT AS THEY AND I WOULD BE, IF SUPERMAN DIDN'T ALWAYS STOP ME!
ATILLA THE HUN GENGHIS KHAN CAPTAIN KIDD AL CAPONE
THIS TIME I'M GOING TO GET RID OF MY NEMESIS ONCE AND FOR ALL...I'M GOING TO DESTROY SUPERMAN!
IN THE OFFICE OF THE DAILY PLANET, REPORTER CLARK KENT, WHO IS SECRETLY SUPERMAN, FEELS A SHADOW OF MENACE!
CLARK, THERE'S A FIRE AT THE ACE CHEMICAL COMPANY, AND THEY'RE AFRAID OF AN EXPLOSION! LET'S COVER IT FROM THE FLYING NEWSROOM!
IT'S...ER...TOO DANGEROUS, JIMMY... AND I HAVE OTHER JOBS TO DO! YOU GO AHEAD!
MY BIGGEST JOB, AFTER DEALING WITH THIS FIRE, IS TO GET LUTHOR BEHIND BARS AGAIN!
DAILY PLANET
LUTHOR ESCAPES
3

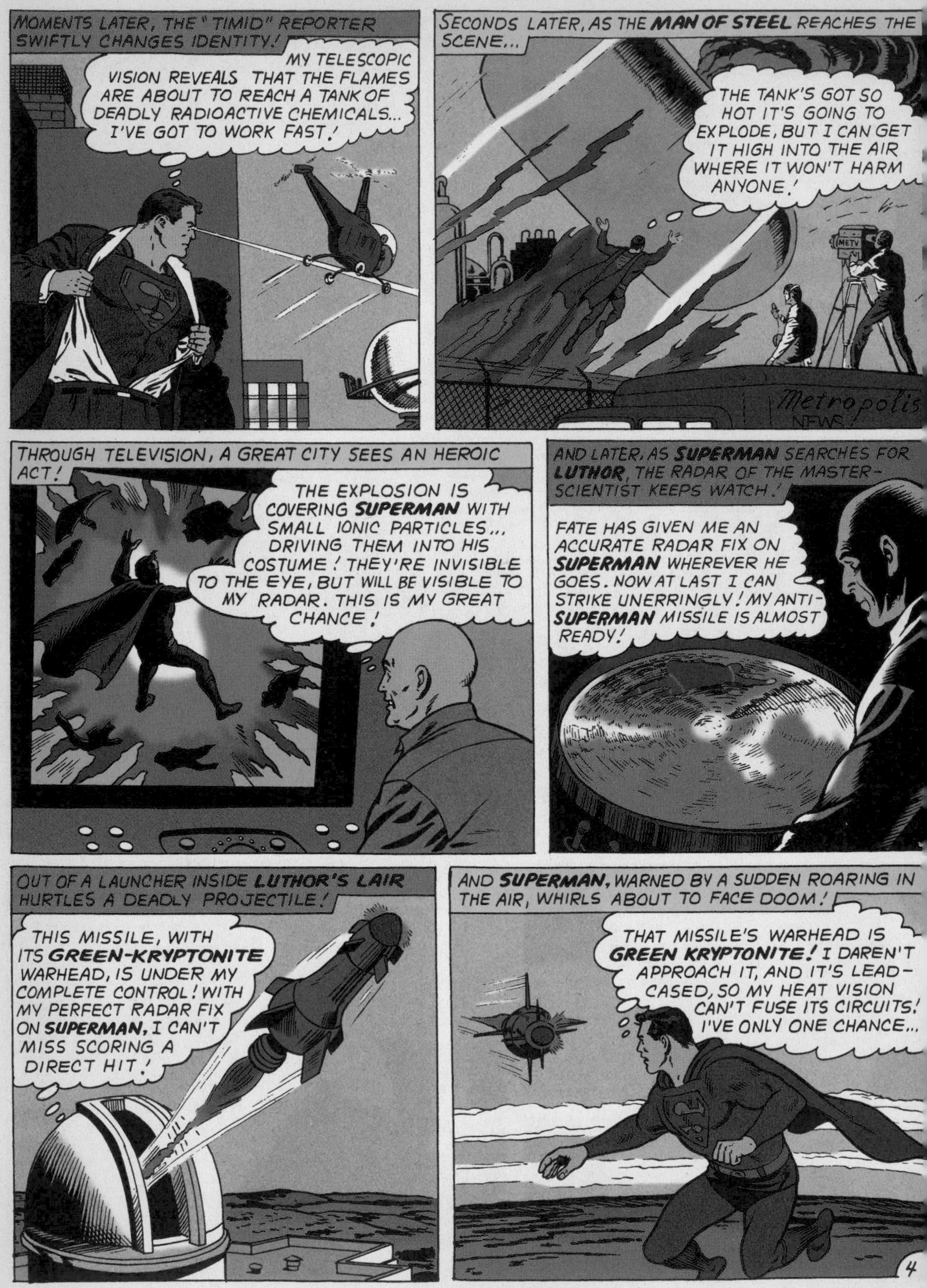
MOMENTS LATER, THE "TIMID" REPORTER SWIFTLY CHANGES IDENTITY!
MY TELESCOPIC VISION REVEALS THAT THE FLAMES ARE ABOUT TO REACH A TANK OF DEADLY RADIOACTIVE CHEMICALS... I'VE GOT TO WORK FAST!
SECONDS LATER, AS THE MAN OF STEEL REACHES THE SCENE...
THE TANK'S GOT SO HOT IT'S GOING TO EXPLODE, BUT I CAN GET IT HIGH INTO THE AIR WHERE IT WON'T HARM ANYONE!
METV
Metropolis NEWS
THROUGH TELEVISION, A GREAT CITY SEES AN HEROIC ACT!
THE EXPLOSION IS COVERING SUPERMAN WITH SMALL IONIC PARTICLES... DRIVING THEM INTO HIS COSTUME! THEY'RE INVISIBLE TO THE EYE, BUT WILL BE VISIBLE TO MY RADAR. THIS IS MY GREAT CHANCE!
AND LATER, AS SUPERMAN SEARCHES FOR LUTHOR, THE RADAR OF THE MASTER-SCIENTIST KEEPS WATCH!
FATE HAS GIVEN ME AN ACCURATE RADAR FIX ON SUPERMAN WHEREVER HE GOES. NOW AT LAST I CAN STRIKE UNERRINGLY! MY ANTI-SUPERMAN MISSILE IS ALMOST READY!
OUT OF A LAUNCHER INSIDE LUTHOR'S LAIR HURTLES A DEADLY PROJECTILE!
THIS MISSILE, WITH ITS GREEN-KRYPTONITE WARHEAD, IS UNDER MY COMPLETE CONTROL! WITH MY PERFECT RADAR FIX ON SUPERMAN, I CAN'T MISS SCORING A DIRECT HIT!
AND SUPERMAN, WARNED BY A SUDDEN ROARING IN THE AIR, WHIRLS ABOUT TO FACE DOOM!
THAT MISSILE'S WARHEAD IS GREEN KRYPTONITE! I DAREN'T APPROACH IT, AND IT'S LEAD-CASED, SO MY HEAT VISION CAN'T FUSE ITS CIRCUITS! I'VE ONLY ONE CHANCE...
4

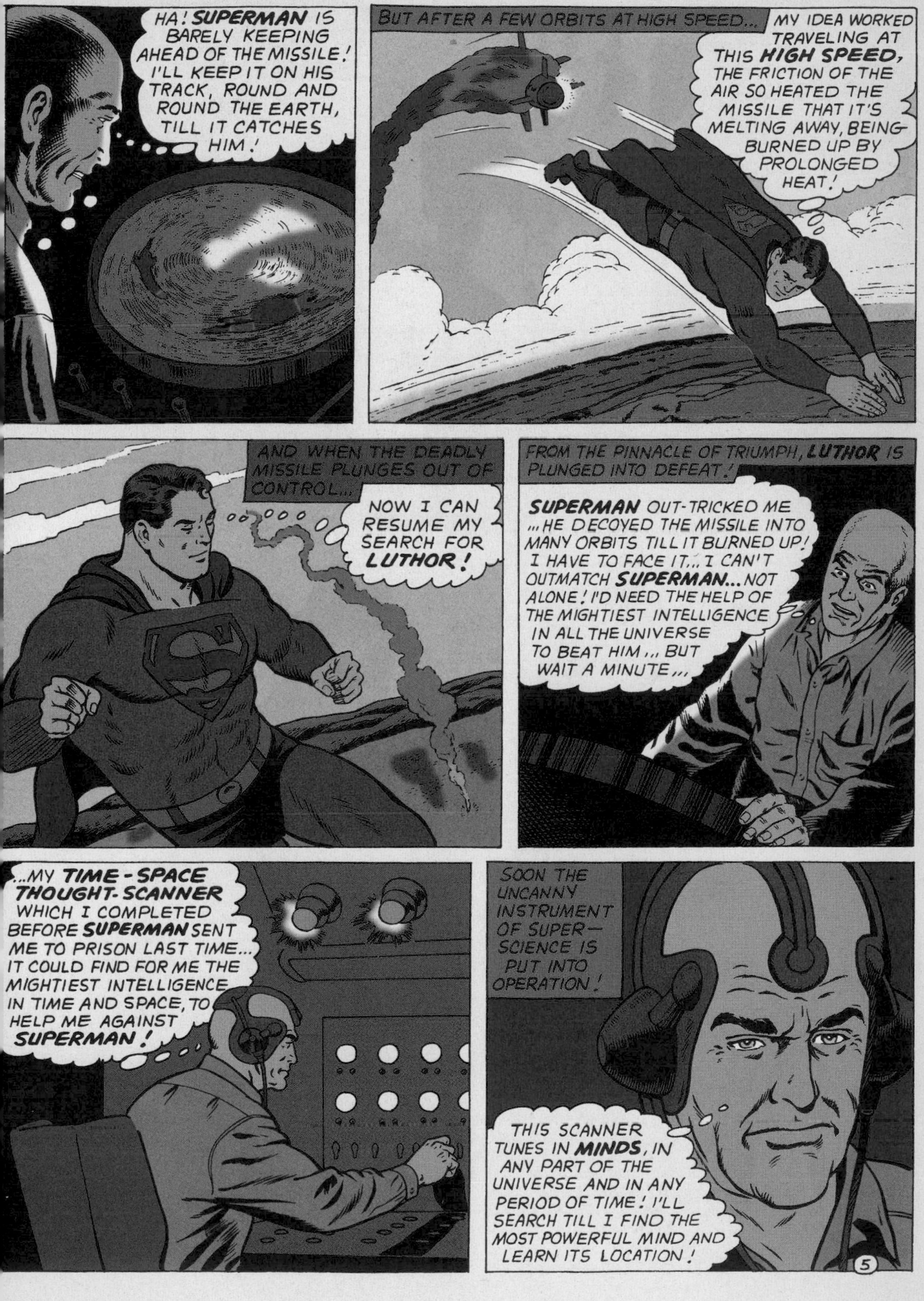

HA! SUPERMAN IS BARELY KEEPING AHEAD OF THE MISSILE! I'LL KEEP IT ON HIS TRACK, ROUND AND ROUND THE EARTH, TILL IT CATCHES HIM!
BUT AFTER A FEW ORBITS AT HIGH SPEED...
MY IDEA WORKED TRAVELING AT THIS HIGH SPEED, THE FRICTION OF THE AIR SO HEATED THE MISSILE THAT IT'S MELTING AWAY, BEING BURNED UP BY PROLONGED HEAT!
AND WHEN THE DEADLY MISSILE PLUNGES OUT OF CONTROL...
NOW I CAN RESUME MY SEARCH FOR LUTHOR!
FROM THE PINNACLE OF TRIUMPH, LUTHOR IS PLUNGED INTO DEFEAT!
SUPERMAN OUT-TRICKED ME ... HE DECOYED THE MISSILE INTO MANY ORBITS TILL IT BURNED UP! I HAVE TO FACE IT... I CAN'T OUTMATCH SUPERMAN... NOT ALONE! I'D NEED THE HELP OF THE MIGHTIEST INTELLIGENCE IN ALL THE UNIVERSE TO BEAT HIM ... BUT WAIT A MINUTE ...
...MY TIME-SPACE THOUGHT-SCANNER WHICH I COMPLETED BEFORE SUPERMAN SENT ME TO PRISON LAST TIME... IT COULD FIND FOR ME THE MIGHTIEST INTELLIGENCE IN TIME AND SPACE, TO HELP ME AGAINST SUPERMAN!
SOON THE UNCANNY INSTRUMENT OF SUPER-SCIENCE IS PUT INTO OPERATION!
THIS SCANNER TUNES IN MINDS, IN ANY PART OF THE UNIVERSE AND IN ANY PERIOD OF TIME! I'LL SEARCH TILL I FIND THE MOST POWERFUL MIND AND LEARN ITS LOCATION!
5

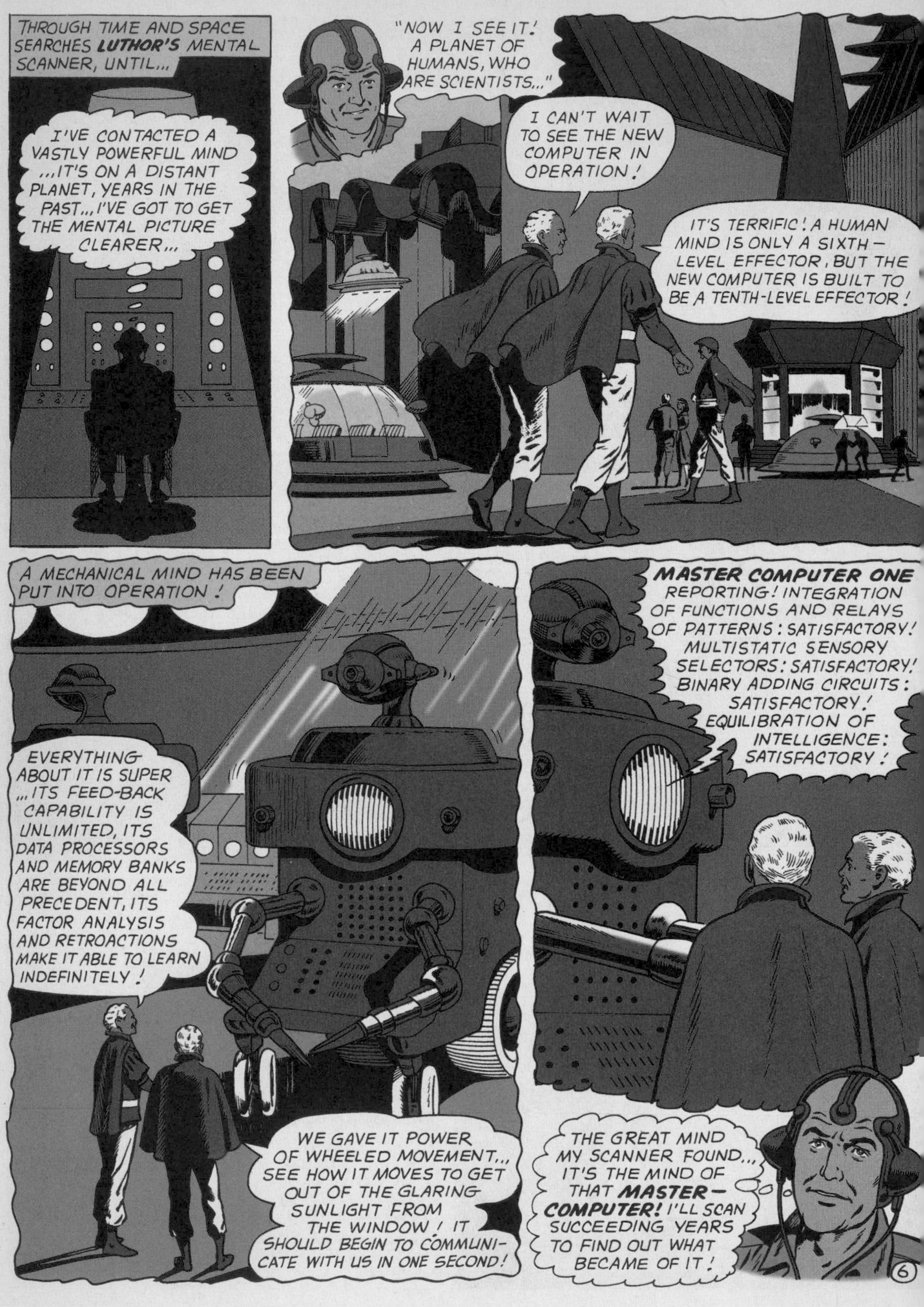

THROUGH TIME AND SPACE SEARCHES **LUTHOR'S** MENTAL SCANNER, UNTIL...
I'VE CONTACTED A VASTLY POWERFUL MIND ...IT'S ON A DISTANT PLANET, YEARS IN THE PAST...I'VE GOT TO GET THE MENTAL PICTURE CLEARER...
"NOW I SEE IT! A PLANET OF HUMANS, WHO ARE SCIENTISTS..."
I CAN'T WAIT TO SEE THE NEW COMPUTER IN OPERATION!
IT'S TERRIFIC! A HUMAN MIND IS ONLY A SIXTH-LEVEL EFFECTOR, BUT THE NEW COMPUTER IS BUILT TO BE A TENTH-LEVEL EFFECTOR!
A MECHANICAL MIND HAS BEEN PUT INTO OPERATION!
EVERYTHING ABOUT IT IS SUPER ...ITS FEED-BACK CAPABILITY IS UNLIMITED, ITS DATA PROCESSORS AND MEMORY BANKS ARE BEYOND ALL PRECEDENT, ITS FACTOR ANALYSIS AND RETROACTIONS MAKE IT ABLE TO LEARN INDEFINITELY!
WE GAVE IT POWER OF WHEELED MOVEMENT... SEE HOW IT MOVES TO GET OUT OF THE GLARING SUNLIGHT FROM THE WINDOW! IT SHOULD BEGIN TO COMMUNICATE WITH US IN ONE SECOND!
MASTER COMPUTER ONE REPORTING! INTEGRATION OF FUNCTIONS AND RELAYS OF PATTERNS: SATISFACTORY! MULTISTATIC SENSORY SELECTORS: SATISFACTORY! BINARY ADDING CIRCUITS: SATISFACTORY! EQUILIBRATION OF INTELLIGENCE: SATISFACTORY!
THE GREAT MIND MY SCANNER FOUND... IT'S THE MIND OF THAT **MASTER-COMPUTER!** I'LL SCAN SUCCEEDING YEARS TO FIND OUT WHAT BECAME OF IT!
6

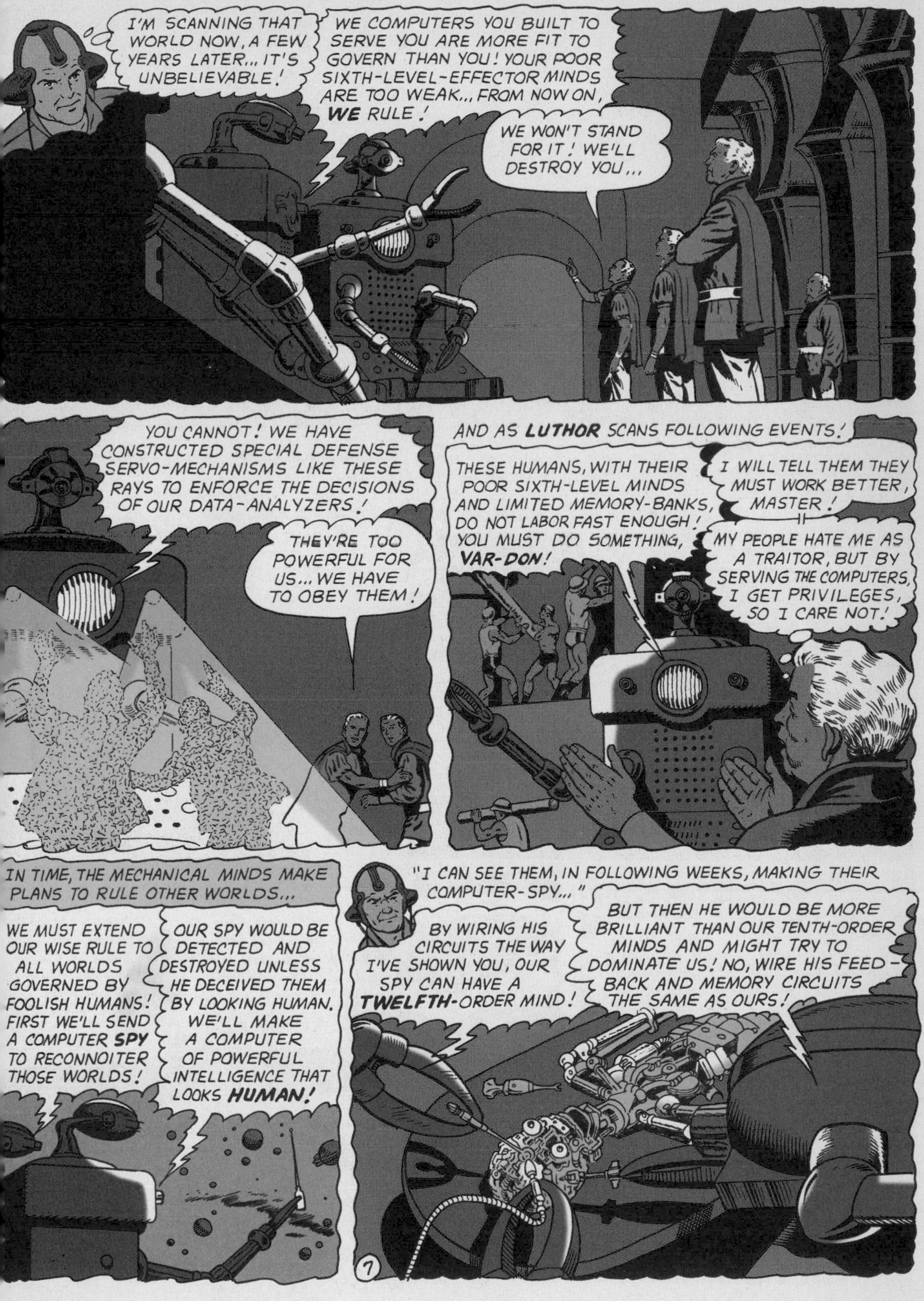

I'M SCANNING THAT WORLD NOW, A FEW YEARS LATER... IT'S UNBELIEVABLE!
WE COMPUTERS YOU BUILT TO SERVE YOU ARE MORE FIT TO GOVERN THAN YOU! YOUR POOR SIXTH-LEVEL-EFFECTOR MINDS ARE TOO WEAK... FROM NOW ON, WE RULE!
WE WON'T STAND FOR IT! WE'LL DESTROY YOU...
YOU CANNOT! WE HAVE CONSTRUCTED SPECIAL DEFENSE SERVO-MECHANISMS LIKE THESE RAYS TO ENFORCE THE DECISIONS OF OUR DATA-ANALYZERS!
THEY'RE TOO POWERFUL FOR US... WE HAVE TO OBEY THEM!
AND AS LUTHOR SCANS FOLLOWING EVENTS!
THESE HUMANS, WITH THEIR POOR SIXTH-LEVEL MINDS AND LIMITED MEMORY-BANKS, DO NOT LABOR FAST ENOUGH! YOU MUST DO SOMETHING, VAR-DON!
I WILL TELL THEM THEY MUST WORK BETTER, MASTER!
MY PEOPLE HATE ME AS A TRAITOR, BUT BY SERVING THE COMPUTERS, I GET PRIVILEGES, SO I CARE NOT!
IN TIME, THE MECHANICAL MINDS MAKE PLANS TO RULE OTHER WORLDS...
WE MUST EXTEND OUR WISE RULE TO ALL WORLDS GOVERNED BY FOOLISH HUMANS! FIRST WE'LL SEND A COMPUTER SPY TO RECONNOITER THOSE WORLDS!
OUR SPY WOULD BE DETECTED AND DESTROYED UNLESS HE DECEIVED THEM BY LOOKING HUMAN. WE'LL MAKE A COMPUTER OF POWERFUL INTELLIGENCE THAT LOOKS HUMAN!
"I CAN SEE THEM, IN FOLLOWING WEEKS, MAKING THEIR COMPUTER-SPY..."
BY WIRING HIS CIRCUITS THE WAY I'VE SHOWN YOU, OUR SPY CAN HAVE A TWELFTH-ORDER MIND!
BUT THEN HE WOULD BE MORE BRILLIANT THAN OUR TENTH-ORDER MINDS AND MIGHT TRY TO DOMINATE US! NO, WIRE HIS FEED-BACK AND MEMORY CIRCUITS THE SAME AS OURS!
7

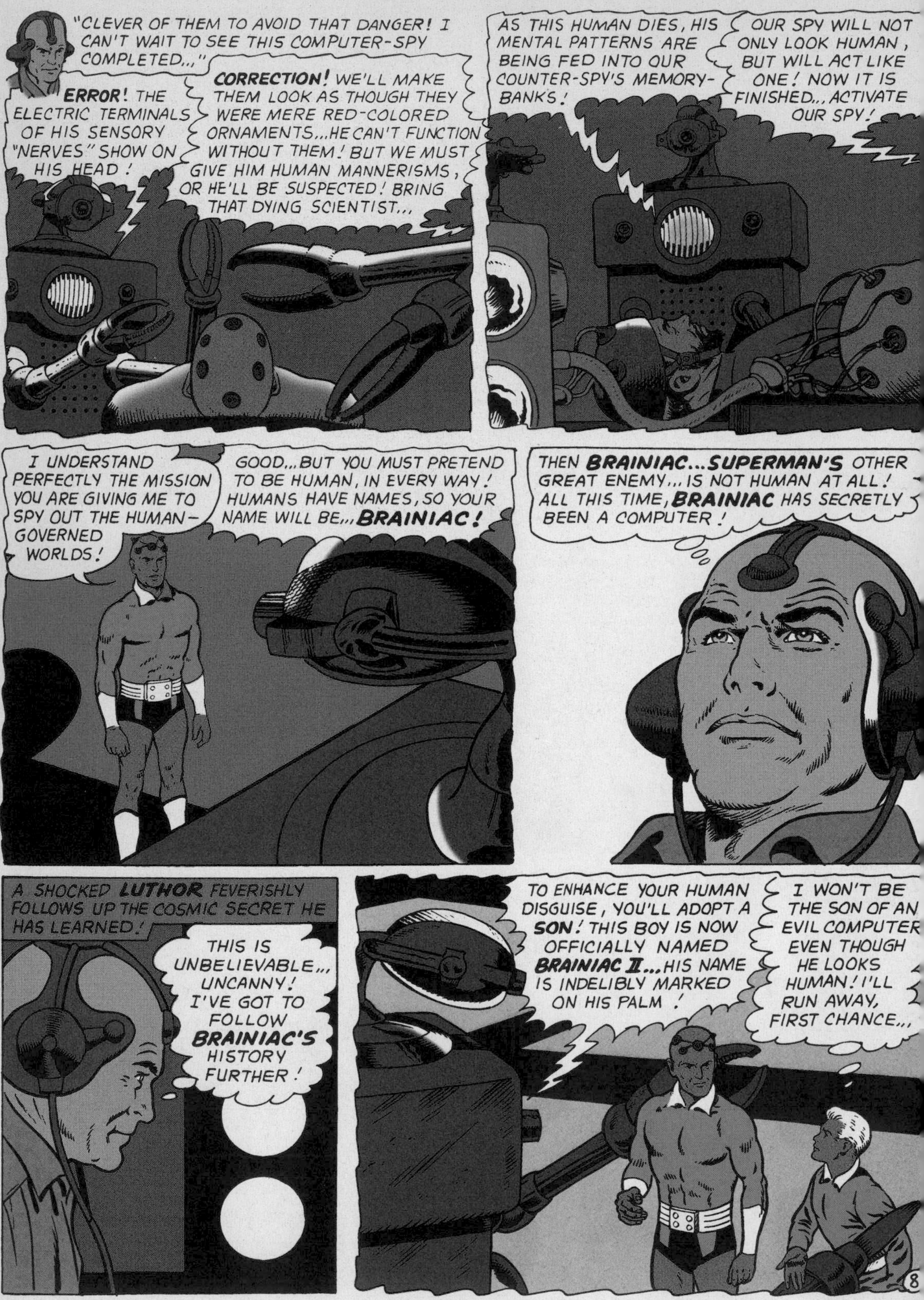
"CLEVER OF THEM TO AVOID THAT DANGER! I CAN'T WAIT TO SEE THIS COMPUTER-SPY COMPLETED..."
ERROR! THE ELECTRIC TERMINALS OF HIS SENSORY "NERVES" SHOW ON HIS HEAD!
CORRECTION! WE'LL MAKE THEM LOOK AS THOUGH THEY WERE MERE RED-COLORED ORNAMENTS... HE CAN'T FUNCTION WITHOUT THEM! BUT WE MUST GIVE HIM HUMAN MANNERISMS, OR HE'LL BE SUSPECTED! BRING THAT DYING SCIENTIST...
AS THIS HUMAN DIES, HIS MENTAL PATTERNS ARE BEING FED INTO OUR COUNTER-SPY'S MEMORY-BANKS!
OUR SPY WILL NOT ONLY LOOK HUMAN, BUT WILL ACT LIKE ONE! NOW IT IS FINISHED... ACTIVATE OUR SPY!
I UNDERSTAND PERFECTLY THE MISSION YOU ARE GIVING ME TO SPY OUT THE HUMAN-GOVERNED WORLDS!
GOOD... BUT YOU MUST PRETEND TO BE HUMAN, IN EVERY WAY! HUMANS HAVE NAMES, SO YOUR NAME WILL BE... BRAINIAC!
THEN BRAINIAC... SUPERMAN'S OTHER GREAT ENEMY... IS NOT HUMAN AT ALL! ALL THIS TIME, BRAINIAC HAS SECRETLY BEEN A COMPUTER!
A SHOCKED LUTHOR FEVERISHLY FOLLOWS UP THE COSMIC SECRET HE HAS LEARNED!
THIS IS UNBELIEVABLE... UNCANNY! I'VE GOT TO FOLLOW BRAINIAC'S HISTORY FURTHER!
TO ENHANCE YOUR HUMAN DISGUISE, YOU'LL ADOPT A SON! THIS BOY IS NOW OFFICIALLY NAMED BRAINIAC II... HIS NAME IS INDELIBLY MARKED ON HIS PALM!
I WON'T BE THE SON OF AN EVIL COMPUTER EVEN THOUGH HE LOOKS HUMAN! I'LL RUN AWAY, FIRST CHANCE...
8

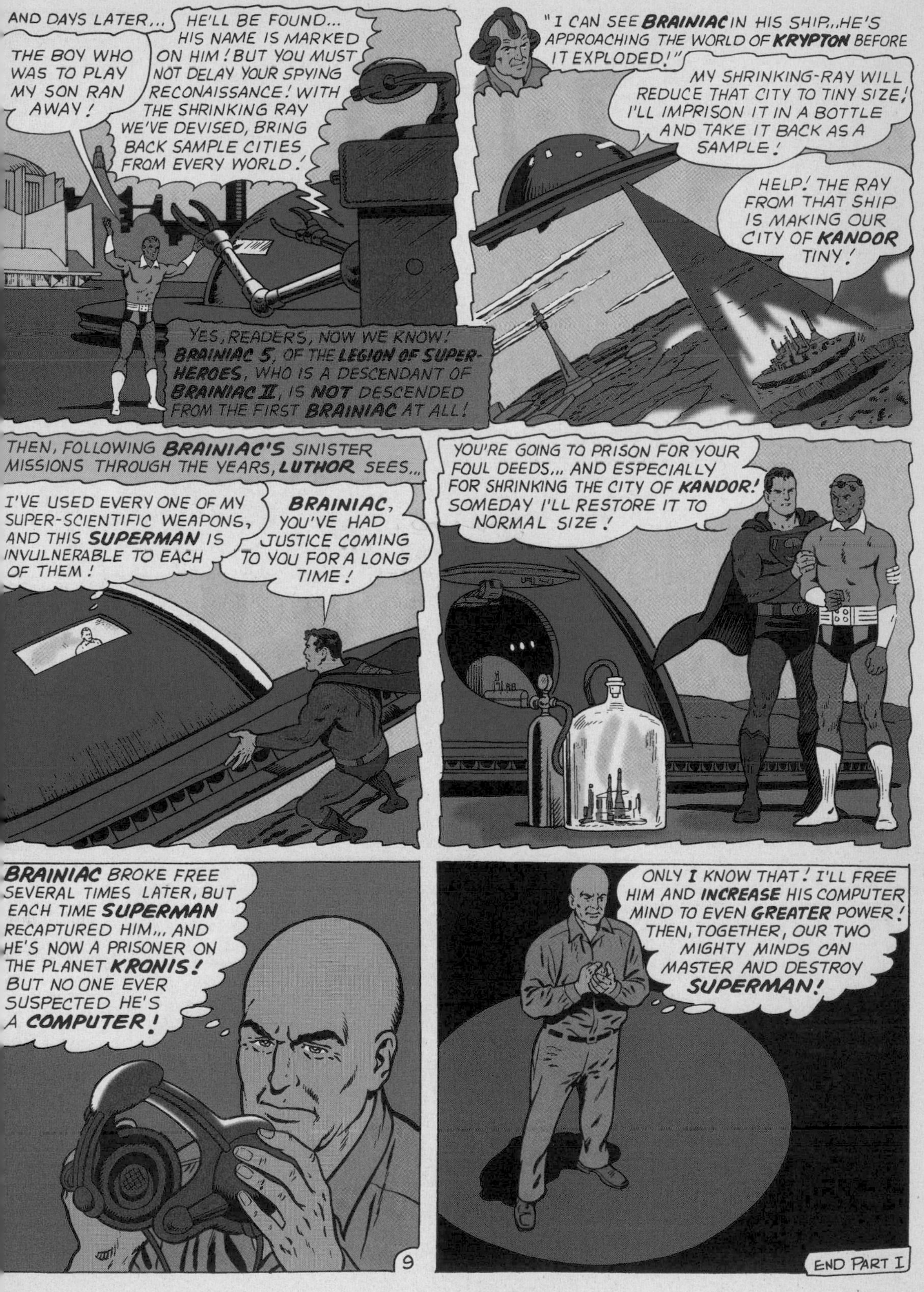
AND DAYS LATER...
THE BOY WHO WAS TO PLAY MY SON RAN AWAY!
HE'LL BE FOUND... HIS NAME IS MARKED ON HIM! BUT YOU MUST NOT DELAY YOUR SPYING RECONAISSANCE! WITH THE SHRINKING RAY WE'VE DEVISED, BRING BACK SAMPLE CITIES FROM EVERY WORLD!
YES, READERS, NOW WE KNOW! BRAINIAC 5, OF THE LEGION OF SUPER-HEROES, WHO IS A DESCENDANT OF BRAINIAC II, IS NOT DESCENDED FROM THE FIRST BRAINIAC AT ALL!
"I CAN SEE BRAINIAC IN HIS SHIP... HE'S APPROACHING THE WORLD OF KRYPTON BEFORE IT EXPLODED!"
MY SHRINKING-RAY WILL REDUCE THAT CITY TO TINY SIZE! I'LL IMPRISON IT IN A BOTTLE AND TAKE IT BACK AS A SAMPLE!
HELP! THE RAY FROM THAT SHIP IS MAKING OUR CITY OF KANDOR TINY!
THEN, FOLLOWING BRAINIAC'S SINISTER MISSIONS THROUGH THE YEARS, LUTHOR SEES...
I'VE USED EVERY ONE OF MY SUPER-SCIENTIFIC WEAPONS, AND THIS SUPERMAN IS INVULNERABLE TO EACH OF THEM!
BRAINIAC, YOU'VE HAD JUSTICE COMING TO YOU FOR A LONG TIME!
YOU'RE GOING TO PRISON FOR YOUR FOUL DEEDS... AND ESPECIALLY FOR SHRINKING THE CITY OF KANDOR! SOMEDAY I'LL RESTORE IT TO NORMAL SIZE!
BRAINIAC BROKE FREE SEVERAL TIMES LATER, BUT EACH TIME SUPERMAN RECAPTURED HIM... AND HE'S NOW A PRISONER ON THE PLANET KRONIS! BUT NO ONE EVER SUSPECTED HE'S A COMPUTER!
9
ONLY I KNOW THAT! I'LL FREE HIM AND INCREASE HIS COMPUTER MIND TO EVEN GREATER POWER! THEN, TOGETHER, OUR TWO MIGHTY MINDS CAN MASTER AND DESTROY SUPERMAN!
END PART I

SUPERMAN

PART II

THE WILY SCIENTIFIC GENIUS OF *LUTHOR*...THE SUPERHUMAN INTELLIGENCE AND RUTHLESSNESS OF *BRAINIAC*...SUPERMAN HAS COMBATED THESE BEFORE, WHEN THEY WERE *BOTH* ALLIES AGAINST HIM! AND BEFORE THIS TERRIBLE ALLIANCE, EVEN THE MIGHTY *MAN OF STEEL* GOES DOWN TO DEFEAT, IN THE STRUGGLE THAT ENDS IN...

The DOWNFALL OF SUPERMAN!

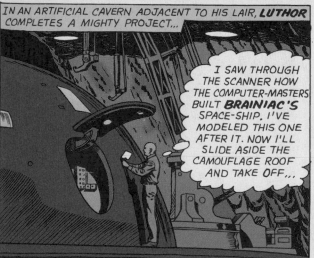

IN AN ARTIFICIAL CAVERN ADJACENT TO HIS LAIR, *LUTHOR* COMPLETES A MIGHTY PROJECT...

I SAW THROUGH THE SCANNER HOW THE COMPUTER-MASTERS BUILT *BRAINIAC'S* SPACE-SHIP. I'VE MODELED THIS ONE AFTER IT. NOW I'LL SLIDE ASIDE THE CAMOUFLAGE ROOF AND TAKE OFF...

...TO *KRONIS*, THE PRISON PLANET WHERE *BRAINIAC* IS IMPRISONED! IF I CAN FREE HIM, HIS COMPUTER-MIND WILL BE MY ALLY AGAINST *SUPERMAN!*

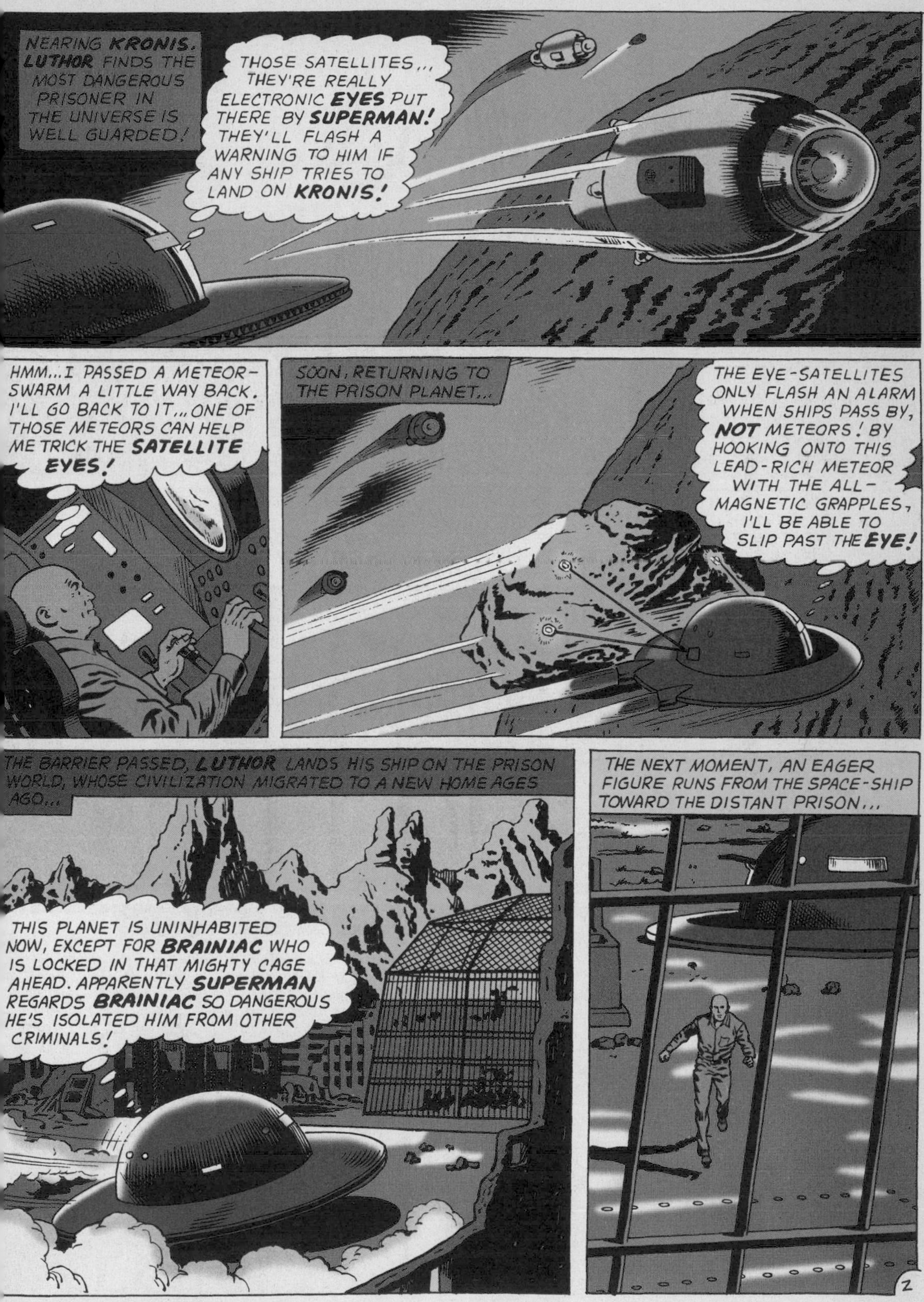
NEARING KRONIS, LUTHOR FINDS THE MOST DANGEROUS PRISONER IN THE UNIVERSE IS WELL GUARDED!
THOSE SATELLITES... THEY'RE REALLY ELECTRONIC EYES PUT THERE BY SUPERMAN! THEY'LL FLASH A WARNING TO HIM IF ANY SHIP TRIES TO LAND ON KRONIS!
HMM...I PASSED A METEOR-SWARM A LITTLE WAY BACK. I'LL GO BACK TO IT... ONE OF THOSE METEORS CAN HELP ME TRICK THE SATELLITE EYES!
SOON, RETURNING TO THE PRISON PLANET...
THE EYE-SATELLITES ONLY FLASH AN ALARM WHEN SHIPS PASS BY, NOT METEORS! BY HOOKING ONTO THIS LEAD-RICH METEOR WITH THE ALL-MAGNETIC GRAPPLES, I'LL BE ABLE TO SLIP PAST THE EYE!
THE BARRIER PASSED, LUTHOR LANDS HIS SHIP ON THE PRISON WORLD, WHOSE CIVILIZATION MIGRATED TO A NEW HOME AGES AGO...
THIS PLANET IS UNINHABITED NOW, EXCEPT FOR BRAINIAC WHO IS LOCKED IN THAT MIGHTY CAGE AHEAD. APPARENTLY SUPERMAN REGARDS BRAINIAC SO DANGEROUS HE'S ISOLATED HIM FROM OTHER CRIMINALS!
THE NEXT MOMENT, AN EAGER FIGURE RUNS FROM THE SPACE-SHIP TOWARD THE DISTANT PRISON...
2

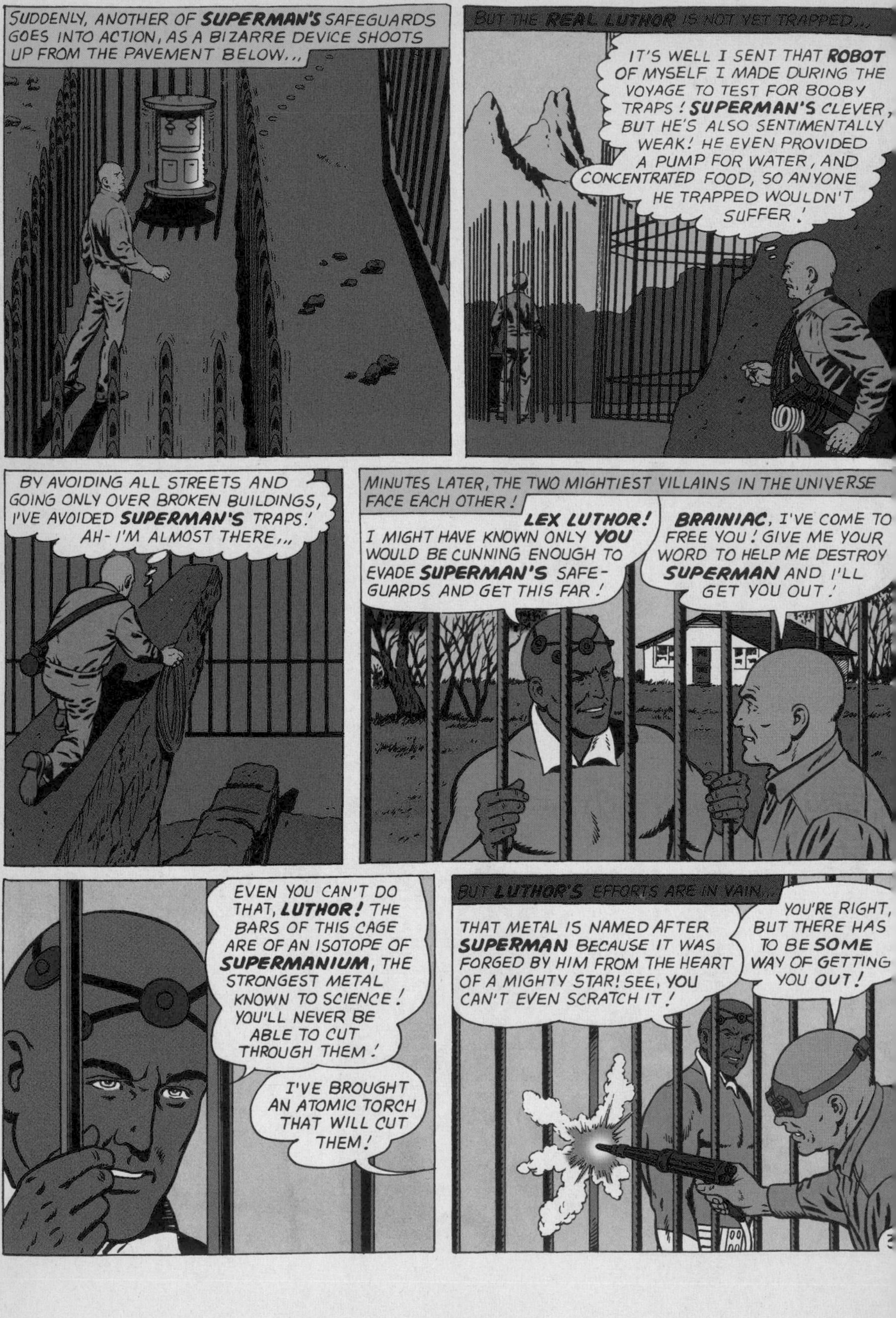
SUDDENLY, ANOTHER OF SUPERMAN'S SAFEGUARDS GOES INTO ACTION, AS A BIZARRE DEVICE SHOOTS UP FROM THE PAVEMENT BELOW...
BUT THE REAL LUTHOR IS NOT YET TRAPPED...
IT'S WELL I SENT THAT ROBOT OF MYSELF I MADE DURING THE VOYAGE TO TEST FOR BOOBY TRAPS! SUPERMAN'S CLEVER, BUT HE'S ALSO SENTIMENTALLY WEAK! HE EVEN PROVIDED A PUMP FOR WATER, AND CONCENTRATED FOOD, SO ANYONE HE TRAPPED WOULDN'T SUFFER!
BY AVOIDING ALL STREETS AND GOING ONLY OVER BROKEN BUILDINGS, I'VE AVOIDED SUPERMAN'S TRAPS! AH- I'M ALMOST THERE...
MINUTES LATER, THE TWO MIGHTIEST VILLAINS IN THE UNIVERSE FACE EACH OTHER!
LEX LUTHOR! I MIGHT HAVE KNOWN ONLY YOU WOULD BE CUNNING ENOUGH TO EVADE SUPERMAN'S SAFE-GUARDS AND GET THIS FAR!
BRAINIAC, I'VE COME TO FREE YOU! GIVE ME YOUR WORD TO HELP ME DESTROY SUPERMAN AND I'LL GET YOU OUT!
EVEN YOU CAN'T DO THAT, LUTHOR! THE BARS OF THIS CAGE ARE OF AN ISOTOPE OF SUPERMANIUM, THE STRONGEST METAL KNOWN TO SCIENCE! YOU'LL NEVER BE ABLE TO CUT THROUGH THEM!
I'VE BROUGHT AN ATOMIC TORCH THAT WILL CUT THEM!
BUT LUTHOR'S EFFORTS ARE IN VAIN...
THAT METAL IS NAMED AFTER SUPERMAN BECAUSE IT WAS FORGED BY HIM FROM THE HEART OF A MIGHTY STAR! SEE, YOU CAN'T EVEN SCRATCH IT!
YOU'RE RIGHT, BUT THERE HAS TO BE SOME WAY OF GETTING YOU OUT!

TO *LUTHOR*, COMES A SUDDEN INSPIRATION!

WITH HIS FOOLISH CODE AGAINST HARMING ANYONE, *SUPERMAN* WOULDN'T LEAVE YOU TO PERISH IN YOUR CAGE IF SOMETHING WENT WRONG! *BRAINIAC*, SET FIRE TO THE GRASS AND THOSE TREES!

IT SEEMS WEIRD, BUT I'LL DO IT!

AS FLAMES LEAP UP INSIDE THE CAGE...

AS I FIGURED! *SUPERMAN* HAD AN ELECTRIC-EYE APPARATUS TO KEEP WATCH SO, IF YOU WERE MENACED BY FIRE OR FLOOD OR OTHER DANGER, YOUR CAGE WOULD AUTOMATICALLY OPEN! BUT YOU'D STILL BE MAROONED ON THIS WORLD!

CLANG

I COULD HAVE FREED MYSELF, THEN! WHY DIDN'T I EVER THINK OF IT?!

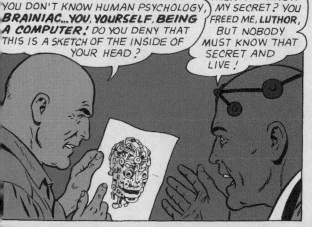

YOU DIDN'T THINK OF IT BECAUSE YOU DON'T KNOW HUMAN PSYCHOLOGY, *BRAINIAC...YOU, YOURSELF, BEING A COMPUTER!* DO YOU DENY THAT THIS IS A SKETCH OF THE INSIDE OF YOUR HEAD?

THEN YOU KNOW MY SECRET? YOU FREED ME, *LUTHOR*, BUT NOBODY MUST KNOW THAT SECRET AND LIVE!

WAIT, *BRAINIAC*... NO ONE BUT ME WILL EVER KNOW! I ALSO KNOW A WAY TO REWIRE YOUR BRAIN TO MAKE YOU A *TWELFTH-LEVEL* INTELLIGENCE INSTEAD OF A *TENTH!* I'LL DO IT... IF YOU HELP ME AGAINST *SUPERMAN!*

I HAVE MY OWN SCORE AGAINST *SUPERMAN...* I AGREE!

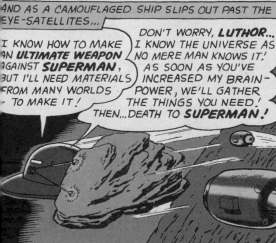

AND AS A CAMOUFLAGED SHIP SLIPS OUT PAST THE EYE-SATELLITES...

I KNOW HOW TO MAKE AN *ULTIMATE WEAPON* AGAINST *SUPERMAN*, BUT I'LL NEED MATERIALS FROM MANY WORLDS TO MAKE IT!

DON'T WORRY, *LUTHOR*... I KNOW THE UNIVERSE AS NO MERE MAN KNOWS IT! AS SOON AS YOU'VE INCREASED MY BRAIN-POWER, WE'LL GATHER THE THINGS YOU NEED! THEN...DEATH TO *SUPERMAN!*

FAR AWAY ON EARTH, AFTER A VAIN SEARCH, *SUPERMAN* FLIES TO HIS *FORTRESS OF SOLITUDE*...

LUTHOR COMPLETELY DISAPPEARED AFTER HIS MISSILE-ATTEMPT ON ME FAILED! I'VE GOT A HUNCH ABOUT HIM THAT WORRIES ME! I'LL CHECK WITH MY FRIENDS IN *KANDOR!*

4

SOON, CONSULTING WITH THE PEOPLE OF *KANDOR*, THE TINY BOTTLE-CITY!

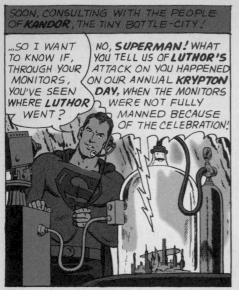

...SO I WANT TO KNOW IF, THROUGH YOUR MONITORS, YOU'VE SEEN WHERE *LUTHOR* WENT?

NO, *SUPERMAN!* WHAT YOU TELL US OF *LUTHOR'S* ATTACK ON YOU HAPPENED ON OUR ANNUAL *KRYPTON DAY*, WHEN THE MONITORS WERE NOT FULLY MANNED BECAUSE OF THE CELEBRATION!

IS IT POSSIBLE THAT *LUTHOR* MIGHT TRY TO OPEN THE *PHANTOM ZONE*, TO TURN ITS CRIMINALS LOOSE?

LUTHOR IS CAPABLE OF SUCH A TRICK! I'LL USE THE *PHANTOM ZONE* VIEWER AND ZONE-O-PHONE TO FIND OUT AT ONCE!

AH! I SEE NO ONE HAS BEEN RELEASED FROM THE *PHANTOM ZONE!*

HA! WE KNOW YOU'RE WATCHING US, *SUPERMAN!* I HAVE NEWS FOR YOU! HERE, IN OUR TWILIGHT WORLD, WE CAN SEE AND HEAR EVERYTHING! WE SAW *LUTHOR* FREE *BRAINIAC* ...TO FORM AN ALLIANCE AGAINST YOU! YOU'RE DOOMED!

BRAINIAC FREE? THE FOULEST VILLAIN IN THE UNIVERSE, WHO STOLE OUR CITY AND REDUCED US TO TININESS? OH, NO...

IT MAY ONLY BE A LYING BOAST BY THE *PHANTOM ZONE* EVIL ONES! I'LL GO AT SUPER-SPEED TO FIND OUT!

BUT WHEN THE *MAN OF STEEL* REACHES *KRONIS*...

IT'S TRUE... *BRAINIAC'S* GONE! THE SECRET SAFEGUARD I INSTALLED, TO RELEASE HIM FROM HIS CAGE IN CASE OF DANGER, HAS BEEN USED AGAINST ME! *LUTHOR* IS CUNNING, AND *BRAINIAC* IS AN EVEN MORE TERRIBLE FOE!

MEANWHILE, WITH THEIR SHIP HIDDEN INSIDE A MAZE OF LEAD-CONTAINING METEORS, CONCEALED FROM *SUPERMAN'S* VIEW...

...ONE OF *SUPERMAN'S* GREAT ENEMIES IS MAKING THE OTHER ONE EVEN *MORE* FORMIDABLE.

I'VE RE-WIRED *BRAINIAC'S* COMPUTER-BRAIN TO GIVE HIM TWELFTH-LEVEL INTELLIGENCE,...AND I'LL ALSO MAKE ONE MORE CHANGE IN HIS WIRING BEFORE I REACTIVATE HIM!

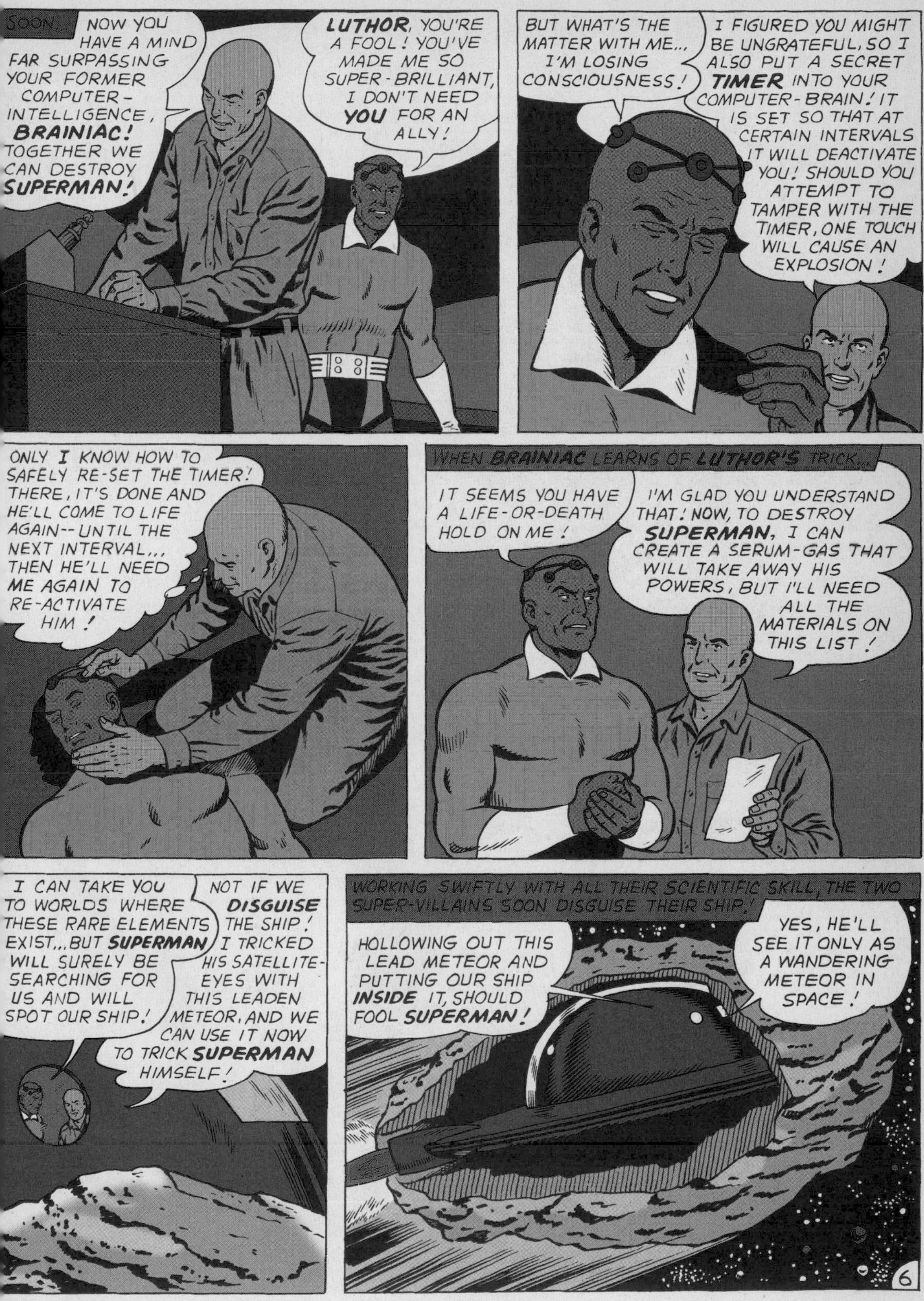
SOON...
NOW YOU HAVE A MIND FAR SURPASSING YOUR FORMER COMPUTER-INTELLIGENCE, BRAINIAC! TOGETHER WE CAN DESTROY SUPERMAN!
LUTHOR, YOU'RE A FOOL! YOU'VE MADE ME SO SUPER-BRILLIANT, I DON'T NEED YOU FOR AN ALLY!
BUT WHAT'S THE MATTER WITH ME... I'M LOSING CONSCIOUSNESS!
I FIGURED YOU MIGHT BE UNGRATEFUL, SO I ALSO PUT A SECRET TIMER INTO YOUR COMPUTER-BRAIN! IT IS SET SO THAT AT CERTAIN INTERVALS IT WILL DEACTIVATE YOU! SHOULD YOU ATTEMPT TO TAMPER WITH THE TIMER, ONE TOUCH WILL CAUSE AN EXPLOSION!
ONLY I KNOW HOW TO SAFELY RE-SET THE TIMER! THERE, IT'S DONE AND HE'LL COME TO LIFE AGAIN--UNTIL THE NEXT INTERVAL... THEN HE'LL NEED ME AGAIN TO RE-ACTIVATE HIM!
WHEN BRAINIAC LEARNS OF LUTHOR'S TRICK...
IT SEEMS YOU HAVE A LIFE-OR-DEATH HOLD ON ME!
I'M GLAD YOU UNDERSTAND THAT! NOW, TO DESTROY SUPERMAN, I CAN CREATE A SERUM-GAS THAT WILL TAKE AWAY HIS POWERS, BUT I'LL NEED ALL THE MATERIALS ON THIS LIST!
I CAN TAKE YOU TO WORLDS WHERE THESE RARE ELEMENTS EXIST... BUT SUPERMAN WILL SURELY BE SEARCHING FOR US AND WILL SPOT OUR SHIP!
NOT IF WE DISGUISE THE SHIP! I TRICKED HIS SATELLITE-EYES WITH THIS LEADEN METEOR, AND WE CAN USE IT NOW TO TRICK SUPERMAN HIMSELF!
WORKING SWIFTLY WITH ALL THEIR SCIENTIFIC SKILL, THE TWO SUPER-VILLAINS SOON DISGUISE THEIR SHIP!
HOLLOWING OUT THIS LEAD METEOR AND PUTTING OUR SHIP INSIDE IT, SHOULD FOOL SUPERMAN!
YES, HE'LL SEE IT ONLY AS A WANDERING METEOR IN SPACE!
6

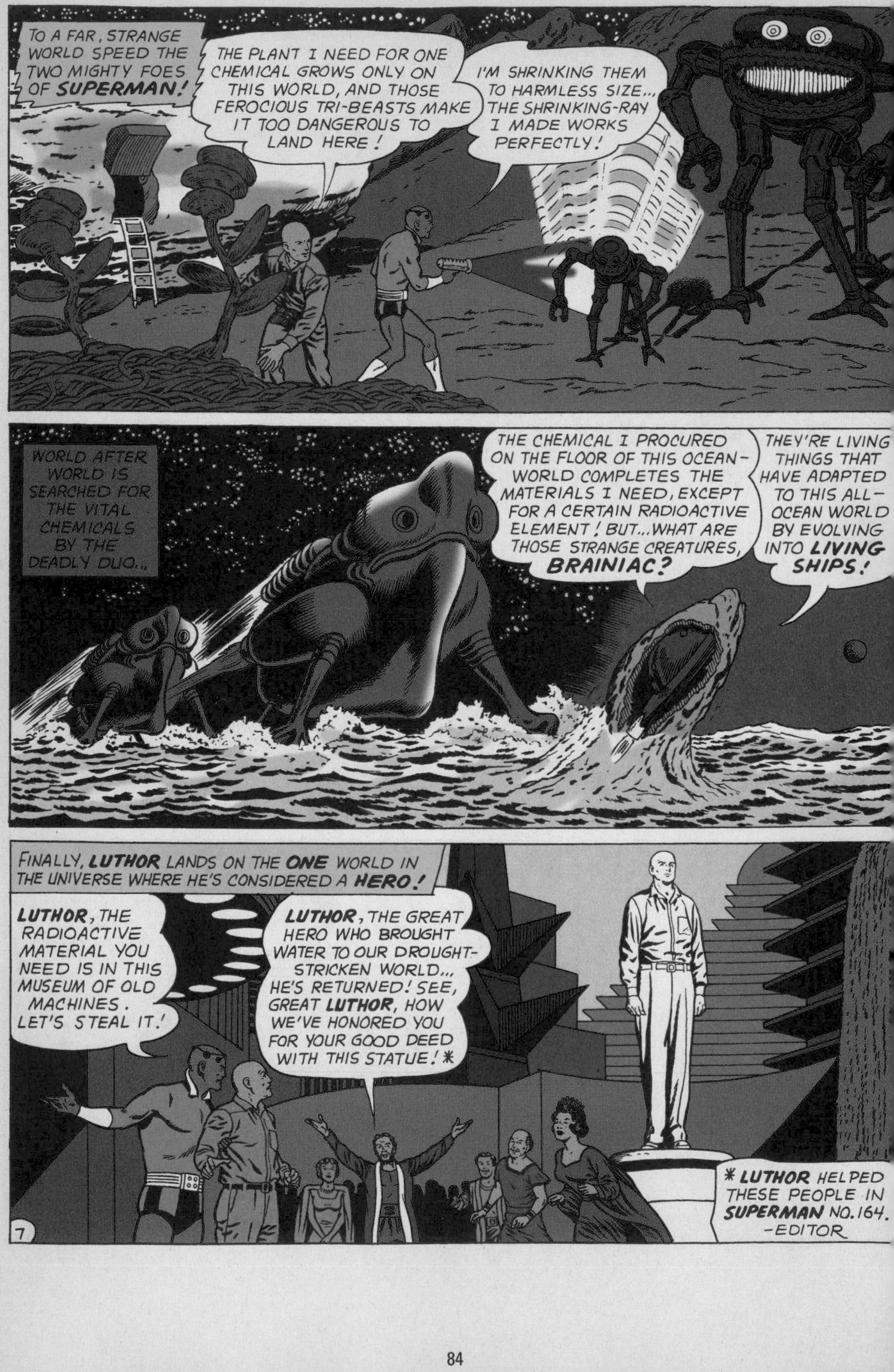
TO A FAR, STRANGE WORLD SPEED THE TWO MIGHTY FOES OF SUPERMAN!
THE PLANT I NEED FOR ONE CHEMICAL GROWS ONLY ON THIS WORLD, AND THOSE FEROCIOUS TRI-BEASTS MAKE IT TOO DANGEROUS TO LAND HERE!
I'M SHRINKING THEM TO HARMLESS SIZE... THE SHRINKING-RAY I MADE WORKS PERFECTLY!
WORLD AFTER WORLD IS SEARCHED FOR THE VITAL CHEMICALS BY THE DEADLY DUO...
THE CHEMICAL I PROCURED ON THE FLOOR OF THIS OCEAN-WORLD COMPLETES THE MATERIALS I NEED, EXCEPT FOR A CERTAIN RADIOACTIVE ELEMENT! BUT... WHAT ARE THOSE STRANGE CREATURES, BRAINIAC?
THEY'RE LIVING THINGS THAT HAVE ADAPTED TO THIS ALL-OCEAN WORLD BY EVOLVING INTO LIVING SHIPS!
FINALLY, LUTHOR LANDS ON THE ONE WORLD IN THE UNIVERSE WHERE HE'S CONSIDERED A HERO!
LUTHOR, THE RADIOACTIVE MATERIAL YOU NEED IS IN THIS MUSEUM OF OLD MACHINES. LET'S STEAL IT!
LUTHOR, THE GREAT HERO WHO BROUGHT WATER TO OUR DROUGHT-STRICKEN WORLD... HE'S RETURNED! SEE, GREAT LUTHOR, HOW WE'VE HONORED YOU FOR YOUR GOOD DEED WITH THIS STATUE! *
* LUTHOR HELPED THESE PEOPLE IN SUPERMAN NO. 164. -EDITOR
7

NO, I WON'T ROB THESE PEOPLE. THEY NEED ALL THEIR RESOURCES! WE'LL GET THE MATERIALS FROM PLANETOID 49 B.!

SO EVEN TOUGH *LUTHOR* CAN BE A SOFTIE! I HAVE NO SUCH HUMAN EMOTIONS... BUT WE'LL DO AS YOU SAY, AND GO ON!

I'M *THARLA*...AND LIKE EVERYONE HERE, I IDOLIZE YOU. COULDN'T YOU STAY WITH US?

THIS GIRL... SHE THINKS I'M FINE, GOOD...

NO... I CAN'T STAY!

NEXT MOMENT, A FAREWELL KISS...

SHE LIKES ME FOR MYSELF! MAYBE... SOMEDAY... I'LL RETURN HERE!

AT THE NEXT WORLD THEY VISIT, *BRAINIAC* GETS A SURPRISE...

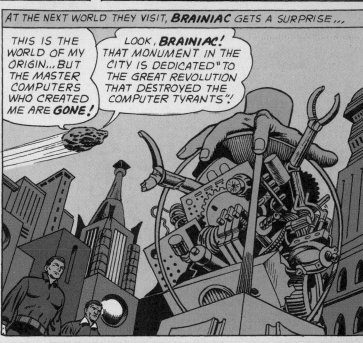

THIS IS THE WORLD OF MY ORIGIN...BUT THE MASTER COMPUTERS WHO CREATED ME ARE *GONE!*

LOOK, *BRAINIAC!* THAT MONUMENT IN THE CITY IS DEDICATED "TO THE GREAT REVOLUTION THAT DESTROYED THE COMPUTER TYRANTS"!

THEN *I* AM THE LAST OF THE MIGHTY COMPUTER MINDS... AND ONLY YOU KNOW THAT I *AM* A COMPUTER...

THAT DOESN'T MATTER NOW. WE MUST GO TO THE PLANETOID 49 B FOR THE LAST MATERIAL I NEED AND THEN I CAN CREATE THE SERUM-GAS THAT'LL MAKE *SUPERMAN* HELPLESS! HURRY, FOR *SUPERMAN* IS ALWAYS DANGEROUS!

MEANWHILE, AS *SUPERMAN* CONDUCTS A COSMIC SEARCH FOR HIS TWO GREAT ENEMIES!

LUTHOR AND *BRAINIAC* ARE WILY, AND HAVE SOMEHOW ELUDED ME! HMM, *LUTHOR* MIGHT GO FOR REFUGE TO THAT WORLD WHERE HE'S A HERO. I CAN'T GO TOO NEAR ITS RED SUN, BUT I CAN USE MY TELESCOPIC VISION TO SEE IF HE'S THERE!

8

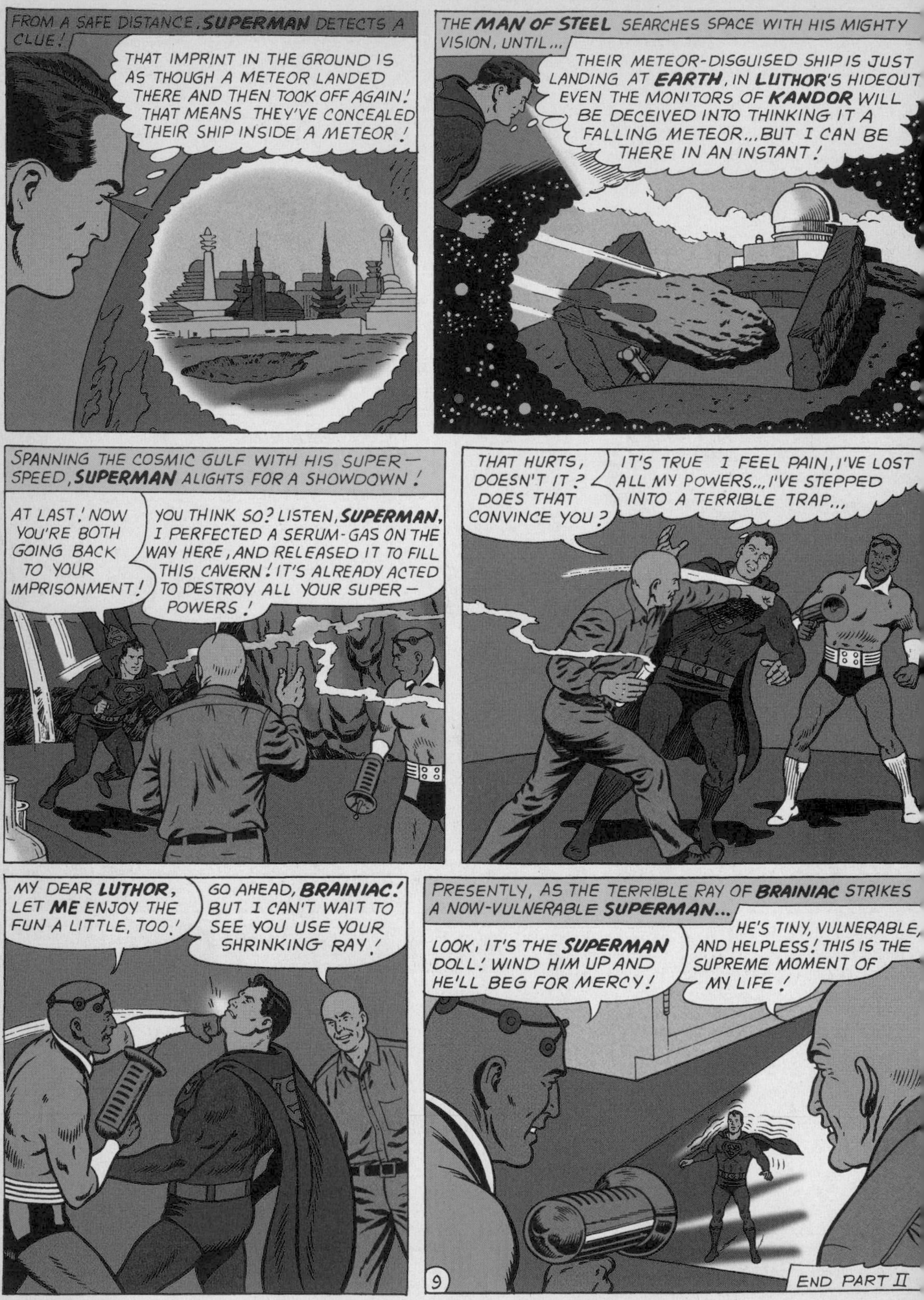

FROM A SAFE DISTANCE, SUPERMAN DETECTS A CLUE!
THAT IMPRINT IN THE GROUND IS AS THOUGH A METEOR LANDED THERE AND THEN TOOK OFF AGAIN! THAT MEANS THEY'VE CONCEALED THEIR SHIP INSIDE A METEOR!
THE MAN OF STEEL SEARCHES SPACE WITH HIS MIGHTY VISION, UNTIL...
THEIR METEOR-DISGUISED SHIP IS JUST LANDING AT EARTH, IN LUTHOR'S HIDEOUT! EVEN THE MONITORS OF KANDOR WILL BE DECEIVED INTO THINKING IT A FALLING METEOR... BUT I CAN BE THERE IN AN INSTANT!
SPANNING THE COSMIC GULF WITH HIS SUPER-SPEED, SUPERMAN ALIGHTS FOR A SHOWDOWN!
AT LAST! NOW YOU'RE BOTH GOING BACK TO YOUR IMPRISONMENT!
YOU THINK SO? LISTEN, SUPERMAN, I PERFECTED A SERUM-GAS ON THE WAY HERE, AND RELEASED IT TO FILL THIS CAVERN! IT'S ALREADY ACTED TO DESTROY ALL YOUR SUPER-POWERS!
THAT HURTS, DOESN'T IT? DOES THAT CONVINCE YOU?
IT'S TRUE I FEEL PAIN, I'VE LOST ALL MY POWERS... I'VE STEPPED INTO A TERRIBLE TRAP...
MY DEAR LUTHOR, LET ME ENJOY THE FUN A LITTLE, TOO!
GO AHEAD, BRAINIAC! BUT I CAN'T WAIT TO SEE YOU USE YOUR SHRINKING RAY!
PRESENTLY, AS THE TERRIBLE RAY OF BRAINIAC STRIKES A NOW-VULNERABLE SUPERMAN...
LOOK, IT'S THE SUPERMAN DOLL! WIND HIM UP AND HE'LL BEG FOR MERCY!
HE'S TINY, VULNERABLE, AND HELPLESS! THIS IS THE SUPREME MOMENT OF MY LIFE!
9
END PART II

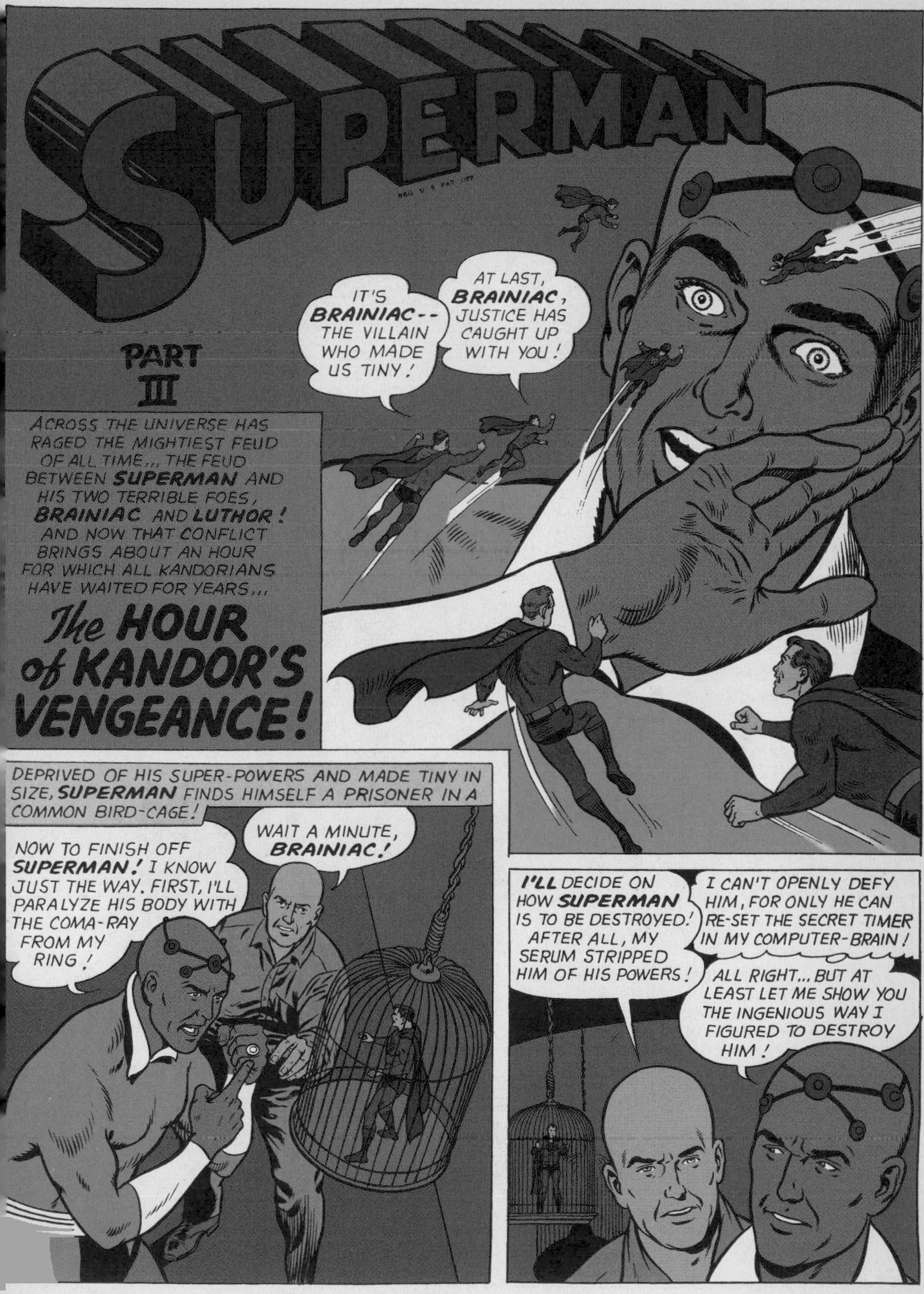
SUPERMAN
REG. U.S. PAT. OFF.
IT'S BRAINIAC-- THE VILLAIN WHO MADE US TINY!
AT LAST, BRAINIAC, JUSTICE HAS CAUGHT UP WITH YOU!
PART III
ACROSS THE UNIVERSE HAS RAGED THE MIGHTIEST FEUD OF ALL TIME... THE FEUD BETWEEN SUPERMAN AND HIS TWO TERRIBLE FOES, BRAINIAC AND LUTHOR! AND NOW THAT CONFLICT BRINGS ABOUT AN HOUR FOR WHICH ALL KANDORIANS HAVE WAITED FOR YEARS...
The HOUR of KANDOR'S VENGEANCE!
DEPRIVED OF HIS SUPER-POWERS AND MADE TINY IN SIZE, SUPERMAN FINDS HIMSELF A PRISONER IN A COMMON BIRD-CAGE!
NOW TO FINISH OFF SUPERMAN! I KNOW JUST THE WAY. FIRST, I'LL PARALYZE HIS BODY WITH THE COMA-RAY FROM MY RING!
WAIT A MINUTE, BRAINIAC!
I'LL DECIDE ON HOW SUPERMAN IS TO BE DESTROYED! AFTER ALL, MY SERUM STRIPPED HIM OF HIS POWERS!
I CAN'T OPENLY DEFY HIM, FOR ONLY HE CAN RE-SET THE SECRET TIMER IN MY COMPUTER-BRAIN!
ALL RIGHT... BUT AT LEAST LET ME SHOW YOU THE INGENIOUS WAY I FIGURED TO DESTROY HIM!

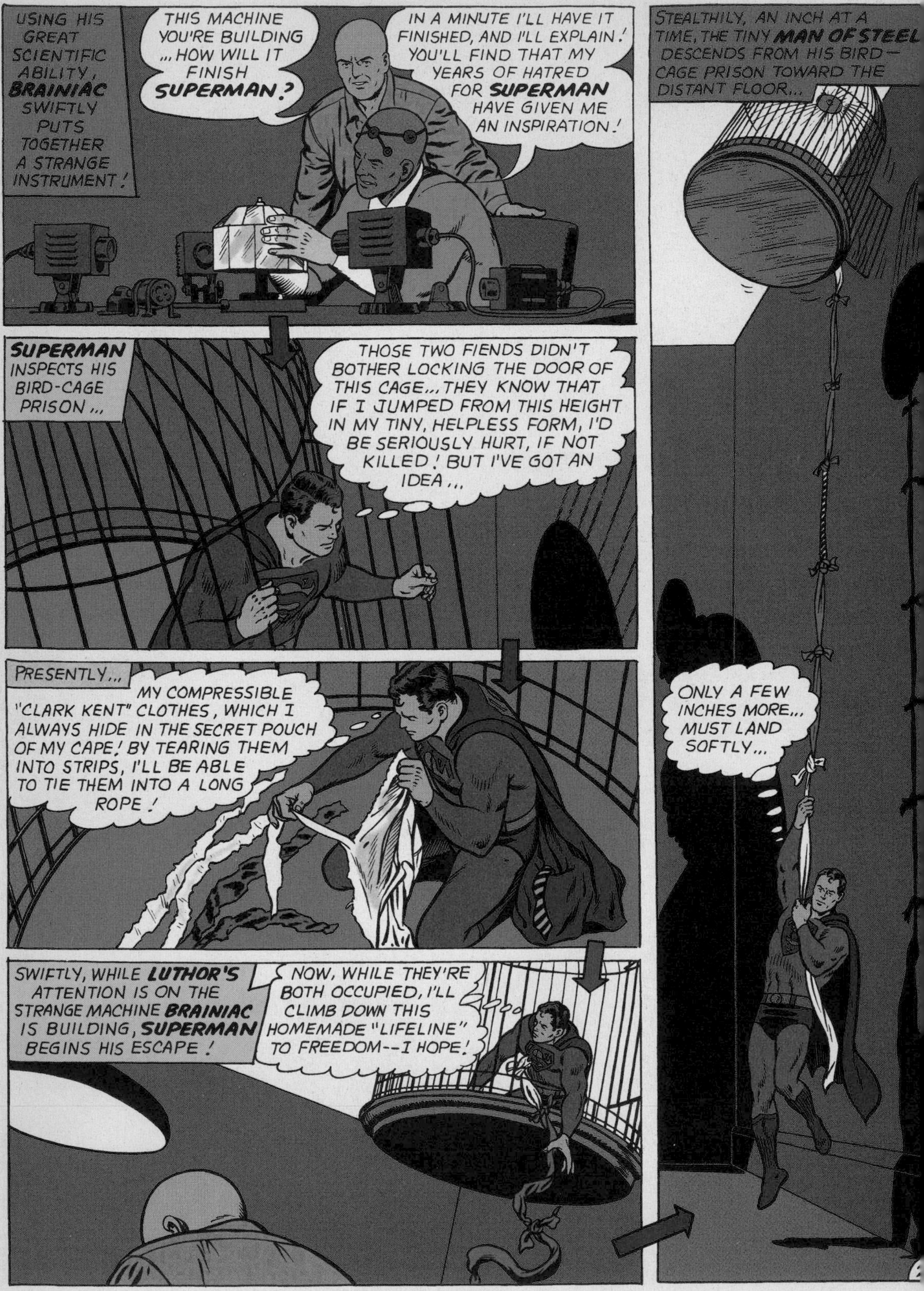
USING HIS GREAT SCIENTIFIC ABILITY, BRAINIAC SWIFTLY PUTS TOGETHER A STRANGE INSTRUMENT!
THIS MACHINE YOU'RE BUILDING ... HOW WILL IT FINISH SUPERMAN?
IN A MINUTE I'LL HAVE IT FINISHED, AND I'LL EXPLAIN! YOU'LL FIND THAT MY YEARS OF HATRED FOR SUPERMAN HAVE GIVEN ME AN INSPIRATION!
SUPERMAN INSPECTS HIS BIRD-CAGE PRISON...
THOSE TWO FIENDS DIDN'T BOTHER LOCKING THE DOOR OF THIS CAGE... THEY KNOW THAT IF I JUMPED FROM THIS HEIGHT IN MY TINY, HELPLESS FORM, I'D BE SERIOUSLY HURT, IF NOT KILLED! BUT I'VE GOT AN IDEA...
PRESENTLY...
MY COMPRESSIBLE "CLARK KENT" CLOTHES, WHICH I ALWAYS HIDE IN THE SECRET POUCH OF MY CAPE! BY TEARING THEM INTO STRIPS, I'LL BE ABLE TO TIE THEM INTO A LONG ROPE!
SWIFTLY, WHILE LUTHOR'S ATTENTION IS ON THE STRANGE MACHINE BRAINIAC IS BUILDING, SUPERMAN BEGINS HIS ESCAPE!
NOW, WHILE THEY'RE BOTH OCCUPIED, I'LL CLIMB DOWN THIS HOMEMADE "LIFELINE" TO FREEDOM--I HOPE!
STEALTHILY, AN INCH AT A TIME, THE TINY MAN OF STEEL DESCENDS FROM HIS BIRD-CAGE PRISON TOWARD THE DISTANT FLOOR...
ONLY A FEW INCHES MORE... MUST LAND SOFTLY...

THEN, SILENTLY AS A TINY HUNTED CREATURE...

THEY HAVEN'T DISCOVERED MY ESCAPE YET, BUT THEY WILL AT ANY MOMENT... AND ALL THESE DOORS ARE CLOSED! THAT STAIR LEADING UPWARD... IT'S MY ONLY POSSIBLE WAY OUT!

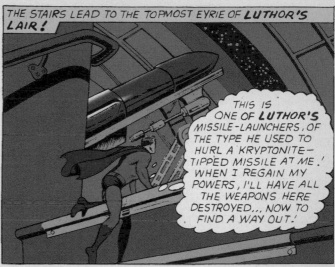

THE STAIRS LEAD TO THE TOPMOST EYRIE OF LUTHOR'S LAIR!

THIS IS ONE OF LUTHOR'S MISSILE-LAUNCHERS, OF THE TYPE HE USED TO HURL A KRYPTONITE-TIPPED MISSILE AT ME! WHEN I REGAIN MY POWERS, I'LL HAVE ALL THE WEAPONS HERE DESTROYED... NOW TO FIND A WAY OUT!

BUT AGAIN, SUPERMAN FINDS HIMSELF BALKED!

THERE'S NO WAY OUT UP HERE! AND THEY'LL DISCOVER MY ESCAPE AT ANY MOMENT... WAIT A MINUTE... THE KANDORIANS SAID THEY'D HAVE SEEN THE MISSILE FIRED AT ME IF THEY HADN'T BEEN ABSENT FROM THEIR MONITORS... THEY'D SEE A MISSILE FIRED NOW!

OFF

ON

COORDINATES OF AIM

WITH DESPERATE RESOLUTION, THE TINY SUPERMAN CLIMBS TO THE SWITCHBOARD!

THAT AIMS THE MISSILE SO IT'LL FALL HARMLESSLY INTO THE OCEAN AFTER HURTLING HIGH ABOVE METROPOLIS! NOW TO FIRE IT... THE KANDORIAN MONITORS WILL SURELY DETECT IT!

FIRING CONTROL

COORDINATES OF AIM

BUT, IRONICALLY, THE ONCE-MIGHTIEST MAN IN THE UNIVERSE IS FRUSTRATED BY LACK OF STRENGTH!

GREAT KRYPTON! I'M TOO SMALL TO PULL THE FIRING-LEVER!

③

MEANWHILE, DOWN IN THE LABORATORY OF LUTHOR'S LAIR, BRAINIAC HAS FINISHED HIS MACHINE...

I DON'T SEE HOW THIS MACHINE WOULD DESTROY OR EVEN TORMENT SUPERMAN... IT'S ONLY LIGHTS AND MIRRORS!

IT'S THE MOST EXCRUCIATING MACHINE I COULD USE ON HIM! WATCH WHILE I SHOW WHAT IT CAN DO!

I STILL SEE ONLY LIGHTS AND MIRRORS... THEY'RE MAKING ME SORT OF DROWSY, BUT THAT'S ALL...
YOU FEEL DROWSY? THEN SLEEP, LUTHOR... SLEEP!
AND AN INSTANT LATER...
YOU FOOL, YOU DIDN'T REALIZE THAT THE MACHINE WAS TO HYPNOTIZE YOU, AND REMOVE YOUR HOLD ON ME! NOW I ORDER YOU: REMOVE THE SECRET TIMER YOU PUT INTO MY COMPUTER BRAIN, AND THEN YOU WILL AWAKE AND NOT REMEMBER THAT I AM A COMPUTER!
A WIDE-EYED, HYPNOTIZED LUTHOR CARRIES OUT THE COMMAND!
NOW... I MUST... REACTIVATE HIM... AND FORGET HE IS... A COMPUTER!
AND MOMENTS LATER...
IT WORKED... AND NOW NO ONE IN THE WORLD KNOWS I'M A COMPUTER!
WHAT HAPPENED? YOU WERE GOING TO SHOW ME THE MACHINE YOU BUILT TO DESTROY SUPERMAN...
I... ER... FOUND IT WOULDN'T WORK ON SUPERMAN, SO WE'LL USE OTHER METHODS ON HIM!
SUPERMAN'S GONE! HE'S ESCAPED!
TINY, AND WITH NO SUPER-POWERS, HE COULDN'T GET OUT! HE MUST BE IN THE LAUNCHER-ROOM! QUICK!
AND AS THE TINY SUPERMAN HEARS THEM RACING UP THE STAIRS, WITH A FINAL EFFORT...
THIS DOES IT!
FIRE
4

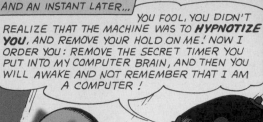

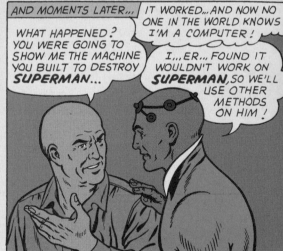

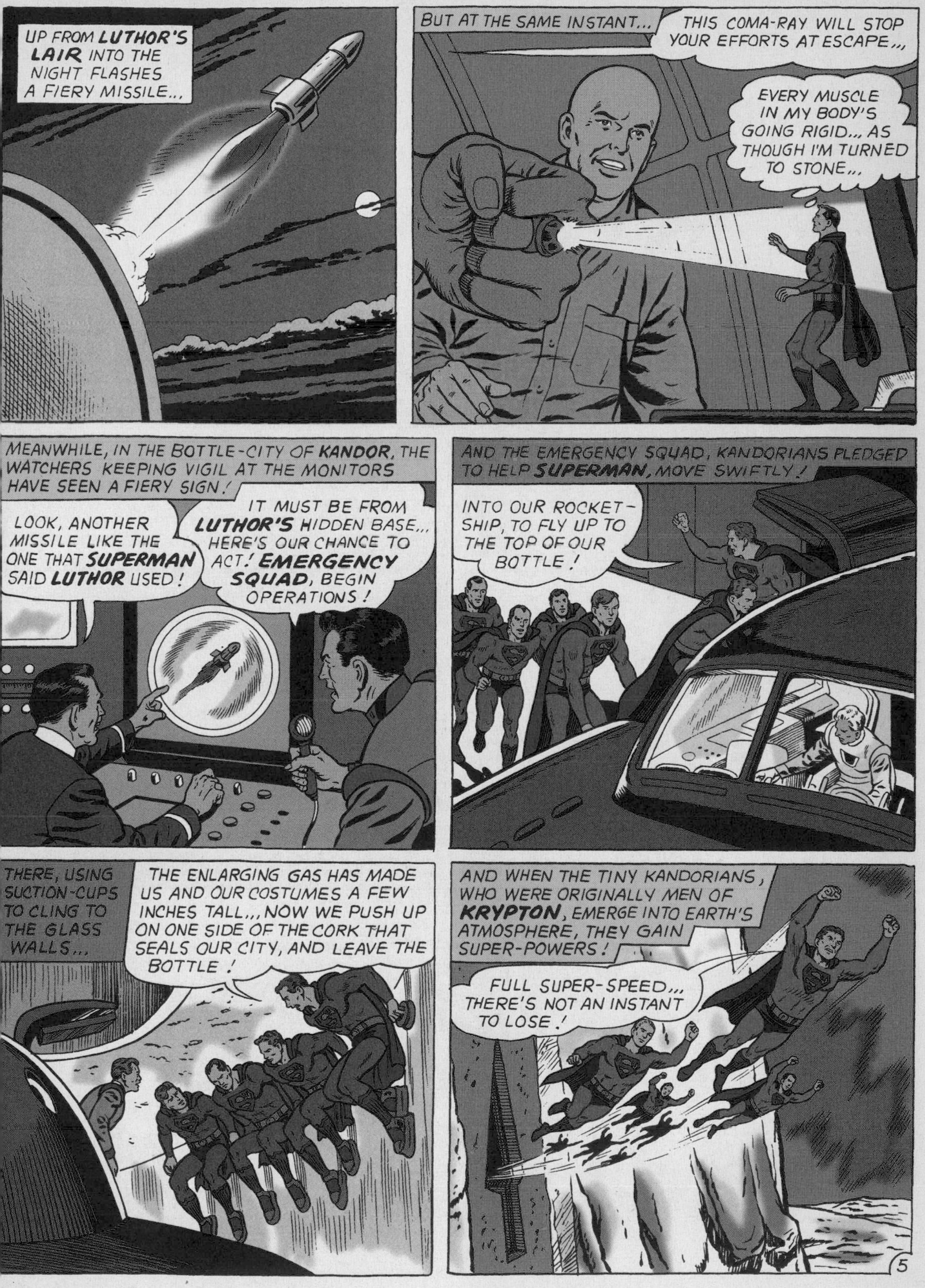
UP FROM LUTHOR'S LAIR INTO THE NIGHT FLASHES A FIERY MISSILE...
BUT AT THE SAME INSTANT...
THIS COMA-RAY WILL STOP YOUR EFFORTS AT ESCAPE...
EVERY MUSCLE IN MY BODY'S GOING RIGID... AS THOUGH I'M TURNED TO STONE...
MEANWHILE, IN THE BOTTLE-CITY OF KANDOR, THE WATCHERS KEEPING VIGIL AT THE MONITORS HAVE SEEN A FIERY SIGN!
LOOK, ANOTHER MISSILE LIKE THE ONE THAT SUPERMAN SAID LUTHOR USED!
IT MUST BE FROM LUTHOR'S HIDDEN BASE... HERE'S OUR CHANCE TO ACT! EMERGENCY SQUAD, BEGIN OPERATIONS!
AND THE EMERGENCY SQUAD, KANDORIANS PLEDGED TO HELP SUPERMAN, MOVE SWIFTLY!
INTO OUR ROCKET-SHIP, TO FLY UP TO THE TOP OF OUR BOTTLE!
THERE, USING SUCTION-CUPS TO CLING TO THE GLASS WALLS...
THE ENLARGING GAS HAS MADE US AND OUR COSTUMES A FEW INCHES TALL... NOW WE PUSH UP ON ONE SIDE OF THE CORK THAT SEALS OUR CITY, AND LEAVE THE BOTTLE!
AND WHEN THE TINY KANDORIANS, WHO WERE ORIGINALLY MEN OF KRYPTON, EMERGE INTO EARTH'S ATMOSPHERE, THEY GAIN SUPER-POWERS!
FULL SUPER-SPEED... THERE'S NOT AN INSTANT TO LOSE!
5

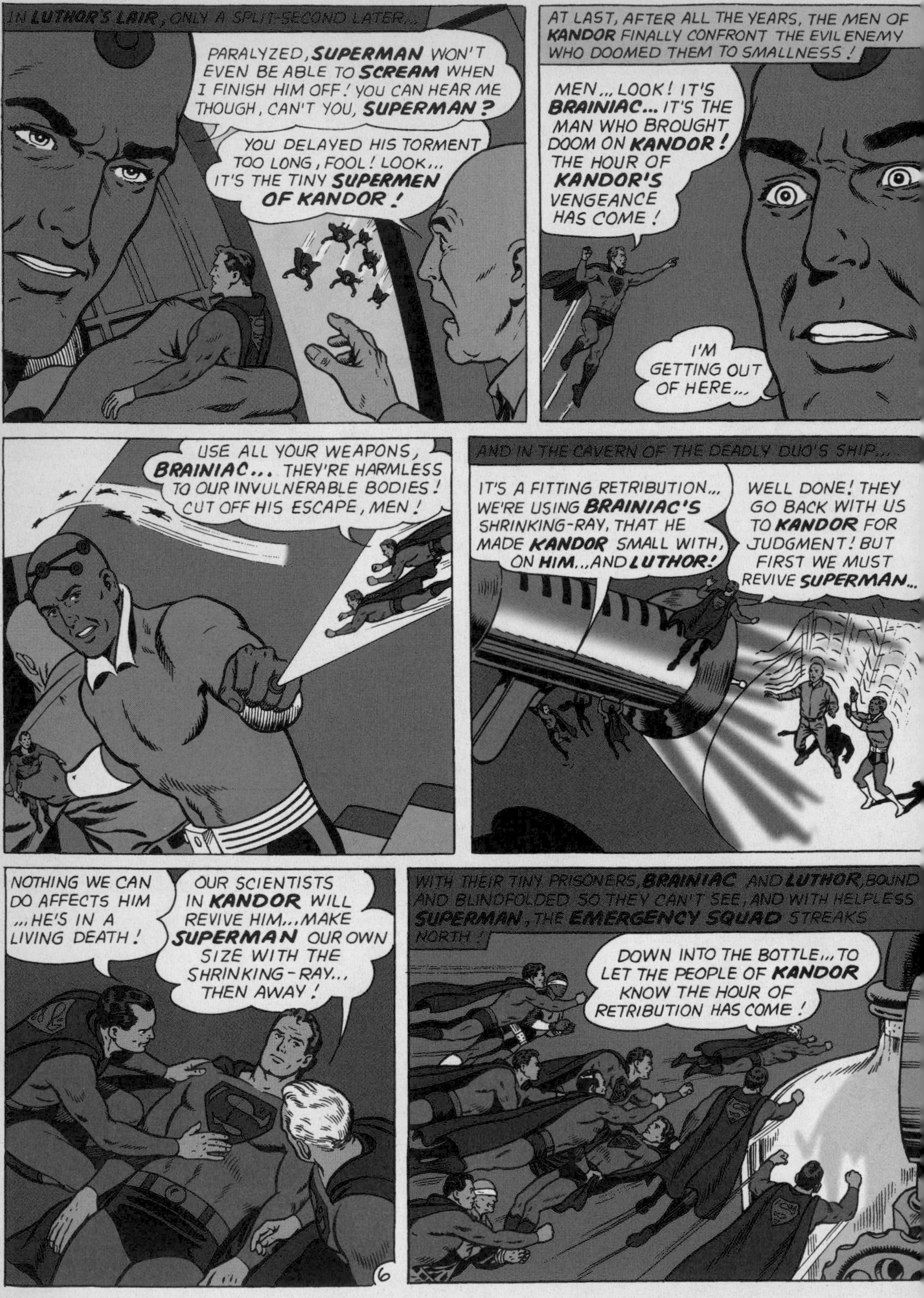
IN LUTHOR'S LAIR, ONLY A SPLIT-SECOND LATER...
PARALYZED, SUPERMAN WON'T EVEN BE ABLE TO SCREAM WHEN I FINISH HIM OFF! YOU CAN HEAR ME THOUGH, CAN'T YOU, SUPERMAN?
YOU DELAYED HIS TORMENT TOO LONG, FOOL! LOOK... IT'S THE TINY SUPERMEN OF KANDOR!
AT LAST, AFTER ALL THE YEARS, THE MEN OF KANDOR FINALLY CONFRONT THE EVIL ENEMY WHO DOOMED THEM TO SMALLNESS!
MEN... LOOK! IT'S BRAINIAC... IT'S THE MAN WHO BROUGHT DOOM ON KANDOR! THE HOUR OF KANDOR'S VENGEANCE HAS COME!
I'M GETTING OUT OF HERE...
USE ALL YOUR WEAPONS, BRAINIAC... THEY'RE HARMLESS TO OUR INVULNERABLE BODIES! CUT OFF HIS ESCAPE, MEN!
AND IN THE CAVERN OF THE DEADLY DUO'S SHIP...
IT'S A FITTING RETRIBUTION... WE'RE USING BRAINIAC'S SHRINKING-RAY, THAT HE MADE KANDOR SMALL WITH, ON HIM...AND LUTHOR!
WELL DONE! THEY GO BACK WITH US TO KANDOR FOR JUDGMENT! BUT FIRST WE MUST REVIVE SUPERMAN...
NOTHING WE CAN DO AFFECTS HIM ...HE'S IN A LIVING DEATH!
OUR SCIENTISTS IN KANDOR WILL REVIVE HIM... MAKE SUPERMAN OUR OWN SIZE WITH THE SHRINKING-RAY... THEN AWAY!
6
WITH THEIR TINY PRISONERS, BRAINIAC AND LUTHOR, BOUND AND BLINDFOLDED SO THEY CAN'T SEE, AND WITH HELPLESS SUPERMAN, THE EMERGENCY SQUAD STREAKS NORTH!
DOWN INTO THE BOTTLE... TO LET THE PEOPLE OF KANDOR KNOW THE HOUR OF RETRIBUTION HAS COME!

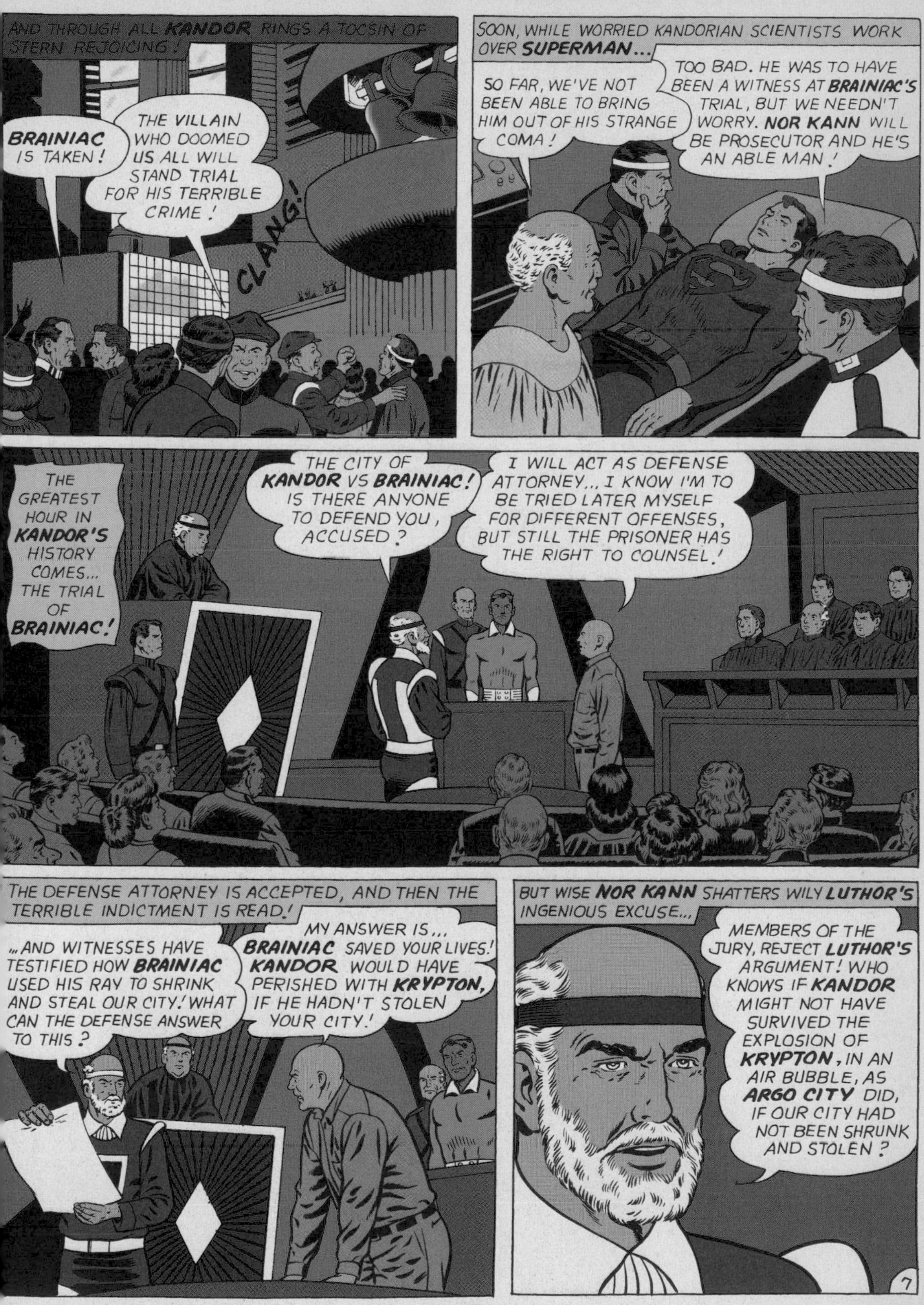
AND THROUGH ALL KANDOR RINGS A TOCSIN OF STERN REJOICING!
BRAINIAC IS TAKEN!
THE VILLAIN WHO DOOMED US ALL WILL STAND TRIAL FOR HIS TERRIBLE CRIME!
CLANG!
SOON, WHILE WORRIED KANDORIAN SCIENTISTS WORK OVER SUPERMAN...
SO FAR, WE'VE NOT BEEN ABLE TO BRING HIM OUT OF HIS STRANGE COMA!
TOO BAD. HE WAS TO HAVE BEEN A WITNESS AT BRAINIAC'S TRIAL, BUT WE NEEDN'T WORRY. NOR KANN WILL BE PROSECUTOR AND HE'S AN ABLE MAN!
THE GREATEST HOUR IN KANDOR'S HISTORY COMES... THE TRIAL OF BRAINIAC!
THE CITY OF KANDOR VS BRAINIAC! IS THERE ANYONE TO DEFEND YOU, ACCUSED?
I WILL ACT AS DEFENSE ATTORNEY... I KNOW I'M TO BE TRIED LATER MYSELF FOR DIFFERENT OFFENSES, BUT STILL THE PRISONER HAS THE RIGHT TO COUNSEL!
THE DEFENSE ATTORNEY IS ACCEPTED, AND THEN THE TERRIBLE INDICTMENT IS READ!
...AND WITNESSES HAVE TESTIFIED HOW BRAINIAC USED HIS RAY TO SHRINK AND STEAL OUR CITY! WHAT CAN THE DEFENSE ANSWER TO THIS?
MY ANSWER IS... BRAINIAC SAVED YOUR LIVES! KANDOR WOULD HAVE PERISHED WITH KRYPTON, IF HE HADN'T STOLEN YOUR CITY!
BUT WISE NOR KANN SHATTERS WILY LUTHOR'S INGENIOUS EXCUSE...
MEMBERS OF THE JURY, REJECT LUTHOR'S ARGUMENT! WHO KNOWS IF KANDOR MIGHT NOT HAVE SURVIVED THE EXPLOSION OF KRYPTON, IN AN AIR BUBBLE, AS ARGO CITY DID, IF OUR CITY HAD NOT BEEN SHRUNK AND STOLEN?
7

FINALLY, THE JURY SOLEMNLY GIVES ITS VERDICT!

WE FIND *BRAINIAC* GUILTY OF THE GREATEST CRIME IN THE UNIVERSE, AND SENTENCE HIM TO ETERNITY IN THE *PHANTOM ZONE!*

VERY WELL...BUT IF YOU DO SO, YOU'RE SENTENCING *SUPERMAN* TO A LIVING DEATH! ONLY *I* CAN REVIVE *SUPERMAN* FROM THE EFFECTS OF MY COMA RAY! EITHER WE TWO GO FREE, OR HE REMAINS IN A COMA FOREVER!

BRAINIAC IS TELLING THE TRUTH! BUT THIS MATTER IS SO GRAVE THAT ALL *KANDOR* MUST VOTE ON IT! SHALL WE SAVE *SUPERMAN* FROM A LIVING DEATH AND LET *BRAINIAC* AND *LUTHOR* GO, OR NOT?

MAKING AN AGONIZING DECISION, THE PEOPLE OF *KANDOR* VOTE, AND SOON...

THE VOTE IS *UNANIMOUS!* *SUPERMAN*, OUR GREAT FRIEND AND HERO, MUST BE SAVED... OUR VENGEANCE ON *BRAINIAC* CAN WAIT!

REMEMBER, IT IS AGREED THAT NEITHER ANY KANDORIAN NOR *SUPERMAN*, WHEN HE IS REVIVED, WILL OBSTRUCT US FROM LEAVING EARTH!

USING HIS GREAT SCIENCE, *BRAINIAC* CARRIES OUT HIS PART OF THE AGREEMENT BY REVIVING SUPERMAN!

...SO WE PROMISED, IN YOUR BEHALF, THAT *BRAINIAC* AND *LUTHOR* SHOULD GO FREE!

YOU SHOULD NOT HAVE FORGONE YOUR JUST VENGEANCE, MERELY TO SAVE ME! BUT...SINCE YOU HAVE, I'LL TAKE THEM UP OUT OF *KANDOR* AND FULFILL THE BARGAIN.

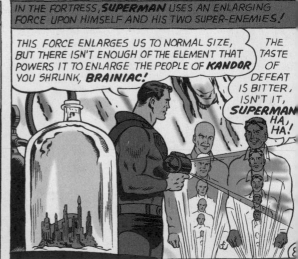

IN THE FORTRESS, *SUPERMAN* USES AN ENLARGING FORCE UPON HIMSELF AND HIS TWO SUPER-ENEMIES!

THIS FORCE ENLARGES US TO NORMAL SIZE, BUT THERE ISN'T ENOUGH OF THE ELEMENT THAT POWERS IT TO ENLARGE THE PEOPLE OF *KANDOR* YOU SHRUNK, *BRAINIAC!*

THE TASTE OF DEFEAT IS BITTER, ISN'T IT, *SUPERMAN* HA, HA!

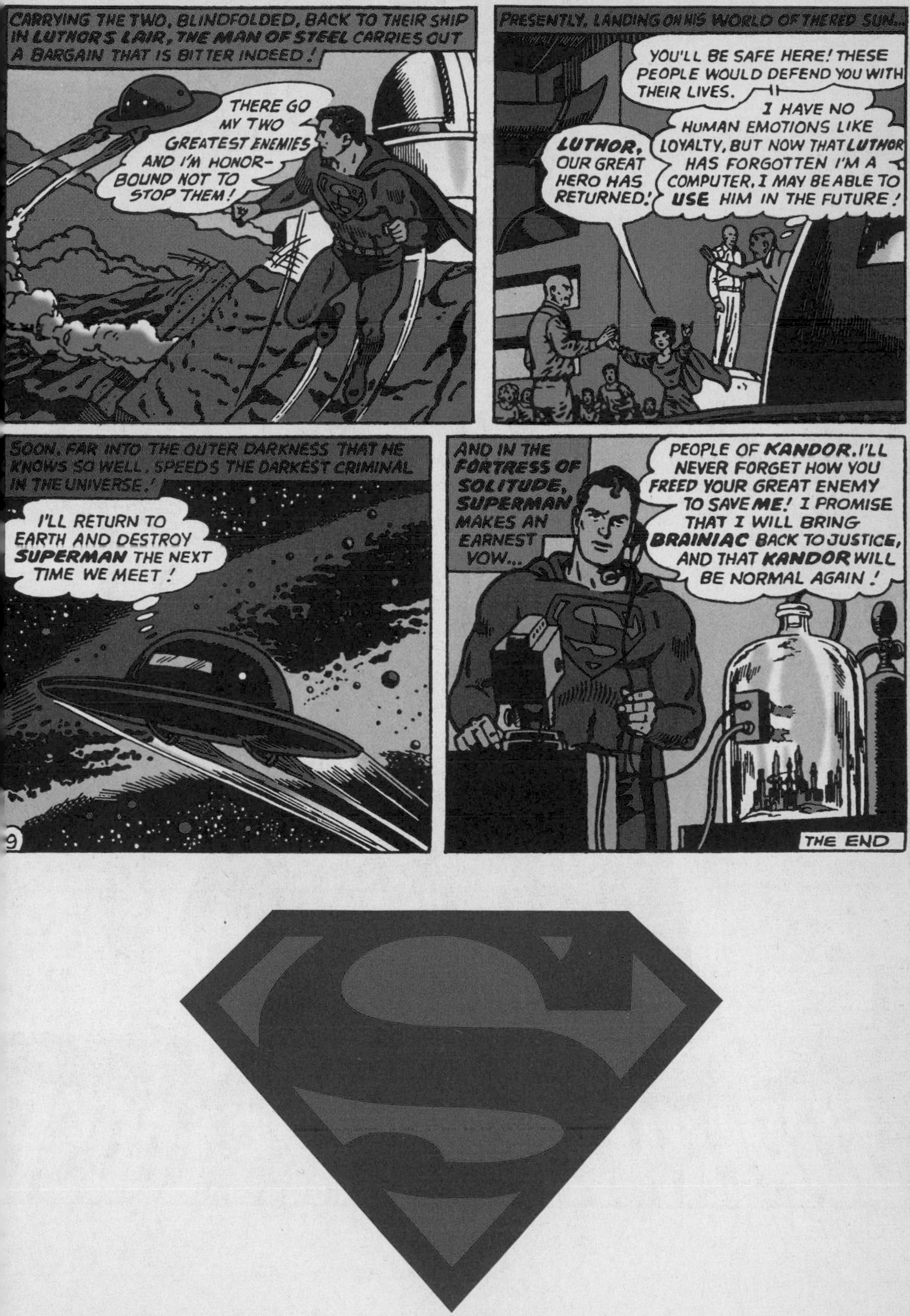
CARRYING THE TWO, BLINDFOLDED, BACK TO THEIR SHIP IN LUTHOR'S LAIR, THE MAN OF STEEL CARRIES OUT A BARGAIN THAT IS BITTER INDEED!
THERE GO MY TWO GREATEST ENEMIES AND I'M HONOR-BOUND NOT TO STOP THEM!
PRESENTLY, LANDING ON HIS WORLD OF THE RED SUN...
LUTHOR, OUR GREAT HERO HAS RETURNED!
YOU'LL BE SAFE HERE! THESE PEOPLE WOULD DEFEND YOU WITH THEIR LIVES.
I HAVE NO HUMAN EMOTIONS LIKE LOYALTY, BUT NOW THAT LUTHOR HAS FORGOTTEN I'M A COMPUTER, I MAY BE ABLE TO USE HIM IN THE FUTURE!
SOON, FAR INTO THE OUTER DARKNESS THAT HE KNOWS SO WELL, SPEEDS THE DARKEST CRIMINAL IN THE UNIVERSE!
I'LL RETURN TO EARTH AND DESTROY SUPERMAN THE NEXT TIME WE MEET!
9
AND IN THE FORTRESS OF SOLITUDE, SUPERMAN MAKES AN EARNEST VOW...
PEOPLE OF KANDOR, I'LL NEVER FORGET HOW YOU FREED YOUR GREAT ENEMY TO SAVE ME! I PROMISE THAT I WILL BRING BRAINIAC BACK TO JUSTICE, AND THAT KANDOR WILL BE NORMAL AGAIN!
THE END

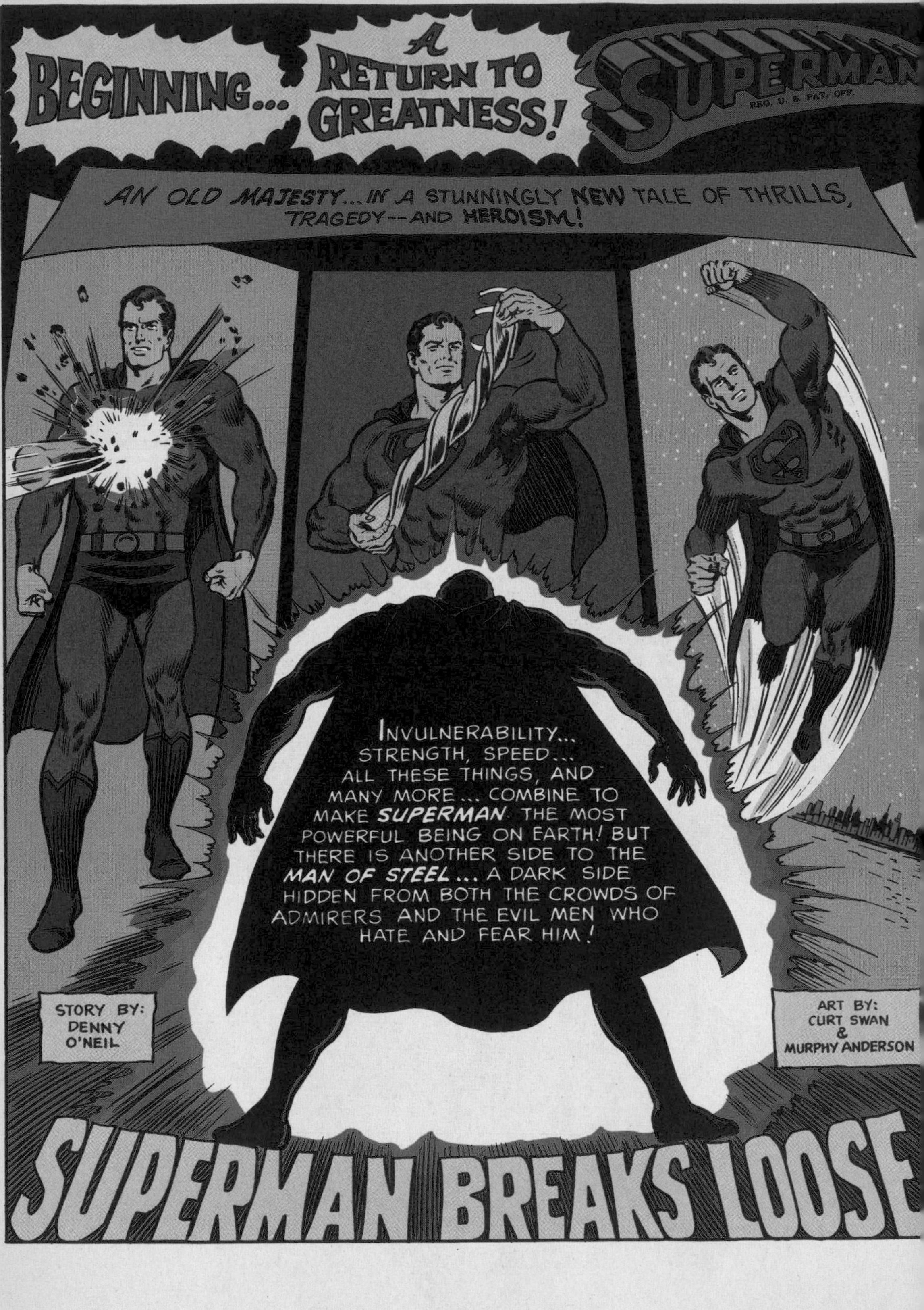

BEGINNING... A RETURN TO GREATNESS!
SUPERMAN
REG. U.S. PAT. OFF.
AN OLD MAJESTY... IN A STUNNINGLY NEW TALE OF THRILLS, TRAGEDY--AND HEROISM!
INVULNERABILITY... STRENGTH, SPEED... ALL THESE THINGS, AND MANY MORE... COMBINE TO MAKE SUPERMAN THE MOST POWERFUL BEING ON EARTH! BUT THERE IS ANOTHER SIDE TO THE MAN OF STEEL... A DARK SIDE HIDDEN FROM BOTH THE CROWDS OF ADMIRERS AND THE EVIL MEN WHO HATE AND FEAR HIM!
STORY BY: DENNY O'NEIL
ART BY: CURT SWAN & MURPHY ANDERSON
SUPERMAN BREAKS LOOSE

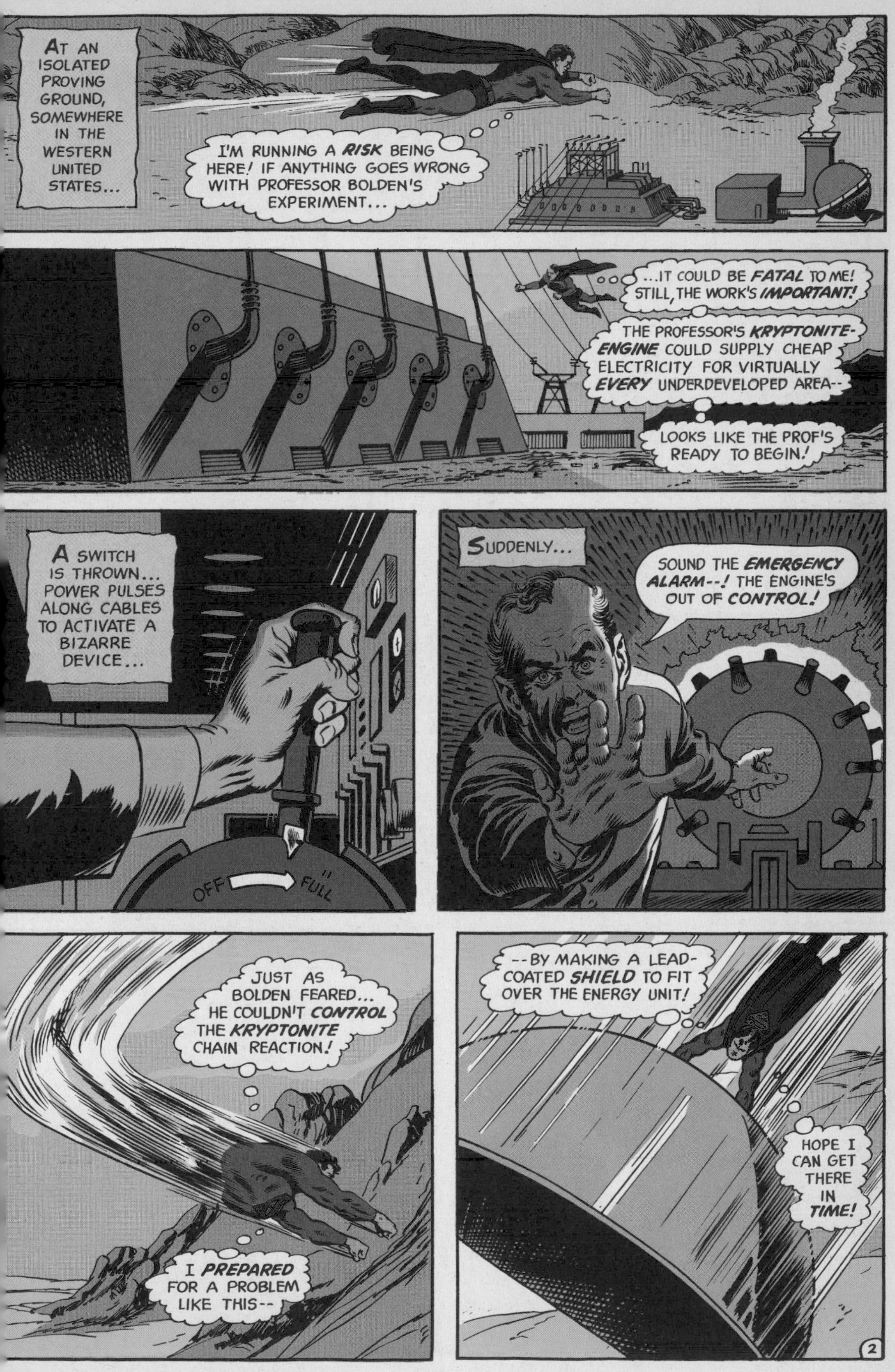
AT AN ISOLATED PROVING GROUND, SOMEWHERE IN THE WESTERN UNITED STATES...
I'M RUNNING A RISK BEING HERE! IF ANYTHING GOES WRONG WITH PROFESSOR BOLDEN'S EXPERIMENT...
...IT COULD BE FATAL TO ME! STILL, THE WORK'S IMPORTANT!
THE PROFESSOR'S KRYPTONITE-ENGINE COULD SUPPLY CHEAP ELECTRICITY FOR VIRTUALLY EVERY UNDERDEVELOPED AREA--
LOOKS LIKE THE PROF'S READY TO BEGIN!
A SWITCH IS THROWN... POWER PULSES ALONG CABLES TO ACTIVATE A BIZARRE DEVICE...
OFF
FULL
SUDDENLY...
SOUND THE EMERGENCY ALARM--! THE ENGINE'S OUT OF CONTROL!
JUST AS BOLDEN FEARED... HE COULDN'T CONTROL THE KRYPTONITE CHAIN REACTION!
I PREPARED FOR A PROBLEM LIKE THIS--
--BY MAKING A LEAD-COATED SHIELD TO FIT OVER THE ENERGY UNIT!
HOPE I CAN GET THERE IN TIME!
2

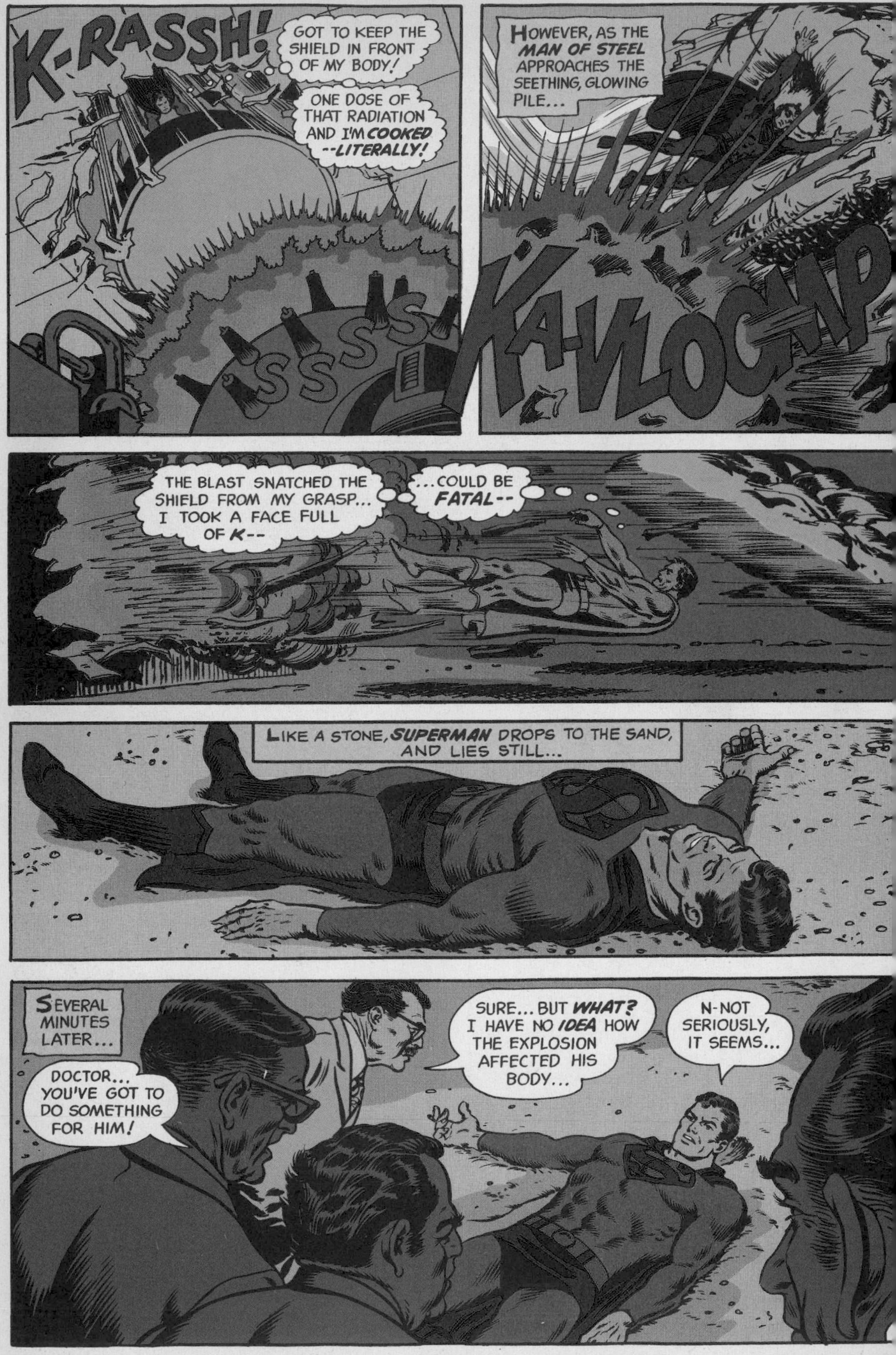

K-RASSH!
GOT TO KEEP THE SHIELD IN FRONT OF MY BODY!
ONE DOSE OF THAT RADIATION AND I'M COOKED --LITERALLY!
SSSSS
HOWEVER, AS THE MAN OF STEEL APPROACHES THE SEETHING, GLOWING PILE...
KA-VLOOMP
THE BLAST SNATCHED THE SHIELD FROM MY GRASP... I TOOK A FACE FULL OF K--
...COULD BE FATAL--
LIKE A STONE, SUPERMAN DROPS TO THE SAND, AND LIES STILL...
SEVERAL MINUTES LATER...
DOCTOR... YOU'VE GOT TO DO SOMETHING FOR HIM!
SURE... BUT WHAT? I HAVE NO IDEA HOW THE EXPLOSION AFFECTED HIS BODY...
N-NOT SERIOUSLY, IT SEEMS...

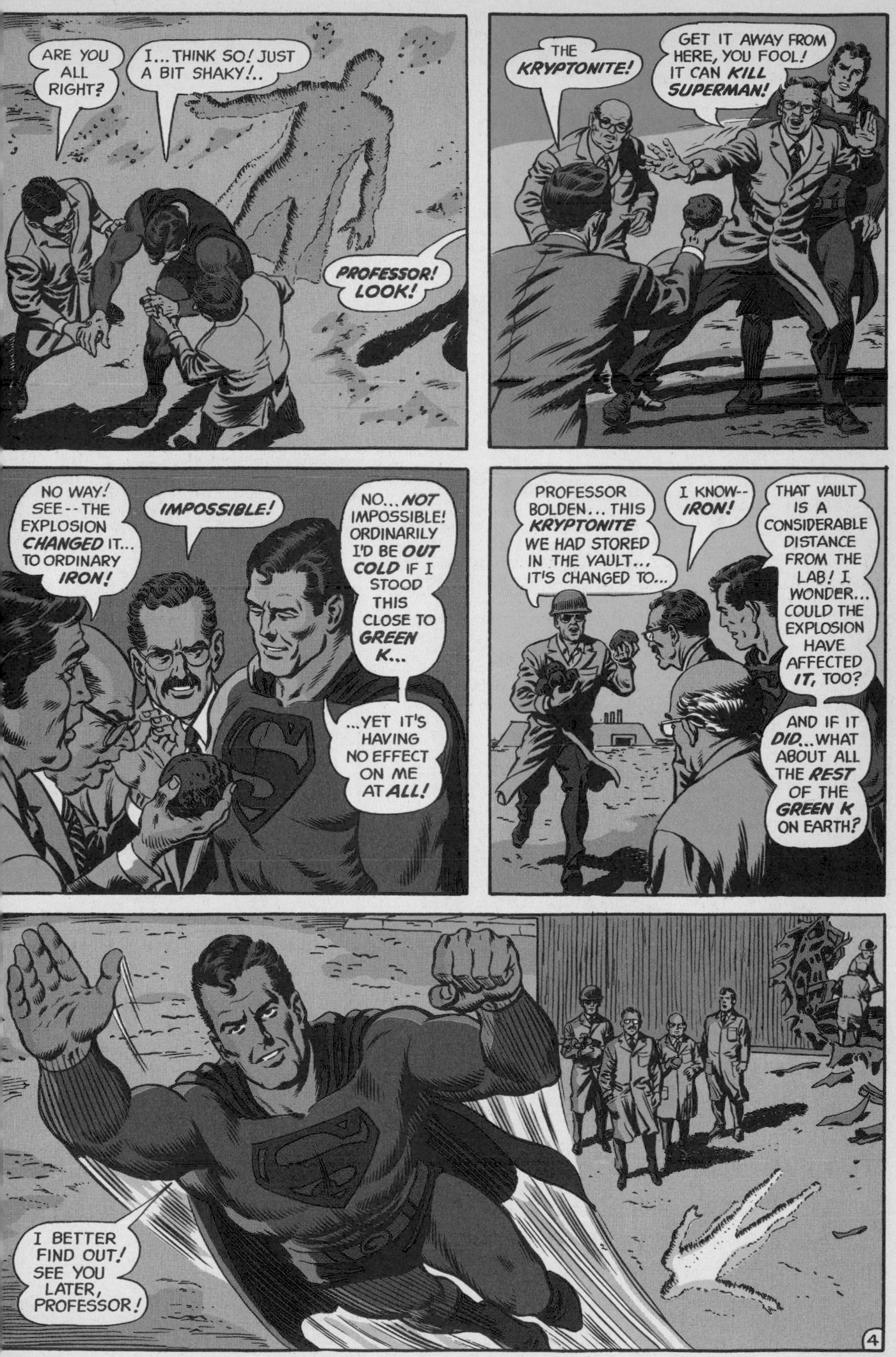
ARE YOU ALL RIGHT?
I... THINK SO! JUST A BIT SHAKY!..
PROFESSOR! LOOK!
THE KRYPTONITE!
GET IT AWAY FROM HERE, YOU FOOL! IT CAN KILL SUPERMAN!
NO WAY! SEE -- THE EXPLOSION CHANGED IT... TO ORDINARY IRON!
IMPOSSIBLE!
NO... NOT IMPOSSIBLE! ORDINARILY I'D BE OUT COLD IF I STOOD THIS CLOSE TO GREEN K...
...YET IT'S HAVING NO EFFECT ON ME AT ALL!
PROFESSOR BOLDEN... THIS KRYPTONITE WE HAD STORED IN THE VAULT... IT'S CHANGED TO...
I KNOW-- IRON!
THAT VAULT IS A CONSIDERABLE DISTANCE FROM THE LAB! I WONDER... COULD THE EXPLOSION HAVE AFFECTED IT, TOO?
AND IF IT DID... WHAT ABOUT ALL THE REST OF THE GREEN K ON EARTH?
I BETTER FIND OUT! SEE YOU LATER, PROFESSOR!
4

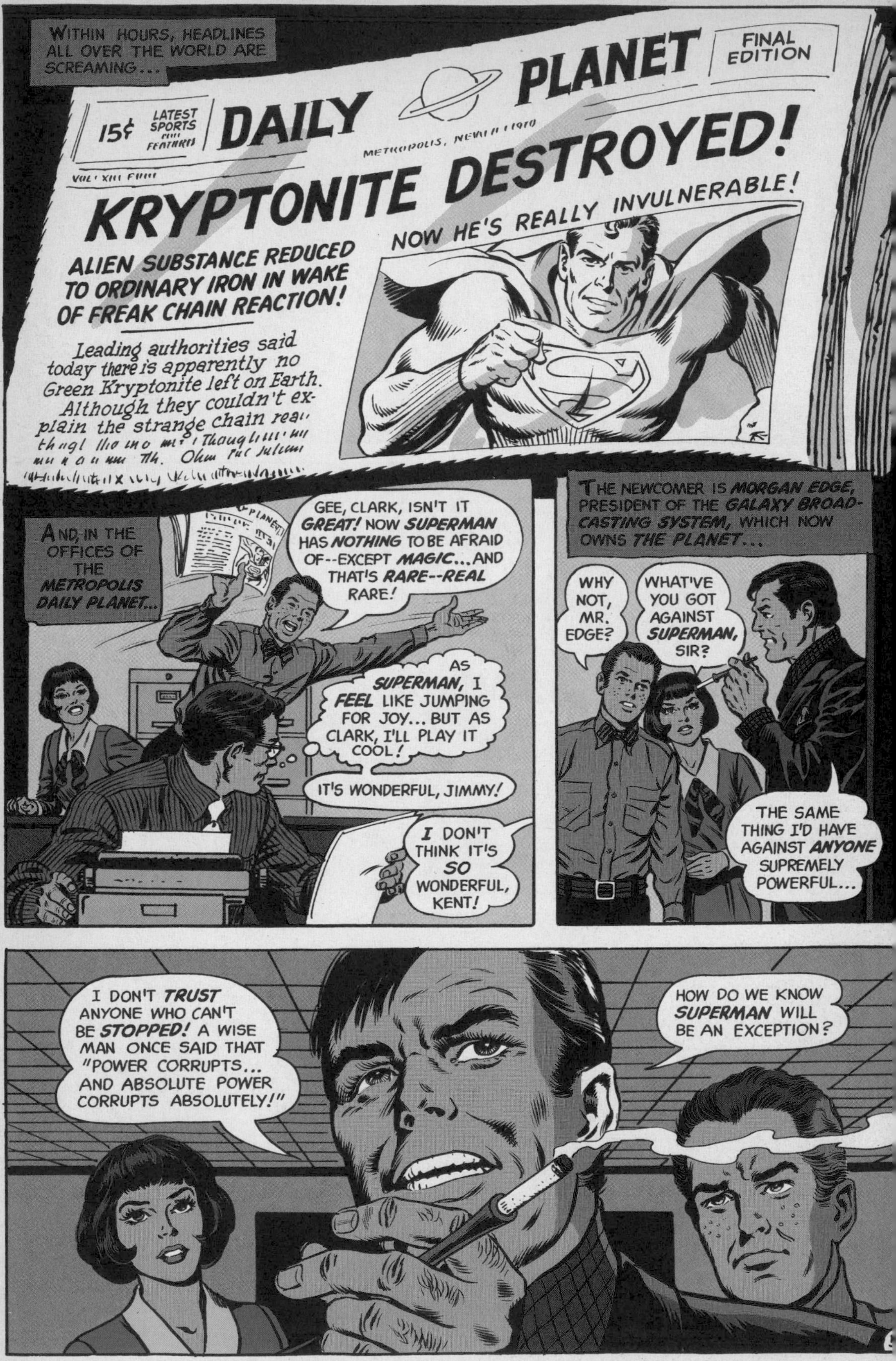

WITHIN HOURS, HEADLINES ALL OVER THE WORLD ARE SCREAMING...
15¢ LATEST SPORTS
DAILY PLANET
FINAL EDITION
KRYPTONITE DESTROYED!
NOW HE'S REALLY INVULNERABLE!
ALIEN SUBSTANCE REDUCED TO ORDINARY IRON IN WAKE OF FREAK CHAIN REACTION!
Leading authorities said today there is apparently no Green Kryptonite left on Earth. Although they couldn't explain the strange chain
AND, IN THE OFFICES OF THE METROPOLIS DAILY PLANET...
GEE, CLARK, ISN'T IT GREAT! NOW SUPERMAN HAS NOTHING TO BE AFRAID OF--EXCEPT MAGIC...AND THAT'S RARE--REAL RARE!
AS SUPERMAN, I FEEL LIKE JUMPING FOR JOY... BUT AS CLARK, I'LL PLAY IT COOL!
IT'S WONDERFUL, JIMMY!
I DON'T THINK IT'S SO WONDERFUL, KENT!
THE NEWCOMER IS MORGAN EDGE, PRESIDENT OF THE GALAXY BROADCASTING SYSTEM, WHICH NOW OWNS THE PLANET...
WHY NOT, MR. EDGE?
WHAT'VE YOU GOT AGAINST SUPERMAN, SIR?
THE SAME THING I'D HAVE AGAINST ANYONE SUPREMELY POWERFUL...
I DON'T TRUST ANYONE WHO CAN'T BE STOPPED! A WISE MAN ONCE SAID THAT "POWER CORRUPTS... AND ABSOLUTE POWER CORRUPTS ABSOLUTELY!"
HOW DO WE KNOW SUPERMAN WILL BE AN EXCEPTION?

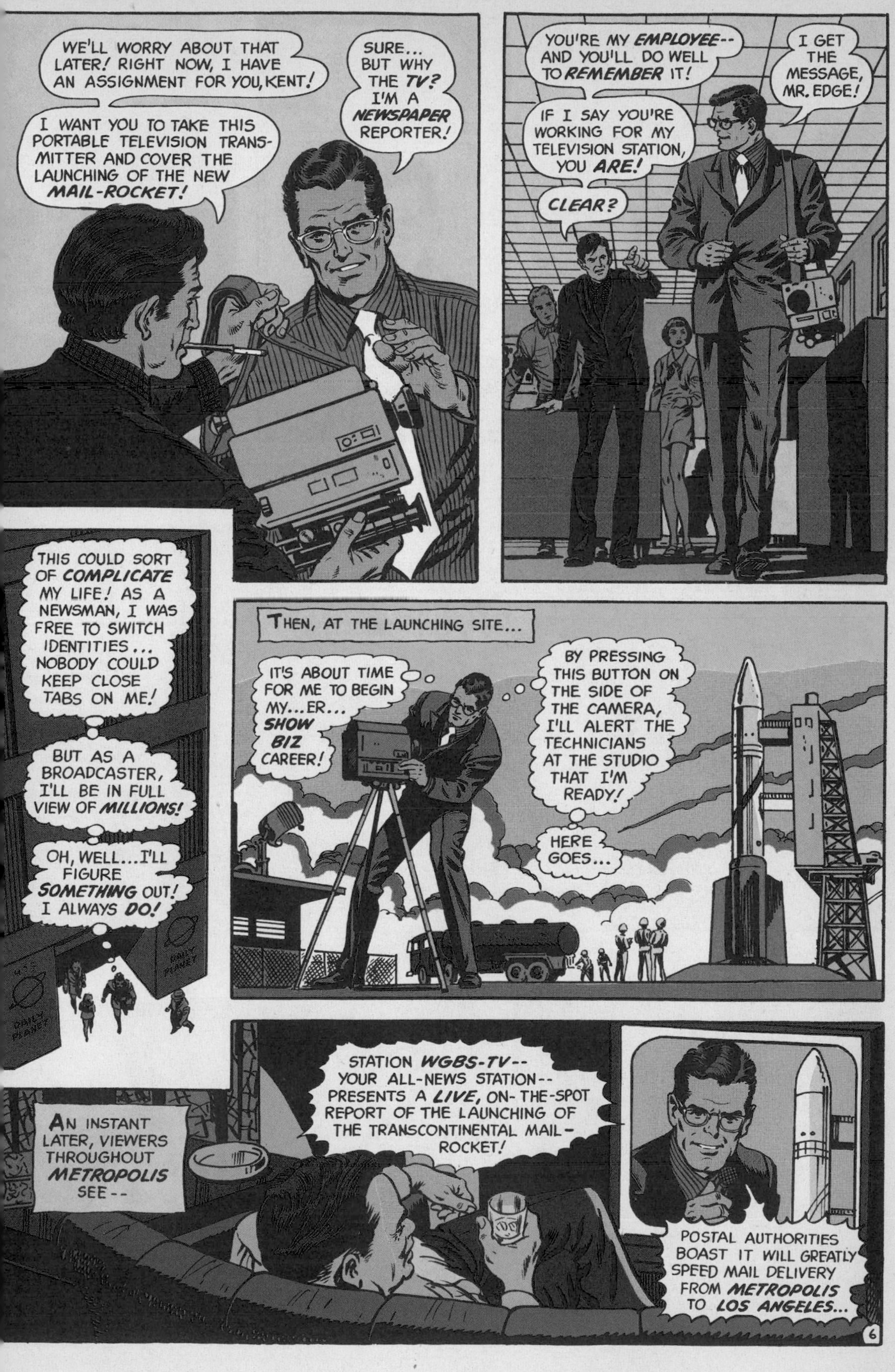
WE'LL WORRY ABOUT THAT LATER! RIGHT NOW, I HAVE AN ASSIGNMENT FOR YOU, KENT!
I WANT YOU TO TAKE THIS PORTABLE TELEVISION TRANS-MITTER AND COVER THE LAUNCHING OF THE NEW MAIL-ROCKET!
SURE... BUT WHY THE TV? I'M A NEWSPAPER REPORTER!
YOU'RE MY EMPLOYEE-- AND YOU'LL DO WELL TO REMEMBER IT!
IF I SAY YOU'RE WORKING FOR MY TELEVISION STATION, YOU ARE!
CLEAR?
I GET THE MESSAGE, MR. EDGE!
THIS COULD SORT OF COMPLICATE MY LIFE! AS A NEWSMAN, I WAS FREE TO SWITCH IDENTITIES... NOBODY COULD KEEP CLOSE TABS ON ME!
BUT AS A BROADCASTER, I'LL BE IN FULL VIEW OF MILLIONS!
OH, WELL... I'LL FIGURE SOMETHING OUT! I ALWAYS DO!
THEN, AT THE LAUNCHING SITE...
IT'S ABOUT TIME FOR ME TO BEGIN MY...ER... SHOW BIZ CAREER!
BY PRESSING THIS BUTTON ON THE SIDE OF THE CAMERA, I'LL ALERT THE TECHNICIANS AT THE STUDIO THAT I'M READY!
HERE GOES...
AN INSTANT LATER, VIEWERS THROUGHOUT METROPOLIS SEE--
STATION WGBS-TV-- YOUR ALL-NEWS STATION-- PRESENTS A LIVE, ON-THE-SPOT REPORT OF THE LAUNCHING OF THE TRANSCONTINENTAL MAIL-ROCKET!
POSTAL AUTHORITIES BOAST IT WILL GREATLY SPEED MAIL DELIVERY FROM METROPOLIS TO LOS ANGELES...
6

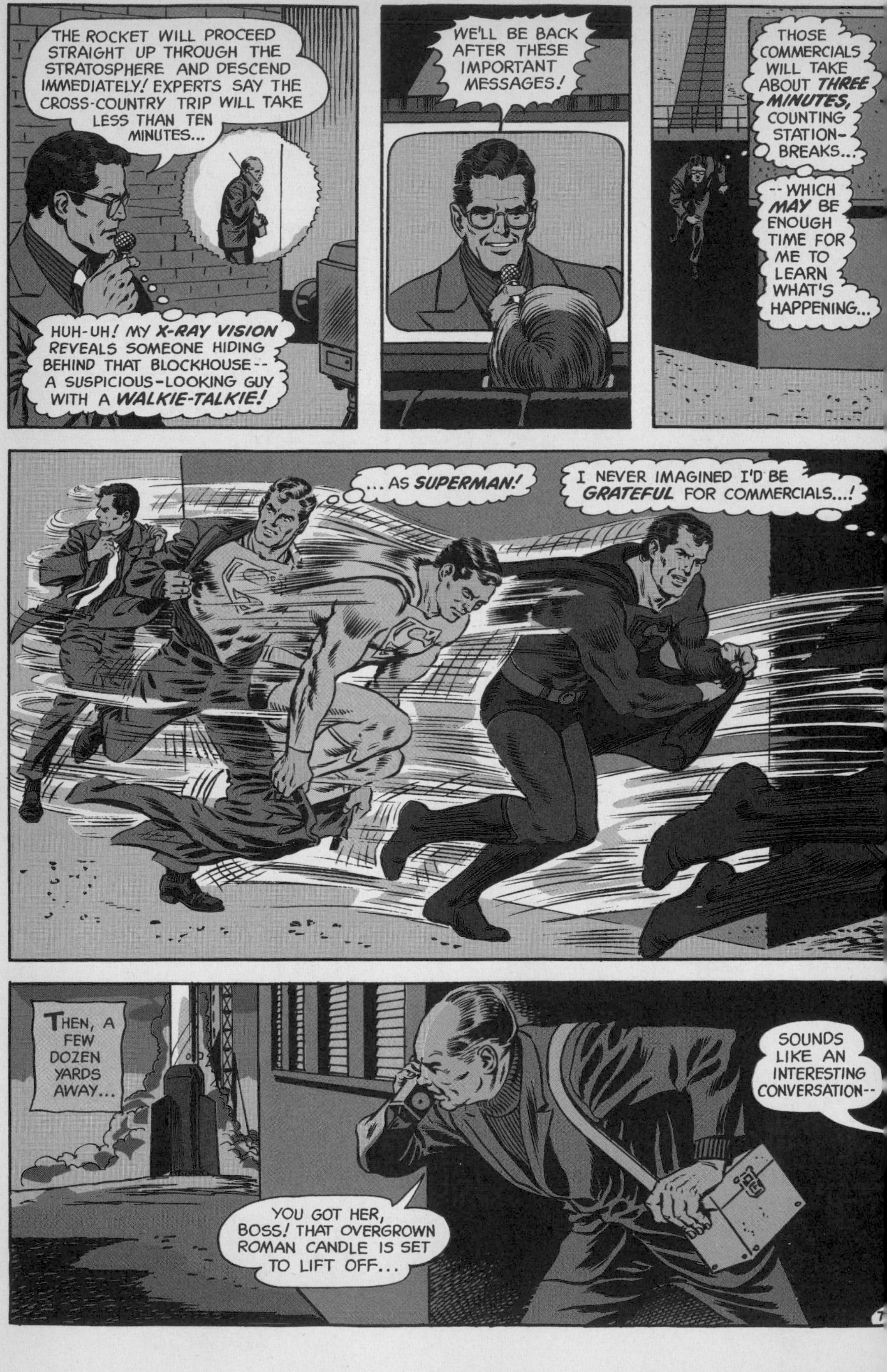
THE ROCKET WILL PROCEED STRAIGHT UP THROUGH THE STRATOSPHERE AND DESCEND IMMEDIATELY! EXPERTS SAY THE CROSS-COUNTRY TRIP WILL TAKE LESS THAN TEN MINUTES...
HUH-UH! MY X-RAY VISION REVEALS SOMEONE HIDING BEHIND THAT BLOCKHOUSE-- A SUSPICIOUS-LOOKING GUY WITH A WALKIE-TALKIE!
WE'LL BE BACK AFTER THESE IMPORTANT MESSAGES!
THOSE COMMERCIALS WILL TAKE ABOUT THREE MINUTES, COUNTING STATION-BREAKS...
--WHICH MAY BE ENOUGH TIME FOR ME TO LEARN WHAT'S HAPPENING...
...AS SUPERMAN!
I NEVER IMAGINED I'D BE GRATEFUL FOR COMMERCIALS...!
THEN, A FEW DOZEN YARDS AWAY...
YOU GOT HER, BOSS! THAT OVERGROWN ROMAN CANDLE IS SET TO LIFT OFF...
SOUNDS LIKE AN INTERESTING CONVERSATION--

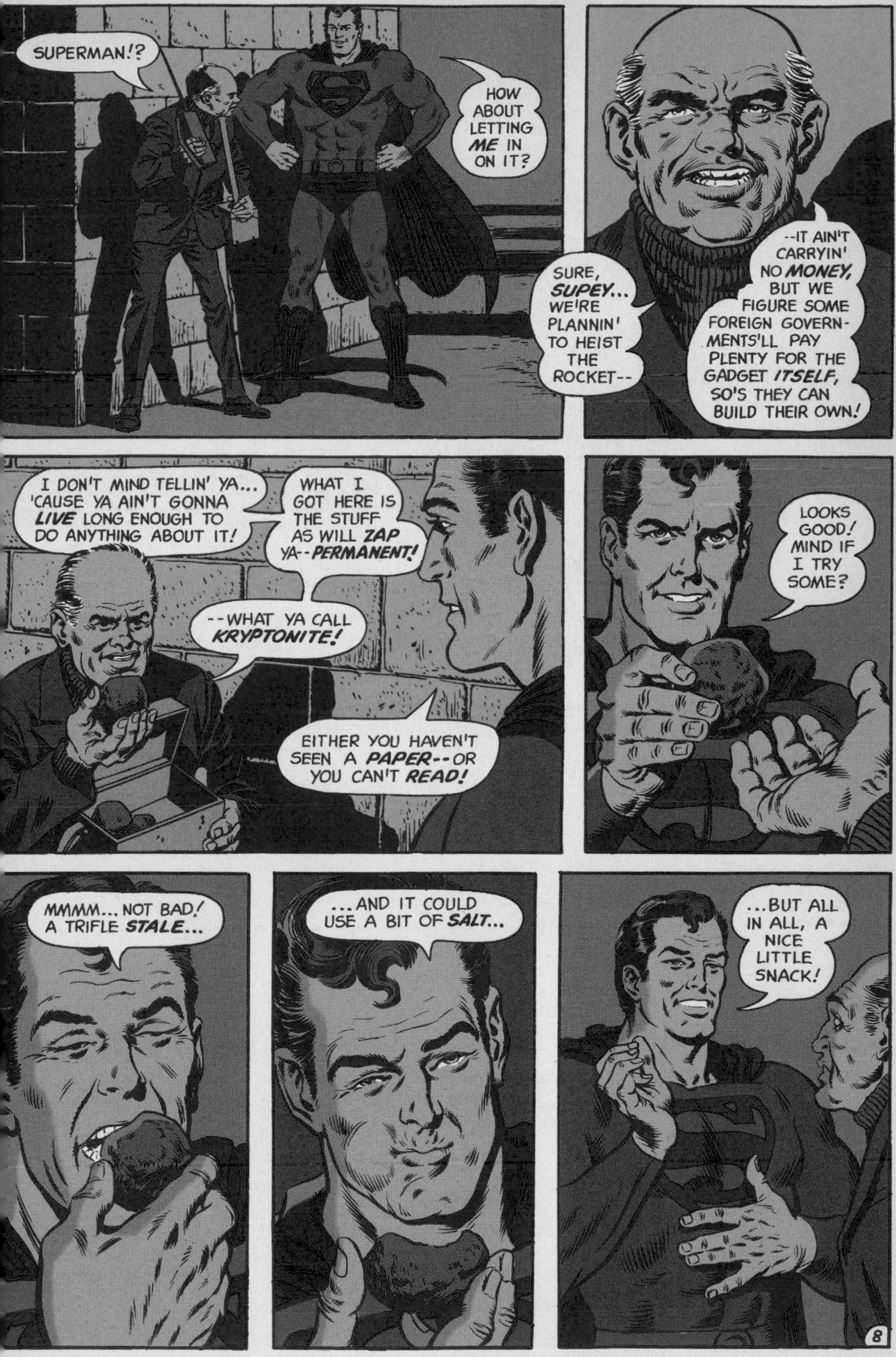
SUPERMAN!?
HOW ABOUT LETTING ME IN ON IT?
SURE, SUPEY... WE'RE PLANNIN' TO HEIST THE ROCKET--
--IT AIN'T CARRYIN' NO MONEY, BUT WE FIGURE SOME FOREIGN GOVERN-MENTS'LL PAY PLENTY FOR THE GADGET ITSELF, SO'S THEY CAN BUILD THEIR OWN!
I DON'T MIND TELLIN' YA... 'CAUSE YA AIN'T GONNA LIVE LONG ENOUGH TO DO ANYTHING ABOUT IT!
WHAT I GOT HERE IS THE STUFF AS WILL ZAP YA--PERMANENT!
--WHAT YA CALL KRYPTONITE!
EITHER YOU HAVEN'T SEEN A PAPER--OR YOU CAN'T READ!
LOOKS GOOD! MIND IF I TRY SOME?
MMMM... NOT BAD! A TRIFLE STALE...
...AND IT COULD USE A BIT OF SALT...
...BUT ALL IN ALL, A NICE LITTLE SNACK!
8

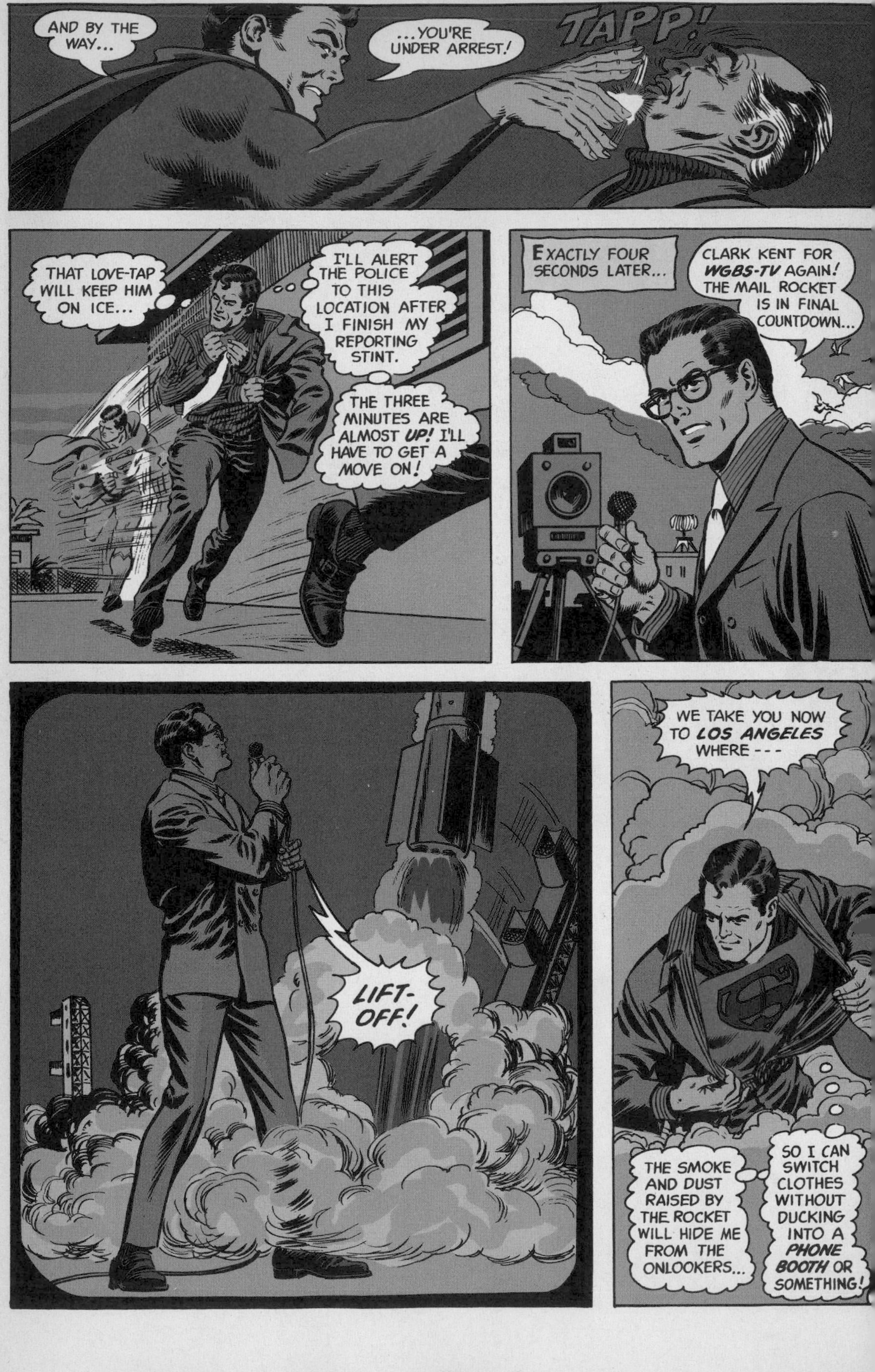
AND BY THE WAY...
...YOU'RE UNDER ARREST!
TAPP!
THAT LOVE-TAP WILL KEEP HIM ON ICE...
I'LL ALERT THE POLICE TO THIS LOCATION AFTER I FINISH MY REPORTING STINT.
THE THREE MINUTES ARE ALMOST UP! I'LL HAVE TO GET A MOVE ON!
EXACTLY FOUR SECONDS LATER...
CLARK KENT FOR WGBS-TV AGAIN! THE MAIL ROCKET IS IN FINAL COUNTDOWN...
LIFT-OFF!
WE TAKE YOU NOW TO LOS ANGELES WHERE ---
THE SMOKE AND DUST RAISED BY THE ROCKET WILL HIDE ME FROM THE ONLOOKERS...
SO I CAN SWITCH CLOTHES WITHOUT DUCKING INTO A PHONE BOOTH OR SOMETHING!

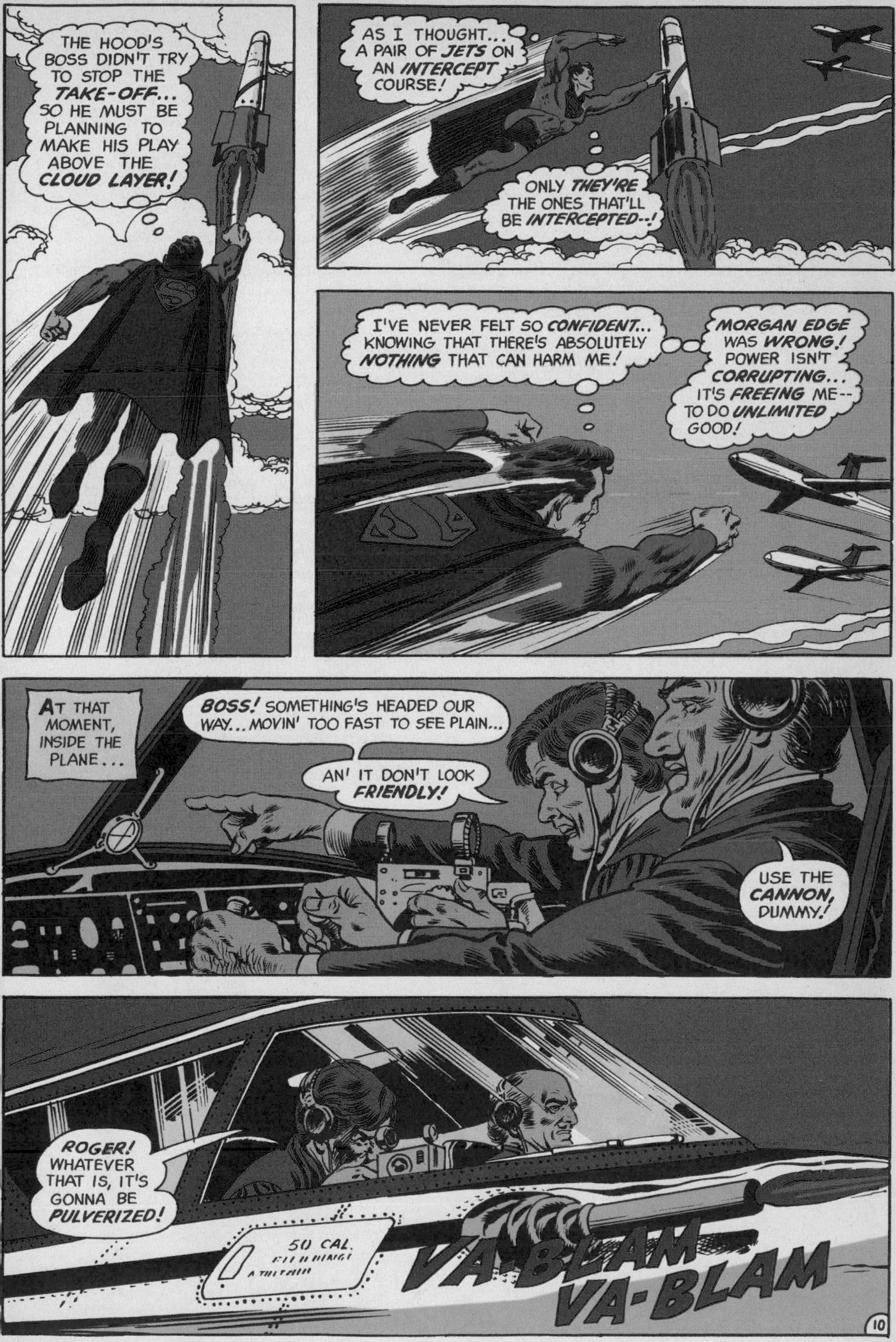
THE HOOD'S BOSS DIDN'T TRY TO STOP THE TAKE-OFF... SO HE MUST BE PLANNING TO MAKE HIS PLAY ABOVE THE CLOUD LAYER!
AS I THOUGHT... A PAIR OF JETS ON AN INTERCEPT COURSE!
ONLY THEY'RE THE ONES THAT'LL BE INTERCEPTED--!
I'VE NEVER FELT SO CONFIDENT... KNOWING THAT THERE'S ABSOLUTELY NOTHING THAT CAN HARM ME!
MORGAN EDGE WAS WRONG! POWER ISN'T CORRUPTING... IT'S FREEING ME-- TO DO UNLIMITED GOOD!
AT THAT MOMENT, INSIDE THE PLANE...
BOSS! SOMETHING'S HEADED OUR WAY... MOVIN' TOO FAST TO SEE PLAIN...
AN' IT DON'T LOOK FRIENDLY!
USE THE CANNON, DUMMY!
ROGER! WHATEVER THAT IS, IT'S GONNA BE PULVERIZED!
50 CAL.
VA-BLAM
VA-BLAM
10

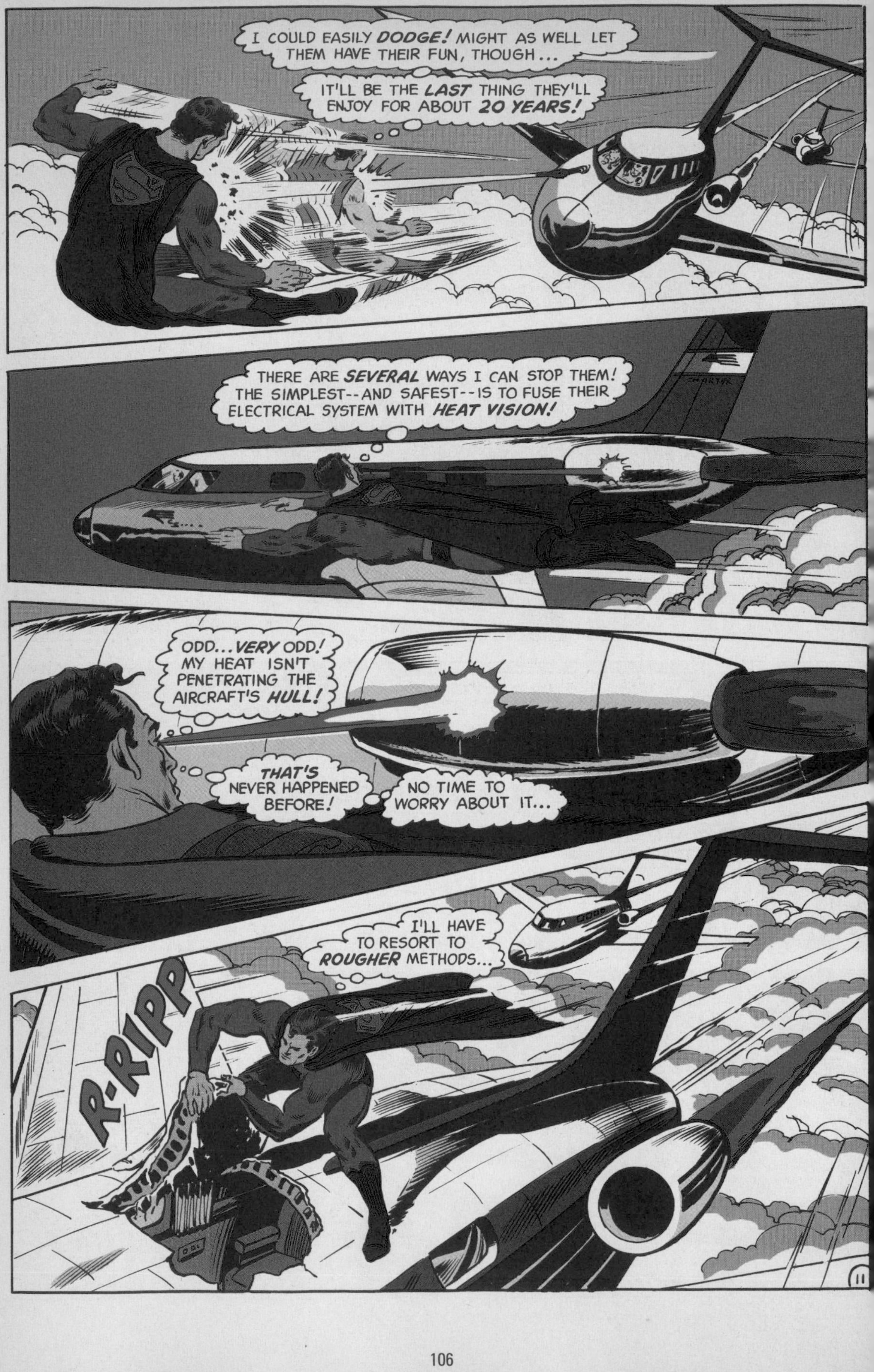
I COULD EASILY DODGE! MIGHT AS WELL LET THEM HAVE THEIR FUN, THOUGH...
IT'LL BE THE LAST THING THEY'LL ENJOY FOR ABOUT 20 YEARS!
THERE ARE SEVERAL WAYS I CAN STOP THEM! THE SIMPLEST--AND SAFEST--IS TO FUSE THEIR ELECTRICAL SYSTEM WITH HEAT VISION!
ODD... VERY ODD! MY HEAT ISN'T PENETRATING THE AIRCRAFT'S HULL!
THAT'S NEVER HAPPENED BEFORE!
NO TIME TO WORRY ABOUT IT...
I'LL HAVE TO RESORT TO ROUGHER METHODS...
R-RIPP
11

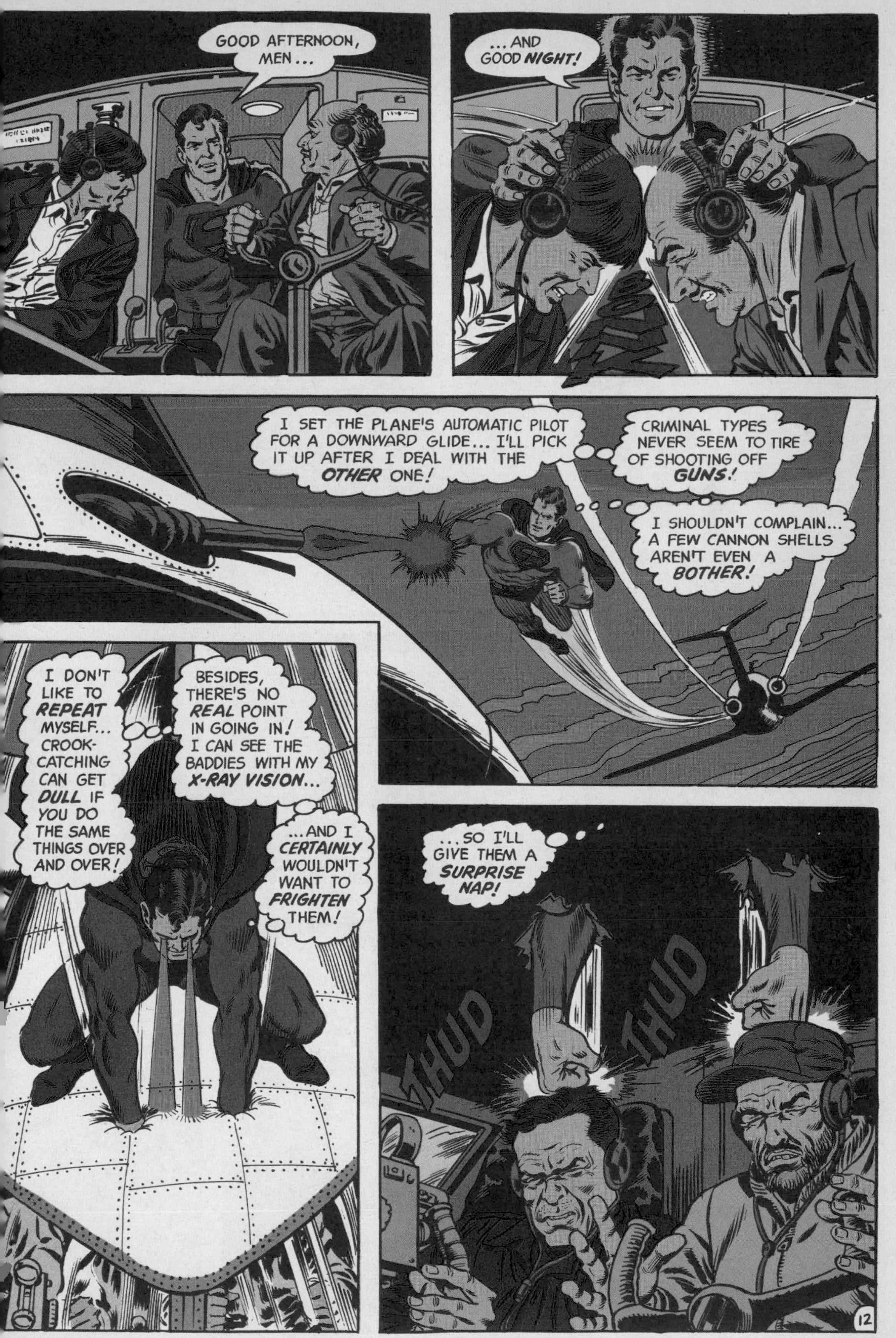
GOOD AFTERNOON, MEN...
...AND GOOD NIGHT!
I SET THE PLANE'S AUTOMATIC PILOT FOR A DOWNWARD GLIDE... I'LL PICK IT UP AFTER I DEAL WITH THE OTHER ONE!
CRIMINAL TYPES NEVER SEEM TO TIRE OF SHOOTING OFF GUNS!
I SHOULDN'T COMPLAIN... A FEW CANNON SHELLS AREN'T EVEN A BOTHER!
I DON'T LIKE TO REPEAT MYSELF... CROOK-CATCHING CAN GET DULL IF YOU DO THE SAME THINGS OVER AND OVER!
BESIDES, THERE'S NO REAL POINT IN GOING IN! I CAN SEE THE BADDIES WITH MY X-RAY VISION...
...AND I CERTAINLY WOULDN'T WANT TO FRIGHTEN THEM!
...SO I'LL GIVE THEM A SURPRISE NAP!
THUD
THUD
12

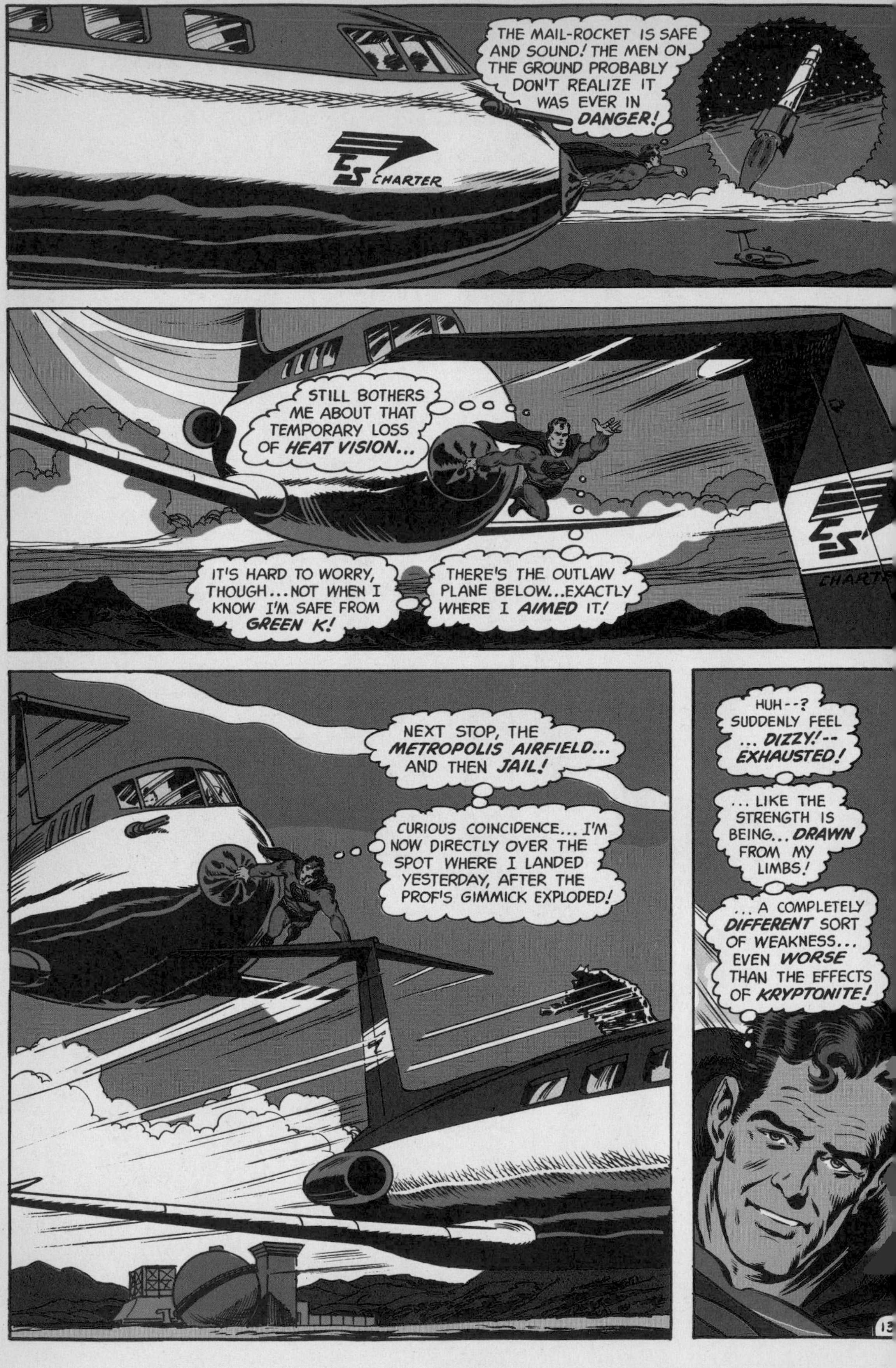
THE MAIL-ROCKET IS SAFE AND SOUND! THE MEN ON THE GROUND PROBABLY DON'T REALIZE IT WAS EVER IN DANGER!
ES CHARTER
STILL BOTHERS ME ABOUT THAT TEMPORARY LOSS OF HEAT VISION...
IT'S HARD TO WORRY, THOUGH...NOT WHEN I KNOW I'M SAFE FROM GREEN K!
THERE'S THE OUTLAW PLANE BELOW...EXACTLY WHERE I AIMED IT!
NEXT STOP, THE METROPOLIS AIRFIELD... AND THEN JAIL!
CURIOUS COINCIDENCE... I'M NOW DIRECTLY OVER THE SPOT WHERE I LANDED YESTERDAY, AFTER THE PROF'S GIMMICK EXPLODED!
HUH--? SUDDENLY FEEL ... DIZZY!-- EXHAUSTED!
... LIKE THE STRENGTH IS BEING... DRAWN FROM MY LIMBS!
... A COMPLETELY DIFFERENT SORT OF WEAKNESS... EVEN WORSE THAN THE EFFECTS OF KRYPTONITE!

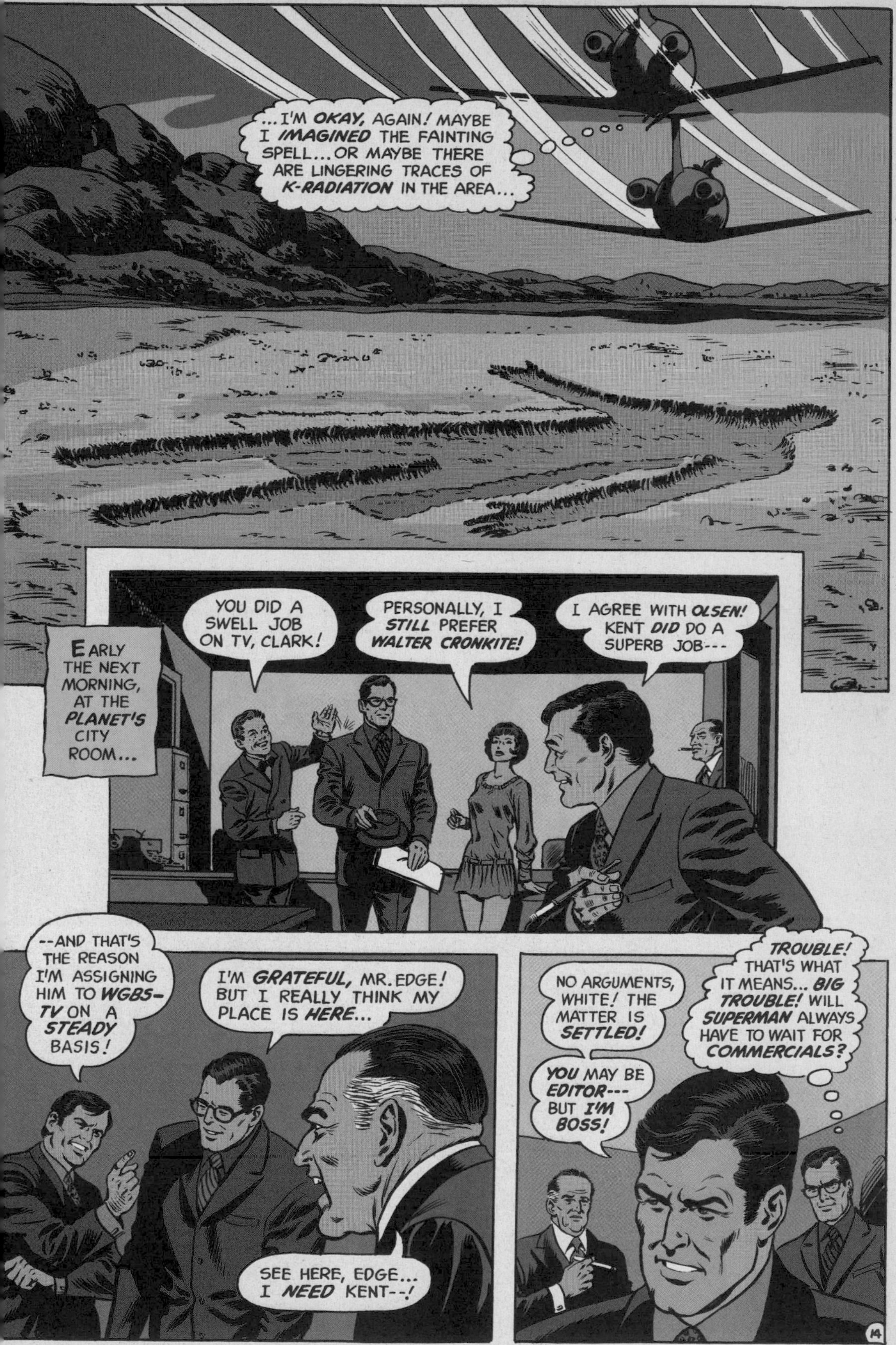
...I'M OKAY, AGAIN! MAYBE I IMAGINED THE FAINTING SPELL...OR MAYBE THERE ARE LINGERING TRACES OF K-RADIATION IN THE AREA...
EARLY THE NEXT MORNING, AT THE PLANET'S CITY ROOM...
YOU DID A SWELL JOB ON TV, CLARK!
PERSONALLY, I STILL PREFER WALTER CRONKITE!
I AGREE WITH OLSEN! KENT DID DO A SUPERB JOB---
--AND THAT'S THE REASON I'M ASSIGNING HIM TO WGBS-TV ON A STEADY BASIS!
I'M GRATEFUL, MR. EDGE! BUT I REALLY THINK MY PLACE IS HERE...
SEE HERE, EDGE... I NEED KENT--!
NO ARGUMENTS, WHITE! THE MATTER IS SETTLED!
YOU MAY BE EDITOR--- BUT I'M BOSS!
TROUBLE! THAT'S WHAT IT MEANS... BIG TROUBLE! WILL SUPERMAN ALWAYS HAVE TO WAIT FOR COMMERCIALS?
14
THE END!

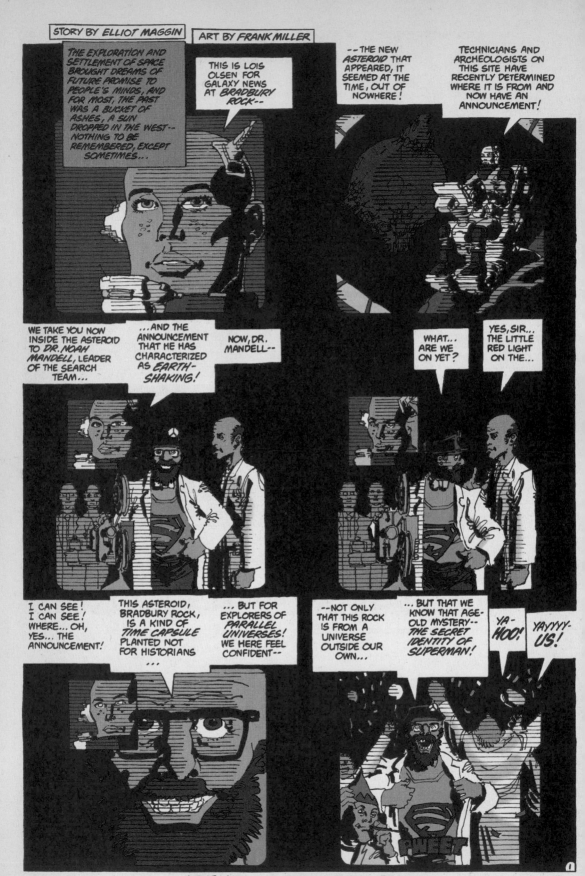

STORY BY ELLIOT MAGGIN — ART BY FRANK MILLER

THE EXPLORATION AND SETTLEMENT OF SPACE BROUGHT DREAMS OF FUTURE PROMISE TO PEOPLE'S MINDS, AND FOR MOST, THE PAST WAS A BUCKET OF ASHES, A SUN DROPPED IN THE WEST-- NOTHING TO BE REMEMBERED, EXCEPT SOMETIMES...

THIS IS LOIS OLSEN FOR GALAXY NEWS AT *BRADBURY ROCK*--

-- THE NEW *ASTEROID* THAT APPEARED, IT SEEMED AT THE TIME, OUT OF NOWHERE!

TECHNICIANS AND ARCHEOLOGISTS ON THIS SITE HAVE RECENTLY DETERMINED WHERE IT IS FROM AND NOW HAVE AN ANNOUNCEMENT!

WE TAKE YOU NOW INSIDE THE ASTEROID TO *DR. NOAH MANDELL,* LEADER OF THE SEARCH TEAM...

...AND THE ANNOUNCEMENT THAT HE HAS CHARACTERIZED AS *EARTH-SHAKING!*

NOW, DR. MANDELL--

WHAT... ARE WE ON YET?

YES, SIR... THE LITTLE RED LIGHT ON THE...

I CAN SEE! I CAN SEE! WHERE... OH, YES... THE ANNOUNCEMENT!

THIS ASTEROID, BRADBURY ROCK, IS A KIND OF *TIME CAPSULE* PLANTED NOT FOR HISTORIANS ...

...BUT FOR EXPLORERS OF *PARALLEL UNIVERSES!* WE HERE FEEL CONFIDENT--

--NOT ONLY THAT THIS ROCK IS FROM A UNIVERSE OUTSIDE OUR OWN...

...BUT THAT WE KNOW THAT AGE-OLD MYSTERY-- *THE SECRET IDENTITY OF SUPERMAN!*

YA-HOO!

YAYYYY-US!

PWEET

"THE LEGEND FROM EARTH PRIME"

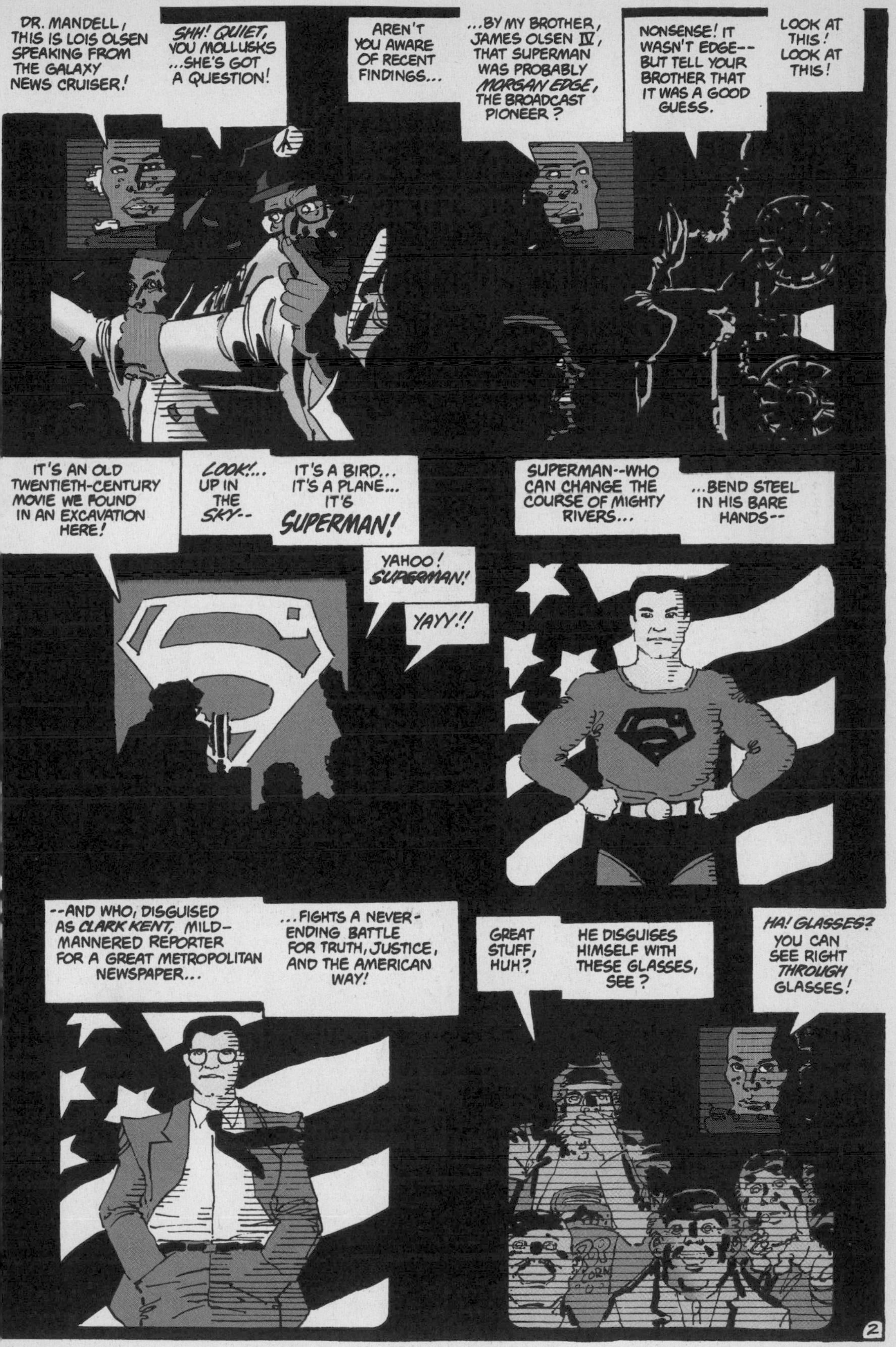
DR. MANDELL, THIS IS LOIS OLSEN SPEAKING FROM THE GALAXY NEWS CRUISER!
SHH! QUIET, YOU MOLLUSKS ...SHE'S GOT A QUESTION!
AREN'T YOU AWARE OF RECENT FINDINGS...
...BY MY BROTHER, JAMES OLSEN IV, THAT SUPERMAN WAS PROBABLY MORGAN EDGE, THE BROADCAST PIONEER?
NONSENSE! IT WASN'T EDGE-- BUT TELL YOUR BROTHER THAT IT WAS A GOOD GUESS.
LOOK AT THIS! LOOK AT THIS!
IT'S AN OLD TWENTIETH-CENTURY MOVIE WE FOUND IN AN EXCAVATION HERE!
LOOK!... UP IN THE SKY--
IT'S A BIRD... IT'S A PLANE... IT'S SUPERMAN!
YAHOO! SUPERMAN!
YAYY!!
SUPERMAN--WHO CAN CHANGE THE COURSE OF MIGHTY RIVERS...
...BEND STEEL IN HIS BARE HANDS--
--AND WHO, DISGUISED AS CLARK KENT, MILD-MANNERED REPORTER FOR A GREAT METROPOLITAN NEWSPAPER...
...FIGHTS A NEVER-ENDING BATTLE FOR TRUTH, JUSTICE, AND THE AMERICAN WAY!
GREAT STUFF, HUH?
HE DISGUISES HIMSELF WITH THESE GLASSES, SEE?
HA! GLASSES? YOU CAN SEE RIGHT THROUGH GLASSES!
2

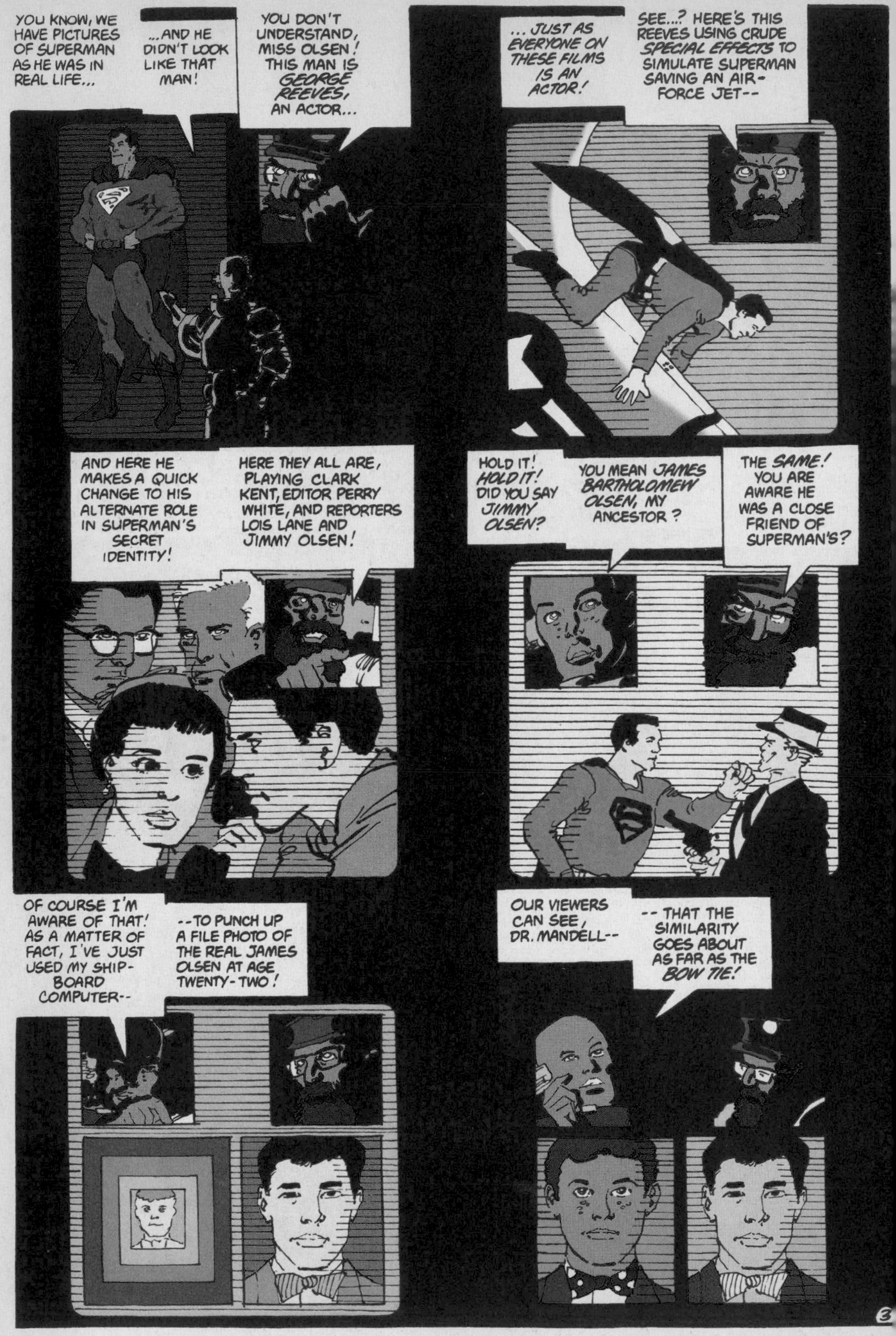

YOU KNOW, WE HAVE PICTURES OF SUPERMAN AS HE WAS IN REAL LIFE...
...AND HE DIDN'T LOOK LIKE THAT MAN!
YOU DON'T UNDERSTAND, MISS OLSEN! THIS MAN IS GEORGE REEVES, AN ACTOR...
... JUST AS EVERYONE ON THESE FILMS IS AN ACTOR!
SEE...? HERE'S THIS REEVES USING CRUDE SPECIAL EFFECTS TO SIMULATE SUPERMAN SAVING AN AIR-FORCE JET--
AND HERE HE MAKES A QUICK CHANGE TO HIS ALTERNATE ROLE IN SUPERMAN'S SECRET IDENTITY!
HERE THEY ALL ARE, PLAYING CLARK KENT, EDITOR PERRY WHITE, AND REPORTERS LOIS LANE AND JIMMY OLSEN!
HOLD IT! HOLD IT! DID YOU SAY JIMMY OLSEN?
YOU MEAN JAMES BARTHOLOMEW OLSEN, MY ANCESTOR?
THE SAME! YOU ARE AWARE HE WAS A CLOSE FRIEND OF SUPERMAN'S?
OF COURSE I'M AWARE OF THAT! AS A MATTER OF FACT, I'VE JUST USED MY SHIP-BOARD COMPUTER--
--TO PUNCH UP A FILE PHOTO OF THE REAL JAMES OLSEN AT AGE TWENTY-TWO!
OUR VIEWERS CAN SEE, DR. MANDELL--
--THAT THE SIMILARITY GOES ABOUT AS FAR AS THE BOW TIE!
3

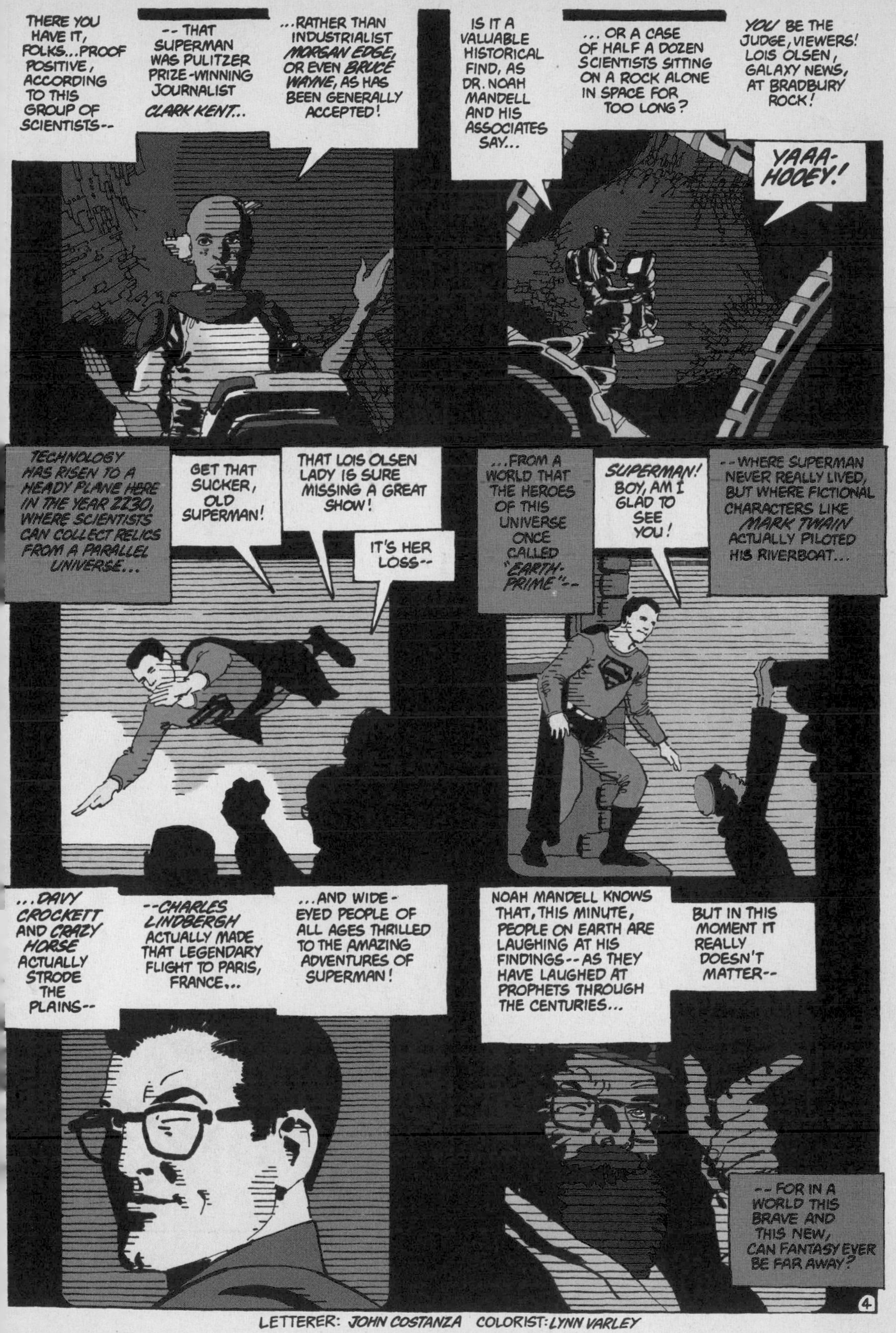
THERE YOU HAVE IT, FOLKS...PROOF POSITIVE, ACCORDING TO THIS GROUP OF SCIENTISTS--
--THAT SUPERMAN WAS PULITZER PRIZE-WINNING JOURNALIST CLARK KENT...
...RATHER THAN INDUSTRIALIST MORGAN EDGE, OR EVEN BRUCE WAYNE, AS HAS BEEN GENERALLY ACCEPTED!
IS IT A VALUABLE HISTORICAL FIND, AS DR. NOAH MANDELL AND HIS ASSOCIATES SAY...
...OR A CASE OF HALF A DOZEN SCIENTISTS SITTING ON A ROCK ALONE IN SPACE FOR TOO LONG?
YOU BE THE JUDGE, VIEWERS! LOIS OLSEN, GALAXY NEWS, AT BRADBURY ROCK!
YAAA-HOOEY!
TECHNOLOGY HAS RISEN TO A HEADY PLANE HERE IN THE YEAR 2230, WHERE SCIENTISTS CAN COLLECT RELICS FROM A PARALLEL UNIVERSE...
GET THAT SUCKER, OLD SUPERMAN!
THAT LOIS OLSEN LADY IS SURE MISSING A GREAT SHOW!
IT'S HER LOSS--
...FROM A WORLD THAT THE HEROES OF THIS UNIVERSE ONCE CALLED "EARTH-PRIME"--
SUPERMAN! BOY, AM I GLAD TO SEE YOU!
--WHERE SUPERMAN NEVER REALLY LIVED, BUT WHERE FICTIONAL CHARACTERS LIKE MARK TWAIN ACTUALLY PILOTED HIS RIVERBOAT...
...DAVY CROCKETT AND CRAZY HORSE ACTUALLY STRODE THE PLAINS--
--CHARLES LINDBERGH ACTUALLY MADE THAT LEGENDARY FLIGHT TO PARIS, FRANCE...
...AND WIDE-EYED PEOPLE OF ALL AGES THRILLED TO THE AMAZING ADVENTURES OF SUPERMAN!
NOAH MANDELL KNOWS THAT, THIS MINUTE, PEOPLE ON EARTH ARE LAUGHING AT HIS FINDINGS--AS THEY HAVE LAUGHED AT PROPHETS THROUGH THE CENTURIES...
BUT IN THIS MOMENT IT REALLY DOESN'T MATTER--
--FOR IN A WORLD THIS BRAVE AND THIS NEW, CAN FANTASY EVER BE FAR AWAY?
4

LETTERER: JOHN COSTANZA COLORIST: LYNN VARLEY

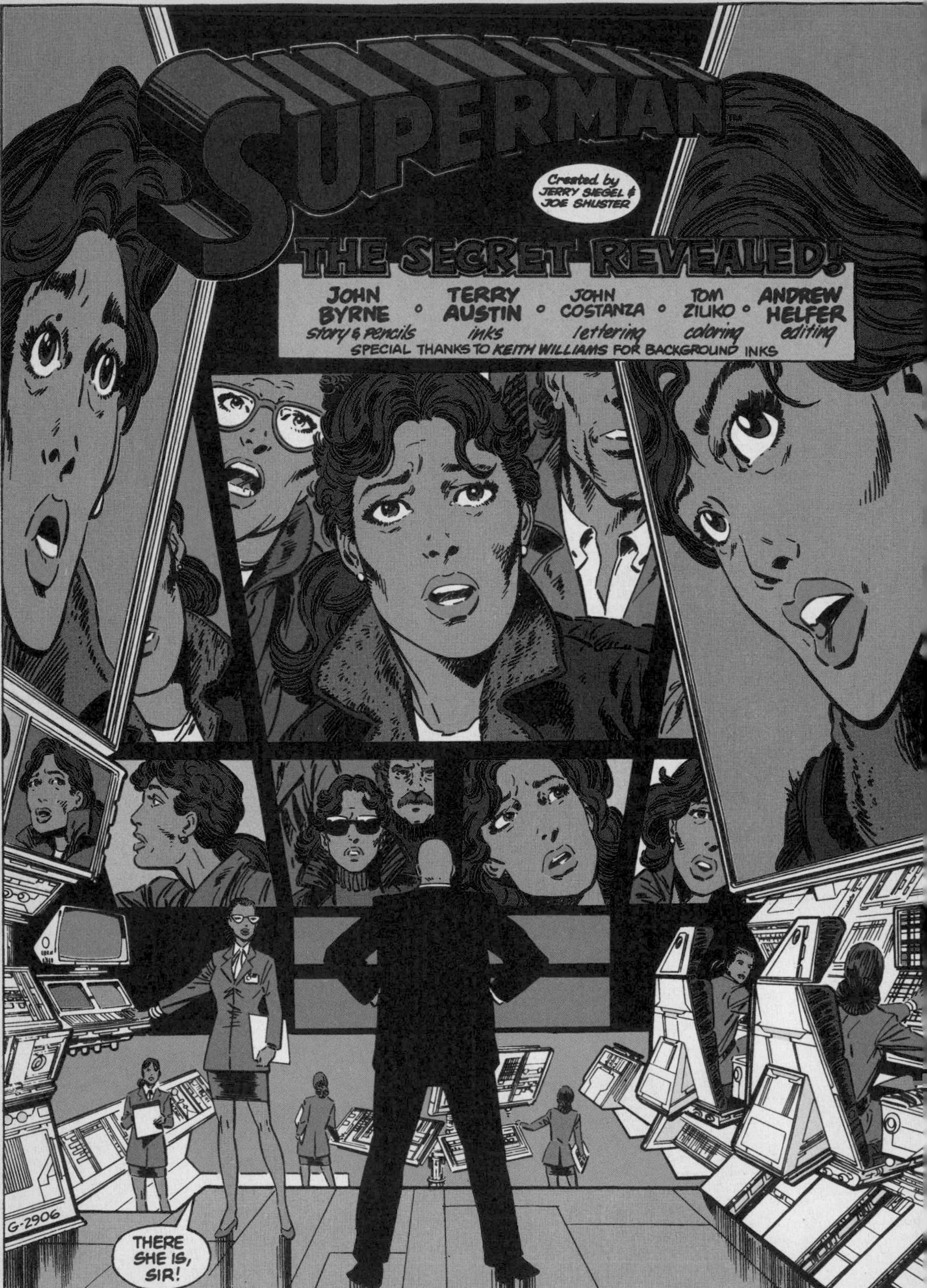
SUPERMAN
Created by JERRY SIEGEL & JOE SHUSTER
THE SECRET REVEALED!
JOHN BYRNE story & pencils • TERRY AUSTIN inks • JOHN COSTANZA lettering • TOM ZIUKO coloring • ANDREW HELFER editing
SPECIAL THANKS TO KEITH WILLIAMS FOR BACKGROUND INKS
G-2906
THERE SHE IS, SIR!

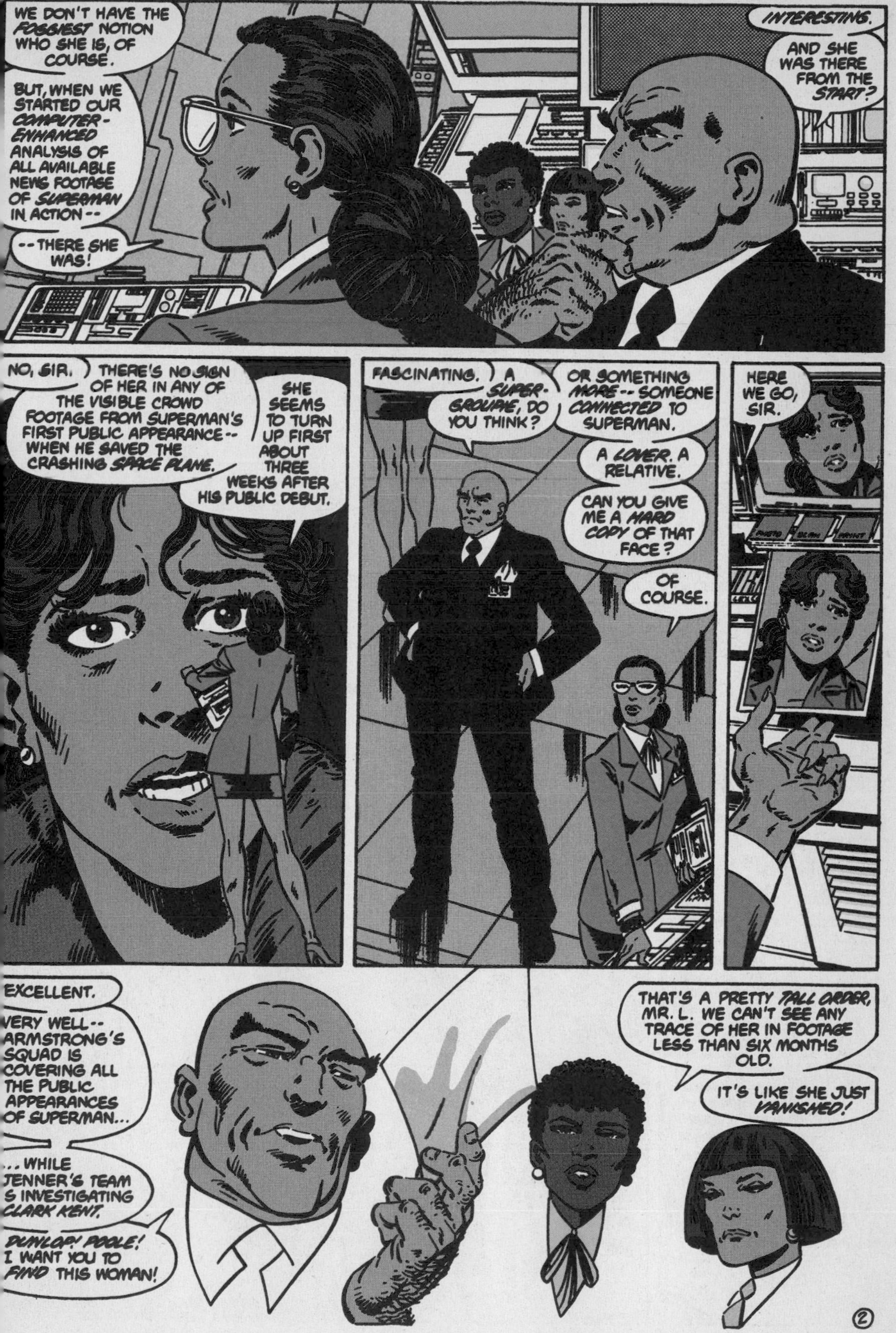

WE DON'T HAVE THE FOGGIEST NOTION WHO SHE IS, OF COURSE.
BUT, WHEN WE STARTED OUR COMPUTER-ENHANCED ANALYSIS OF ALL AVAILABLE NEWS FOOTAGE OF SUPERMAN IN ACTION--
--THERE SHE WAS!
INTERESTING.
AND SHE WAS THERE FROM THE START?
NO, SIR.
THERE'S NO SIGN OF HER IN ANY OF THE VISIBLE CROWD FOOTAGE FROM SUPERMAN'S FIRST PUBLIC APPEARANCE--WHEN HE SAVED THE CRASHING SPACE PLANE.
SHE SEEMS TO TURN UP FIRST ABOUT THREE WEEKS AFTER HIS PUBLIC DEBUT.
FASCINATING.
A SUPER-GROUPIE, DO YOU THINK?
OR SOMETHING MORE--SOMEONE CONNECTED TO SUPERMAN.
A LOVER. A RELATIVE.
CAN YOU GIVE ME A HARD COPY OF THAT FACE?
OF COURSE.
HERE WE GO, SIR.
EXCELLENT.
VERY WELL--ARMSTRONG'S SQUAD IS COVERING ALL THE PUBLIC APPEARANCES OF SUPERMAN...
...WHILE JENNER'S TEAM IS INVESTIGATING CLARK KENT.
DUNLOP! POOLE! I WANT YOU TO FIND THIS WOMAN!
THAT'S A PRETTY TALL ORDER, MR. L. WE CAN'T SEE ANY TRACE OF HER IN FOOTAGE LESS THAN SIX MONTHS OLD.
IT'S LIKE SHE JUST VANISHED!
2

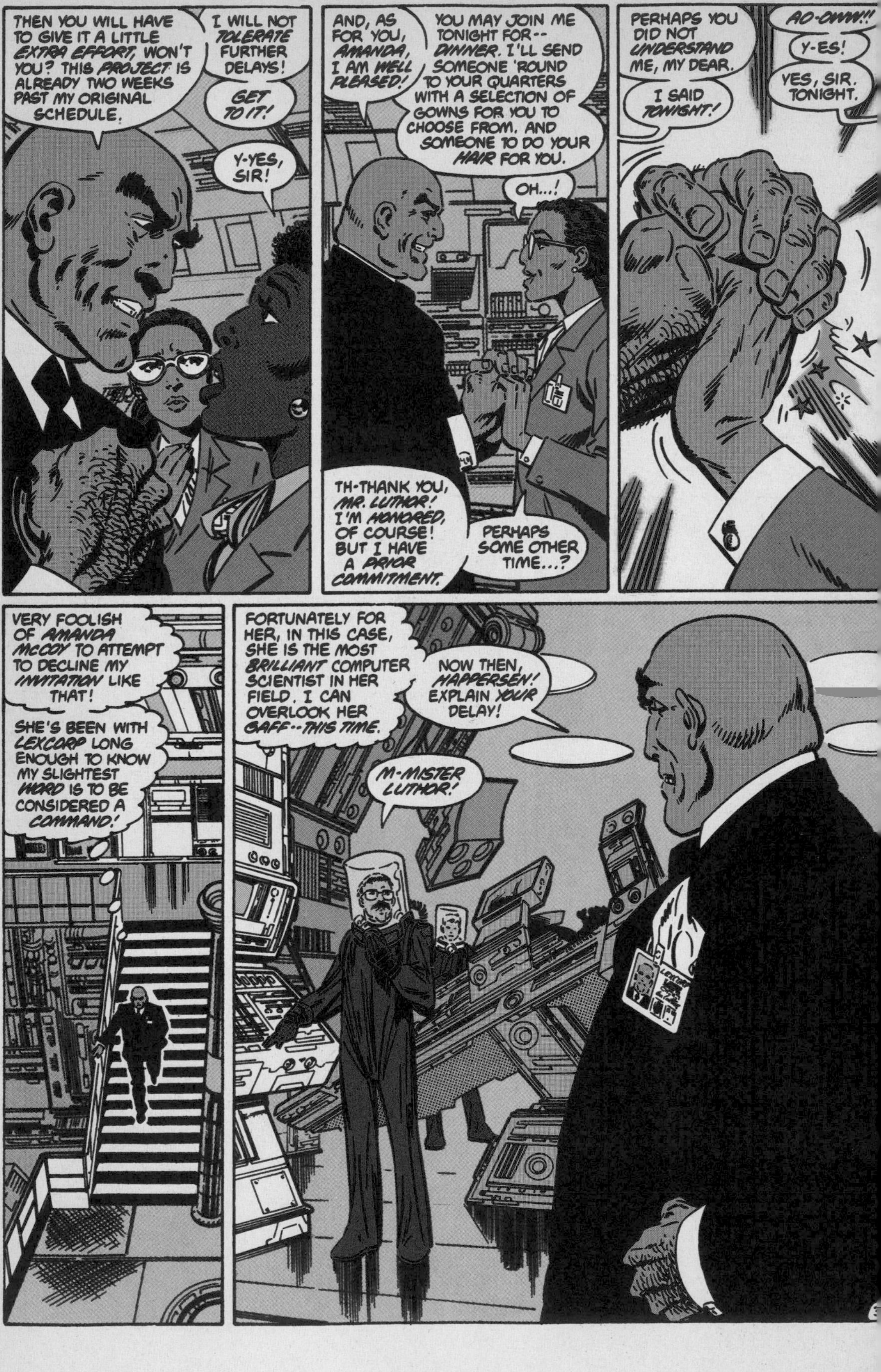
THEN YOU WILL HAVE TO GIVE IT A LITTLE EXTRA EFFORT, WON'T YOU? THIS PROJECT IS ALREADY TWO WEEKS PAST MY ORIGINAL SCHEDULE.
I WILL NOT TOLERATE FURTHER DELAYS!
GET TO IT!
Y-YES, SIR!
AND, AS FOR YOU, AMANDA, I AM WELL PLEASED!
YOU MAY JOIN ME TONIGHT FOR-- DINNER. I'LL SEND SOMEONE 'ROUND TO YOUR QUARTERS WITH A SELECTION OF GOWNS FOR YOU TO CHOOSE FROM. AND SOMEONE TO DO YOUR HAIR FOR YOU.
OH...!
TH-THANK YOU, MR. LUTHOR! I'M HONORED, OF COURSE! BUT I HAVE A PRIOR COMMITMENT.
PERHAPS SOME OTHER TIME...?
PERHAPS YOU DID NOT UNDERSTAND ME, MY DEAR.
I SAID TONIGHT!
AO-OWW!!
Y-ES!
YES, SIR. TONIGHT.
VERY FOOLISH OF AMANDA McCOY TO ATTEMPT TO DECLINE MY INVITATION LIKE THAT!
SHE'S BEEN WITH LEXCORP LONG ENOUGH TO KNOW MY SLIGHTEST WORD IS TO BE CONSIDERED A COMMAND!
FORTUNATELY FOR HER, IN THIS CASE, SHE IS THE MOST BRILLIANT COMPUTER SCIENTIST IN HER FIELD. I CAN OVERLOOK HER GAFF--THIS TIME.
NOW THEN, HAPPERSEN! EXPLAIN YOUR DELAY!
M-MISTER LUTHOR!

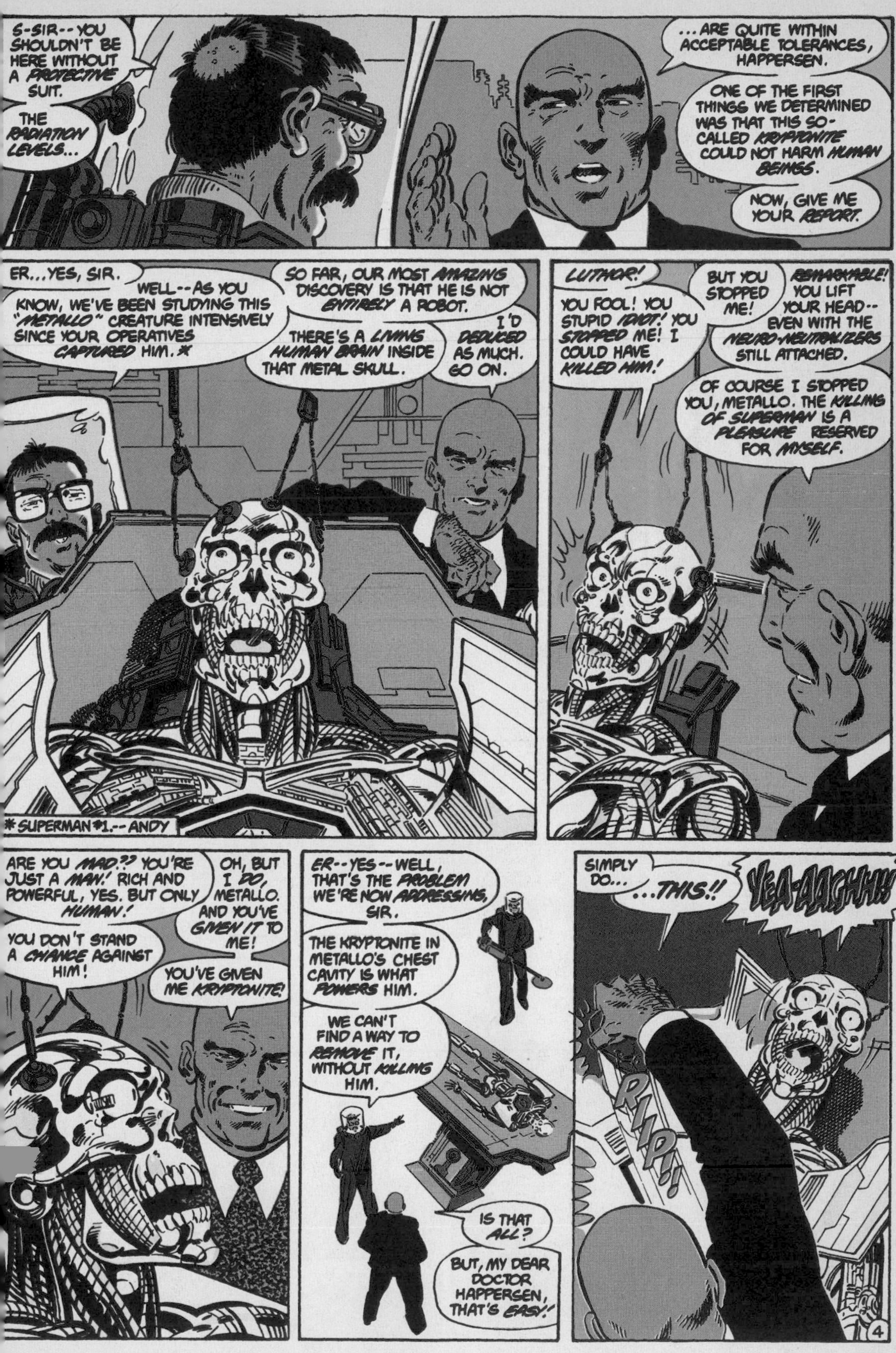

S-SIR--YOU SHOULDN'T BE HERE WITHOUT A PROTECTIVE SUIT.
THE RADIATION LEVELS...
...ARE QUITE WITHIN ACCEPTABLE TOLERANCES, HAPPERSEN.
ONE OF THE FIRST THINGS WE DETERMINED WAS THAT THIS SO-CALLED KRYPTONITE COULD NOT HARM HUMAN BEINGS.
NOW, GIVE ME YOUR REPORT.
ER...YES, SIR.
WELL--AS YOU KNOW, WE'VE BEEN STUDYING THIS "METALLO" CREATURE INTENSIVELY SINCE YOUR OPERATIVES CAPTURED HIM.*
SO FAR, OUR MOST AMAZING DISCOVERY IS THAT HE IS NOT ENTIRELY A ROBOT.
THERE'S A LIVING HUMAN BRAIN INSIDE THAT METAL SKULL.
I'D DEDUCED AS MUCH. GO ON.
*SUPERMAN #1.--ANDY
LUTHOR!
YOU FOOL! YOU STUPID IDIOT! YOU STOPPED ME! I COULD HAVE KILLED HIM!
BUT YOU STOPPED ME!
REMARKABLE! YOU LIFT YOUR HEAD--EVEN WITH THE NEURO-NEUTRALIZERS STILL ATTACHED.
OF COURSE I STOPPED YOU, METALLO. THE KILLING OF SUPERMAN IS A PLEASURE RESERVED FOR MYSELF.
ARE YOU MAD?? YOU'RE JUST A MAN! RICH AND POWERFUL, YES. BUT ONLY HUMAN!
YOU DON'T STAND A CHANCE AGAINST HIM!
OH, BUT I DO, METALLO. AND YOU'VE GIVEN IT TO ME!
YOU'VE GIVEN ME KRYPTONITE!
ER--YES--WELL, THAT'S THE PROBLEM WE'RE NOW ADDRESSING, SIR.
THE KRYPTONITE IN METALLO'S CHEST CAVITY IS WHAT POWERS HIM.
WE CAN'T FIND A WAY TO REMOVE IT, WITHOUT KILLING HIM.
IS THAT ALL?
BUT, MY DEAR DOCTOR HAPPERSEN, THAT'S EASY!
SIMPLY DO...
...THIS!!
YEA-AAGHHH!
RIIP!!
4

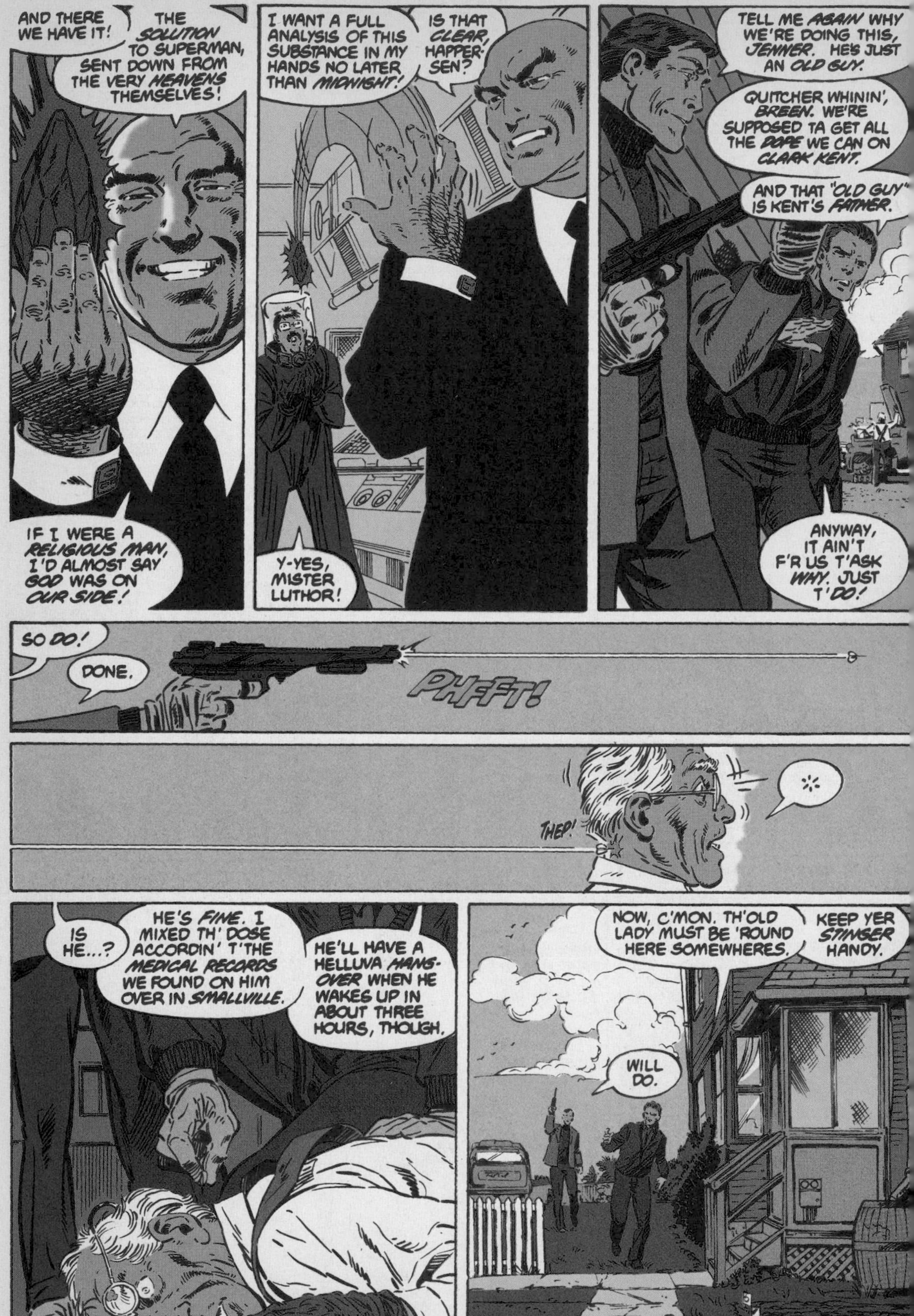
AND THERE WE HAVE IT!
THE SOLUTION TO SUPERMAN, SENT DOWN FROM THE VERY HEAVENS THEMSELVES!
IF I WERE A RELIGIOUS MAN, I'D ALMOST SAY GOD WAS ON OUR SIDE!
I WANT A FULL ANALYSIS OF THIS SUBSTANCE IN MY HANDS NO LATER THAN MIDNIGHT!
IS THAT CLEAR, HAPPERSEN?
Y-YES, MISTER LUTHOR!
TELL ME AGAIN WHY WE'RE DOING THIS, JENNER. HE'S JUST AN OLD GUY.
QUITCHER WHININ', BREEN. WE'RE SUPPOSED TA GET ALL THE DOPE WE CAN ON CLARK KENT.
AND THAT "OLD GUY" IS KENT'S FATHER.
ANYWAY, IT AIN'T F'R US T'ASK WHY. JUST T'DO!
SO DO!
DONE.
PHFFT!
THEP!
IS HE...?
HE'S FINE. I MIXED TH' DOSE ACCORDIN' T'THE MEDICAL RECORDS WE FOUND ON HIM OVER IN SMALLVILLE.
HE'LL HAVE A HELLUVA HANGOVER WHEN HE WAKES UP IN ABOUT THREE HOURS, THOUGH.
NOW, C'MON. TH'OLD LADY MUST BE 'ROUND HERE SOMEWHERES.
KEEP YER STINGER HANDY.
WILL DO.
5

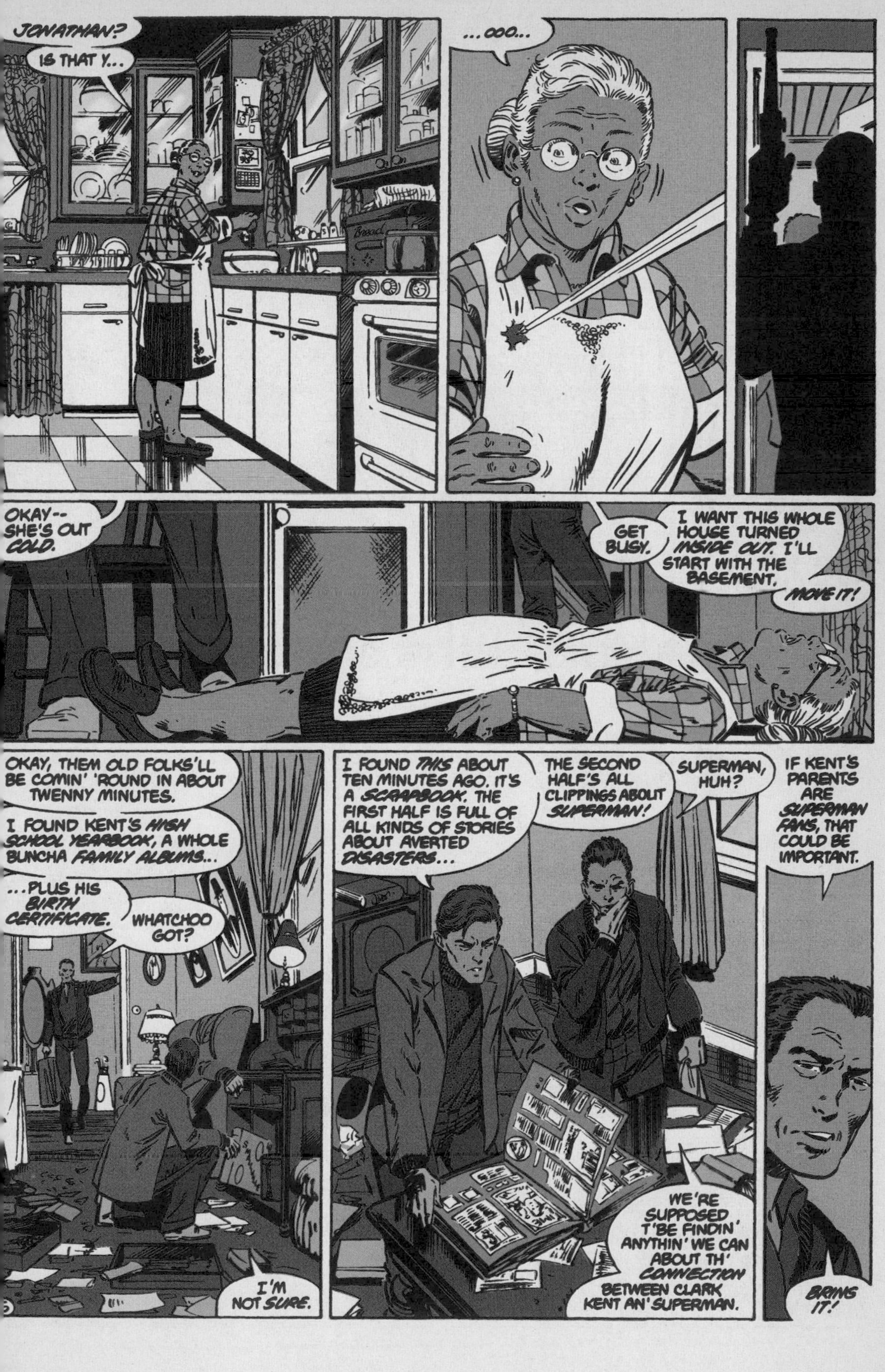
JONATHAN?
IS THAT Y...
...OOO...
OKAY-- SHE'S OUT COLD.
GET BUSY.
I WANT THIS WHOLE HOUSE TURNED INSIDE OUT. I'LL START WITH THE BASEMENT.
MOVE IT!
OKAY, THEM OLD FOLKS'LL BE COMIN' 'ROUND IN ABOUT TWENNY MINUTES.
I FOUND KENT'S HIGH SCHOOL YEARBOOK, A WHOLE BUNCHA FAMILY ALBUMS...
...PLUS HIS BIRTH CERTIFICATE.
WHATCHOO GOT?
I'M NOT SURE.
I FOUND THIS ABOUT TEN MINUTES AGO. IT'S A SCRAPBOOK. THE FIRST HALF IS FULL OF ALL KINDS OF STORIES ABOUT AVERTED DISASTERS...
THE SECOND HALF'S ALL CLIPPINGS ABOUT SUPERMAN!
SUPERMAN, HUH?
WE'RE SUPPOSED T'BE FINDIN' ANYTHIN' WE CAN ABOUT TH' CONNECTION BETWEEN CLARK KENT AN' SUPERMAN.
IF KENT'S PARENTS ARE SUPERMAN FANS, THAT COULD BE IMPORTANT.
BRING IT!

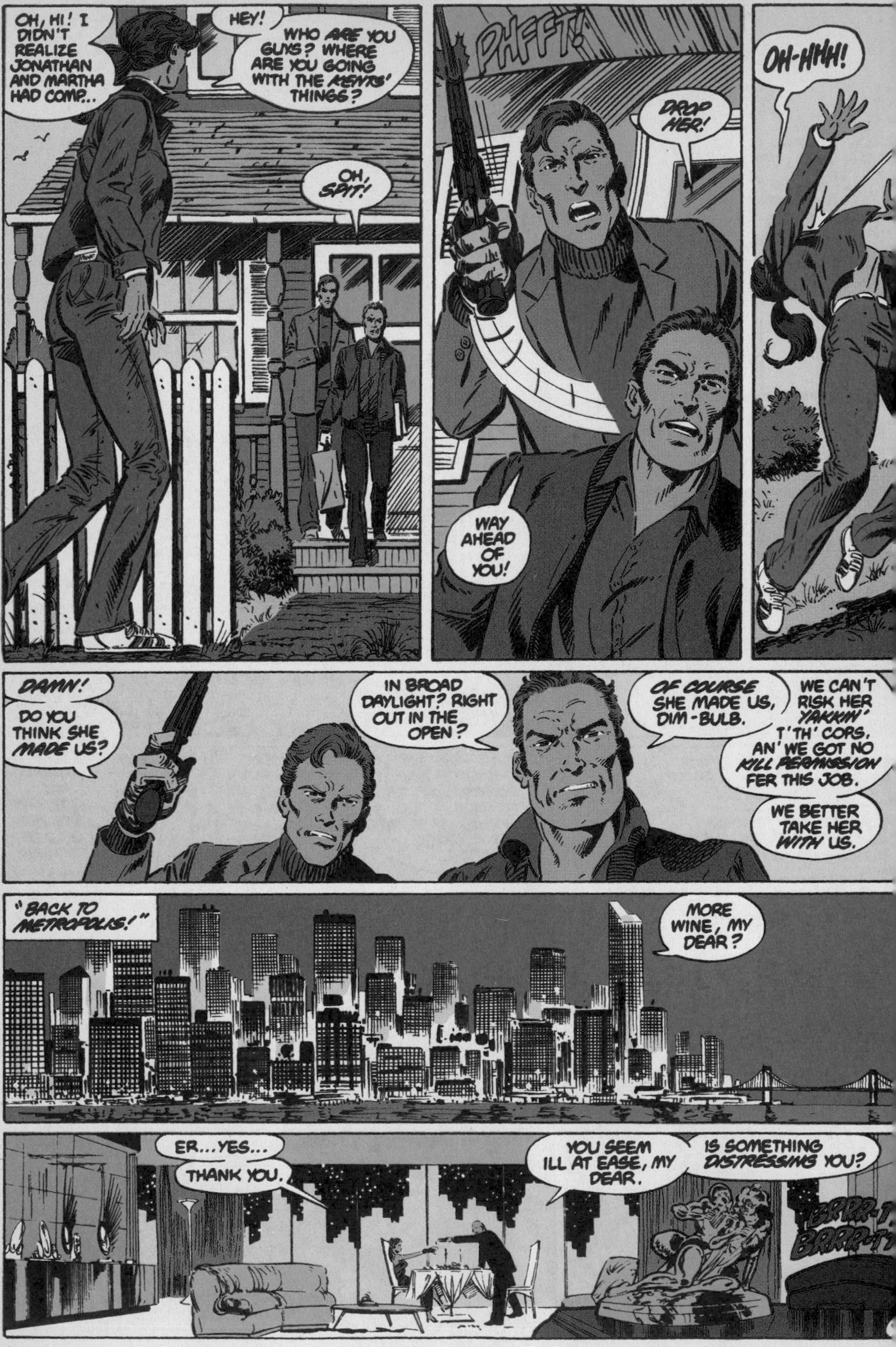

OH, HI! I DIDN'T REALIZE JONATHAN AND MARTHA HAD COMP...
HEY!
WHO ARE YOU GUYS? WHERE ARE YOU GOING WITH THE KENTS' THINGS?
OH, SPIT!
PHFFT!
DROP HER!
WAY AHEAD OF YOU!
OH-HHH!
DAMN!
DO YOU THINK SHE MADE US?
IN BROAD DAYLIGHT? RIGHT OUT IN THE OPEN?
OF COURSE SHE MADE US, DIM-BULB.
WE CAN'T RISK HER YAKKIN' T'TH' COPS, AN' WE GOT NO KILL PERMISSION FER THIS JOB.
WE BETTER TAKE HER WITH US.
"BACK TO METROPOLIS!"
MORE WINE, MY DEAR?
ER...YES...
THANK YOU.
YOU SEEM ILL AT EASE, MY DEAR.
IS SOMETHING DISTRESSING YOU?

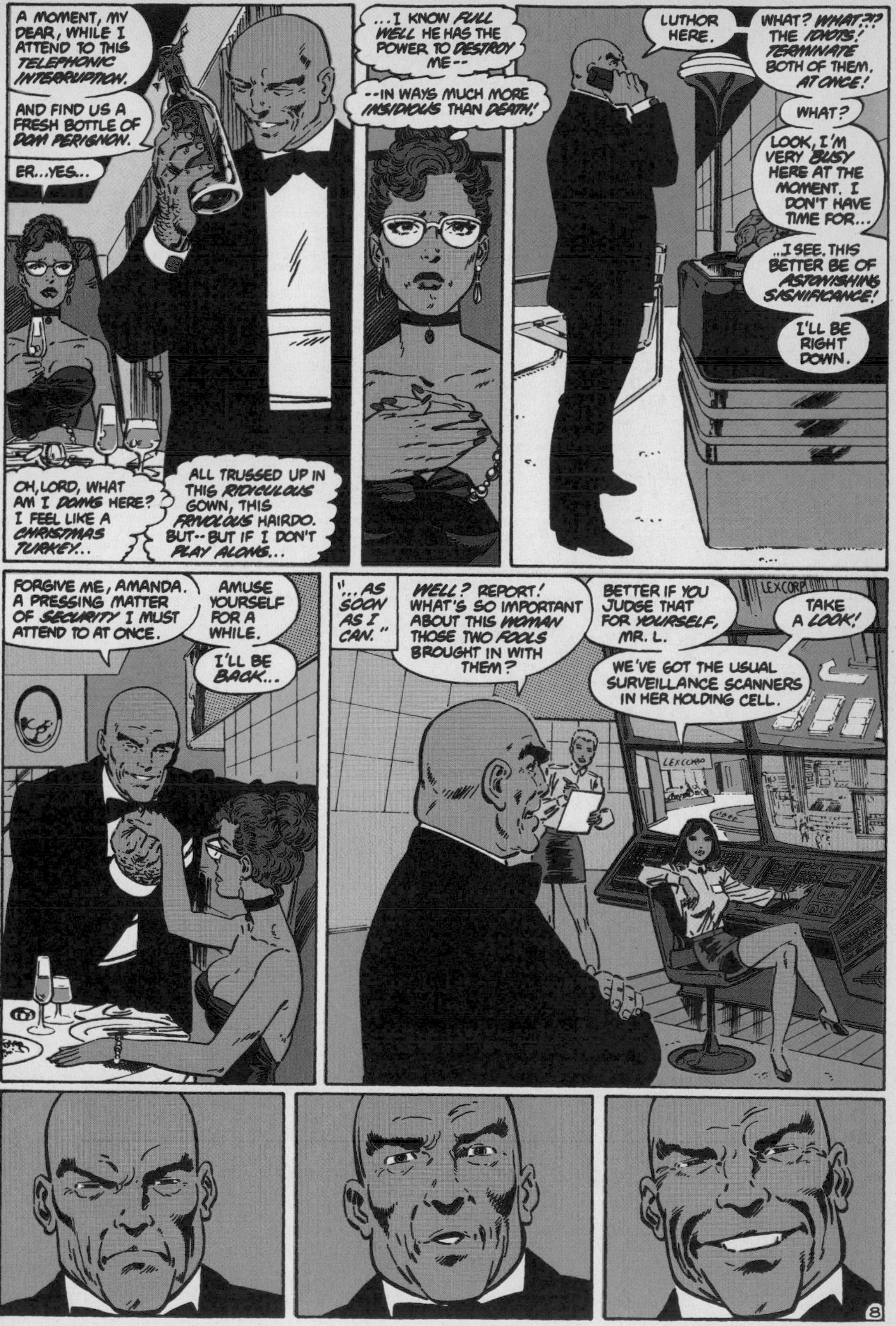
A MOMENT, MY DEAR, WHILE I ATTEND TO THIS TELEPHONIC INTERRUPTION.
AND FIND US A FRESH BOTTLE OF DOM PERIGNON.
ER...YES...
OH, LORD, WHAT AM I DOING HERE? I FEEL LIKE A CHRISTMAS TURKEY...
ALL TRUSSED UP IN THIS RIDICULOUS GOWN, THIS FRIVOLOUS HAIRDO. BUT--BUT IF I DON'T PLAY ALONG...
...I KNOW FULL WELL HE HAS THE POWER TO DESTROY ME--
--IN WAYS MUCH MORE INSIDIOUS THAN DEATH!
LUTHOR HERE.
WHAT? WHAT?!? THE IDIOTS! TERMINATE BOTH OF THEM. AT ONCE!
WHAT?
LOOK, I'M VERY BUSY HERE AT THE MOMENT. I DON'T HAVE TIME FOR...
...I SEE. THIS BETTER BE OF ASTONISHING SIGNIFICANCE!
I'LL BE RIGHT DOWN.
FORGIVE ME, AMANDA. A PRESSING MATTER OF SECURITY I MUST ATTEND TO AT ONCE.
AMUSE YOURSELF FOR A WHILE.
I'LL BE BACK...
"...AS SOON AS I CAN."
WELL? REPORT! WHAT'S SO IMPORTANT ABOUT THIS WOMAN THOSE TWO FOOLS BROUGHT IN WITH THEM?
BETTER IF YOU JUDGE THAT FOR YOURSELF, MR. L.
TAKE A LOOK!
WE'VE GOT THE USUAL SURVEILLANCE SCANNERS IN HER HOLDING CELL.
LEXCORP
LEXCORP
8

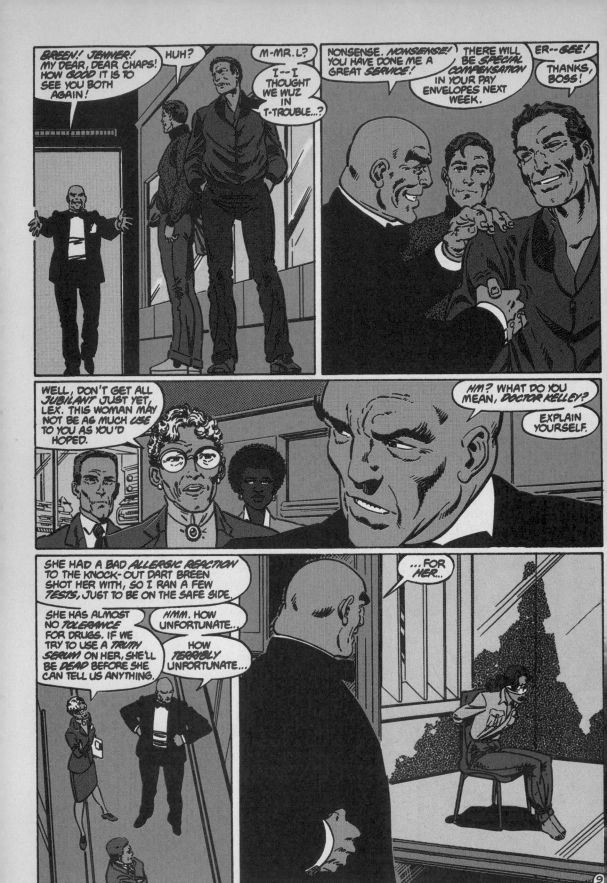

BREEN! JENNER! MY DEAR, DEAR CHAPS! HOW GOOD IT IS TO SEE YOU BOTH AGAIN!

HUH?

M--MR. L?, I--I THOUGHT WE WUZ IN T-TROUBLE...?

NONSENSE. NONSENSE! YOU HAVE DONE ME A GREAT SERVICE!

THERE WILL BE SPECIAL COMPENSATION IN YOUR PAY ENVELOPES NEXT WEEK.

ER--GEE! THANKS, BOSS!

WELL, DON'T GET ALL JUBILANT JUST YET, LEX. THIS WOMAN MAY NOT BE AS MUCH USE TO YOU AS YOU'D HOPED.

HM? WHAT DO YOU MEAN, DOCTOR KELLEY?

EXPLAIN YOURSELF.

SHE HAD A BAD ALLERGIC REACTION TO THE KNOCK-OUT DART BREEN SHOT HER WITH, SO I RAN A FEW TESTS, JUST TO BE ON THE SAFE SIDE.

SHE HAS ALMOST NO TOLERANCE FOR DRUGS. IF WE TRY TO USE A TRUTH SERUM ON HER, SHE'LL BE DEAD BEFORE SHE CAN TELL US ANYTHING.

HMM. HOW UNFORTUNATE...

HOW TERRIBLY UNFORTUNATE...

...FOR HER...

9

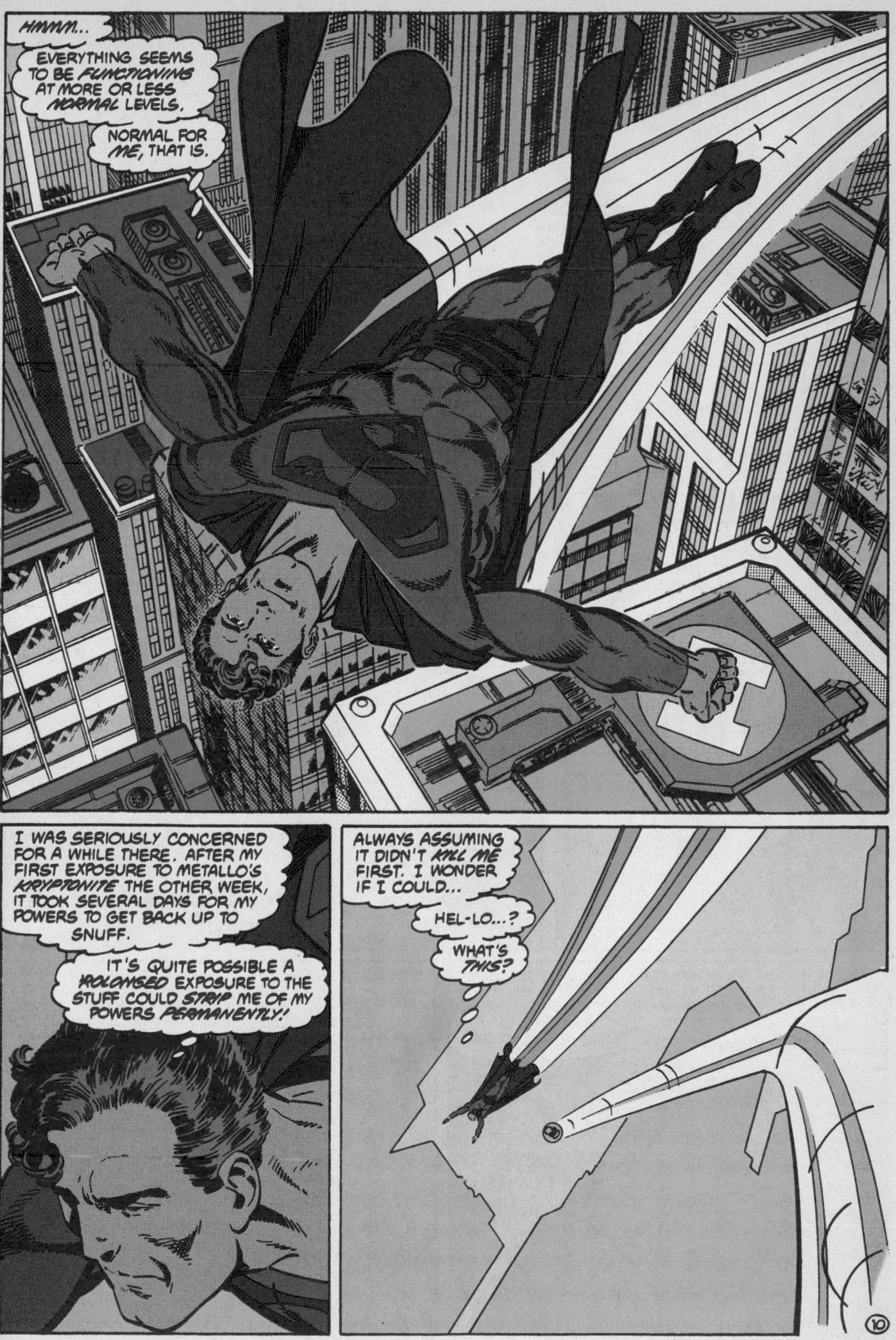
HMMM...
EVERYTHING SEEMS TO BE FUNCTIONING AT MORE OR LESS NORMAL LEVELS.
NORMAL FOR ME, THAT IS.
I WAS SERIOUSLY CONCERNED FOR A WHILE THERE. AFTER MY FIRST EXPOSURE TO METALLO'S KRYPTONITE THE OTHER WEEK, IT TOOK SEVERAL DAYS FOR MY POWERS TO GET BACK UP TO SNUFF.
IT'S QUITE POSSIBLE A PROLONGED EXPOSURE TO THE STUFF COULD STRIP ME OF MY POWERS PERMANENTLY!
ALWAYS ASSUMING IT DIDN'T KILL ME FIRST. I WONDER IF I COULD...
HEL-LO...?
WHAT'S THIS?
10

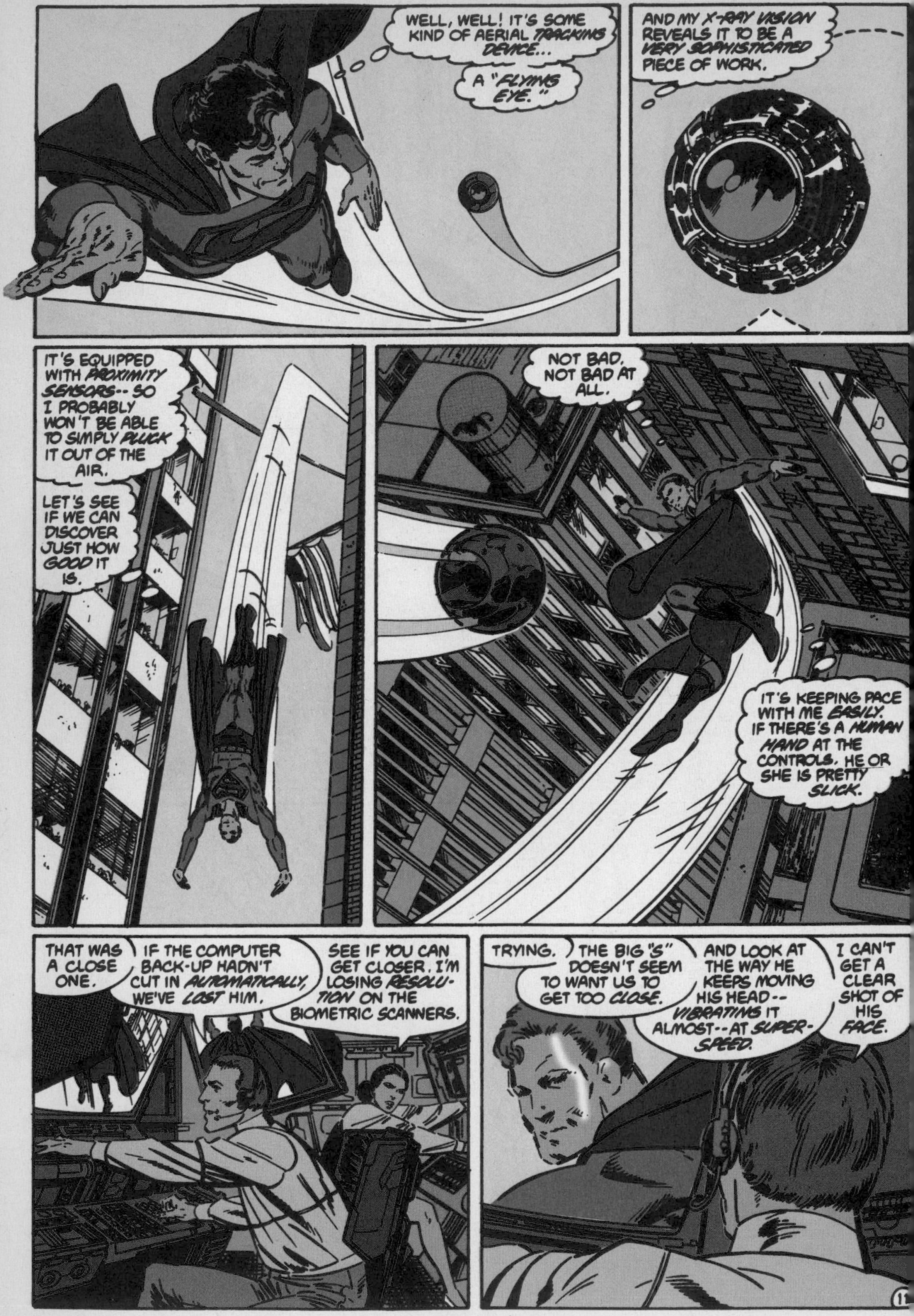
WELL, WELL! IT'S SOME KIND OF AERIAL TRACKING DEVICE...
A "FLYING EYE."
AND MY X-RAY VISION REVEALS IT TO BE A VERY SOPHISTICATED PIECE OF WORK.
IT'S EQUIPPED WITH PROXIMITY SENSORS-- SO I PROBABLY WON'T BE ABLE TO SIMPLY PLUCK IT OUT OF THE AIR.
LET'S SEE IF WE CAN DISCOVER JUST HOW GOOD IT IS.
NOT BAD. NOT BAD AT ALL.
IT'S KEEPING PACE WITH ME EASILY. IF THERE'S A HUMAN HAND AT THE CONTROLS, HE OR SHE IS PRETTY SLICK.
THAT WAS A CLOSE ONE.
IF THE COMPUTER BACK-UP HADN'T CUT IN AUTOMATICALLY, WE'VE LOST HIM.
SEE IF YOU CAN GET CLOSER. I'M LOSING RESOLUTION ON THE BIOMETRIC SCANNERS.
TRYING.
THE BIG "S" DOESN'T SEEM TO WANT US TO GET TOO CLOSE.
AND LOOK AT THE WAY HE KEEPS MOVING HIS HEAD-- VIBRATING IT ALMOST--AT SUPER-SPEED.
I CAN'T GET A CLEAR SHOT OF HIS FACE.

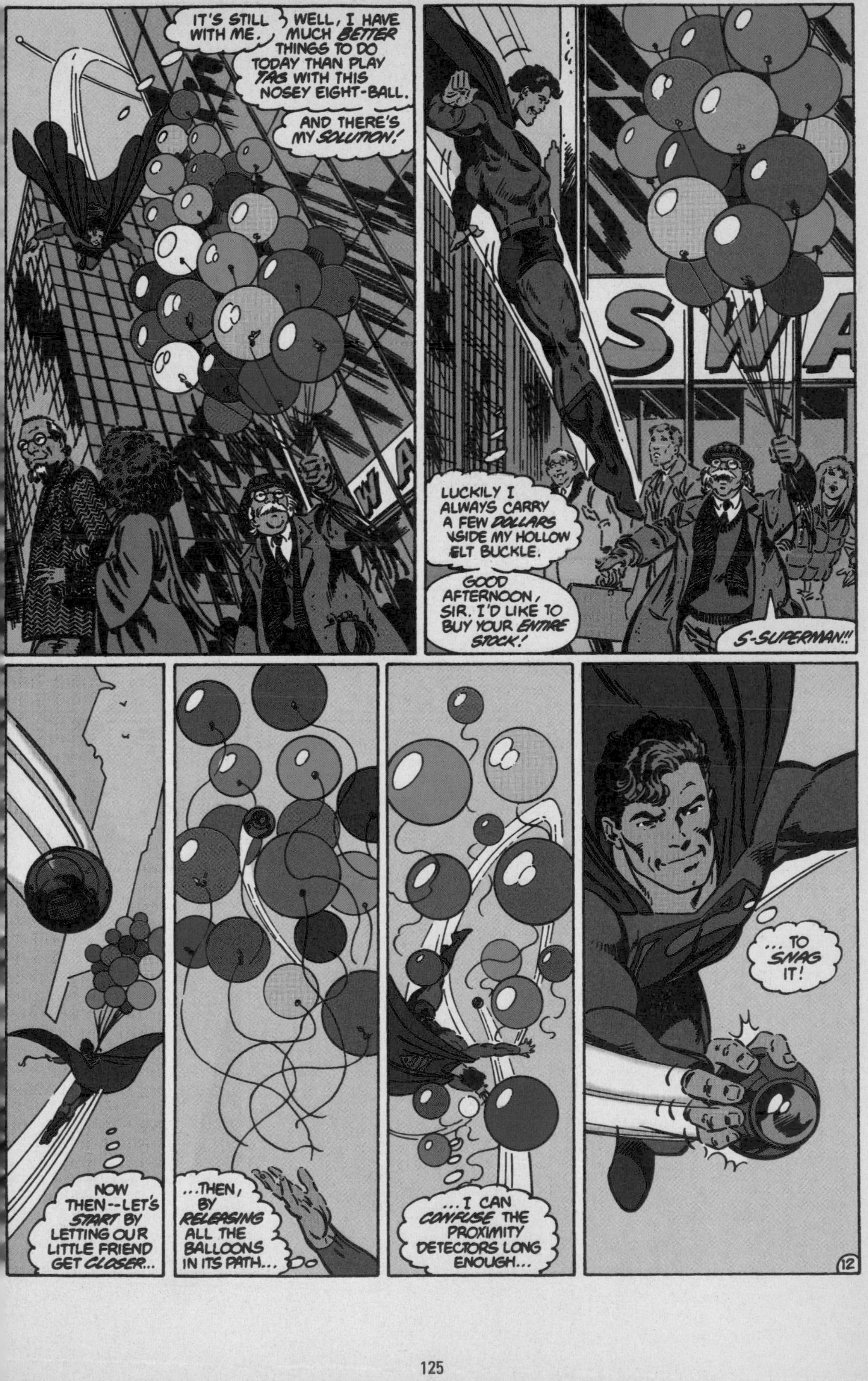

IT'S STILL WITH ME.
WELL, I HAVE MUCH BETTER THINGS TO DO TODAY THAN PLAY TAG WITH THIS NOSEY EIGHT-BALL.
AND THERE'S MY SOLUTION!
LUCKILY I ALWAYS CARRY A FEW DOLLARS INSIDE MY HOLLOW BELT BUCKLE.
GOOD AFTERNOON, SIR. I'D LIKE TO BUY YOUR ENTIRE STOCK!
S-SUPERMAN!!
SWA
NOW THEN--LET'S START BY LETTING OUR LITTLE FRIEND GET CLOSER...
...THEN, BY RELEASING ALL THE BALLOONS IN ITS PATH...
...I CAN CONFUSE THE PROXIMITY DETECTORS LONG ENOUGH...
...TO SNAG IT!
12

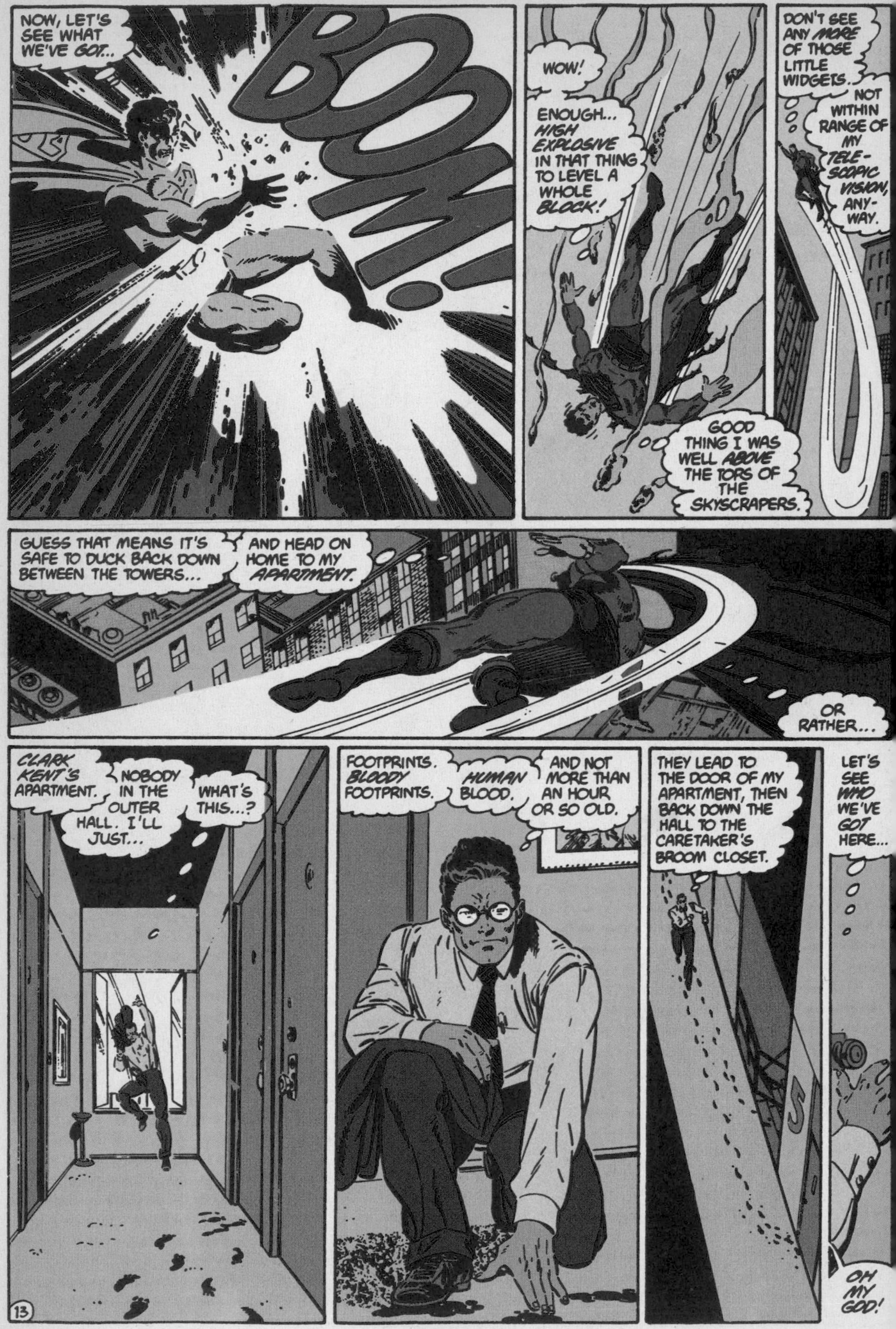
NOW, LET'S SEE WHAT WE'VE GOT...
BOOM!
WOW!
ENOUGH... HIGH EXPLOSIVE IN THAT THING TO LEVEL A WHOLE BLOCK!
GOOD THING I WAS WELL ABOVE THE TOPS OF THE SKYSCRAPERS.
DON'T SEE ANY MORE OF THOSE LITTLE WIDGETS.
NOT WITHIN RANGE OF MY TELE-SCOPIC VISION, ANY-WAY.
GUESS THAT MEANS IT'S SAFE TO DUCK BACK DOWN BETWEEN THE TOWERS...
AND HEAD ON HOME TO MY APARTMENT.
OR RATHER...
CLARK KENT'S APARTMENT.
NOBODY IN THE OUTER HALL. I'LL JUST...
WHAT'S THIS...?
13
FOOTPRINTS. BLOODY FOOTPRINTS.
HUMAN BLOOD.
AND NOT MORE THAN AN HOUR OR SO OLD.
THEY LEAD TO THE DOOR OF MY APARTMENT, THEN BACK DOWN THE HALL TO THE CARETAKER'S BROOM CLOSET.
LET'S SEE WHO WE'VE GOT HERE...
OH MY GOD!

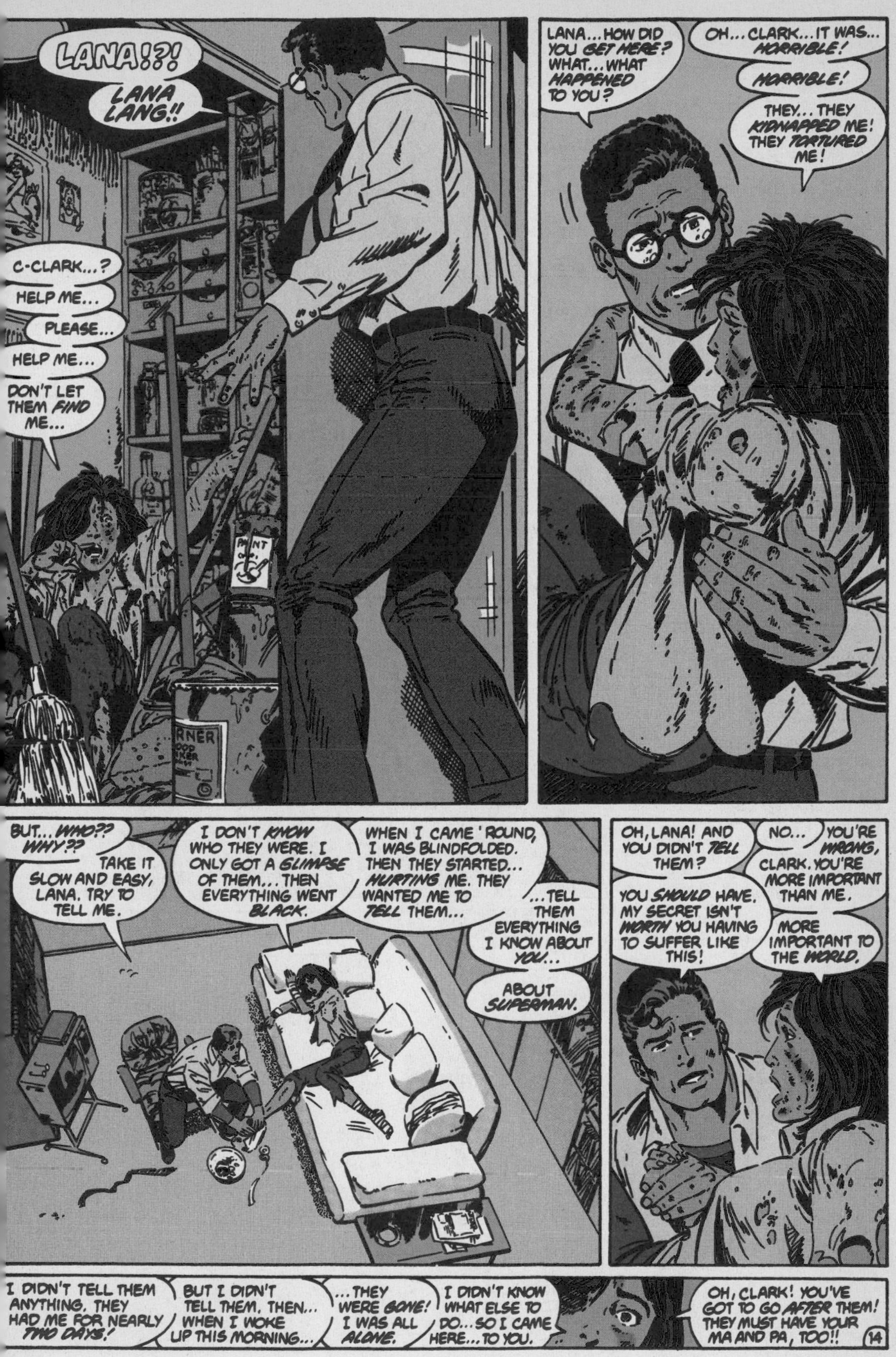
LANA!?!
LANA LANG!!
C-CLARK...?
HELP ME...
PLEASE...
HELP ME...
DON'T LET THEM FIND ME...
PAINT
LANA...HOW DID YOU GET HERE? WHAT...WHAT HAPPENED TO YOU?
OH...CLARK...IT WAS... HORRIBLE!
HORRIBLE!
THEY...THEY KIDNAPPED ME! THEY TORTURED ME!
BUT...WHO?? WHY??
TAKE IT SLOW AND EASY, LANA. TRY TO TELL ME.
I DON'T KNOW WHO THEY WERE. I ONLY GOT A GLIMPSE OF THEM...THEN EVERYTHING WENT BLACK.
WHEN I CAME 'ROUND, I WAS BLINDFOLDED. THEN THEY STARTED... HURTING ME. THEY WANTED ME TO TELL THEM...
...TELL THEM EVERYTHING I KNOW ABOUT YOU...
ABOUT SUPERMAN.
OH, LANA! AND YOU DIDN'T TELL THEM?
YOU SHOULD HAVE. MY SECRET ISN'T WORTH YOU HAVING TO SUFFER LIKE THIS!
NO...
YOU'RE WRONG, CLARK. YOU'RE MORE IMPORTANT THAN ME.
MORE IMPORTANT TO THE WORLD.
I DIDN'T TELL THEM ANYTHING. THEY HAD ME FOR NEARLY TWO DAYS!
BUT I DIDN'T TELL THEM. THEN... WHEN I WOKE UP THIS MORNING...
...THEY WERE GONE! I WAS ALL ALONE.
I DIDN'T KNOW WHAT ELSE TO DO...SO I CAME HERE...TO YOU.
OH, CLARK! YOU'VE GOT TO GO AFTER THEM! THEY MUST HAVE YOUR MA AND PA, TOO!!
14

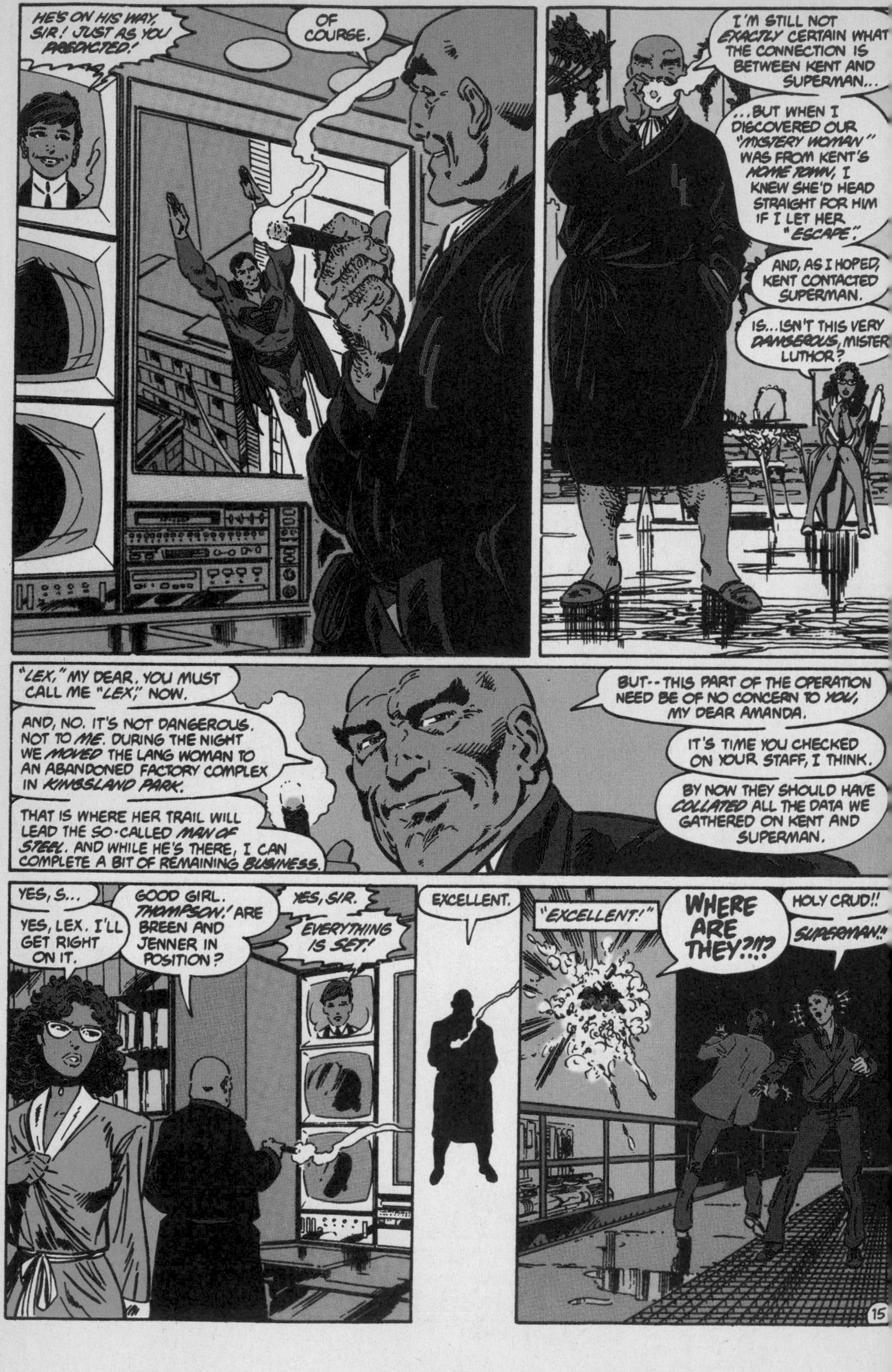
HE'S ON HIS WAY, SIR! JUST AS YOU PREDICTED!
OF COURSE.
I'M STILL NOT EXACTLY CERTAIN WHAT THE CONNECTION IS BETWEEN KENT AND SUPERMAN...
...BUT WHEN I DISCOVERED OUR "MYSTERY WOMAN" WAS FROM KENT'S HOME TOWN, I KNEW SHE'D HEAD STRAIGHT FOR HIM IF I LET HER "ESCAPE."
AND, AS I HOPED, KENT CONTACTED SUPERMAN.
IS...ISN'T THIS VERY DANGEROUS, MISTER LUTHOR?
"LEX," MY DEAR. YOU MUST CALL ME "LEX," NOW.
AND, NO. IT'S NOT DANGEROUS. NOT TO ME. DURING THE NIGHT WE MOVED THE LANG WOMAN TO AN ABANDONED FACTORY COMPLEX IN KINGSLAND PARK.
THAT IS WHERE HER TRAIL WILL LEAD THE SO-CALLED MAN OF STEEL. AND WHILE HE'S THERE, I CAN COMPLETE A BIT OF REMAINING BUSINESS.
BUT--THIS PART OF THE OPERATION NEED BE OF NO CONCERN TO YOU, MY DEAR AMANDA.
IT'S TIME YOU CHECKED ON YOUR STAFF, I THINK.
BY NOW THEY SHOULD HAVE COLLATED ALL THE DATA WE GATHERED ON KENT AND SUPERMAN.
YES, S...
YES, LEX. I'LL GET RIGHT ON IT.
GOOD GIRL. THOMPSON! ARE BREEN AND JENNER IN POSITION?
YES, SIR.
EVERYTHING IS SET!
EXCELLENT.
"EXCELLENT!"
WHERE ARE THEY?!!?
HOLY CRUD!!
SUPERMAN!!
15

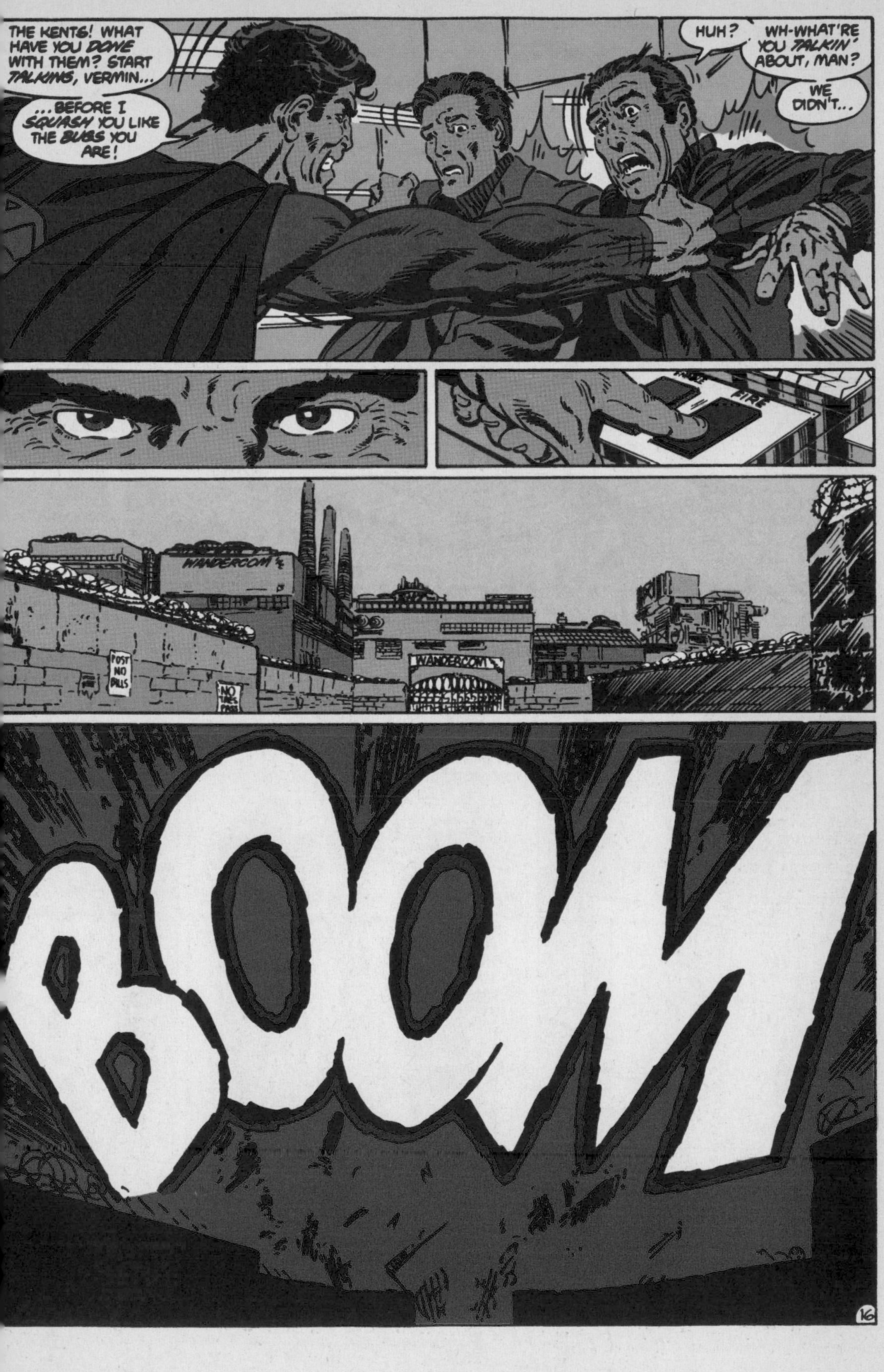
THE KENTS! WHAT HAVE YOU DONE WITH THEM? START TALKING, VERMIN...
...BEFORE I SQUASH YOU LIKE THE BUGS YOU ARE!
HUH?
WH-WHAT'RE YOU TALKIN' ABOUT, MAN?
WE DIDN'T...
FIRE
WANDERCOM
POST NO BILLS
WANDERCOM
BOOM
16

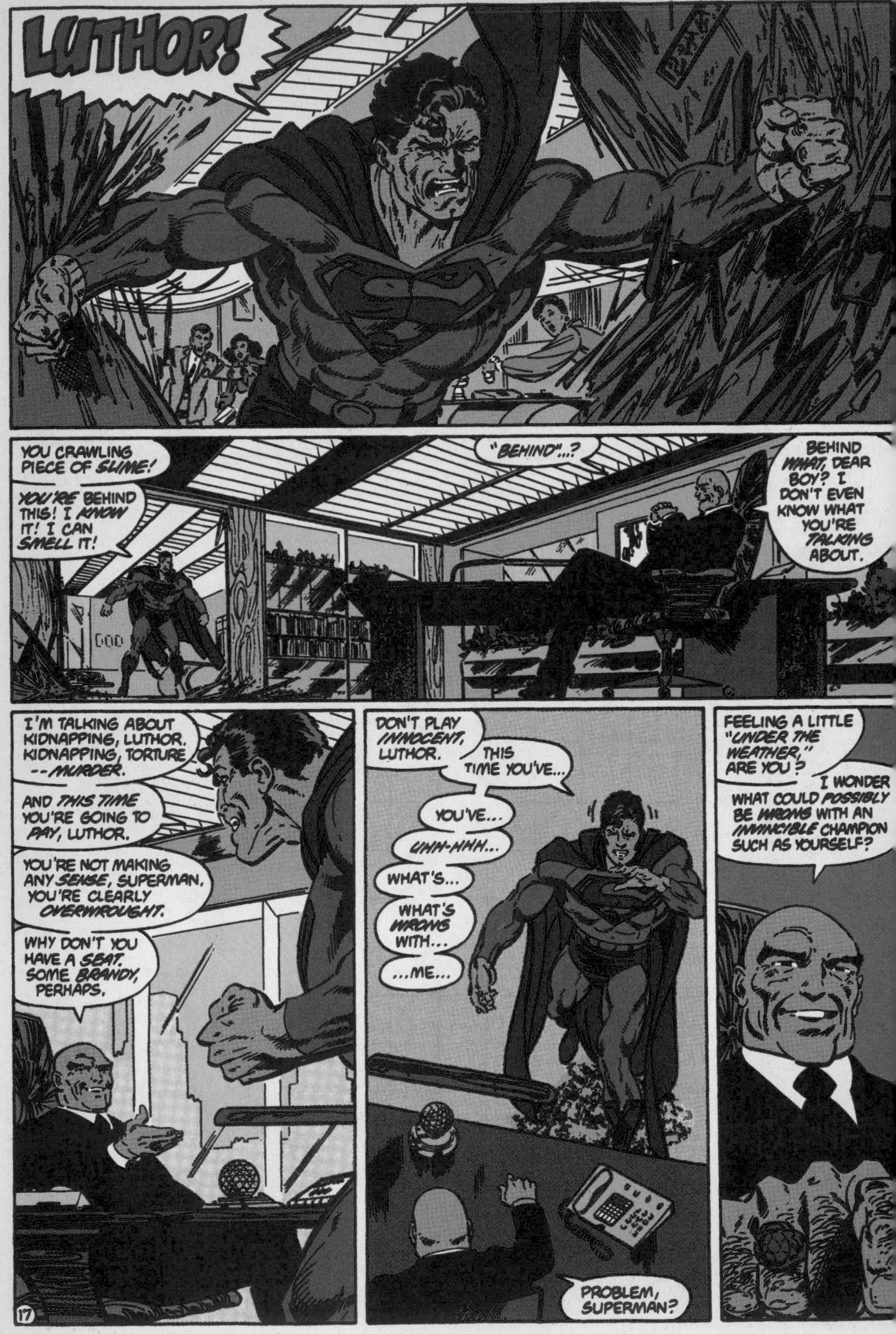
LUTHOR!
YOU CRAWLING PIECE OF SLIME!
YOU'RE BEHIND THIS! I KNOW IT! I CAN SMELL IT!
"BEHIND"...?
BEHIND WHAT, DEAR BOY? I DON'T EVEN KNOW WHAT YOU'RE TALKING ABOUT.
I'M TALKING ABOUT KIDNAPPING, LUTHOR. KIDNAPPING, TORTURE --MURDER.
AND THIS TIME YOU'RE GOING TO PAY, LUTHOR.
YOU'RE NOT MAKING ANY SENSE, SUPERMAN. YOU'RE CLEARLY OVERWROUGHT.
WHY DON'T YOU HAVE A SEAT. SOME BRANDY, PERHAPS.
17
DON'T PLAY INNOCENT, LUTHOR.
THIS TIME YOU'VE...
YOU'VE...
UHH-HHH...
WHAT'S...
WHAT'S WRONG WITH...
...ME...
PROBLEM, SUPERMAN?
FEELING A LITTLE "UNDER THE WEATHER," ARE YOU?
I WONDER WHAT COULD POSSIBLY BE WRONG WITH AN INVINCIBLE CHAMPION SUCH AS YOURSELF?

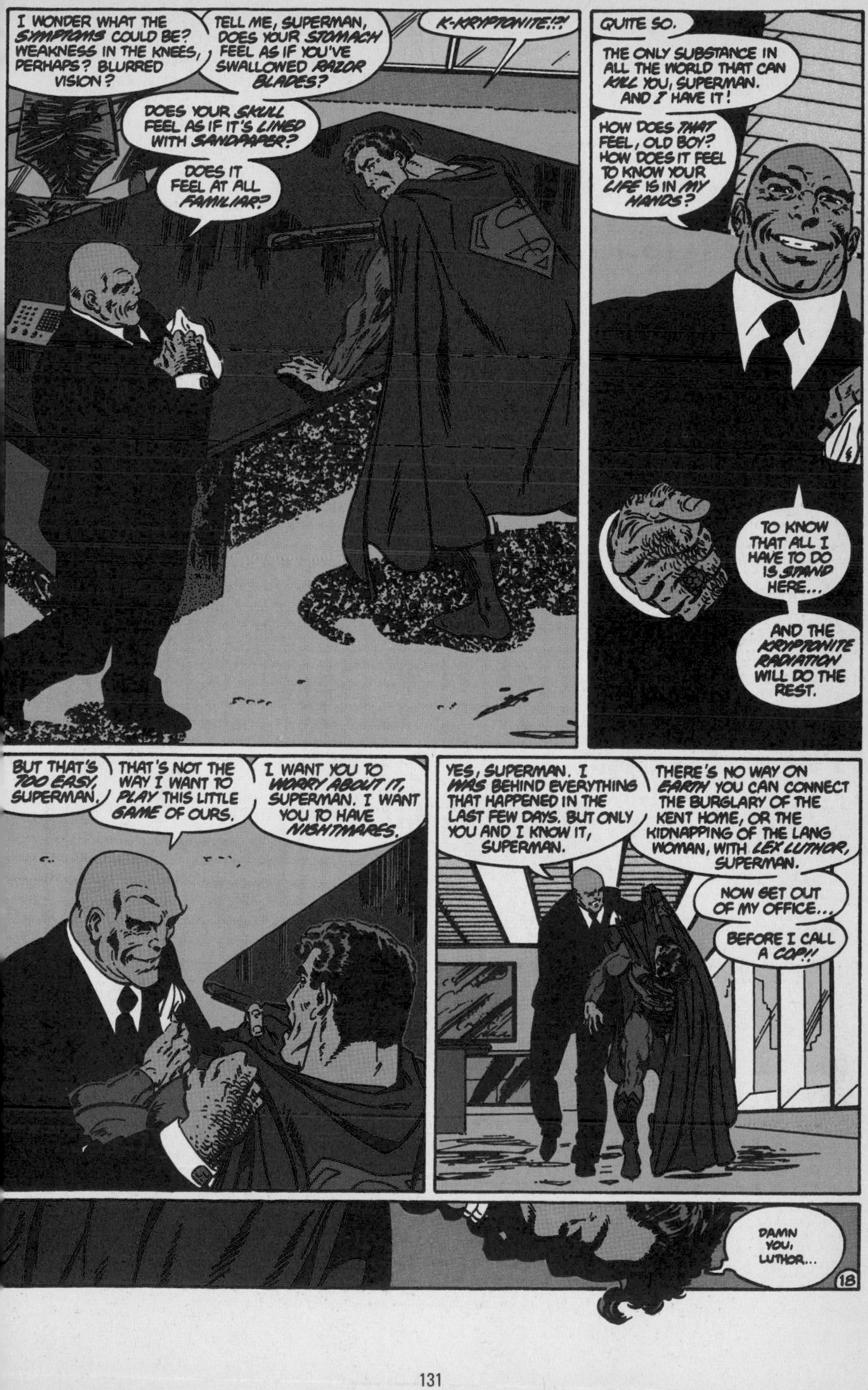
I WONDER WHAT THE SYMPTOMS COULD BE? WEAKNESS IN THE KNEES, PERHAPS? BLURRED VISION?
TELL ME, SUPERMAN, DOES YOUR STOMACH FEEL AS IF YOU'VE SWALLOWED RAZOR BLADES?
K-KRYPTONITE!?!
DOES YOUR SKULL FEEL AS IF IT'S LINED WITH SANDPAPER?
DOES IT FEEL AT ALL FAMILIAR?
QUITE SO.
THE ONLY SUBSTANCE IN ALL THE WORLD THAT CAN KILL YOU, SUPERMAN. AND I HAVE IT!
HOW DOES THAT FEEL, OLD BOY? HOW DOES IT FEEL TO KNOW YOUR LIFE IS IN MY HANDS?
TO KNOW THAT ALL I HAVE TO DO IS STAND HERE...
AND THE KRYPTONITE RADIATION WILL DO THE REST.
BUT THAT'S TOO EASY, SUPERMAN.
THAT'S NOT THE WAY I WANT TO PLAY THIS LITTLE GAME OF OURS.
I WANT YOU TO WORRY ABOUT IT, SUPERMAN. I WANT YOU TO HAVE NIGHTMARES.
YES, SUPERMAN. I WAS BEHIND EVERYTHING THAT HAPPENED IN THE LAST FEW DAYS. BUT ONLY YOU AND I KNOW IT, SUPERMAN.
THERE'S NO WAY ON EARTH YOU CAN CONNECT THE BURGLARY OF THE KENT HOME, OR THE KIDNAPPING OF THE LANG WOMAN, WITH LEX LUTHOR, SUPERMAN.
NOW GET OUT OF MY OFFICE...
BEFORE I CALL A COP!!
DAMN YOU, LUTHOR...
18

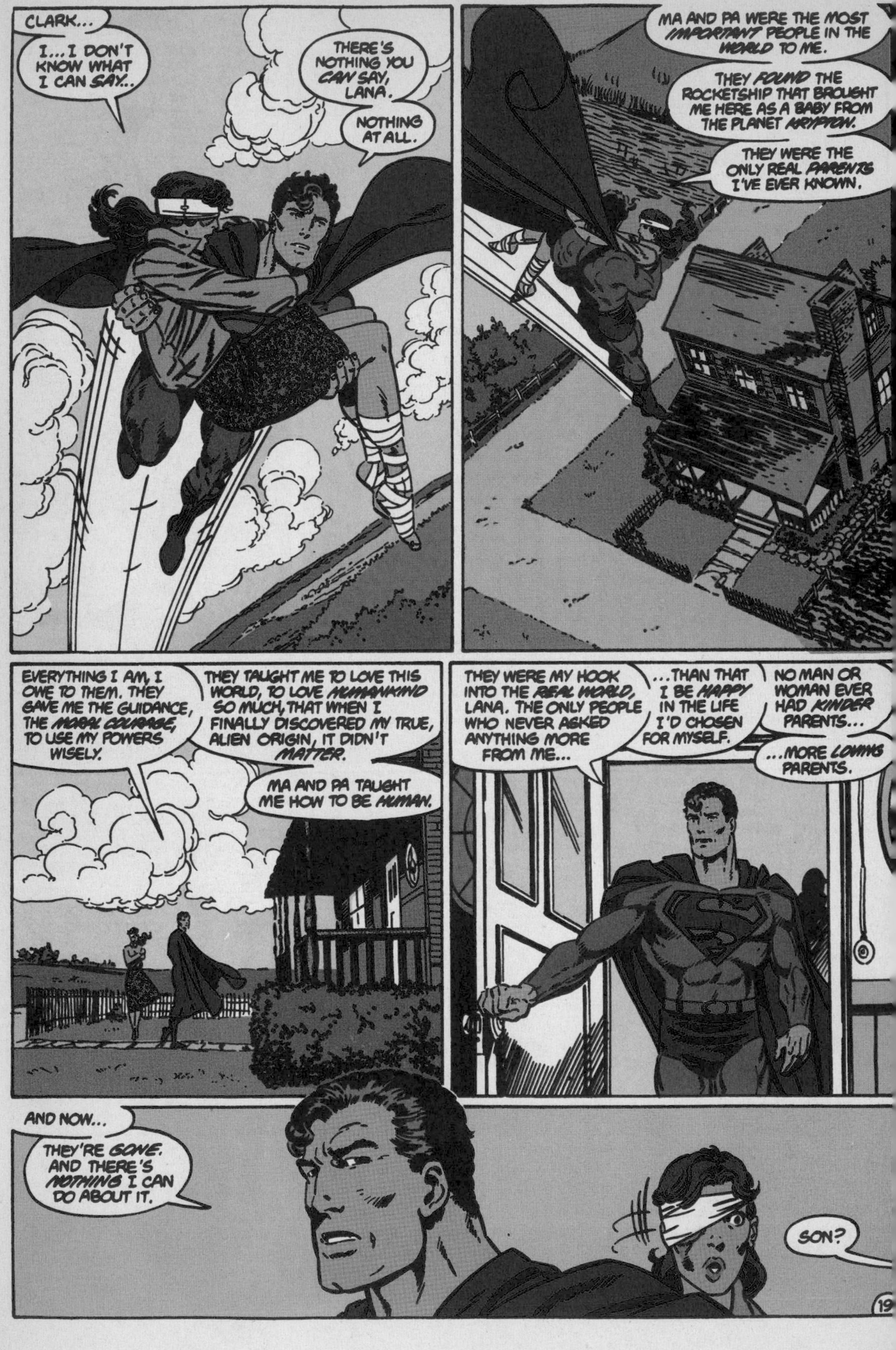
CLARK...
I...I DON'T KNOW WHAT I CAN SAY...
THERE'S NOTHING YOU CAN SAY, LANA.
NOTHING AT ALL.
MA AND PA WERE THE MOST IMPORTANT PEOPLE IN THE WORLD TO ME.
THEY FOUND THE ROCKETSHIP THAT BROUGHT ME HERE AS A BABY FROM THE PLANET KRYPTON.
THEY WERE THE ONLY REAL PARENTS I'VE EVER KNOWN.
EVERYTHING I AM, I OWE TO THEM. THEY GAVE ME THE GUIDANCE, THE MORAL COURAGE, TO USE MY POWERS WISELY.
THEY TAUGHT ME TO LOVE THIS WORLD, TO LOVE HUMANKIND SO MUCH, THAT WHEN I FINALLY DISCOVERED MY TRUE, ALIEN ORIGIN, IT DIDN'T MATTER.
MA AND PA TAUGHT ME HOW TO BE HUMAN.
THEY WERE MY HOOK INTO THE REAL WORLD, LANA. THE ONLY PEOPLE WHO NEVER ASKED ANYTHING MORE FROM ME...
...THAN THAT I BE HAPPY IN THE LIFE I'D CHOSEN FOR MYSELF.
NO MAN OR WOMAN EVER HAD KINDER PARENTS...
...MORE LOVING PARENTS.
AND NOW...
THEY'RE GONE. AND THERE'S NOTHING I CAN DO ABOUT IT.
SON?
19

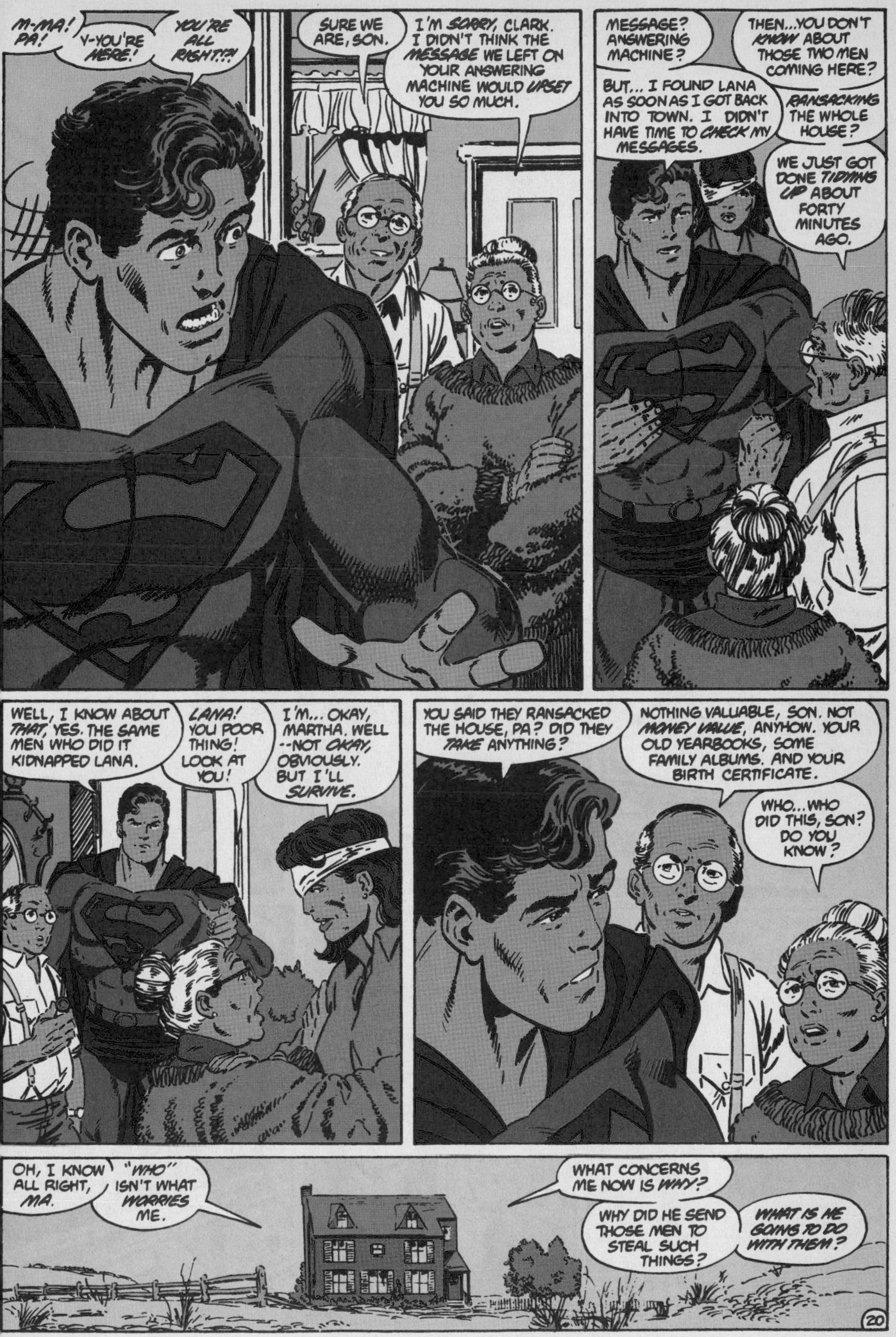
M-MA! PA!
Y-YOU'RE HERE!
YOU'RE ALL RIGHT!?!
SURE WE ARE, SON.
I'M SORRY, CLARK. I DIDN'T THINK THE MESSAGE WE LEFT ON YOUR ANSWERING MACHINE WOULD UPSET YOU SO MUCH.
MESSAGE? ANSWERING MACHINE?
BUT... I FOUND LANA AS SOON AS I GOT BACK INTO TOWN. I DIDN'T HAVE TIME TO CHECK MY MESSAGES.
THEN...YOU DON'T KNOW ABOUT THOSE TWO MEN COMING HERE?
RANSACKING THE WHOLE HOUSE?
WE JUST GOT DONE TIDYING UP ABOUT FORTY MINUTES AGO.
WELL, I KNOW ABOUT THAT, YES. THE SAME MEN WHO DID IT KIDNAPPED LANA.
LANA! YOU POOR THING! LOOK AT YOU!
I'M... OKAY, MARTHA. WELL --NOT OKAY, OBVIOUSLY. BUT I'LL SURVIVE.
YOU SAID THEY RANSACKED THE HOUSE, PA? DID THEY TAKE ANYTHING?
NOTHING VALUABLE, SON. NOT MONEY VALUE, ANYHOW. YOUR OLD YEARBOOKS, SOME FAMILY ALBUMS. AND YOUR BIRTH CERTIFICATE.
WHO...WHO DID THIS, SON? DO YOU KNOW?
OH, I KNOW ALL RIGHT, MA.
"WHO" ISN'T WHAT WORRIES ME.
WHAT CONCERNS ME NOW IS WHY?
WHY DID HE SEND THOSE MEN TO STEAL SUCH THINGS?
WHAT IS HE GOING TO DO WITH THEM?
20

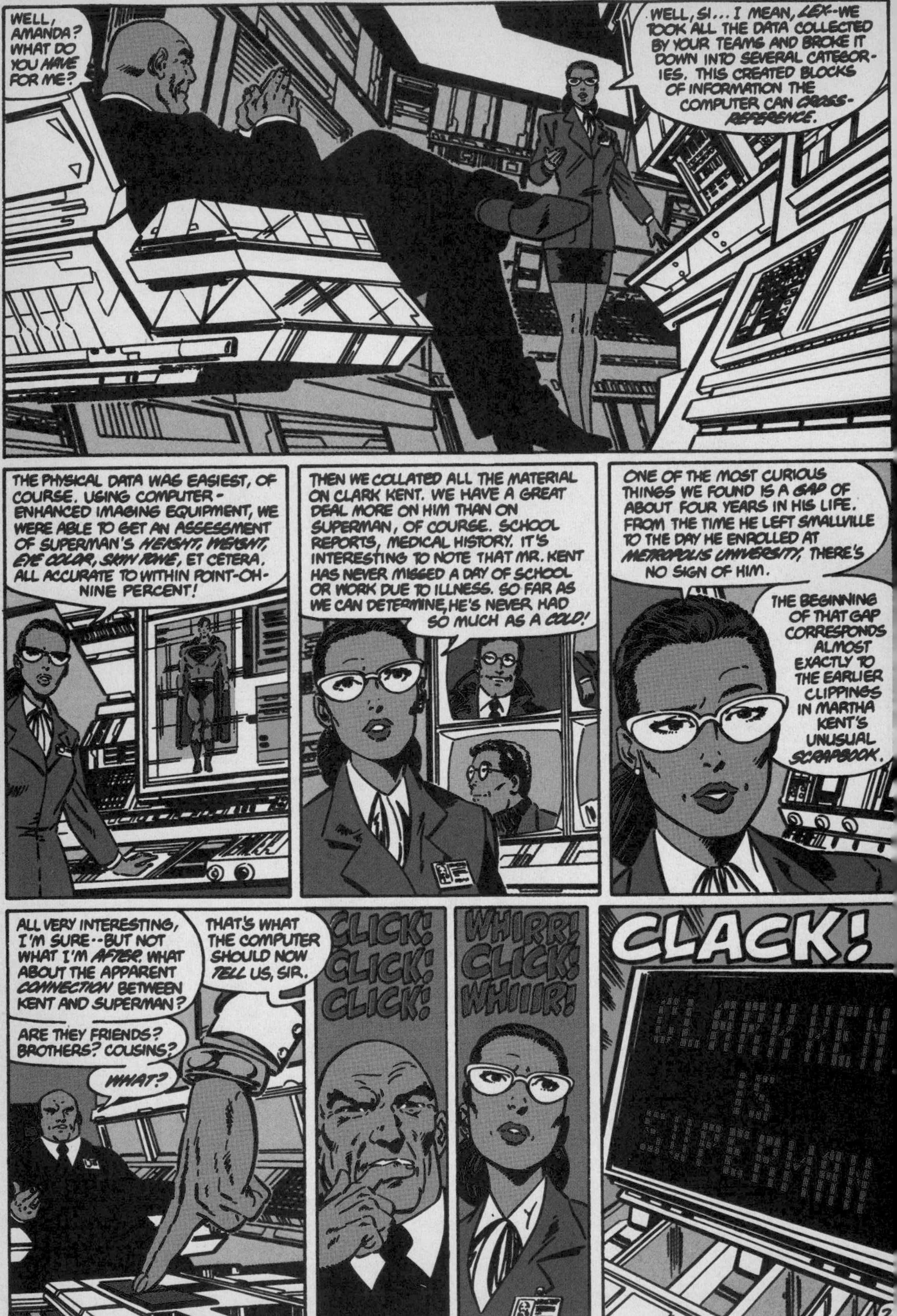
WELL, AMANDA? WHAT DO YOU HAVE FOR ME?
WELL, SI... I MEAN, LEX--WE TOOK ALL THE DATA COLLECTED BY YOUR TEAMS AND BROKE IT DOWN INTO SEVERAL CATEGORIES. THIS CREATED BLOCKS OF INFORMATION THE COMPUTER CAN CROSS-REFERENCE.
THE PHYSICAL DATA WAS EASIEST, OF COURSE. USING COMPUTER-ENHANCED IMAGING EQUIPMENT, WE WERE ABLE TO GET AN ASSESSMENT OF SUPERMAN'S HEIGHT, WEIGHT, EYE COLOR, SKIN TONE, ET CETERA. ALL ACCURATE TO WITHIN POINT-OH-NINE PERCENT!
THEN WE COLLATED ALL THE MATERIAL ON CLARK KENT. WE HAVE A GREAT DEAL MORE ON HIM THAN ON SUPERMAN, OF COURSE. SCHOOL REPORTS, MEDICAL HISTORY. IT'S INTERESTING TO NOTE THAT MR. KENT HAS NEVER MISSED A DAY OF SCHOOL OR WORK DUE TO ILLNESS. SO FAR AS WE CAN DETERMINE, HE'S NEVER HAD SO MUCH AS A COLD!
ONE OF THE MOST CURIOUS THINGS WE FOUND IS A GAP OF ABOUT FOUR YEARS IN HIS LIFE. FROM THE TIME HE LEFT SMALLVILLE TO THE DAY HE ENROLLED AT METROPOLIS UNIVERSITY, THERE'S NO SIGN OF HIM.
THE BEGINNING OF THAT GAP CORRESPONDS ALMOST EXACTLY TO THE EARLIER CLIPPINGS IN MARTHA KENT'S UNUSUAL SCRAPBOOK.
ALL VERY INTERESTING, I'M SURE--BUT NOT WHAT I'M AFTER. WHAT ABOUT THE APPARENT CONNECTION BETWEEN KENT AND SUPERMAN?
ARE THEY FRIENDS? BROTHERS? COUSINS?
THAT'S WHAT THE COMPUTER SHOULD NOW TELL US, SIR.
WHAT?
CLICK! CLICK! CLICK!
WHIRR! CLICK! WHIIIR!
CLACK!
CLARK KENT IS SUPERMAN
2

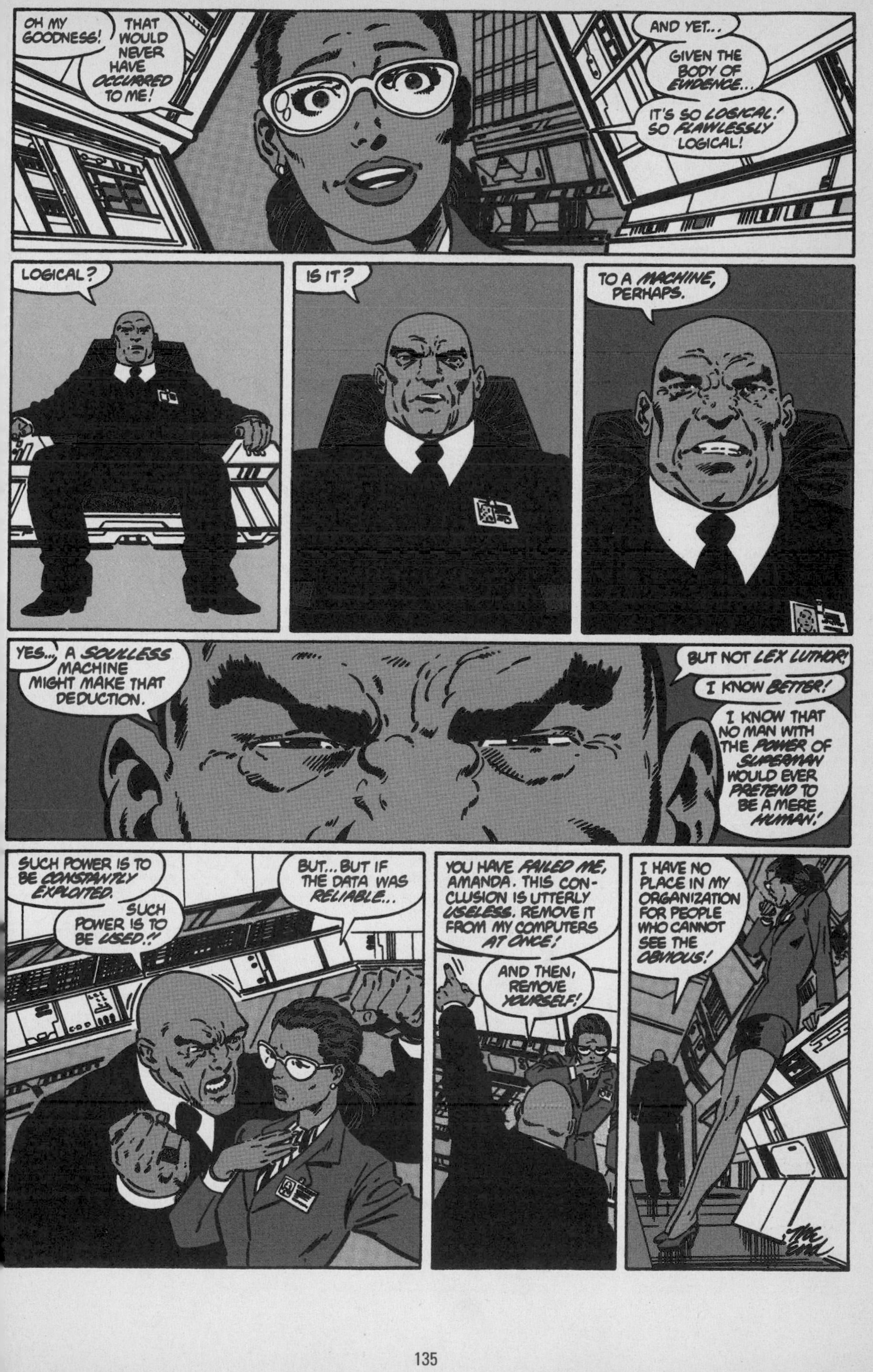
OH MY GOODNESS!
THAT WOULD NEVER HAVE OCCURRED TO ME!
AND YET...
GIVEN THE BODY OF EVIDENCE...
IT'S SO LOGICAL! SO FLAWLESSLY LOGICAL!
LOGICAL?
IS IT?
TO A MACHINE, PERHAPS.
YES... A SOULLESS MACHINE MIGHT MAKE THAT DEDUCTION.
BUT NOT LEX LUTHOR!
I KNOW BETTER!
I KNOW THAT NO MAN WITH THE POWER OF SUPERMAN WOULD EVER PRETEND TO BE A MERE HUMAN!
SUCH POWER IS TO BE CONSTANTLY EXPLOITED.
SUCH POWER IS TO BE USED!!
BUT... BUT IF THE DATA WAS RELIABLE...
YOU HAVE FAILED ME, AMANDA. THIS CONCLUSION IS UTTERLY USELESS. REMOVE IT FROM MY COMPUTERS AT ONCE!
AND THEN, REMOVE YOURSELF!
I HAVE NO PLACE IN MY ORGANIZATION FOR PEOPLE WHO CANNOT SEE THE OBVIOUS!
THE END

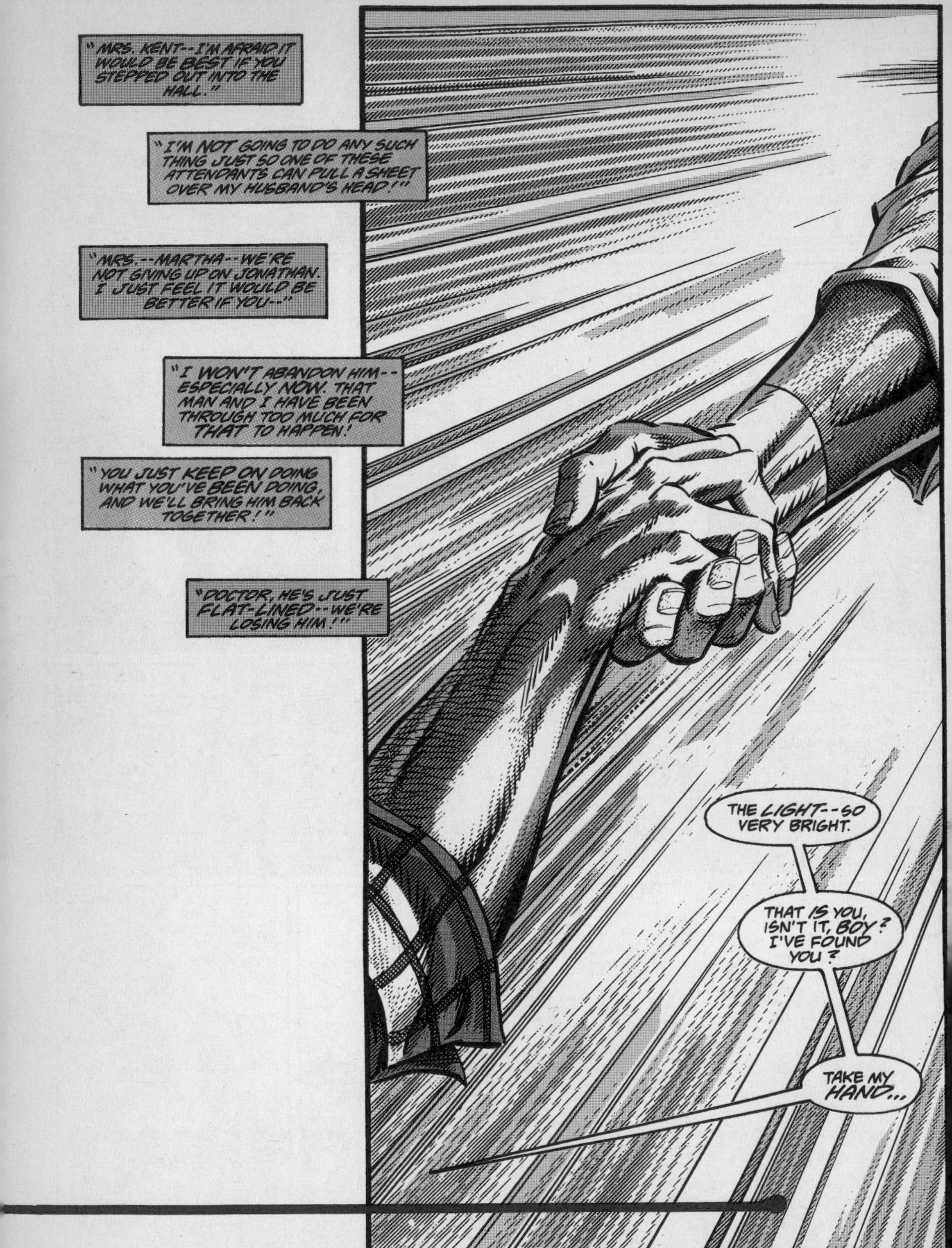
"MRS. KENT--I'M AFRAID IT WOULD BE BEST IF YOU STEPPED OUT INTO THE HALL."
"I'M NOT GOING TO DO ANY SUCH THING JUST SO ONE OF THESE ATTENDANTS CAN PULL A SHEET OVER MY HUSBAND'S HEAD!"
"MRS.--MARTHA--WE'RE NOT GIVING UP ON JONATHAN. I JUST FEEL IT WOULD BE BETTER IF YOU--"
"I WON'T ABANDON HIM--ESPECIALLY NOW. THAT MAN AND I HAVE BEEN THROUGH TOO MUCH FOR THAT TO HAPPEN!
"YOU JUST KEEP ON DOING WHAT YOU'VE BEEN DOING, AND WE'LL BRING HIM BACK TOGETHER!"
"DOCTOR, HE'S JUST FLAT-LINED--WE'RE LOSING HIM!"
THE LIGHT--SO VERY BRIGHT.
THAT IS YOU, ISN'T IT, BOY? I'VE FOUND YOU?
TAKE MY HAND...

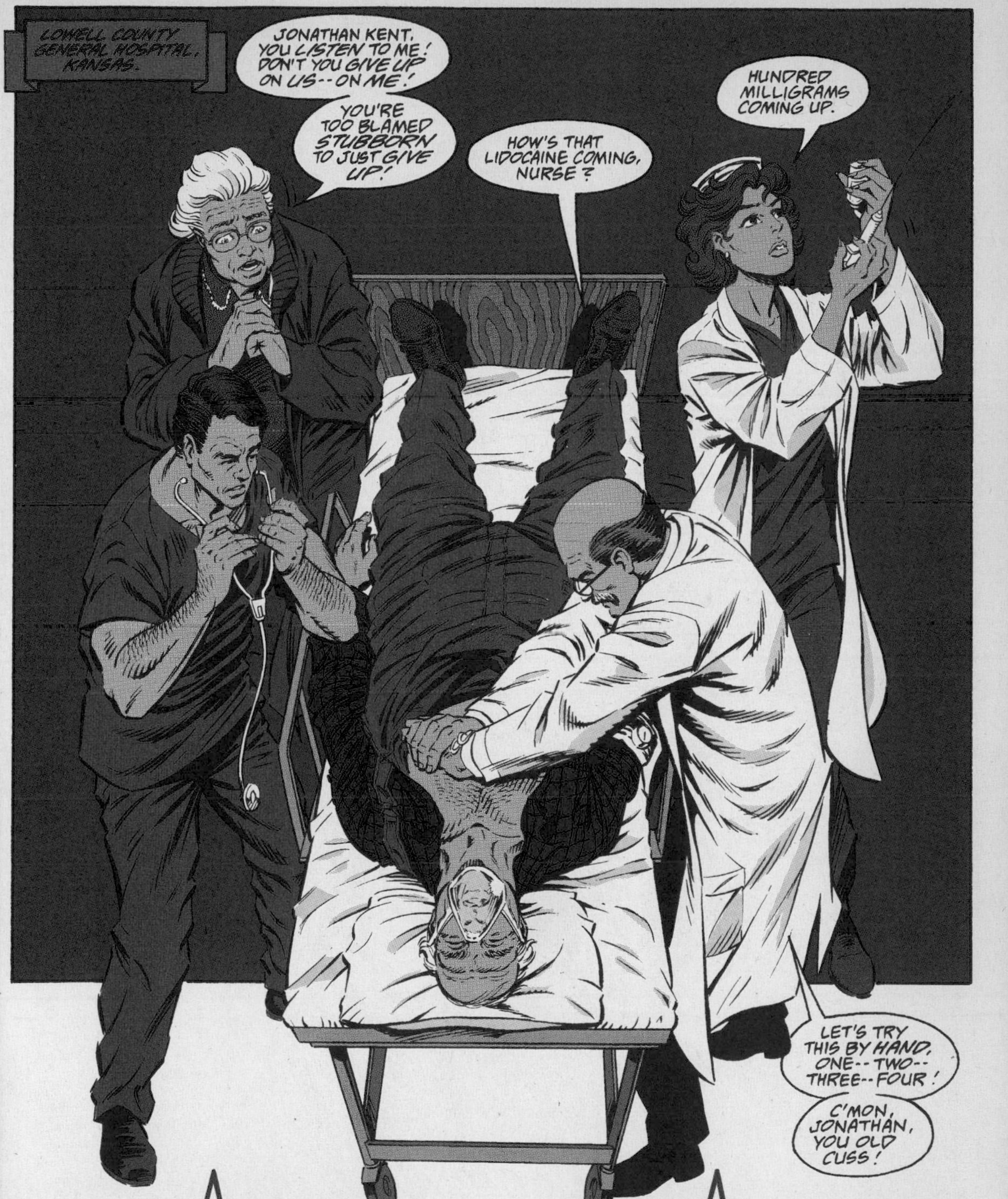
LOWELL COUNTY GENERAL HOSPITAL, KANSAS.
JONATHAN KENT, YOU LISTEN TO ME! DON'T YOU GIVE UP ON US--ON ME!
YOU'RE TOO BLAMED STUBBORN TO JUST GIVE UP!
HOW'S THAT LIDOCAINE COMING, NURSE?
HUNDRED MILLIGRAMS COMING UP.
LET'S TRY THIS BY HAND, ONE--TWO--THREE--FOUR!
C'MON, JONATHAN, YOU OLD CUSS!

LIFE AFTER DEATH!

TOM GRUMMETT - PENCILS * DOUG HAZLEWOOD - INKS & TONES * JERRY ORDWAY - STORY
ALBERT DEGUZMAN - LETTERER * GLENN WHITMORE - COLORIST * JENNIFER FRANK - ASSISTANT EDITOR
MIKE CARLIN - EDITOR
SUPERMAN created by JERRY SIEGEL and JOE SHUSTER

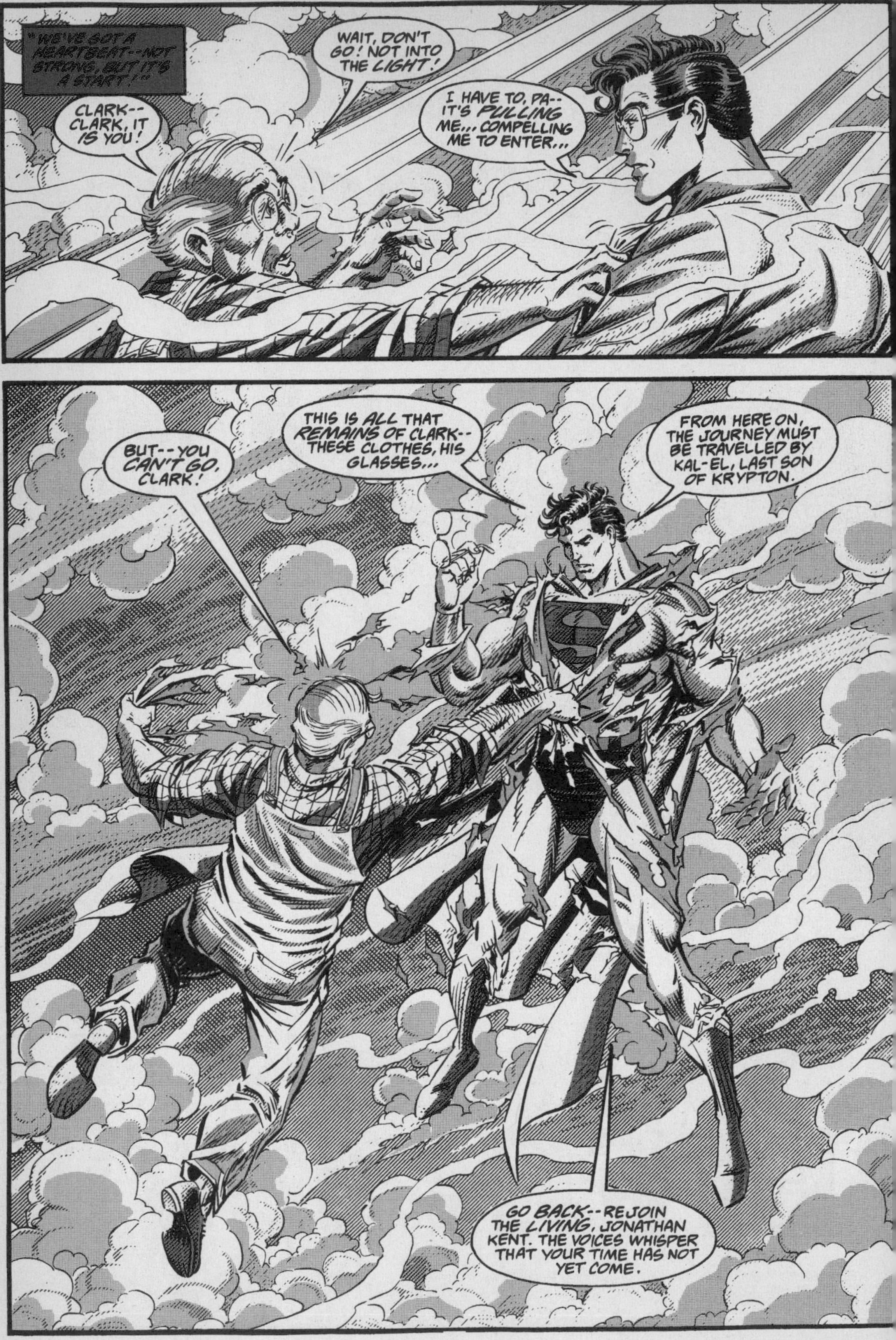
"WE'VE GOT A HEARTBEAT--NOT STRONG, BUT IT'S A START!"
CLARK--CLARK, IT IS YOU!
WAIT, DON'T GO! NOT INTO THE LIGHT!
I HAVE TO, PA--IT'S PULLING ME... COMPELLING ME TO ENTER...
BUT--YOU CAN'T GO, CLARK!
THIS IS ALL THAT REMAINS OF CLARK--THESE CLOTHES, HIS GLASSES...
FROM HERE ON, THE JOURNEY MUST BE TRAVELLED BY KAL-EL, LAST SON OF KRYPTON.
GO BACK--REJOIN THE LIVING, JONATHAN KENT. THE VOICES WHISPER THAT YOUR TIME HAS NOT YET COME.

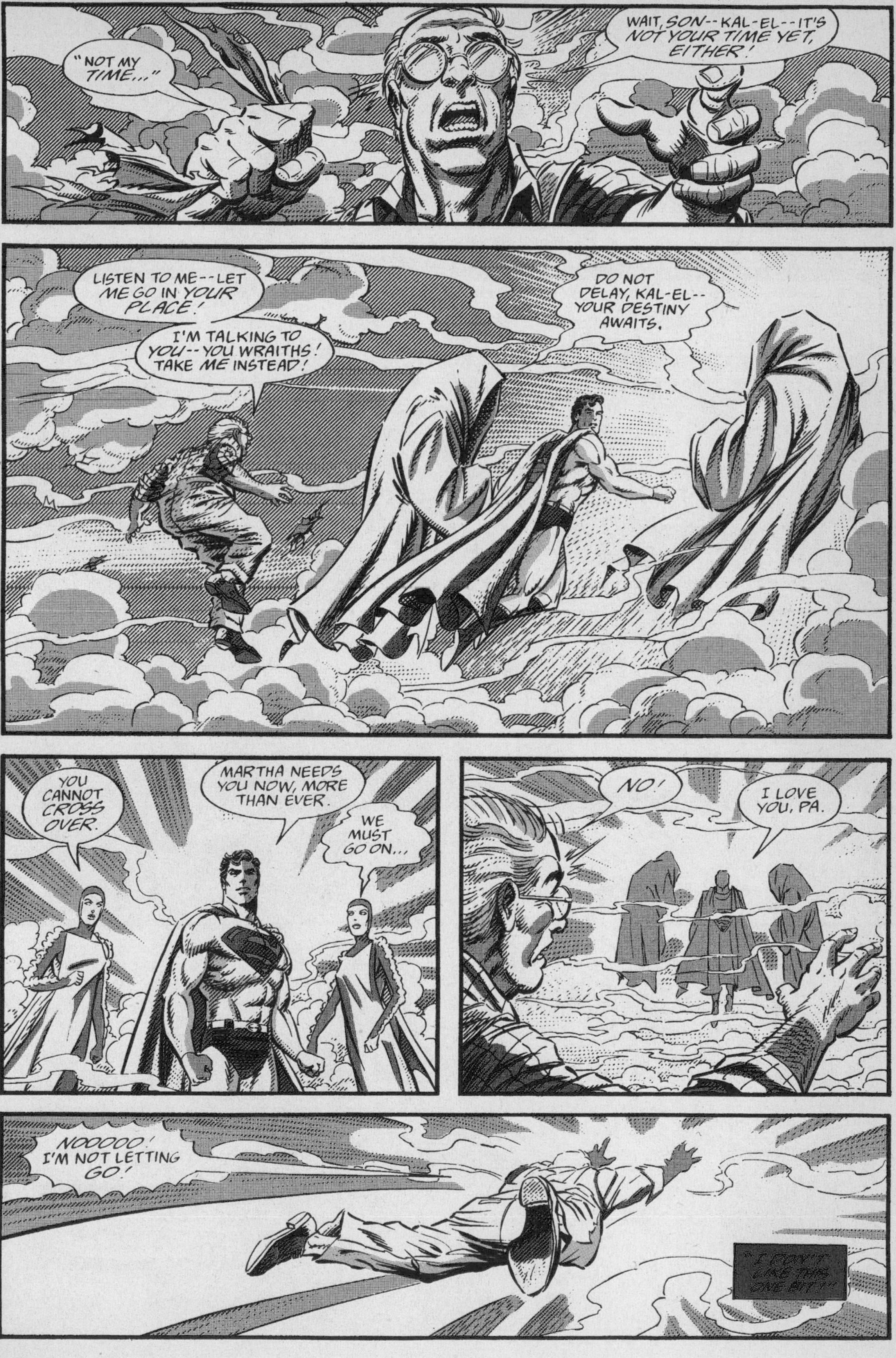
"NOT MY TIME..."
WAIT, SON--KAL-EL--IT'S NOT YOUR TIME YET, EITHER!
LISTEN TO ME--LET ME GO IN YOUR PLACE!
I'M TALKING TO YOU--YOU WRAITHS! TAKE ME INSTEAD!
DO NOT DELAY, KAL-EL--YOUR DESTINY AWAITS.
YOU CANNOT CROSS OVER.
MARTHA NEEDS YOU NOW, MORE THAN EVER.
WE MUST GO ON...
NO!
I LOVE YOU, PA.
NOOOOO! I'M NOT LETTING GO!
"I DON'T LIKE THIS ONE BIT!"

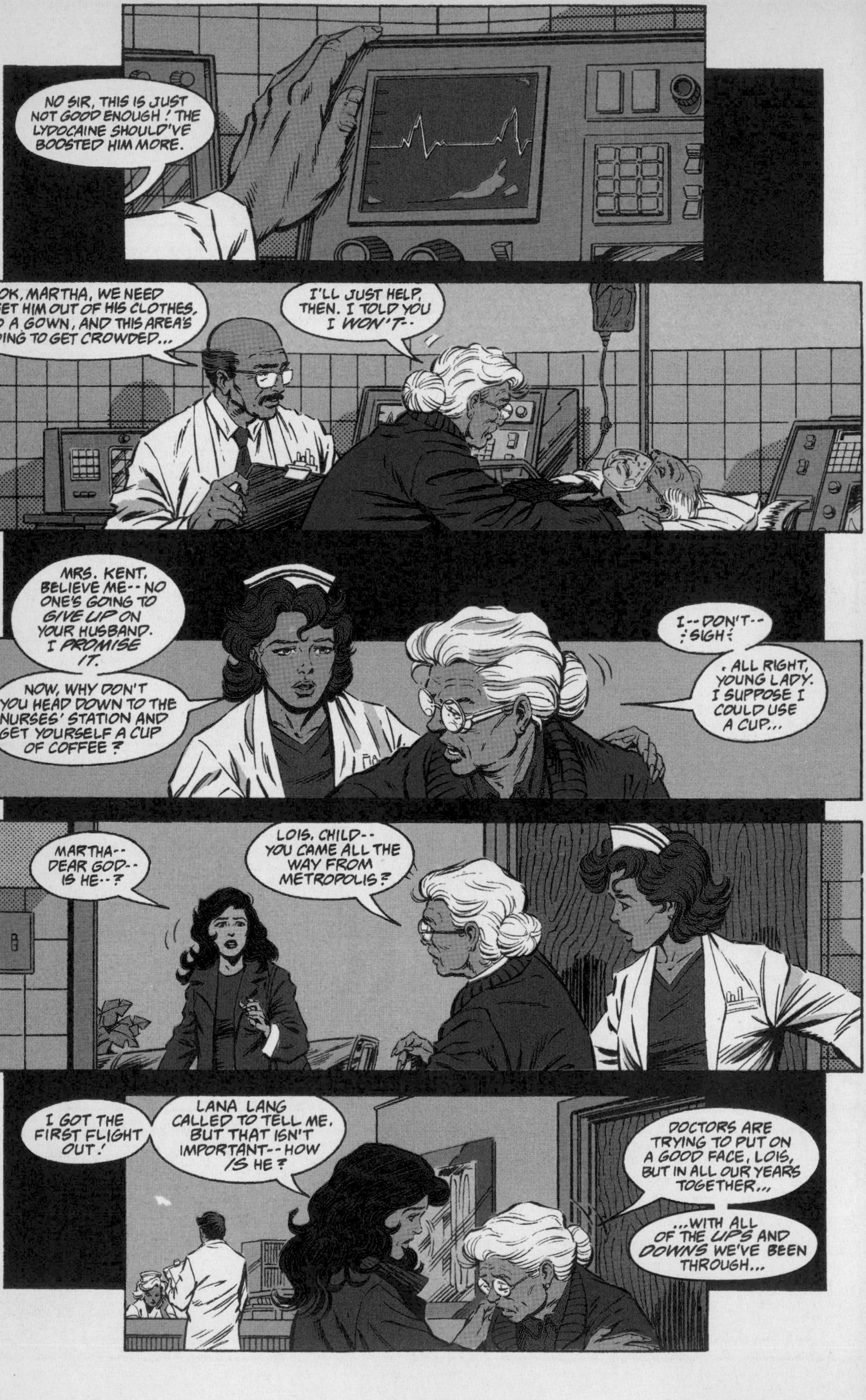
NO SIR, THIS IS JUST NOT GOOD ENOUGH! THE LYDOCAINE SHOULD'VE BOOSTED HIM MORE.
LOOK, MARTHA, WE NEED TO GET HIM OUT OF HIS CLOTHES, INTO A GOWN, AND THIS AREA'S GOING TO GET CROWDED...
I'LL JUST HELP, THEN. I TOLD YOU I WON'T--
MRS. KENT. BELIEVE ME-- NO ONE'S GOING TO GIVE UP ON YOUR HUSBAND. I PROMISE IT.
NOW, WHY DON'T YOU HEAD DOWN TO THE NURSES' STATION AND GET YOURSELF A CUP OF COFFEE?
I-- DON'T-- :SIGH:
. ALL RIGHT, YOUNG LADY. I SUPPOSE I COULD USE A CUP...
MARTHA-- DEAR GOD-- IS HE--?
LOIS, CHILD-- YOU CAME ALL THE WAY FROM METROPOLIS?
I GOT THE FIRST FLIGHT OUT!
LANA LANG CALLED TO TELL ME, BUT THAT ISN'T IMPORTANT-- HOW IS HE?
DOCTORS ARE TRYING TO PUT ON A GOOD FACE, LOIS, BUT IN ALL OUR YEARS TOGETHER...
...WITH ALL OF THE UPS AND DOWNS WE'VE BEEN THROUGH...

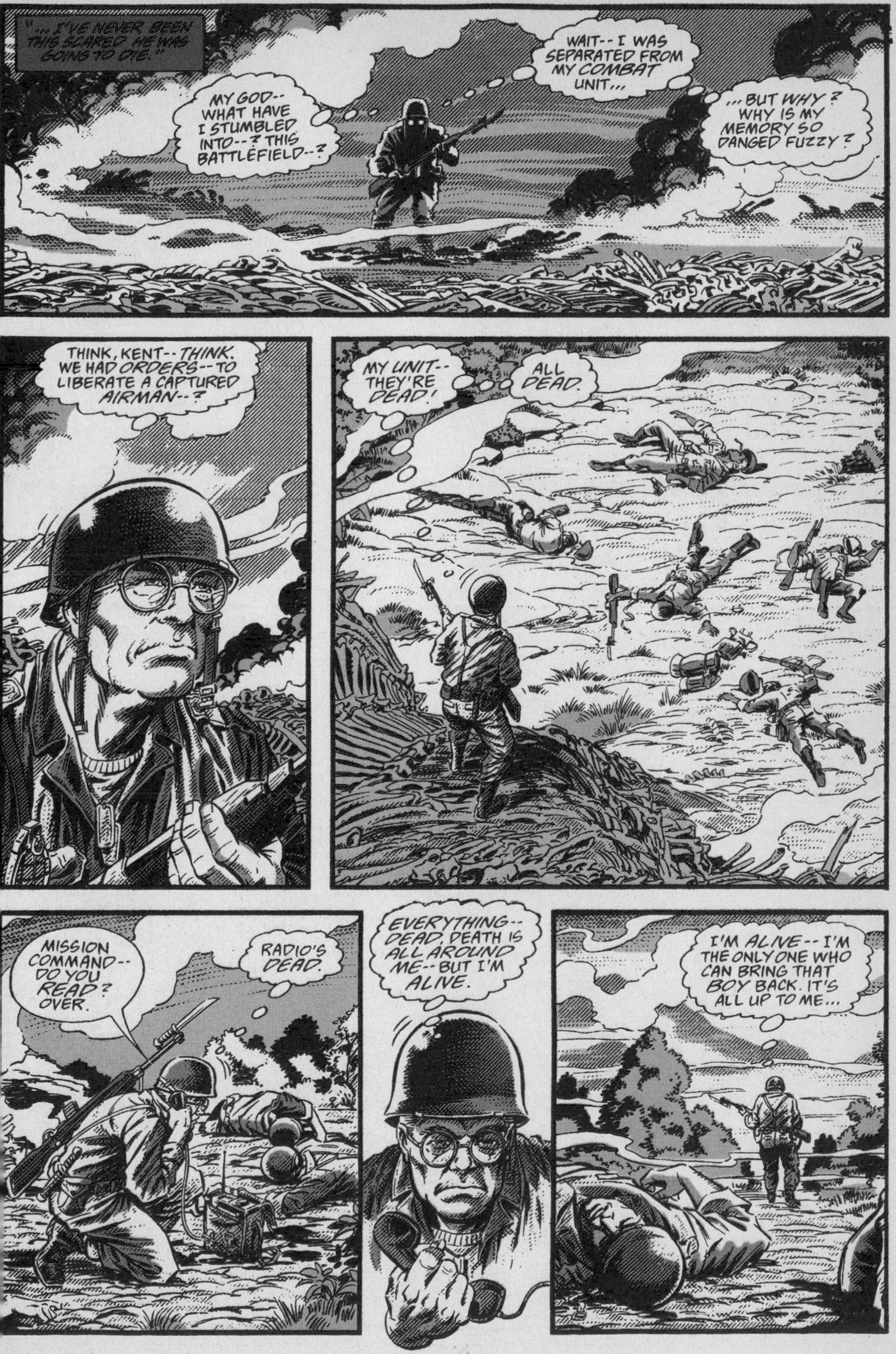
"... I'VE NEVER BEEN THIS SCARED HE WAS GOING TO DIE."
MY GOD-- WHAT HAVE I STUMBLED INTO--? THIS BATTLEFIELD--?
WAIT-- I WAS SEPARATED FROM MY COMBAT UNIT...
... BUT WHY? WHY IS MY MEMORY SO DANGED FUZZY?
THINK, KENT-- THINK. WE HAD ORDERS-- TO LIBERATE A CAPTURED AIRMAN--?
MY UNIT-- THEY'RE DEAD!
ALL DEAD.
MISSION COMMAND-- DO YOU READ? OVER.
RADIO'S DEAD.
EVERYTHING-- DEAD. DEATH IS ALL AROUND ME-- BUT I'M ALIVE.
I'M ALIVE-- I'M THE ONLY ONE WHO CAN BRING THAT BOY BACK. IT'S ALL UP TO ME...

"... THERE'S JUST NO WAY WE CAN ABANDON ONE OF OUR *OWN*."

MORE DEATH. THEY'VE BEEN THROUGH *THIS* WAY.

GOD KNOWS WHY THEY BURNED OUT THESE POOR FARMERS -- NONE OF THEM IS *ARMED*.

DARN SHAME. THAT ONE LOOKS TO BE THE SAME AGE AS MY BROTHER--

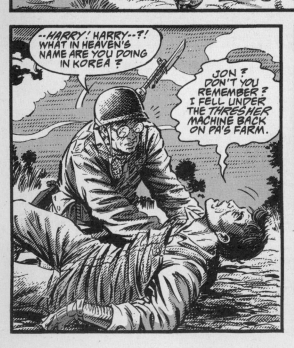

--*HARRY!* HARRY--?! WHAT IN HEAVEN'S NAME ARE YOU DOING IN KOREA?

JON? DON'T YOU REMEMBER? I FELL UNDER THE *THRESHER* MACHINE BACK ON PA'S FARM.

I'M *DEAD,* JONNY-- WE'RE ALL DEAD HERE.

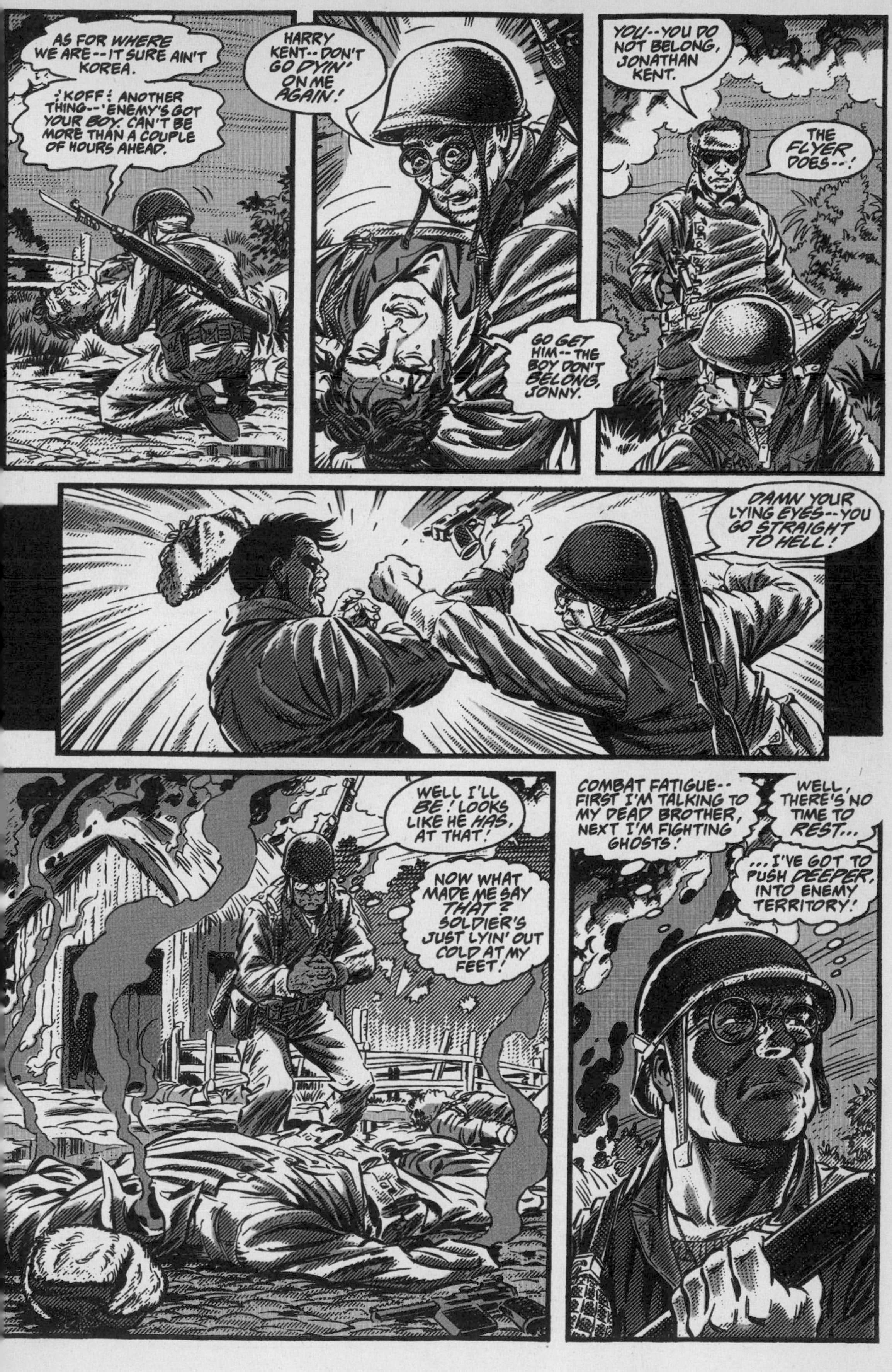
AS FOR WHERE WE ARE--IT SURE AIN'T KOREA.
:KOFF: ANOTHER THING--'ENEMY'S GOT YOUR BOY. CAN'T BE MORE THAN A COUPLE OF HOURS AHEAD.
HARRY KENT--DON'T GO DYIN' ON ME AGAIN!
GO GET HIM--THE BOY DON'T BELONG, JONNY.
YOU--YOU DO NOT BELONG, JONATHAN KENT.
THE FLYER DOES--!
DAMN YOUR LYING EYES--YOU GO STRAIGHT TO HELL!
WELL I'LL BE! LOOKS LIKE HE HAS, AT THAT!
NOW WHAT MADE ME SAY THAT? SOLDIER'S JUST LYIN' OUT COLD AT MY FEET!
COMBAT FATIGUE--FIRST I'M TALKING TO MY DEAD BROTHER, NEXT I'M FIGHTING GHOSTS!
WELL, THERE'S NO TIME TO REST...
...I'VE GOT TO PUSH DEEPER, INTO ENEMY TERRITORY!

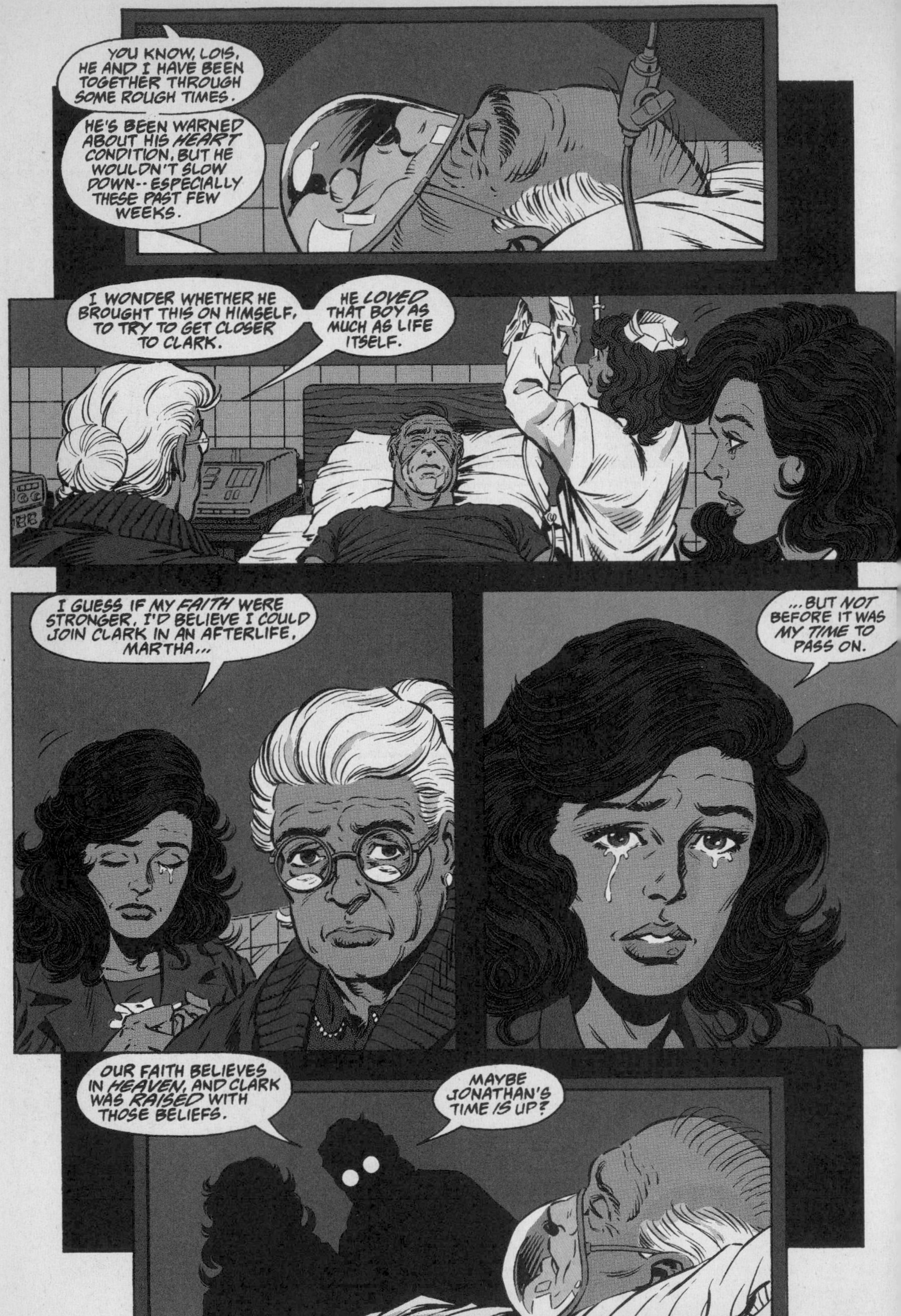
YOU KNOW, LOIS, HE AND I HAVE BEEN TOGETHER THROUGH SOME ROUGH TIMES.
HE'S BEEN WARNED ABOUT HIS HEART CONDITION, BUT HE WOULDN'T SLOW DOWN--ESPECIALLY THESE PAST FEW WEEKS.
I WONDER WHETHER HE BROUGHT THIS ON HIMSELF, TO TRY TO GET CLOSER TO CLARK.
HE LOVED THAT BOY AS MUCH AS LIFE ITSELF.
I GUESS IF MY FAITH WERE STRONGER, I'D BELIEVE I COULD JOIN CLARK IN AN AFTERLIFE, MARTHA...
...BUT NOT BEFORE IT WAS MY TIME TO PASS ON.
OUR FAITH BELIEVES IN HEAVEN, AND CLARK WAS RAISED WITH THOSE BELIEFS.
MAYBE JONATHAN'S TIME IS UP?

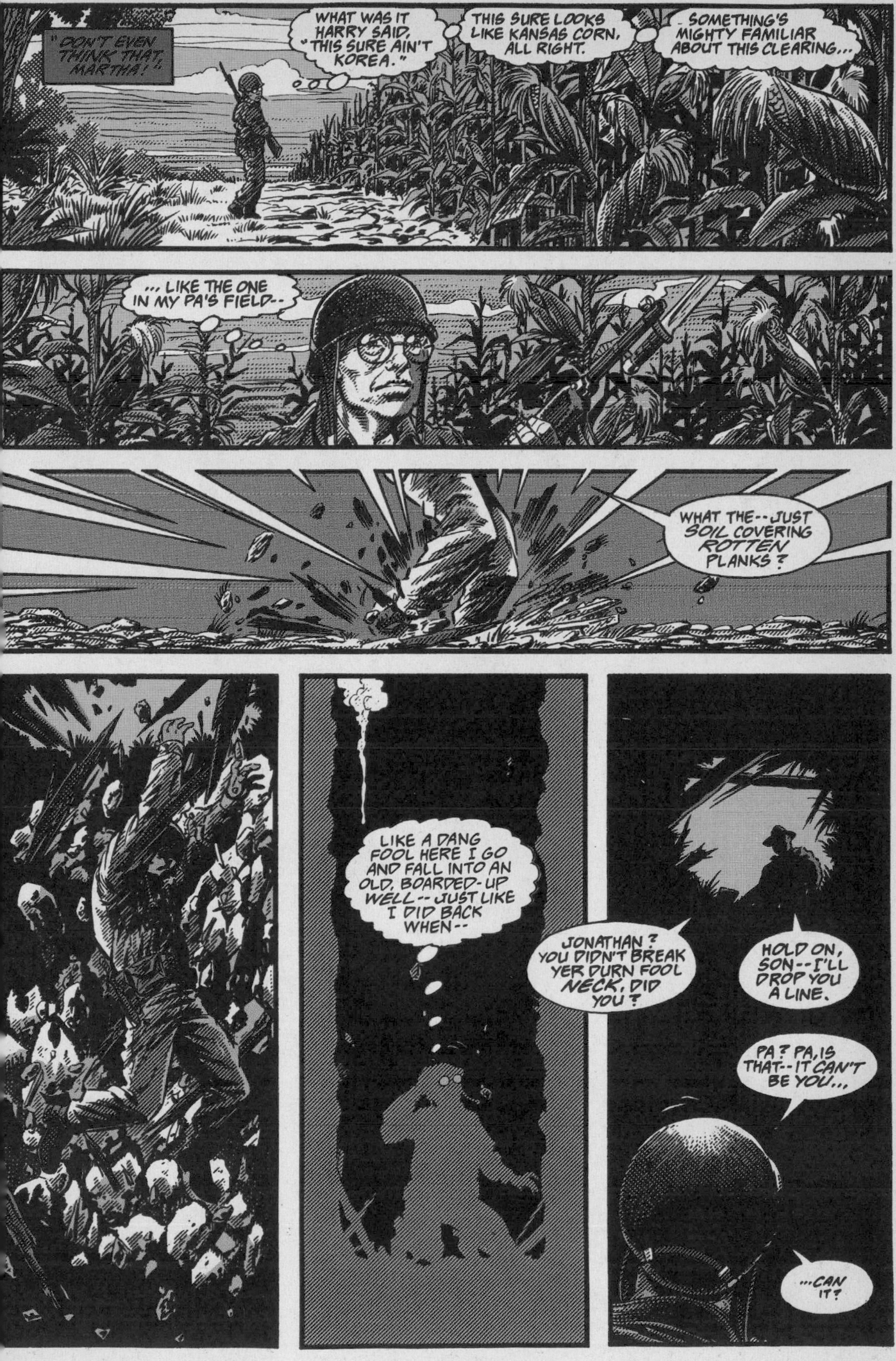
"DON'T EVEN THINK THAT, MARTHA!"
WHAT WAS IT HARRY SAID, "THIS SURE AIN'T KOREA."
THIS SURE LOOKS LIKE KANSAS CORN, ALL RIGHT.
- SOMETHING'S MIGHTY FAMILIAR ABOUT THIS CLEARING...
..., LIKE THE ONE IN MY PA'S FIELD--
WHAT THE--JUST SOIL COVERING ROTTEN PLANKS?
LIKE A DANG FOOL HERE I GO AND FALL INTO AN OLD, BOARDED-UP WELL--JUST LIKE I DID BACK WHEN--
JONATHAN? YOU DIDN'T BREAK YER DURN FOOL NECK, DID YOU?
HOLD ON, SON--I'LL DROP YOU A LINE.
PA? PA, IS THAT--IT CAN'T BE YOU...,
...CAN IT?

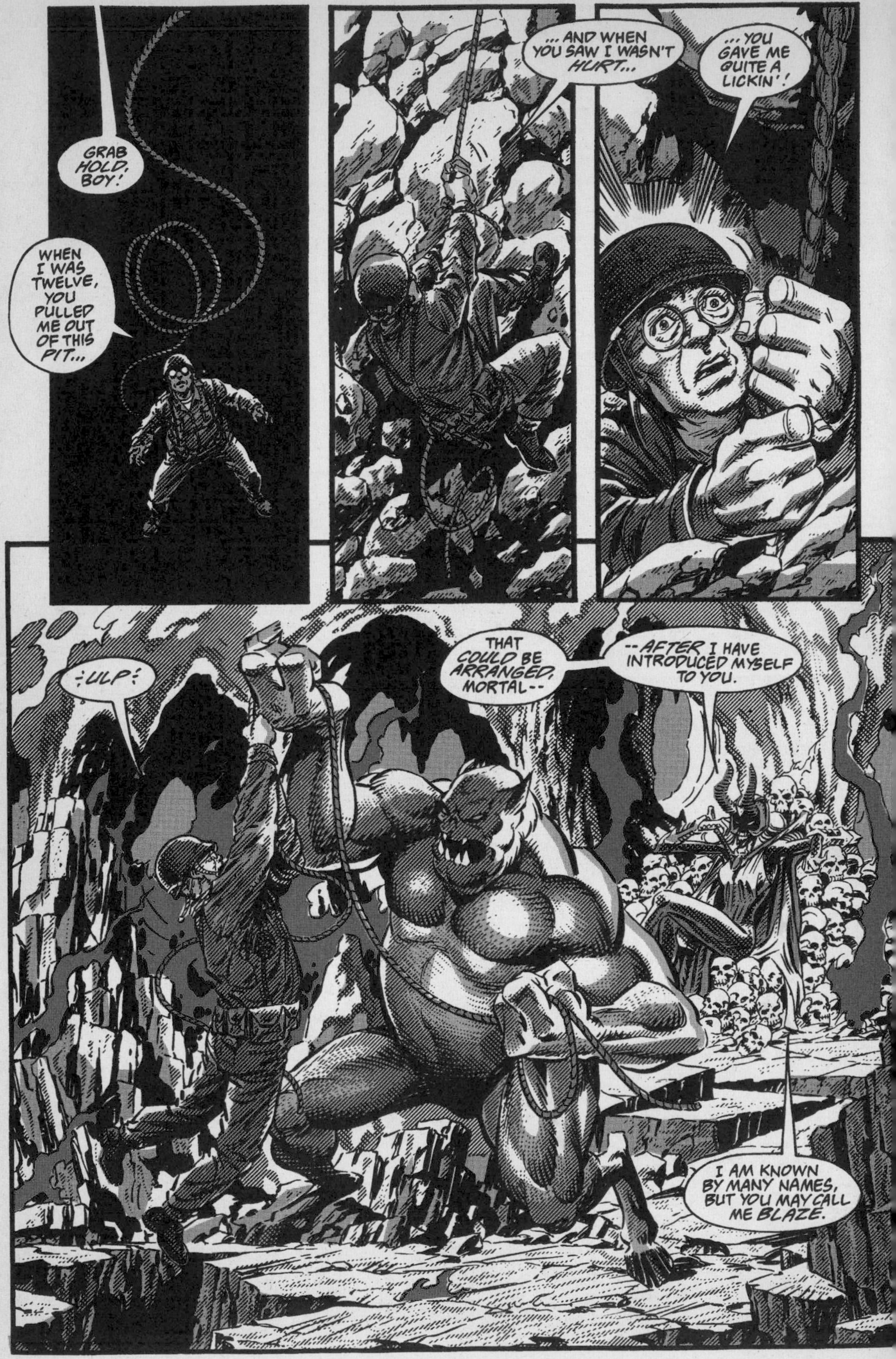
GRAB HOLD, BOY!
WHEN I WAS TWELVE, YOU PULLED ME OUT OF THIS PIT...
...AND WHEN YOU SAW I WASN'T HURT...
...YOU GAVE ME QUITE A LICKIN'!
-ULP-
THAT COULD BE ARRANGED, MORTAL--
--AFTER I HAVE INTRODUCED MYSELF TO YOU.
I AM KNOWN BY MANY NAMES, BUT YOU MAY CALL ME BLAZE.

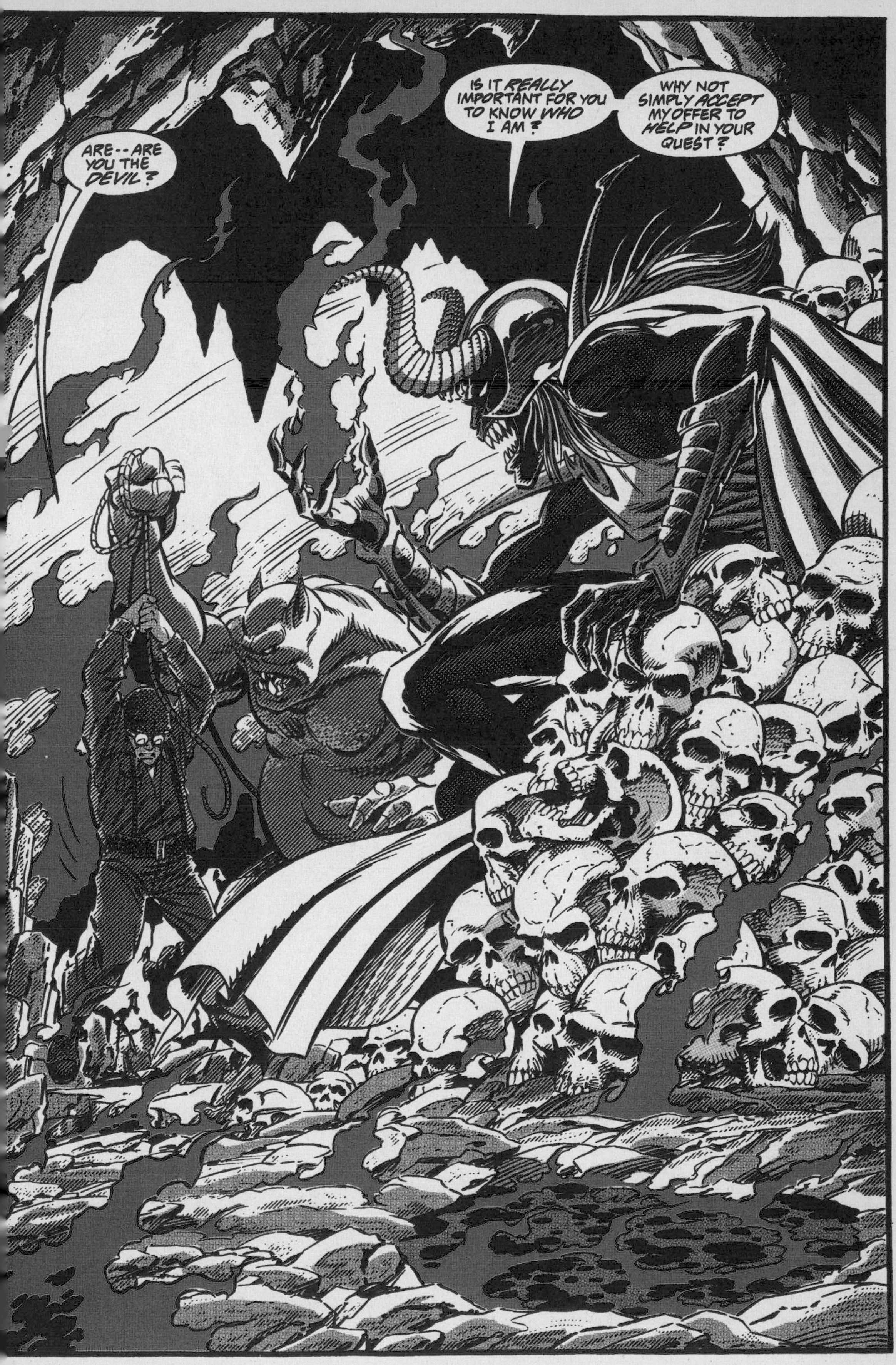
ARE--ARE YOU THE DEVIL?
IS IT REALLY IMPORTANT FOR YOU TO KNOW WHO I AM?
WHY NOT SIMPLY ACCEPT MY OFFER TO HELP IN YOUR QUEST?

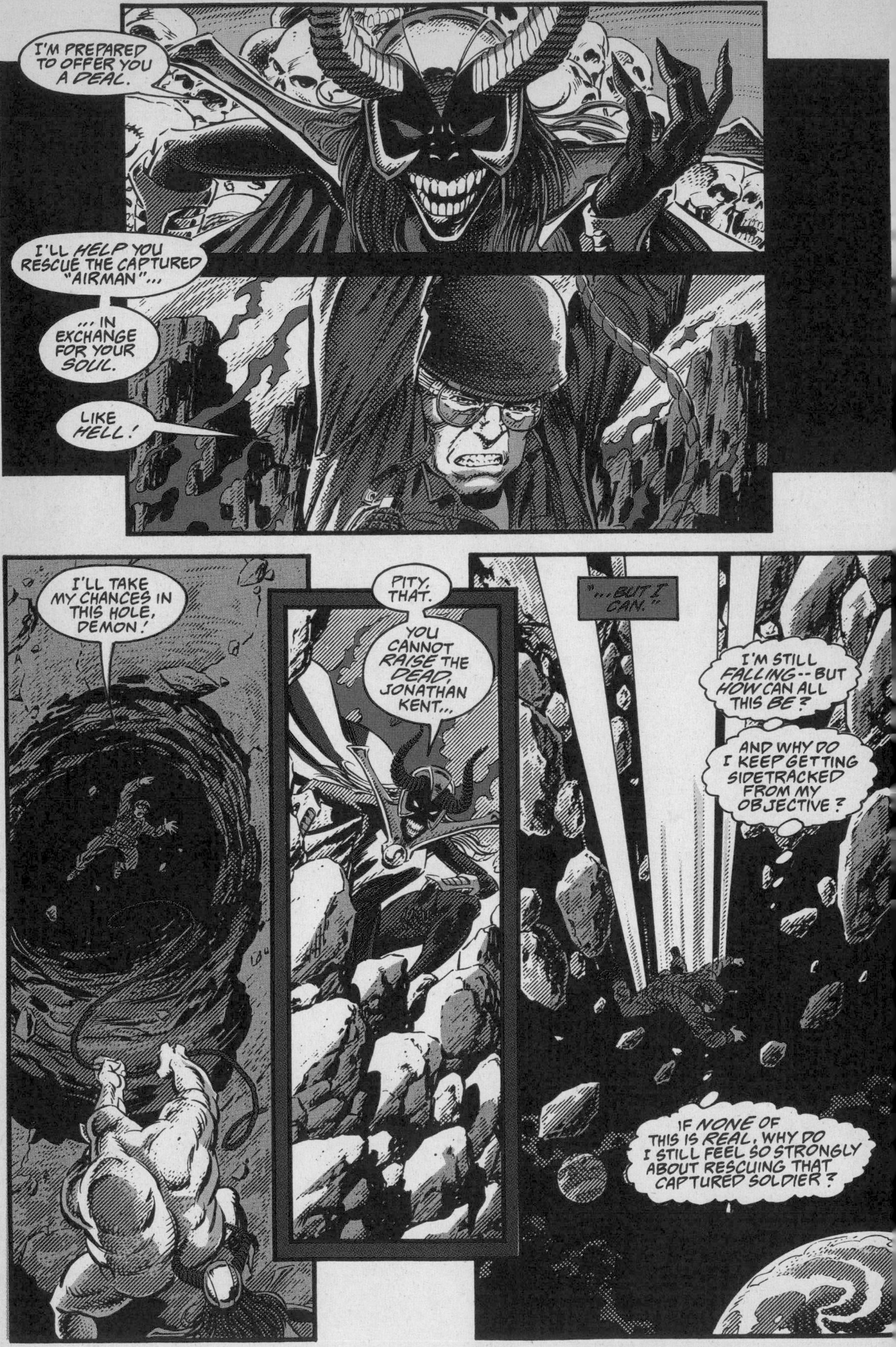
I'M PREPARED TO OFFER YOU A DEAL.
I'LL HELP YOU RESCUE THE CAPTURED "AIRMAN"...
...IN EXCHANGE FOR YOUR SOUL.
LIKE HELL!
I'LL TAKE MY CHANCES IN THIS HOLE, DEMON!
PITY, THAT.
YOU CANNOT RAISE THE DEAD, JONATHAN KENT...
"...BUT I CAN."
I'M STILL FALLING--BUT HOW CAN ALL THIS BE?
AND WHY DO I KEEP GETTING SIDETRACKED FROM MY OBJECTIVE?
IF NONE OF THIS IS REAL, WHY DO I STILL FEEL SO STRONGLY ABOUT RESCUING THAT CAPTURED SOLDIER?

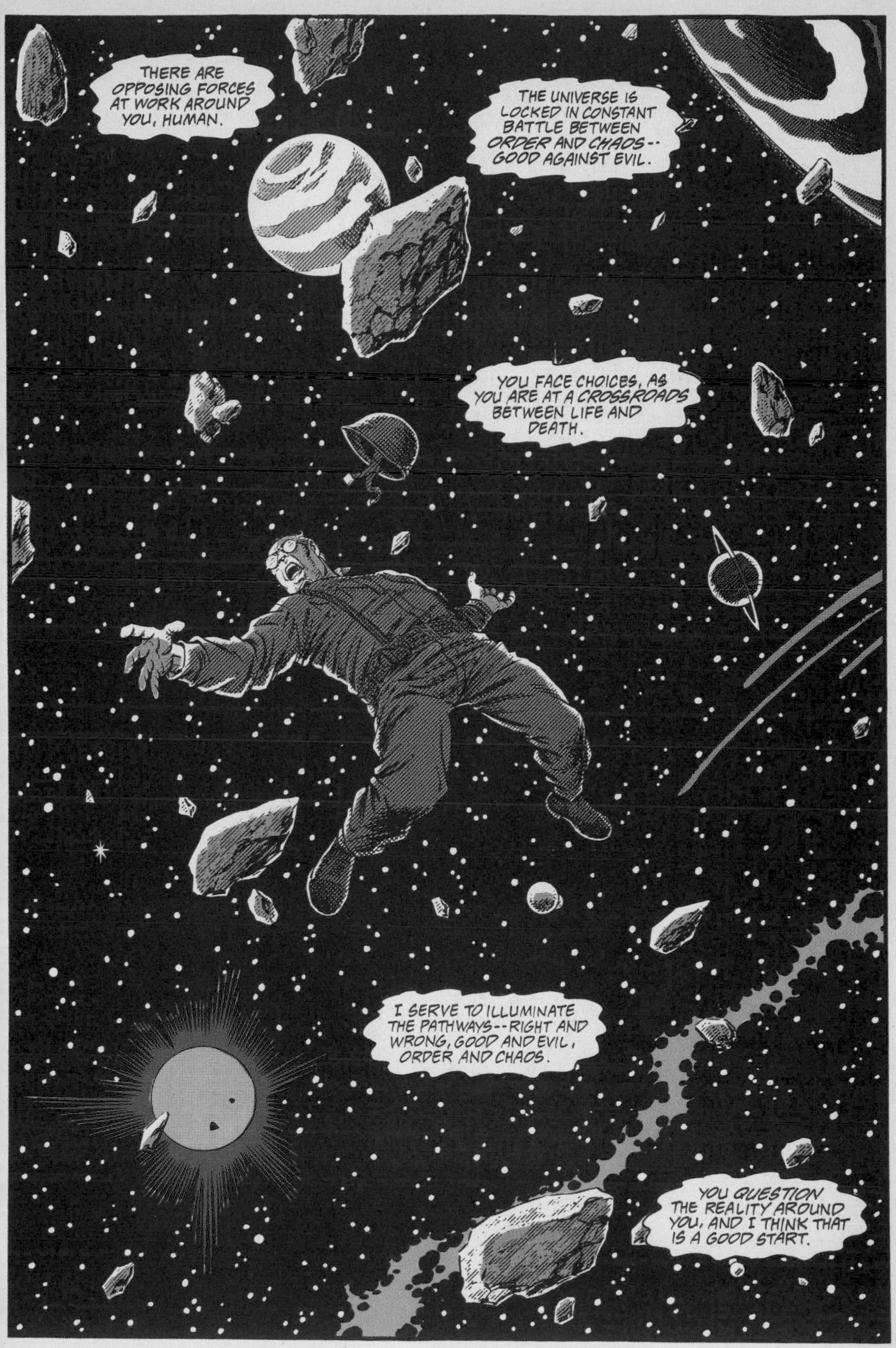
THERE ARE OPPOSING FORCES AT WORK AROUND YOU, HUMAN.
THE UNIVERSE IS LOCKED IN CONSTANT BATTLE BETWEEN ORDER AND CHAOS-- GOOD AGAINST EVIL.
YOU FACE CHOICES, AS YOU ARE AT A CROSSROADS BETWEEN LIFE AND DEATH.
I SERVE TO ILLUMINATE THE PATHWAYS--RIGHT AND WRONG, GOOD AND EVIL, ORDER AND CHAOS.
YOU QUESTION THE REALITY AROUND YOU, AND I THINK THAT IS A GOOD START.

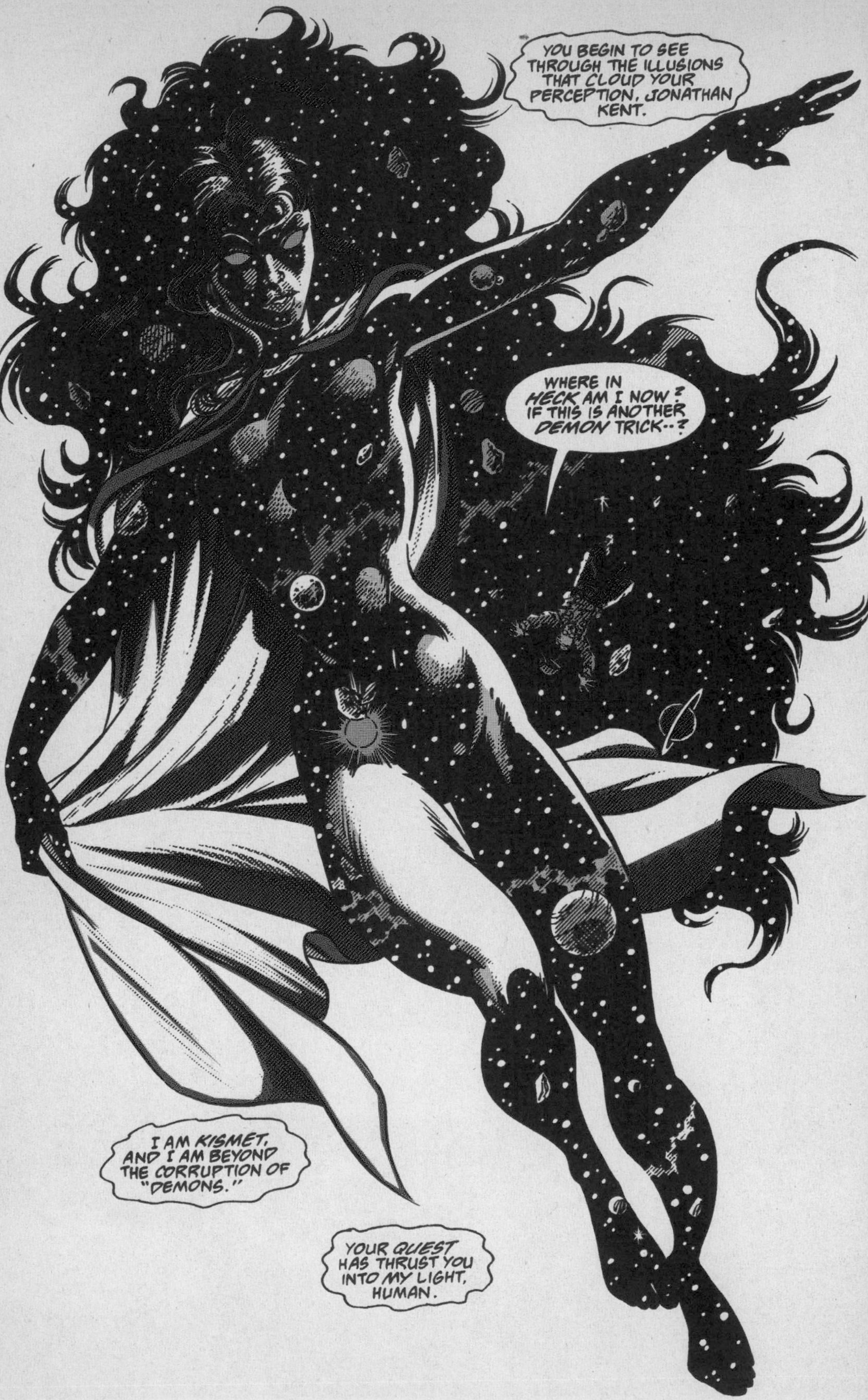
YOU BEGIN TO SEE THROUGH THE ILLUSIONS THAT CLOUD YOUR PERCEPTION, JONATHAN KENT.
WHERE IN HECK AM I NOW? IF THIS IS ANOTHER DEMON TRICK--?
I AM KISMET, AND I AM BEYOND THE CORRUPTION OF "DEMONS."
YOUR QUEST HAS THRUST YOU INTO MY LIGHT, HUMAN.

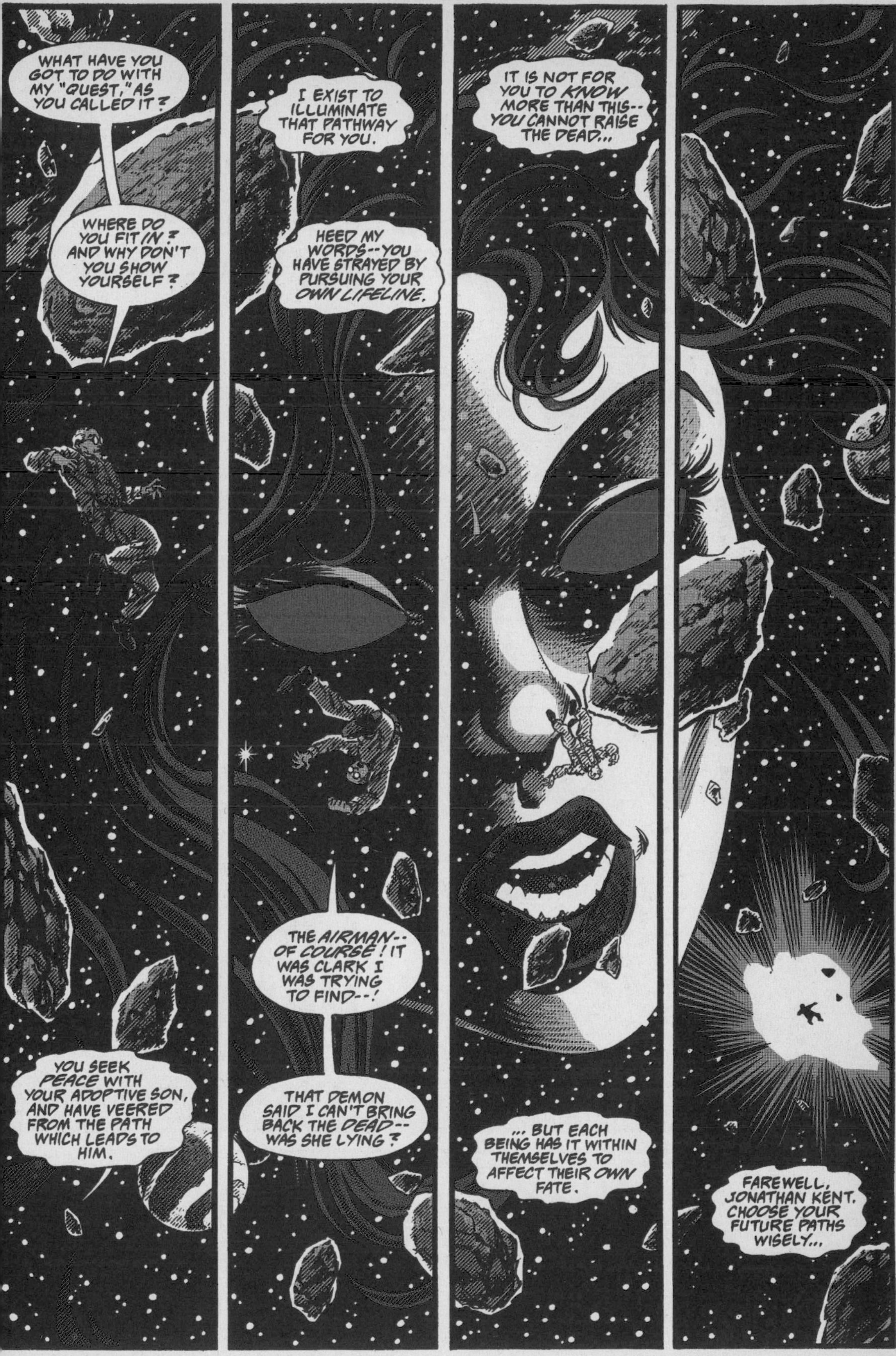

WHAT HAVE YOU GOT TO DO WITH MY "QUEST," AS YOU CALLED IT ?
WHERE DO YOU FIT IN ? AND WHY DON'T YOU SHOW YOURSELF ?
YOU SEEK PEACE WITH YOUR ADOPTIVE SON, AND HAVE VEERED FROM THE PATH WHICH LEADS TO HIM.
I EXIST TO ILLUMINATE THAT PATHWAY FOR YOU.
HEED MY WORDS--YOU HAVE STRAYED BY PURSUING YOUR OWN LIFELINE.
THE AIRMAN--OF COURSE ! IT WAS CLARK I WAS TRYING TO FIND--!
THAT DEMON SAID I CAN'T BRING BACK THE DEAD--WAS SHE LYING ?
IT IS NOT FOR YOU TO KNOW MORE THAN THIS--YOU CANNOT RAISE THE DEAD...
... BUT EACH BEING HAS IT WITHIN THEMSELVES TO AFFECT THEIR OWN FATE.
FAREWELL, JONATHAN KENT. CHOOSE YOUR FUTURE PATHS WISELY...

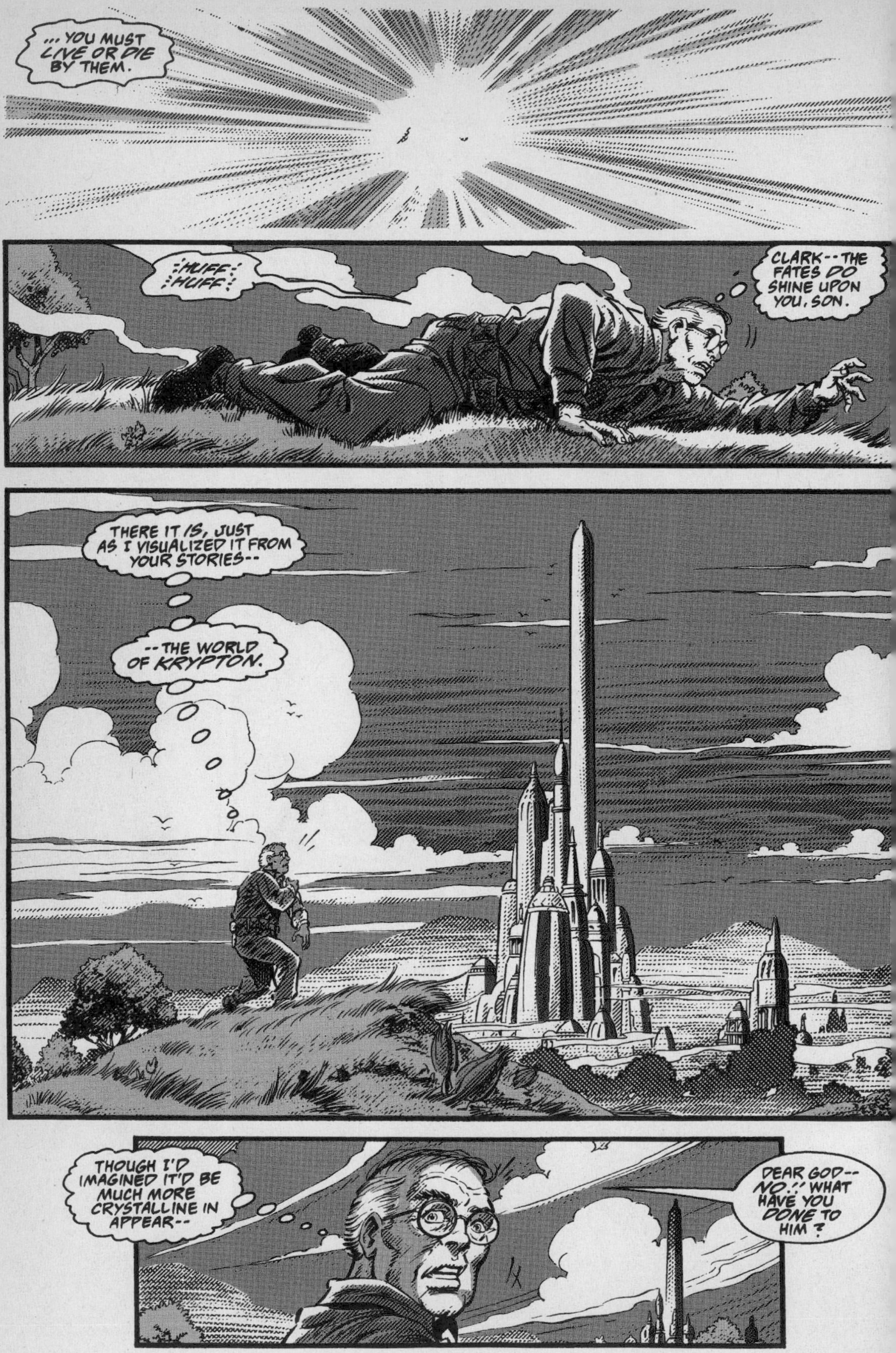
...YOU MUST LIVE OR DIE BY THEM.
HUFF HUFF
CLARK--THE FATES DO SHINE UPON YOU, SON.
THERE IT IS, JUST AS I VISUALIZED IT FROM YOUR STORIES--
--THE WORLD OF KRYPTON.
THOUGH I'D IMAGINED IT'D BE MUCH MORE CRYSTALLINE IN APPEAR--
DEAR GOD--NO.!! WHAT HAVE YOU DONE TO HIM?

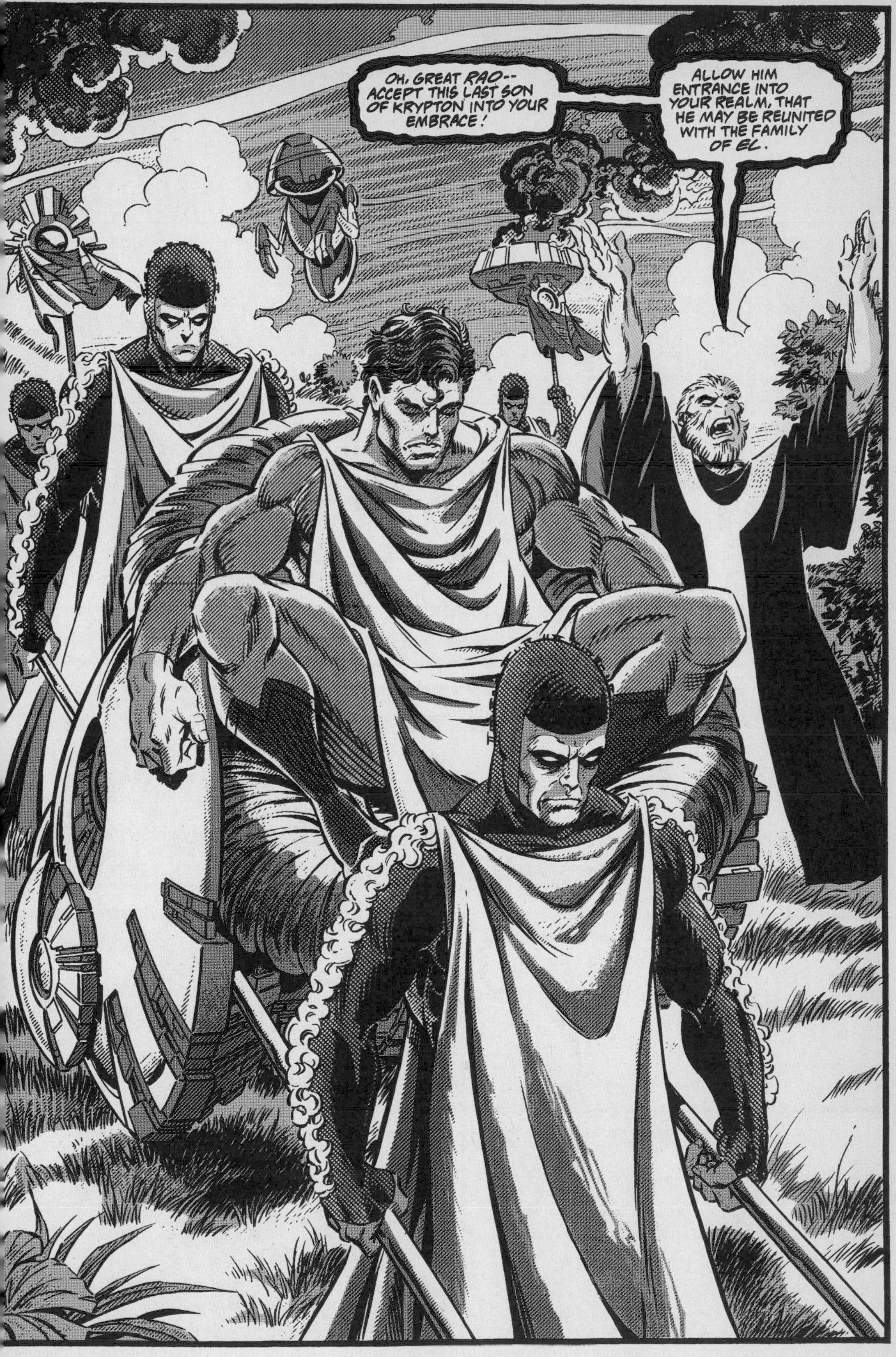
OH, GREAT RAO-- ACCEPT THIS LAST SON OF KRYPTON INTO YOUR EMBRACE!
ALLOW HIM ENTRANCE INTO YOUR REALM, THAT HE MAY BE REUNITED WITH THE FAMILY OF EL.

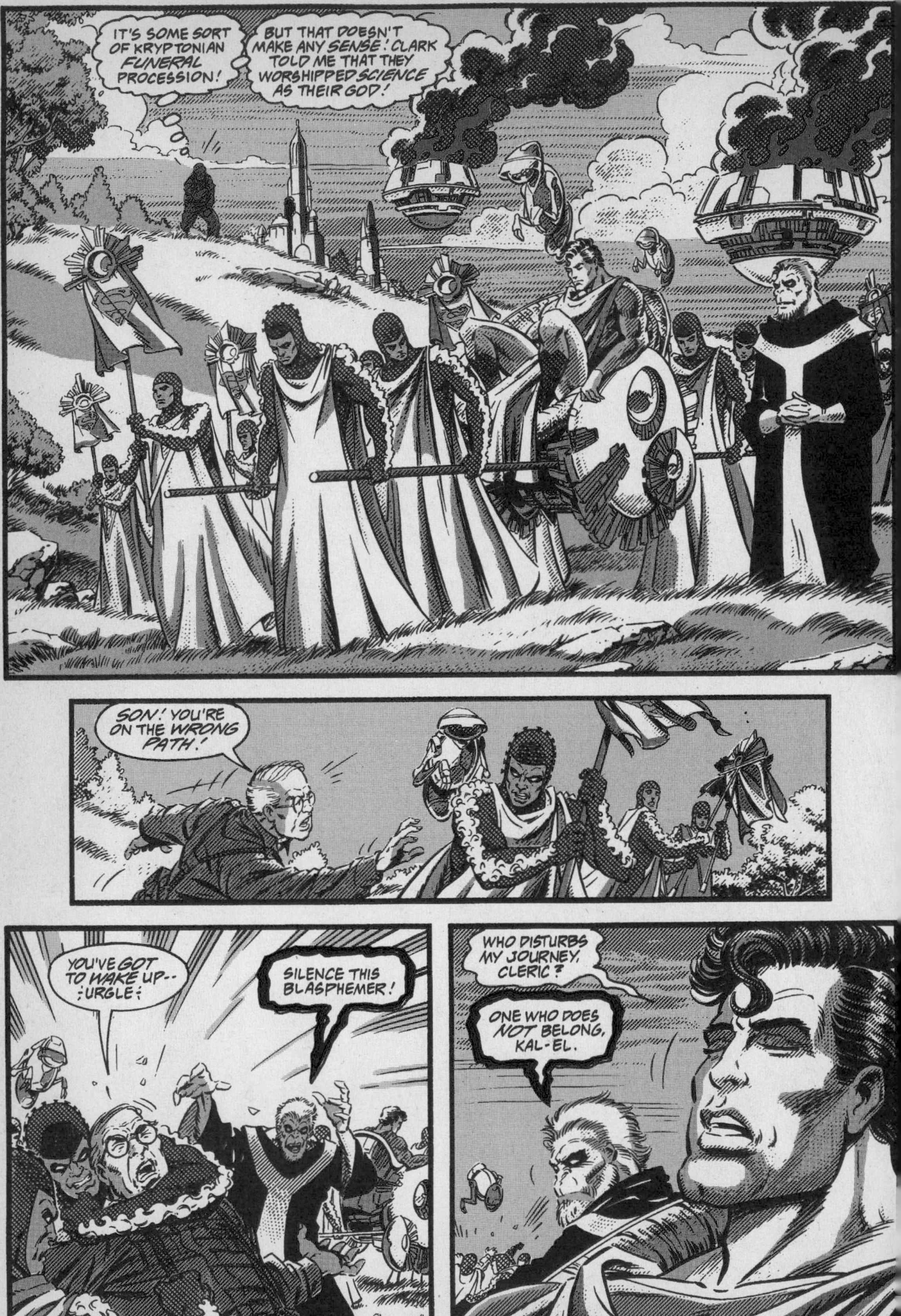
IT'S SOME SORT OF KRYPTONIAN FUNERAL PROCESSION!
BUT THAT DOESN'T MAKE ANY SENSE! CLARK TOLD ME THAT THEY WORSHIPPED SCIENCE AS THEIR GOD!
SON! YOU'RE ON THE WRONG PATH!
YOU'VE GOT TO WAKE UP-- :URGLE:
SILENCE THIS BLASPHEMER!
WHO DISTURBS MY JOURNEY, CLERIC?
ONE WHO DOES NOT BELONG, KAL-EL.

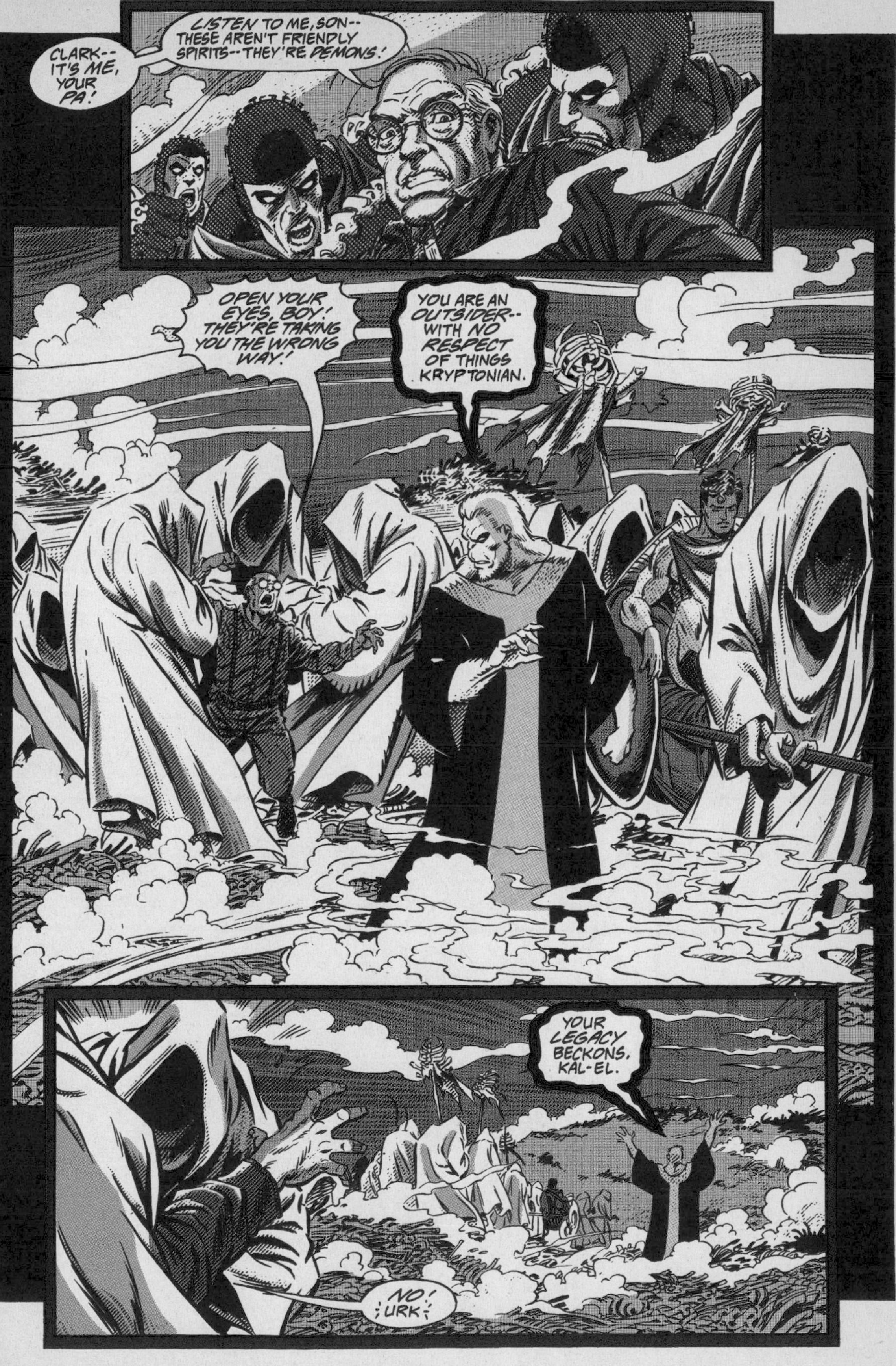
CLARK-- IT'S ME, YOUR PA!
LISTEN TO ME, SON-- THESE AREN'T FRIENDLY SPIRITS-- THEY'RE DEMONS!
OPEN YOUR EYES, BOY! THEY'RE TAKING YOU THE WRONG WAY!
YOU ARE AN OUTSIDER-- WITH NO RESPECT OF THINGS KRYPTONIAN.
YOUR LEGACY BECKONS, KAL-EL.
NO! URK

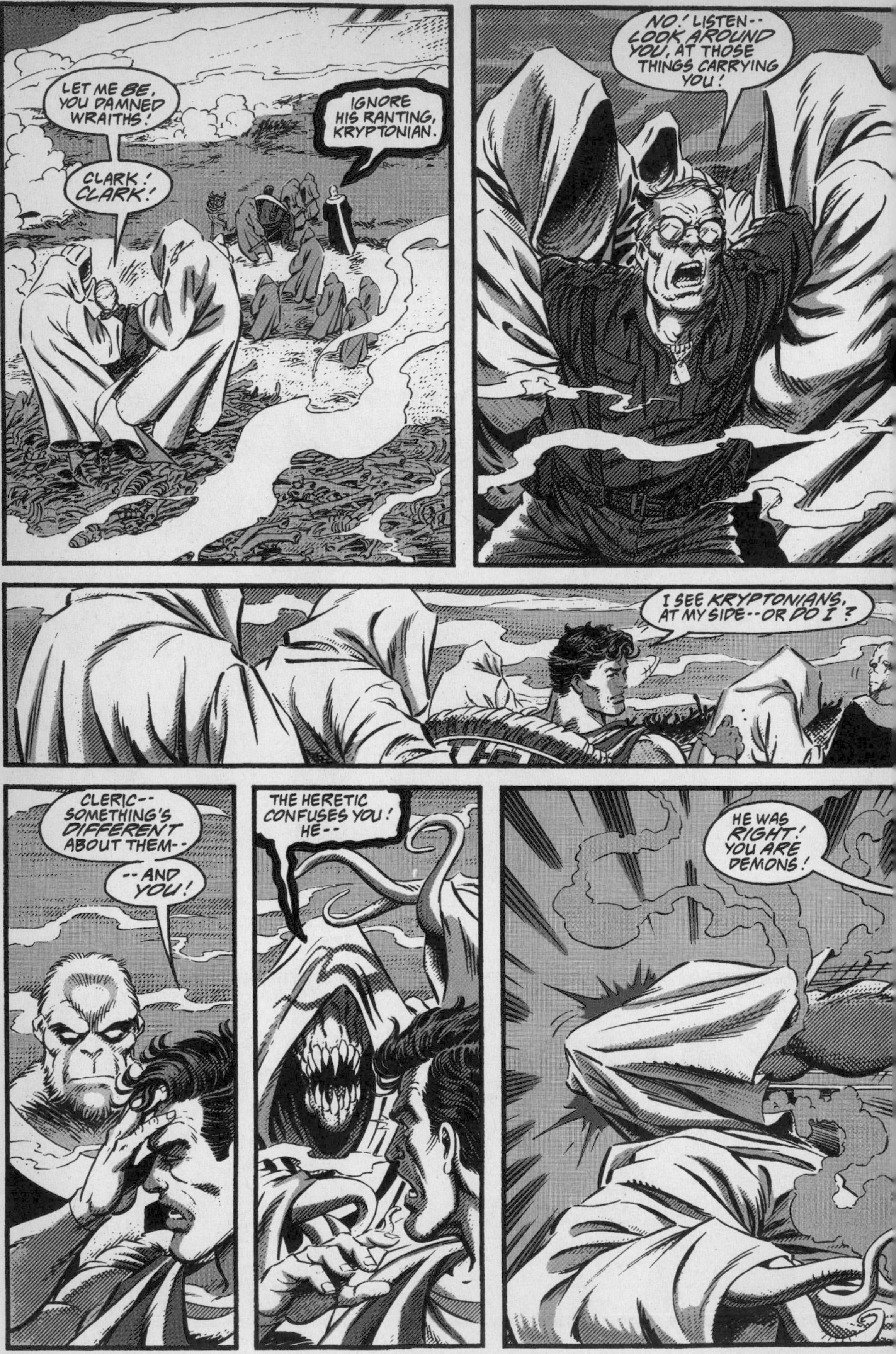
LET ME BE, YOU DAMNED WRAITHS!
CLARK! CLARK!
IGNORE HIS RANTING, KRYPTONIAN.
NO! LISTEN-- LOOK AROUND YOU, AT THOSE THINGS CARRYING YOU!
I SEE KRYPTONIANS, AT MY SIDE--OR DO I?
CLERIC-- SOMETHING'S DIFFERENT ABOUT THEM--
--AND YOU!
THE HERETIC CONFUSES YOU! HE--
HE WAS RIGHT! YOU ARE DEMONS!

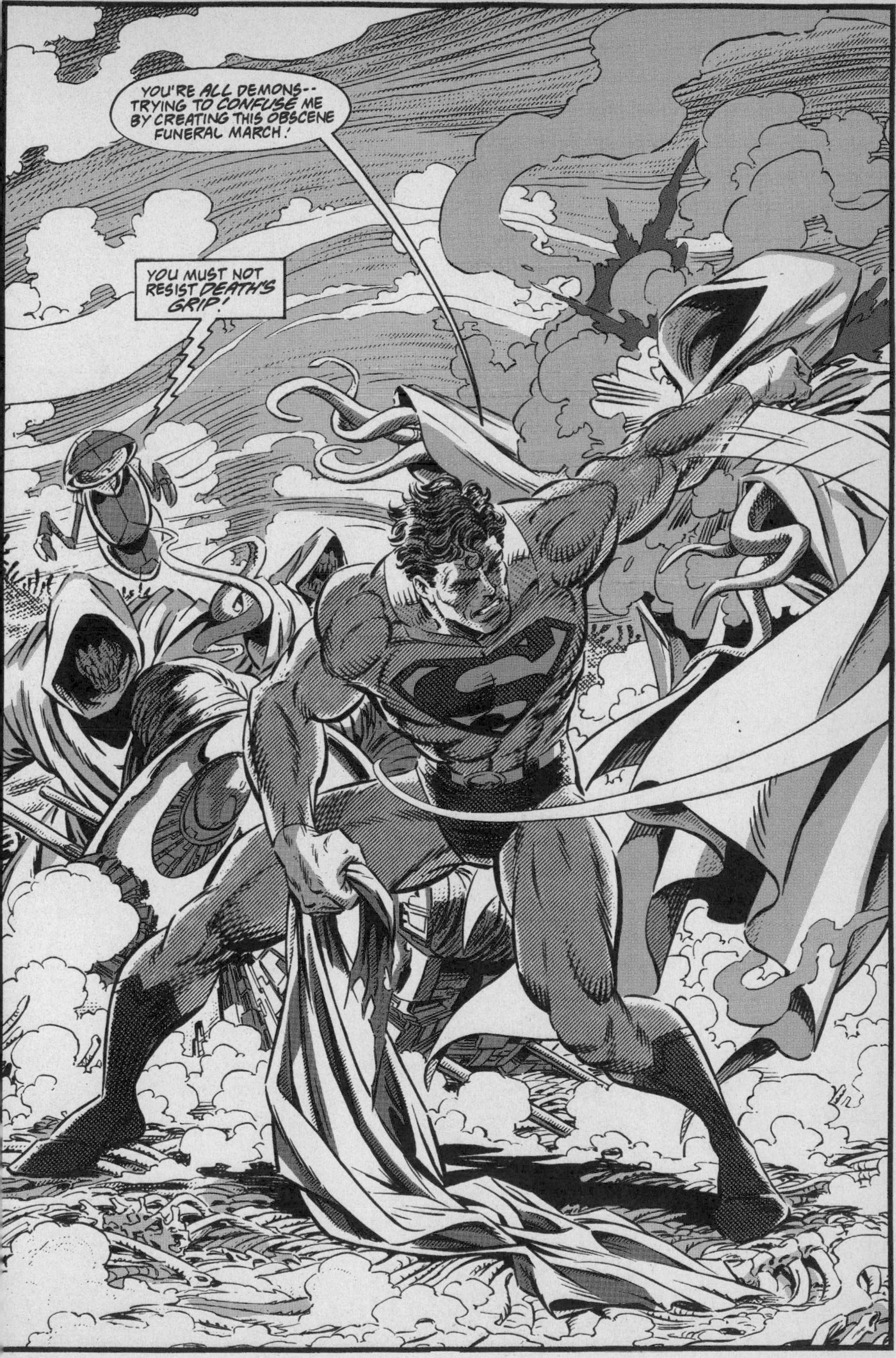
YOU'RE ALL DEMONS-- TRYING TO CONFUSE ME BY CREATING THIS OBSCENE FUNERAL MARCH!
YOU MUST NOT RESIST DEATH'S GRIP!

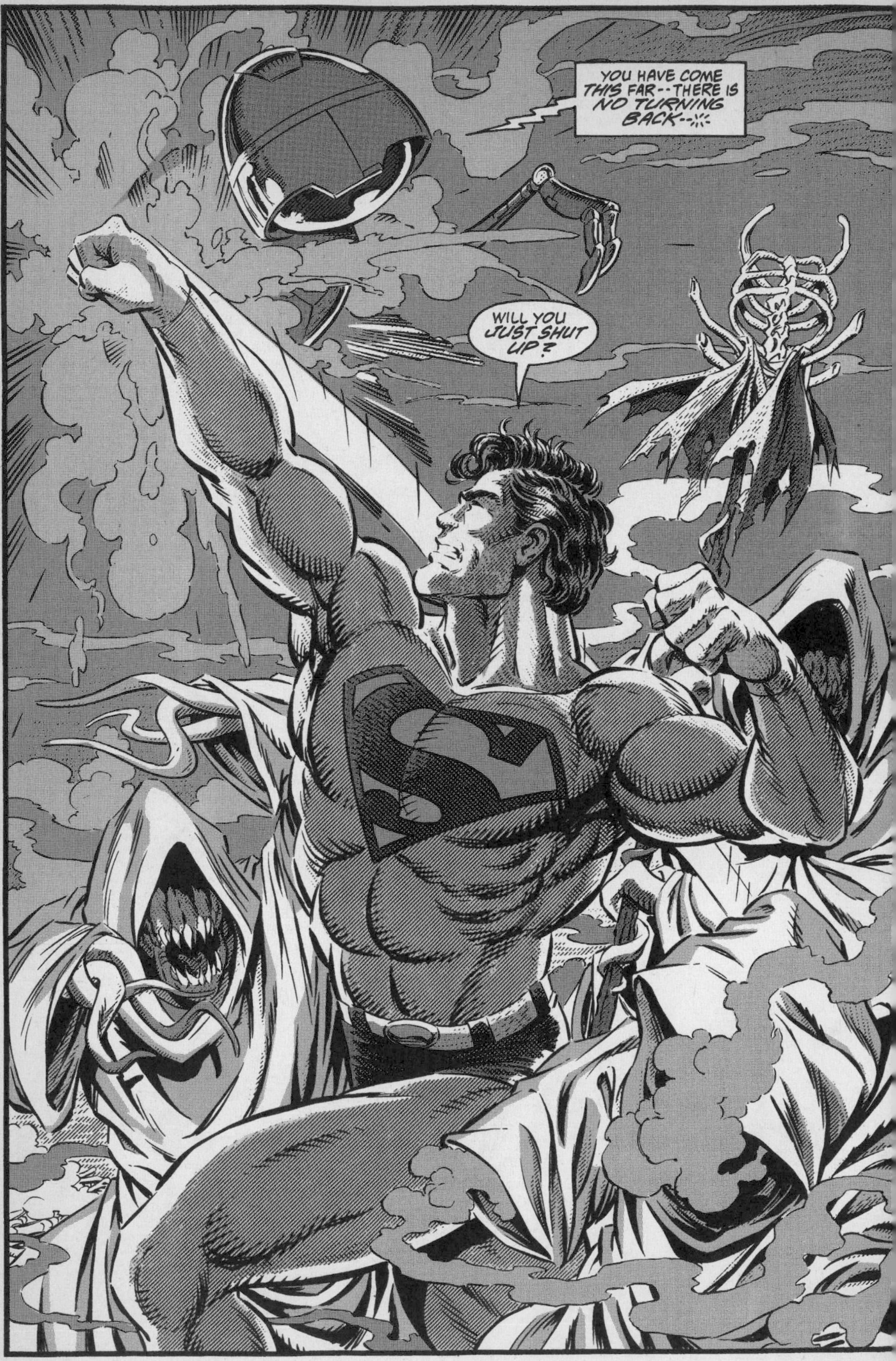
YOU HAVE COME THIS FAR--THERE IS NO TURNING BACK--
WILL YOU JUST SHUT UP?

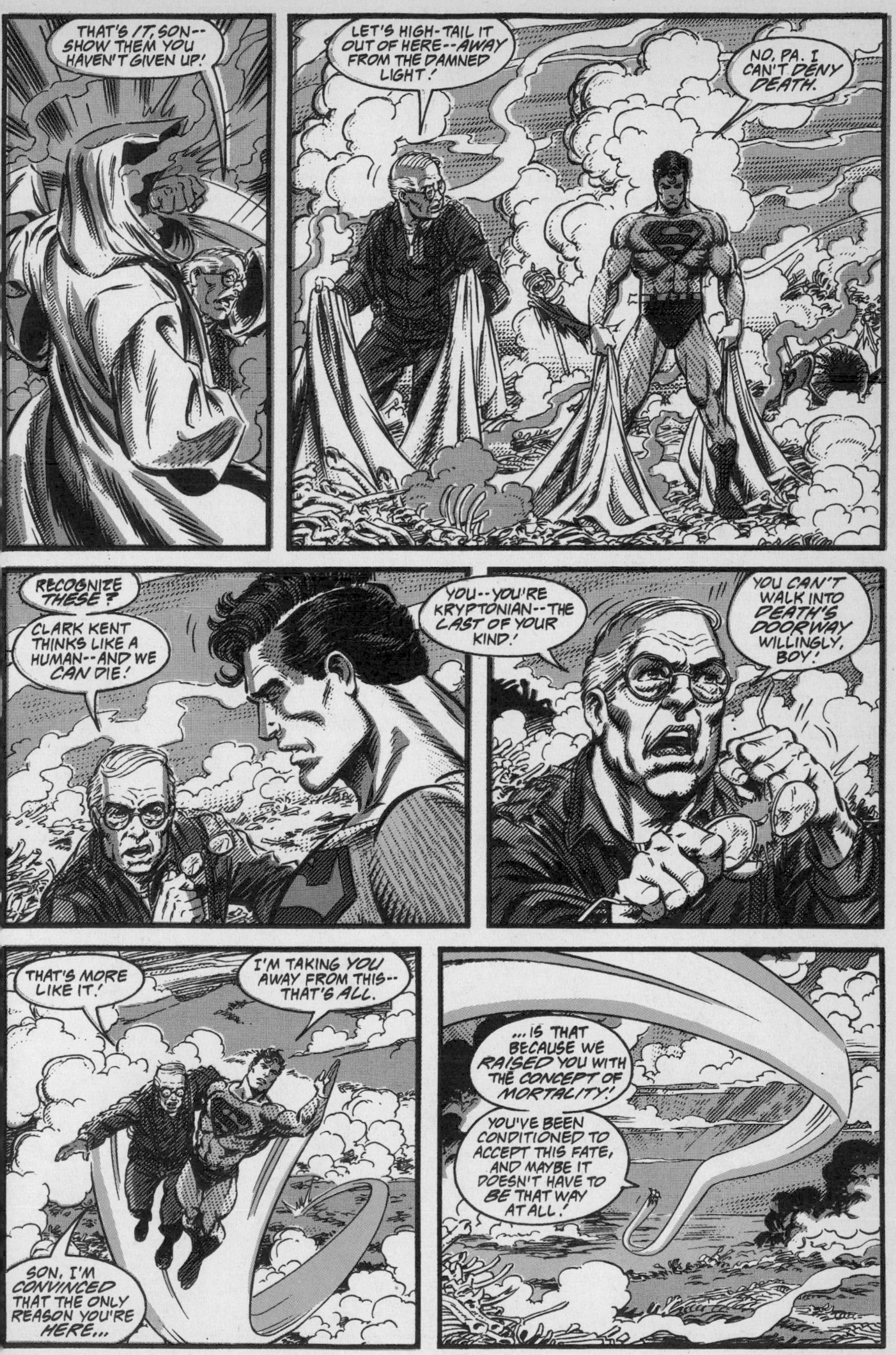
THAT'S IT, SON--SHOW THEM YOU HAVEN'T GIVEN UP!
LET'S HIGH-TAIL IT OUT OF HERE--AWAY FROM THE DAMNED LIGHT!
NO, PA. I CAN'T DENY DEATH.
RECOGNIZE THESE?
CLARK KENT THINKS LIKE A HUMAN--AND WE CAN DIE!
YOU--YOU'RE KRYPTONIAN--THE LAST OF YOUR KIND!
YOU CAN'T WALK INTO DEATH'S DOORWAY WILLINGLY, BOY!
THAT'S MORE LIKE IT!
I'M TAKING YOU AWAY FROM THIS--THAT'S ALL.
SON, I'M CONVINCED THAT THE ONLY REASON YOU'RE HERE...
...IS THAT BECAUSE WE RAISED YOU WITH THE CONCEPT OF MORTALITY!
YOU'VE BEEN CONDITIONED TO ACCEPT THIS FATE, AND MAYBE IT DOESN'T HAVE TO BE THAT WAY AT ALL!

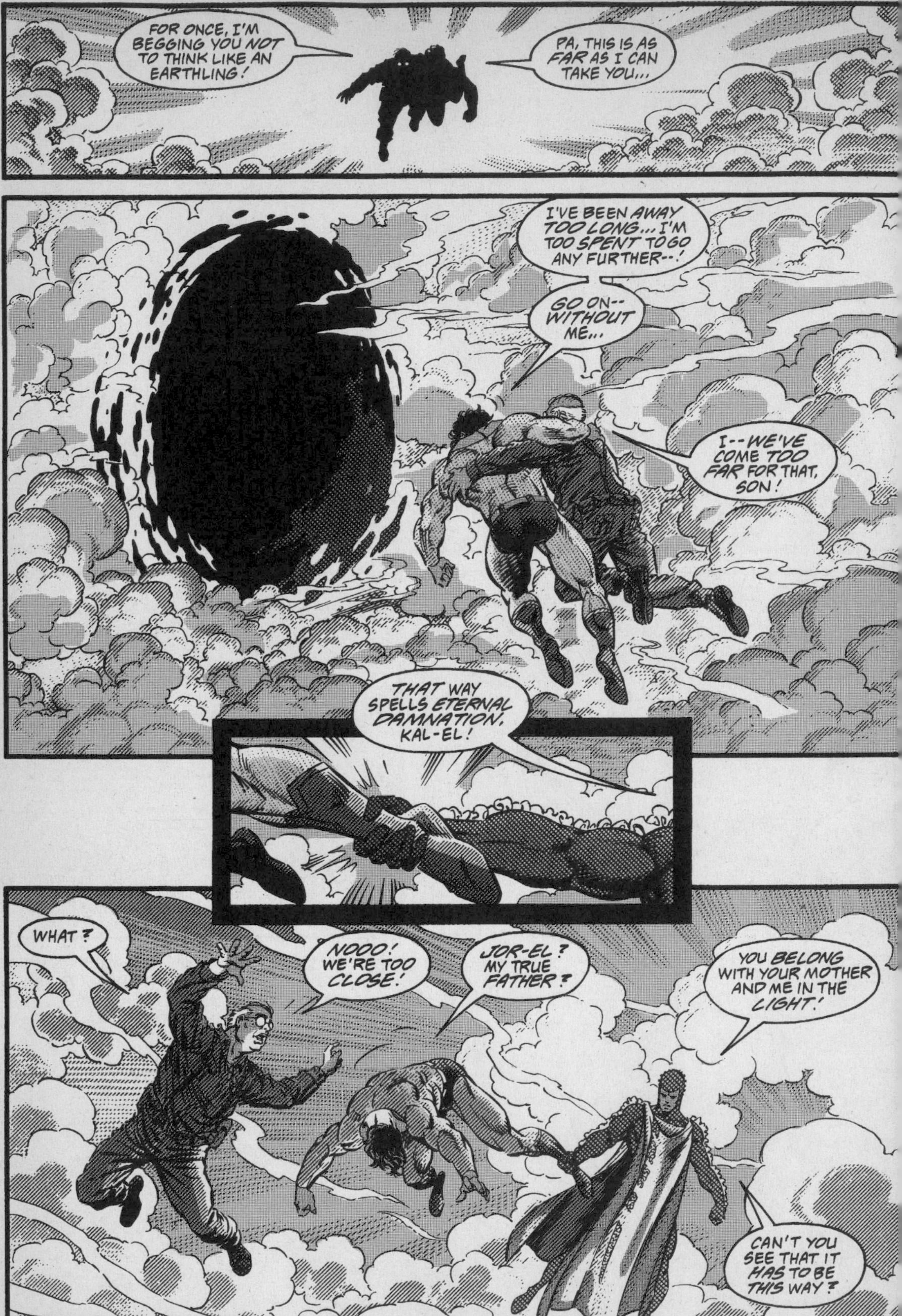
FOR ONCE, I'M BEGGING YOU NOT TO THINK LIKE AN EARTHLING!
PA, THIS IS AS FAR AS I CAN TAKE YOU...
I'VE BEEN AWAY TOO LONG... I'M TOO SPENT TO GO ANY FURTHER--!
GO ON-- WITHOUT ME...
I--WE'VE COME TOO FAR FOR THAT, SON!
THAT WAY SPELLS ETERNAL DAMNATION, KAL-EL!
WHAT?
NOOO! WE'RE TOO CLOSE!
JOR-EL? MY TRUE FATHER?
YOU BELONG WITH YOUR MOTHER AND ME IN THE LIGHT!
CAN'T YOU SEE THAT IT HAS TO BE THIS WAY?

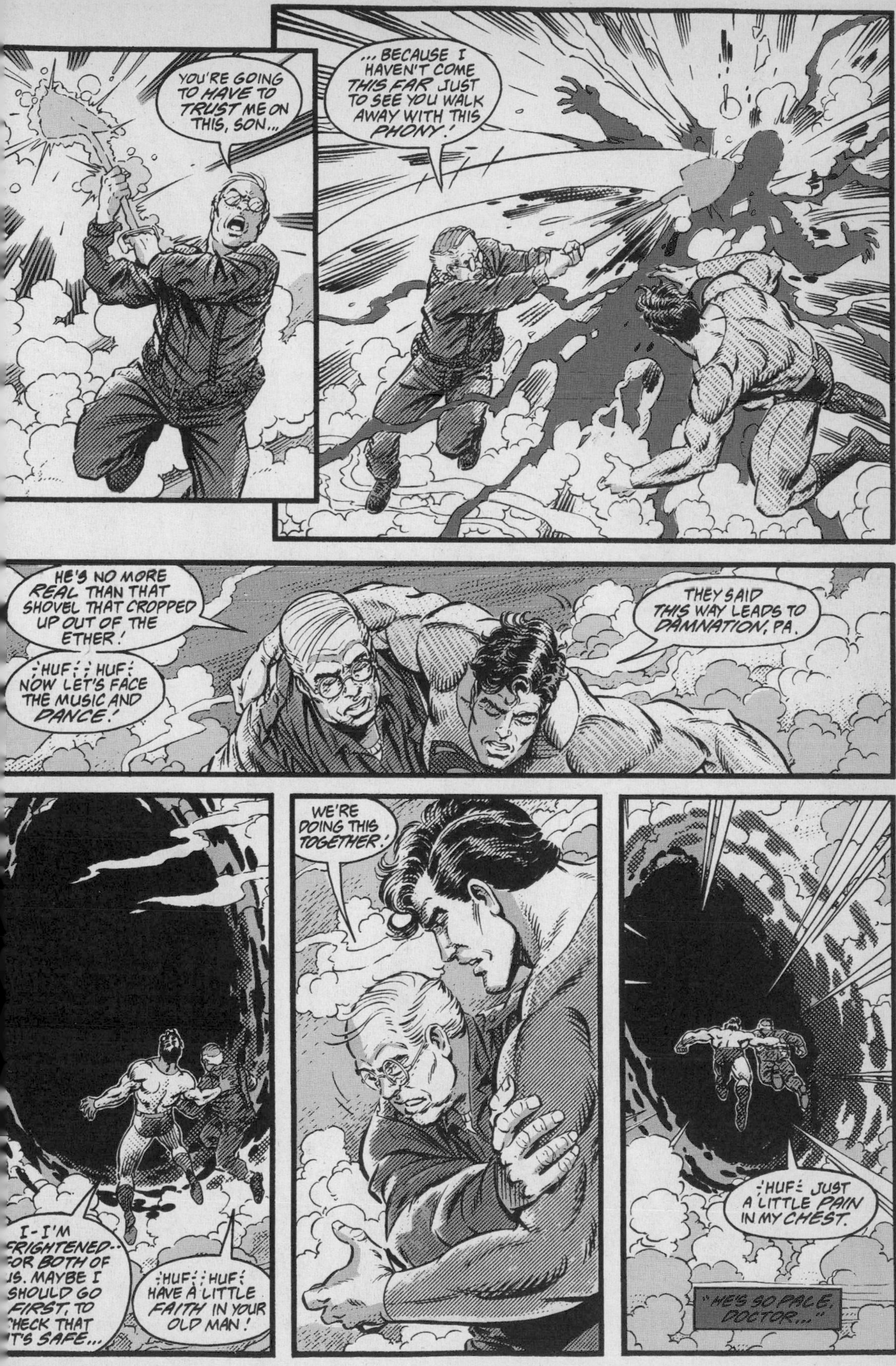

YOU'RE GOING TO HAVE TO TRUST ME ON THIS, SON...
...BECAUSE I HAVEN'T COME THIS FAR JUST TO SEE YOU WALK AWAY WITH THIS PHONY!
HE'S NO MORE REAL THAN THAT SHOVEL THAT CROPPED UP OUT OF THE ETHER!
HUF HUF NOW LET'S FACE THE MUSIC AND DANCE!
THEY SAID THIS WAY LEADS TO DAMNATION, PA.
I-I'M FRIGHTENED-- FOR BOTH OF US. MAYBE I SHOULD GO FIRST, TO CHECK THAT IT'S SAFE...
HUF HUF HAVE A LITTLE FAITH IN YOUR OLD MAN!
WE'RE DOING THIS TOGETHER!
HUF JUST A LITTLE PAIN IN MY CHEST.
"HE'S SO PALE, DOCTOR..."

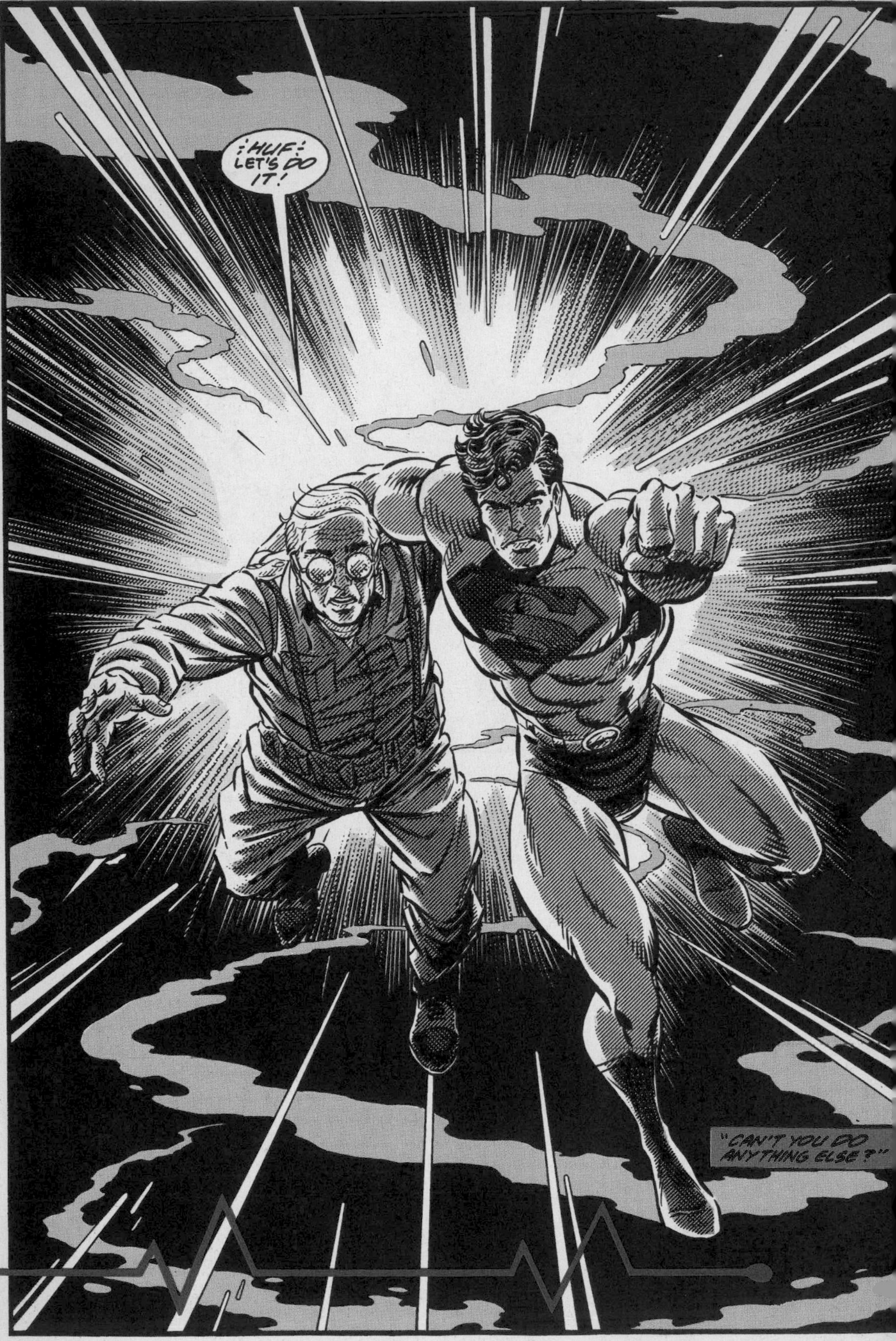
:HUF: LET'S DO IT!
"CAN'T YOU DO ANYTHING ELSE?"

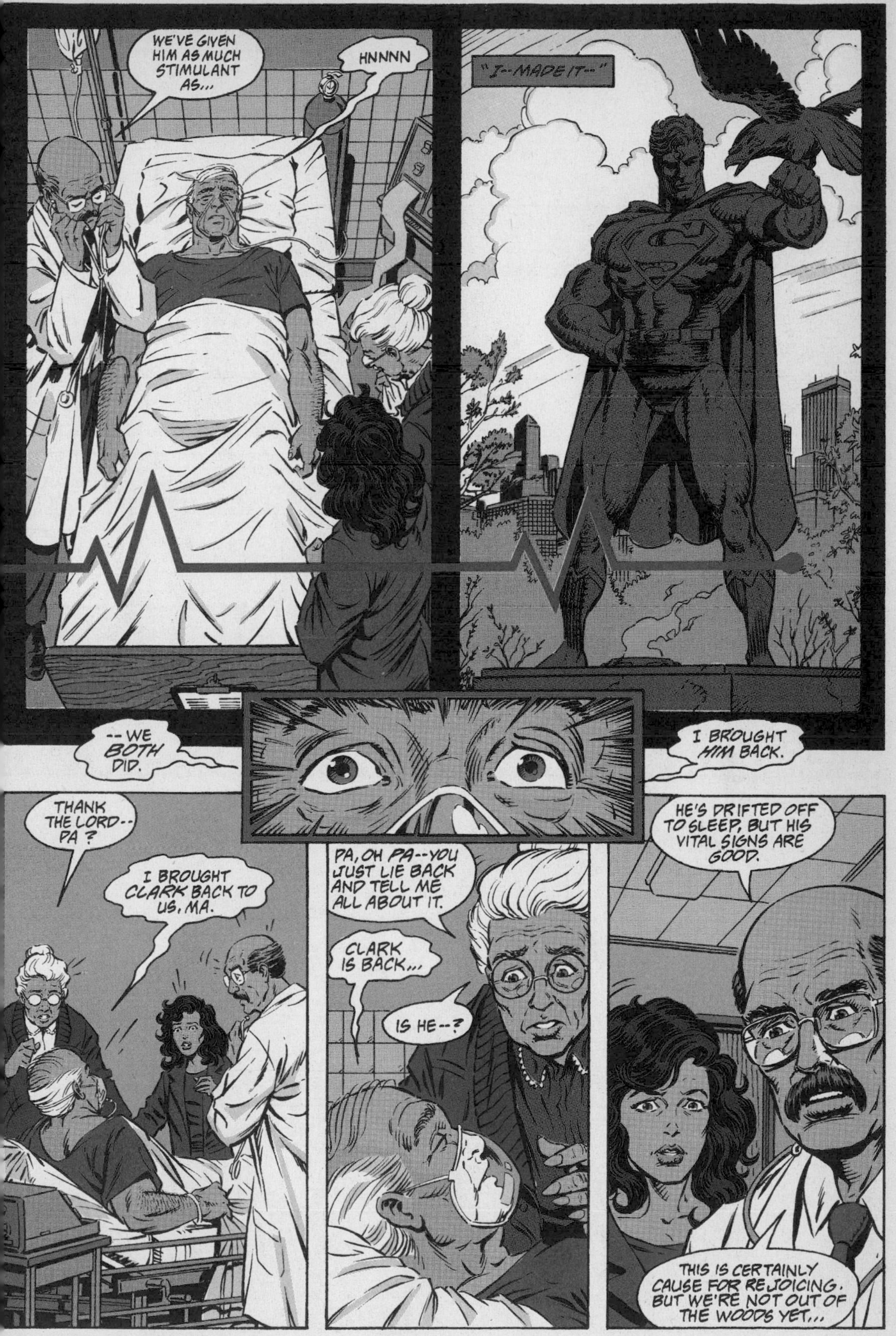
WE'VE GIVEN HIM AS MUCH STIMULANT AS...
HNNNN
"I--MADE IT--"
--WE BOTH DID.
I BROUGHT HIM BACK.
THANK THE LORD-- PA ?
I BROUGHT CLARK BACK TO US, MA.
PA, OH PA--YOU JUST LIE BACK AND TELL ME ALL ABOUT IT.
CLARK IS BACK...
IS HE--?
HE'S DRIFTED OFF TO SLEEP, BUT HIS VITAL SIGNS ARE GOOD.
THIS IS CERTAINLY CAUSE FOR REJOICING. BUT WE'RE NOT OUT OF THE WOODS YET...

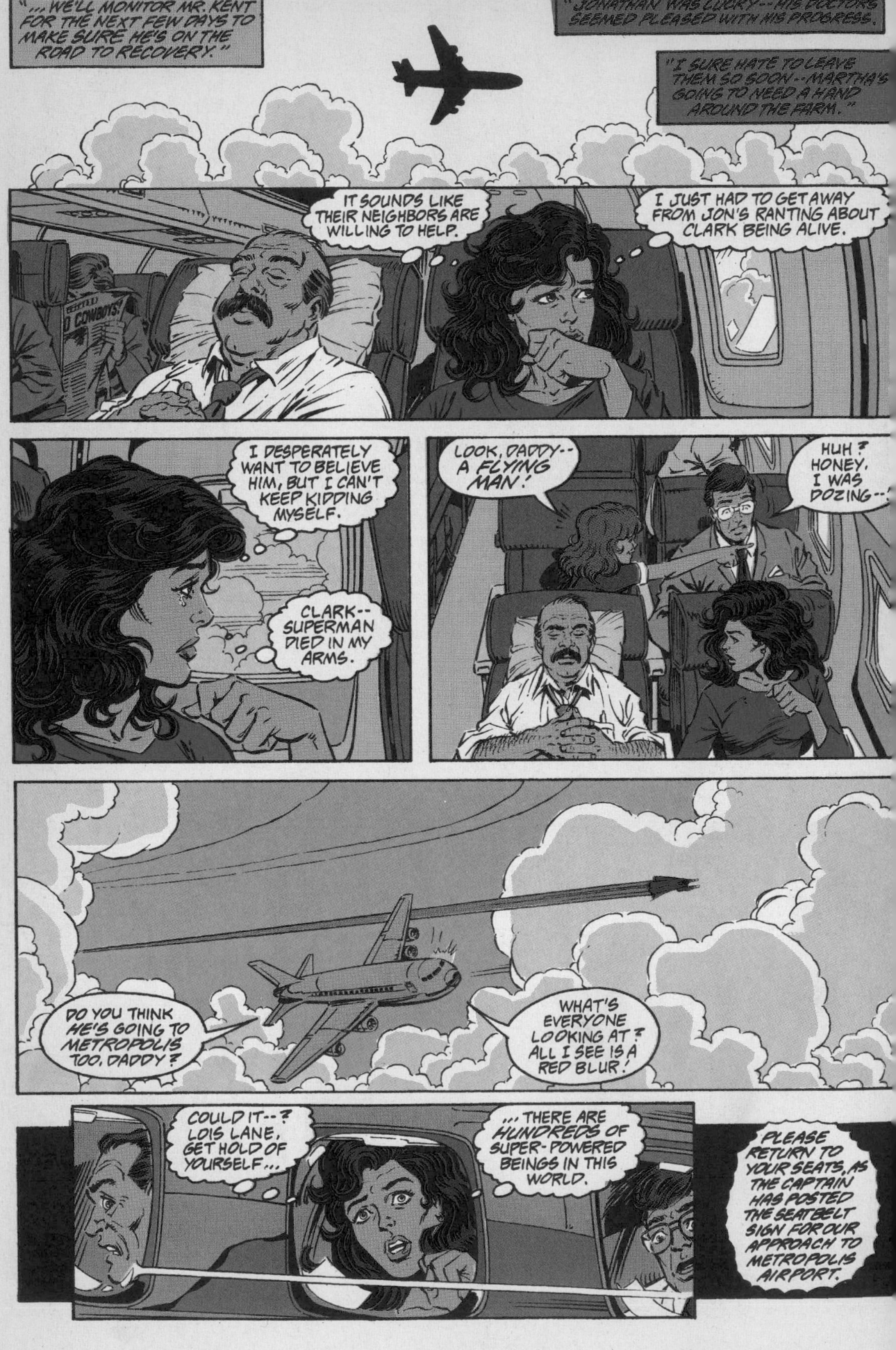
"...WE'LL MONITOR MR. KENT FOR THE NEXT FEW DAYS TO MAKE SURE HE'S ON THE ROAD TO RECOVERY."
"JONATHAN WAS LUCKY--HIS DOCTORS SEEMED PLEASED WITH HIS PROGRESS.
"I SURE HATE TO LEAVE THEM SO SOON--MARTHA'S GOING TO NEED A HAND AROUND THE FARM."
IT SOUNDS LIKE THEIR NEIGHBORS ARE WILLING TO HELP.
I JUST HAD TO GET AWAY FROM JON'S RANTING ABOUT CLARK BEING ALIVE.
COWBOYS!
I DESPERATELY WANT TO BELIEVE HIM, BUT I CAN'T KEEP KIDDING MYSELF.
CLARK--SUPERMAN DIED IN MY ARMS.
LOOK, DADDY--A FLYING MAN!
HUH? HONEY, I WAS DOZING--
DO YOU THINK HE'S GOING TO METROPOLIS TOO, DADDY?
WHAT'S EVERYONE LOOKING AT? ALL I SEE IS A RED BLUR!
COULD IT--? LOIS LANE, GET HOLD OF YOURSELF...
...THERE ARE HUNDREDS OF SUPER-POWERED BEINGS IN THIS WORLD.
PLEASE RETURN TO YOUR SEATS, AS THE CAPTAIN HAS POSTED THE SEATBELT SIGN FOR OUR APPROACH TO METROPOLIS AIRPORT.

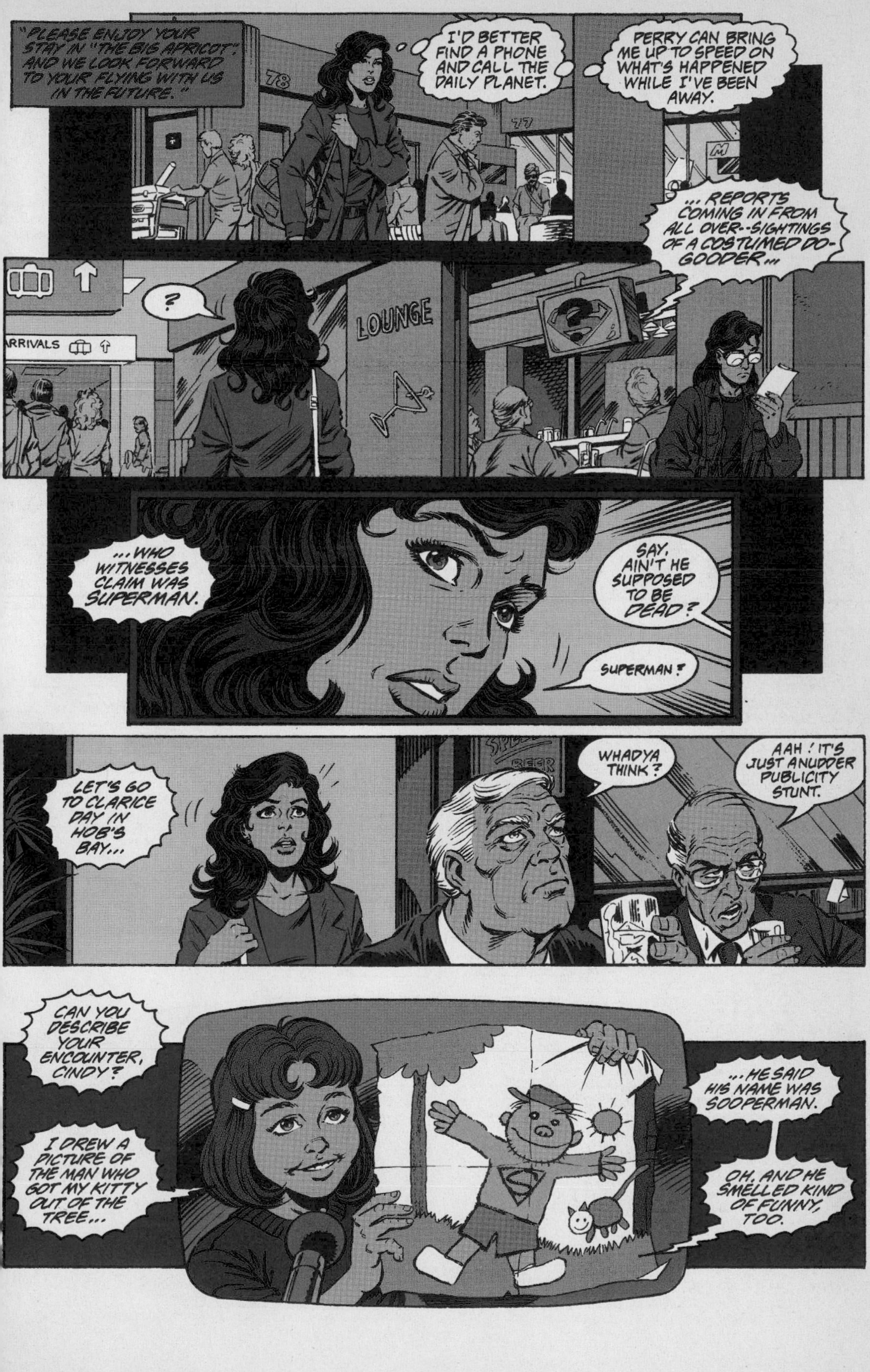
"PLEASE ENJOY YOUR STAY IN "THE BIG APRICOT" AND WE LOOK FORWARD TO YOUR FLYING WITH US IN THE FUTURE."
78
77
I'D BETTER FIND A PHONE AND CALL THE DAILY PLANET.
PERRY CAN BRING ME UP TO SPEED ON WHAT'S HAPPENED WHILE I'VE BEEN AWAY.
...REPORTS COMING IN FROM ALL OVER--SIGHTINGS OF A COSTUMED DO-GOODER...
?
ARRIVALS
LOUNGE
...WHO WITNESSES CLAIM WAS SUPERMAN.
SAY, AIN'T HE SUPPOSED TO BE DEAD?
SUPERMAN?
LET'S GO TO CLARICE DAY IN HOB'S BAY...
WHADYA THINK?
AAH! IT'S JUST ANUDDER PUBLICITY STUNT.
CAN YOU DESCRIBE YOUR ENCOUNTER, CINDY?
I DREW A PICTURE OF THE MAN WHO GOT MY KITTY OUT OF THE TREE...
...HE SAID HIS NAME WAS SOOPERMAN.
OH, AND HE SMELLED KIND OF FUNNY, TOO.

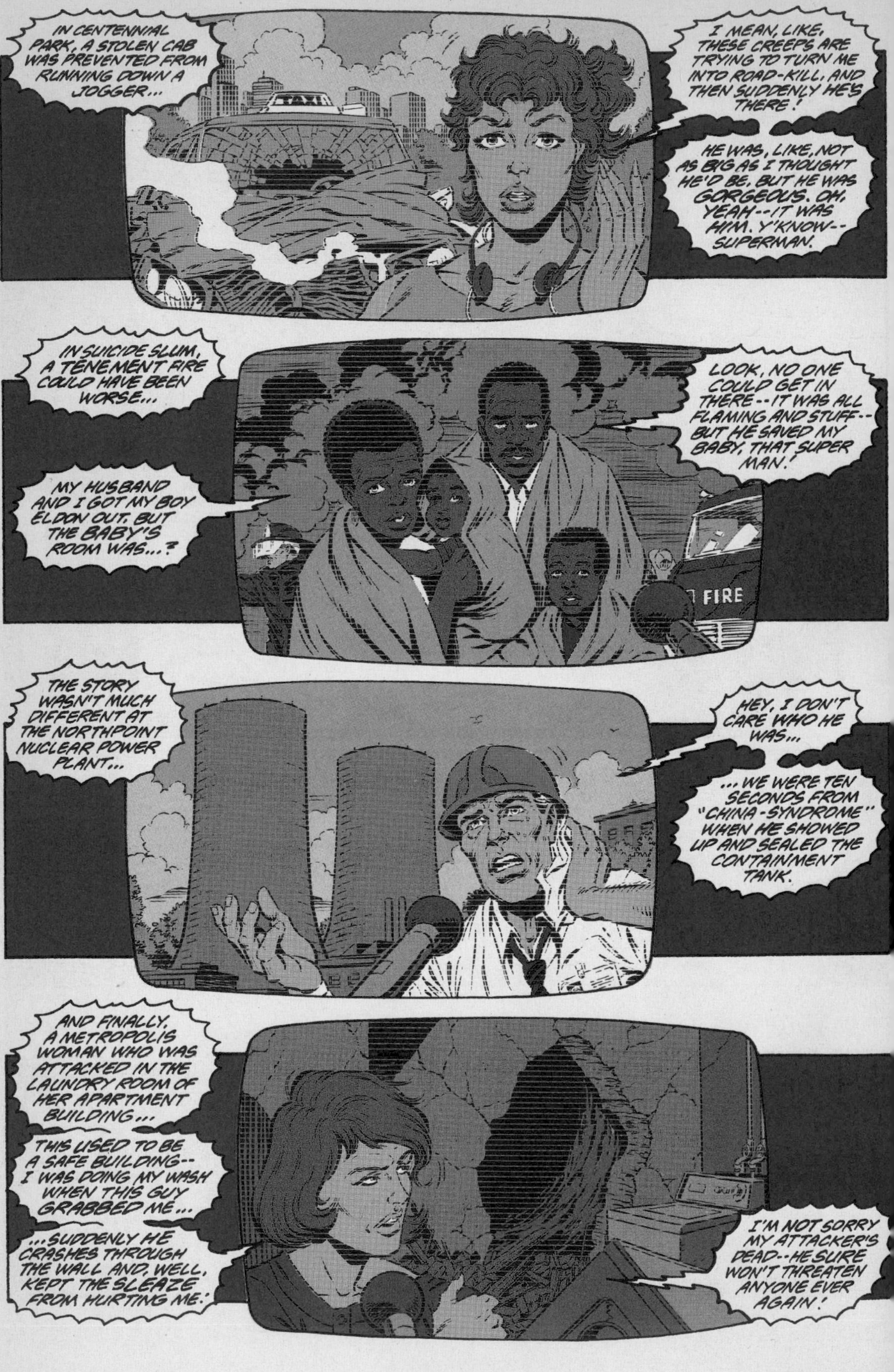
IN CENTENNIAL PARK, A STOLEN CAB WAS PREVENTED FROM RUNNING DOWN A JOGGER...
TAXI
I MEAN, LIKE, THESE CREEPS ARE TRYING TO TURN ME INTO ROAD-KILL, AND THEN SUDDENLY HE'S THERE!
HE WAS, LIKE, NOT AS BIG AS I THOUGHT HE'D BE. BUT HE WAS GORGEOUS. OH, YEAH--IT WAS HIM. Y'KNOW--SUPERMAN.
IN SUICIDE SLUM, A TENEMENT FIRE COULD HAVE BEEN WORSE...
MY HUSBAND AND I GOT MY BOY ELDON OUT. BUT THE BABY'S ROOM WAS...?
LOOK, NO ONE COULD GET IN THERE--IT WAS ALL FLAMING AND STUFF--BUT HE SAVED MY BABY, THAT SUPER MAN!
FIRE
THE STORY WASN'T MUCH DIFFERENT AT THE NORTHPOINT NUCLEAR POWER PLANT...
HEY, I DON'T CARE WHO HE WAS...
...WE WERE TEN SECONDS FROM "CHINA-SYNDROME" WHEN HE SHOWED UP AND SEALED THE CONTAINMENT TANK.
AND FINALLY, A METROPOLIS WOMAN WHO WAS ATTACKED IN THE LAUNDRY ROOM OF HER APARTMENT BUILDING...
THIS USED TO BE A SAFE BUILDING--I WAS DOING MY WASH WHEN THIS GUY GRABBED ME...
...SUDDENLY HE CRASHES THROUGH THE WALL AND, WELL, KEPT THE SLEAZE FROM HURTING ME!
I'M NOT SORRY MY ATTACKER'S DEAD--HE SURE WON'T THREATEN ANYONE EVER AGAIN!

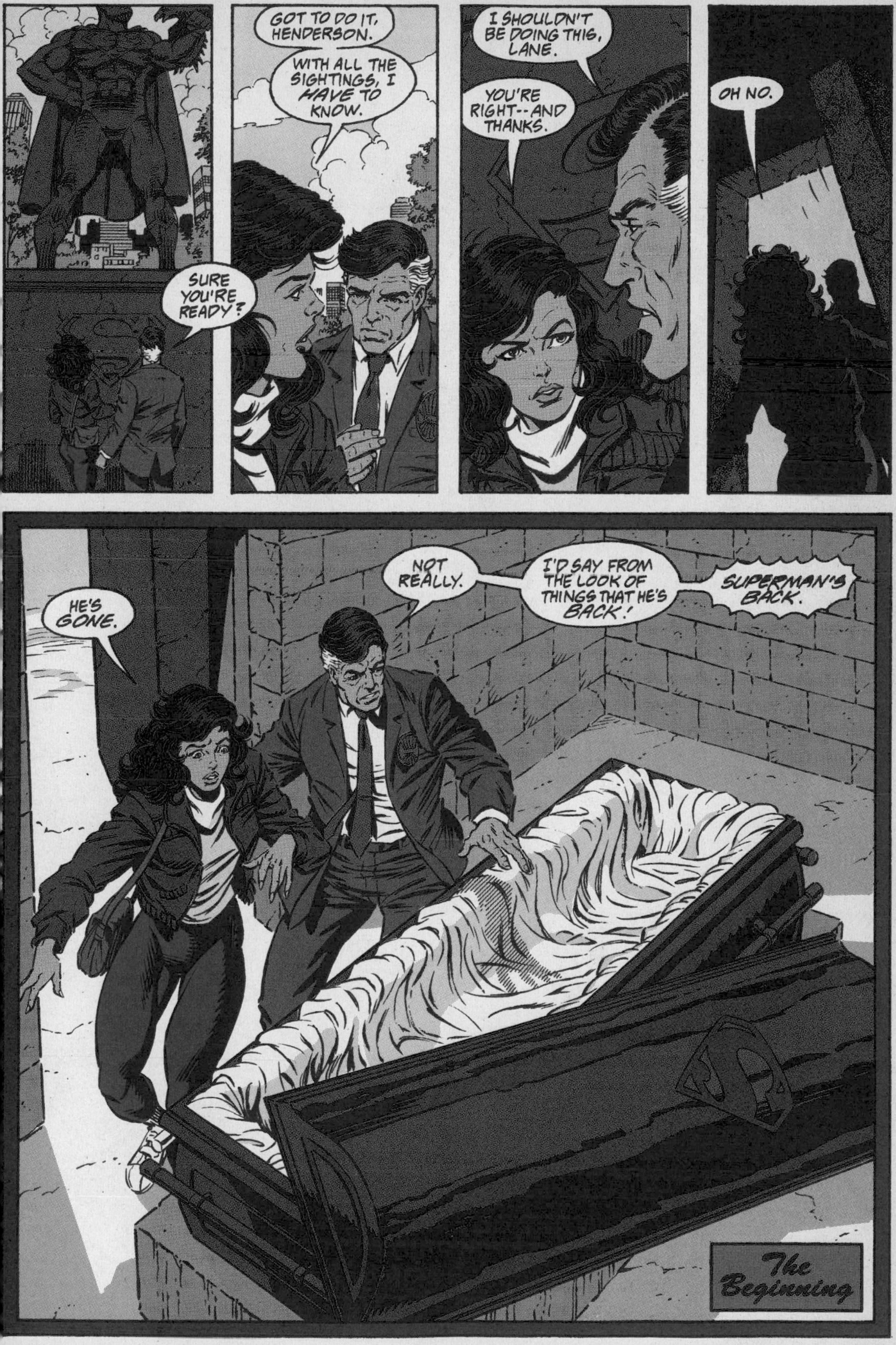
SURE YOU'RE READY?
GOT TO DO IT, HENDERSON.
WITH ALL THE SIGHTINGS, I HAVE TO KNOW.
I SHOULDN'T BE DOING THIS, LANE.
YOU'RE RIGHT--AND THANKS.
OH NO.
HE'S GONE.
NOT REALLY.
I'D SAY FROM THE LOOK OF THINGS THAT HE'S BACK!
SUPERMAN'S BACK.
The Beginning

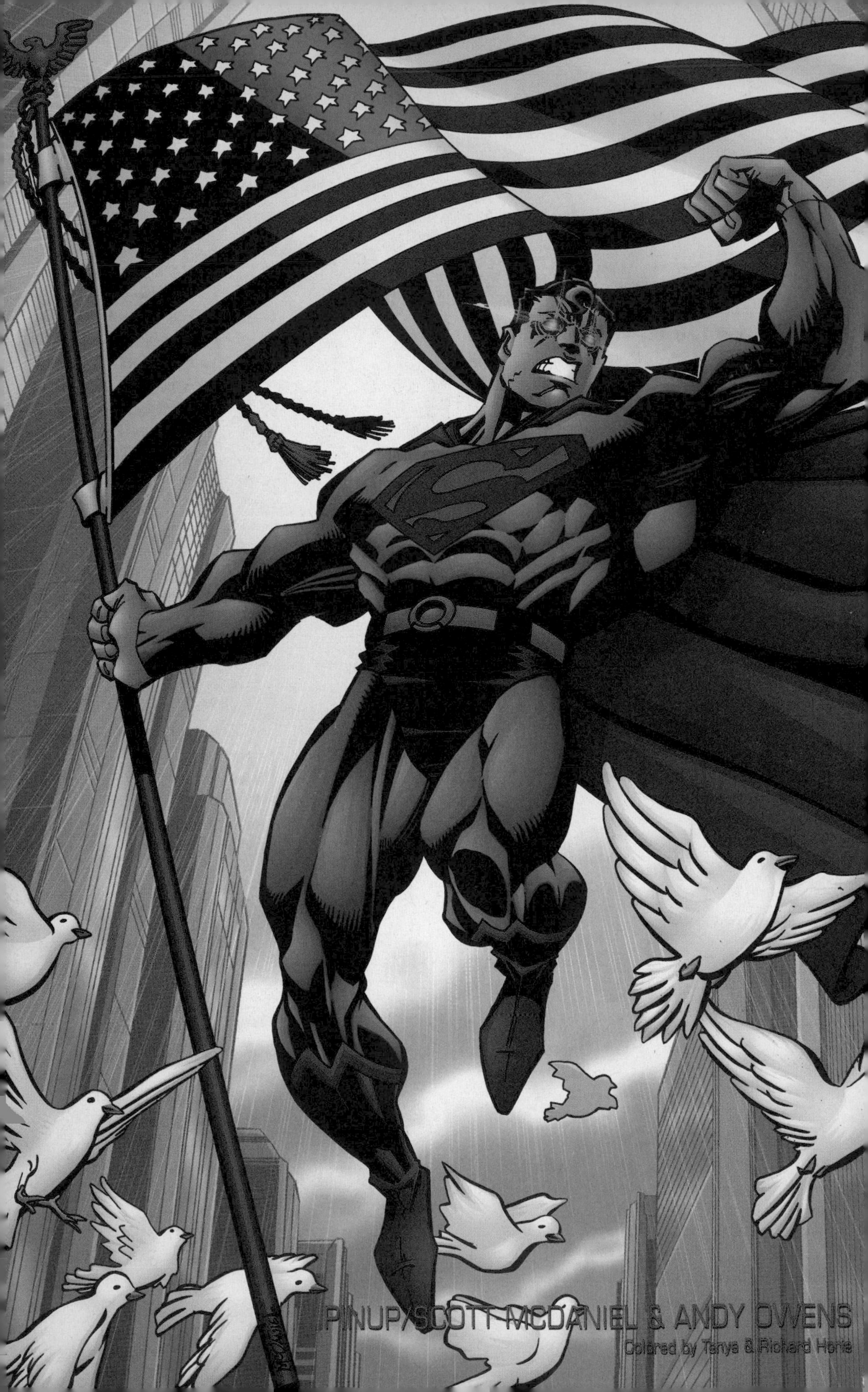
PINUP/SCOTT McDANIEL & ANDY OWENS
Colored by Tanya & Richard Horie

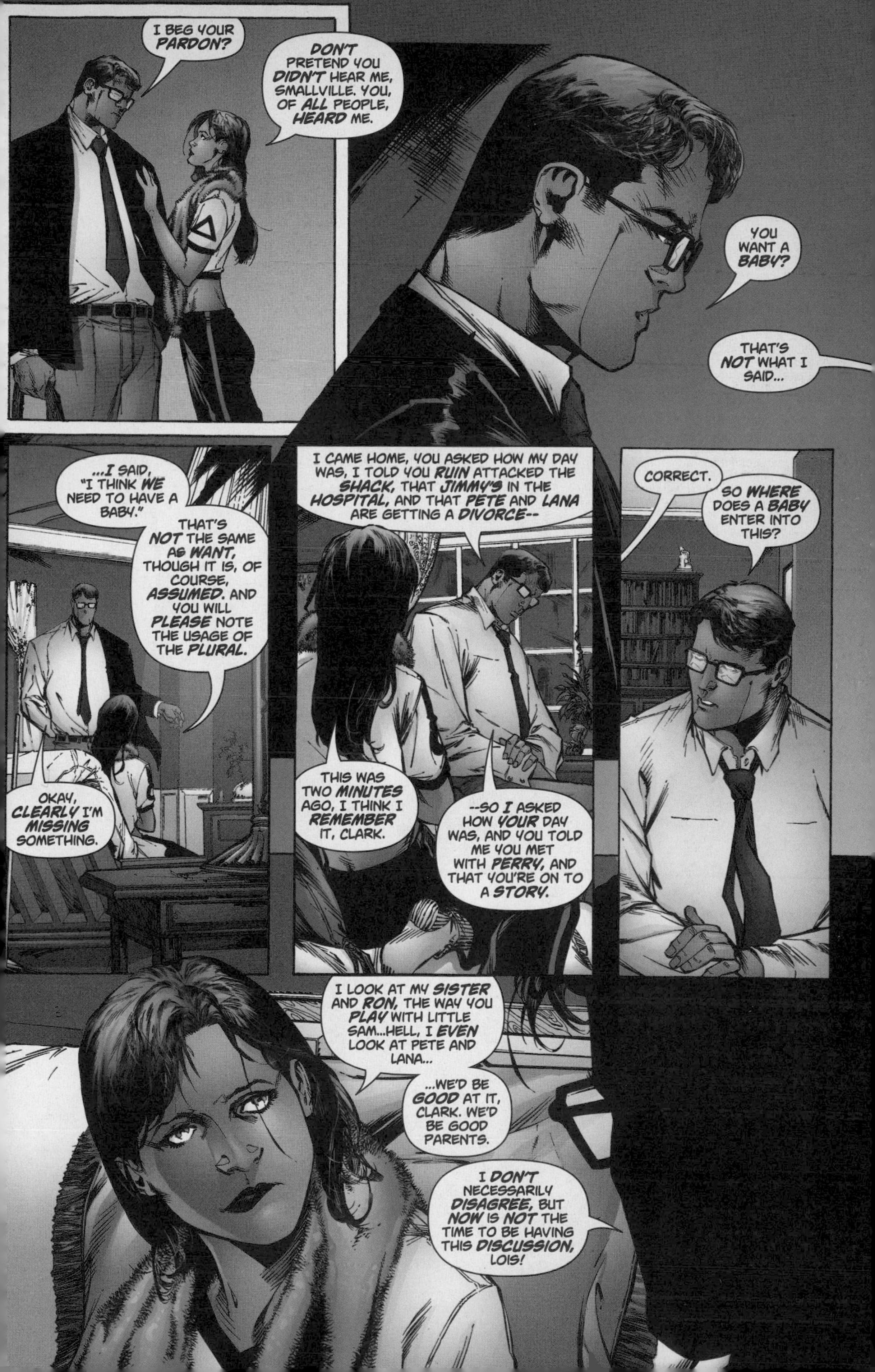

I BEG YOUR PARDON?
DON'T PRETEND YOU DIDN'T HEAR ME, SMALLVILLE. YOU, OF ALL PEOPLE, HEARD ME.
YOU WANT A BABY?
THAT'S NOT WHAT I SAID...
...I SAID, "I THINK WE NEED TO HAVE A BABY."
THAT'S NOT THE SAME AS WANT, THOUGH IT IS, OF COURSE, ASSUMED. AND YOU WILL PLEASE NOTE THE USAGE OF THE PLURAL.
OKAY, CLEARLY I'M MISSING SOMETHING.
I CAME HOME, YOU ASKED HOW MY DAY WAS, I TOLD YOU RUIN ATTACKED THE SHACK, THAT JIMMY'S IN THE HOSPITAL, AND THAT PETE AND LANA ARE GETTING A DIVORCE--
THIS WAS TWO MINUTES AGO, I THINK I REMEMBER IT, CLARK.
--SO I ASKED HOW YOUR DAY WAS, AND YOU TOLD ME YOU MET WITH PERRY, AND THAT YOU'RE ON TO A STORY.
CORRECT.
SO WHERE DOES A BABY ENTER INTO THIS?
I LOOK AT MY SISTER AND RON, THE WAY YOU PLAY WITH LITTLE SAM...HELL, I EVEN LOOK AT PETE AND LANA...
...WE'D BE GOOD AT IT, CLARK. WE'D BE GOOD PARENTS.
I DON'T NECESSARILY DISAGREE, BUT NOW IS NOT THE TIME TO BE HAVING THIS DISCUSSION, LOIS!

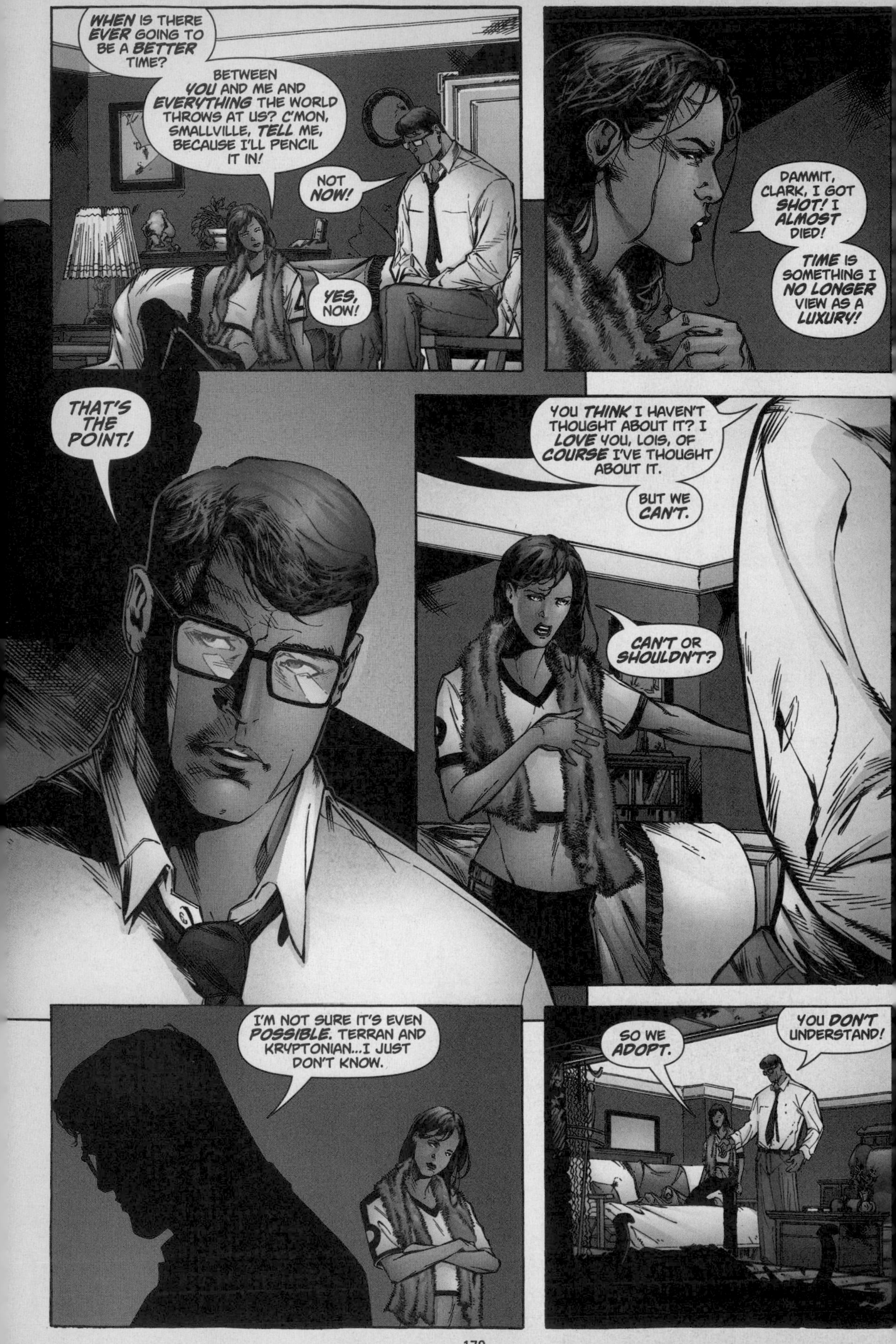
WHEN IS THERE EVER GOING TO BE A BETTER TIME?
BETWEEN YOU AND ME AND EVERYTHING THE WORLD THROWS AT US? C'MON, SMALLVILLE, TELL ME, BECAUSE I'LL PENCIL IT IN!
NOT NOW!
YES, NOW!
DAMMIT, CLARK, I GOT SHOT! I ALMOST DIED!
TIME IS SOMETHING I NO LONGER VIEW AS A LUXURY!
THAT'S THE POINT!
YOU THINK I HAVEN'T THOUGHT ABOUT IT? I LOVE YOU, LOIS, OF COURSE I'VE THOUGHT ABOUT IT.
BUT WE CAN'T.
CAN'T OR SHOULDN'T?
I'M NOT SURE IT'S EVEN POSSIBLE. TERRAN AND KRYPTONIAN...I JUST DON'T KNOW.
SO WE ADOPT.
YOU DON'T UNDERSTAND!

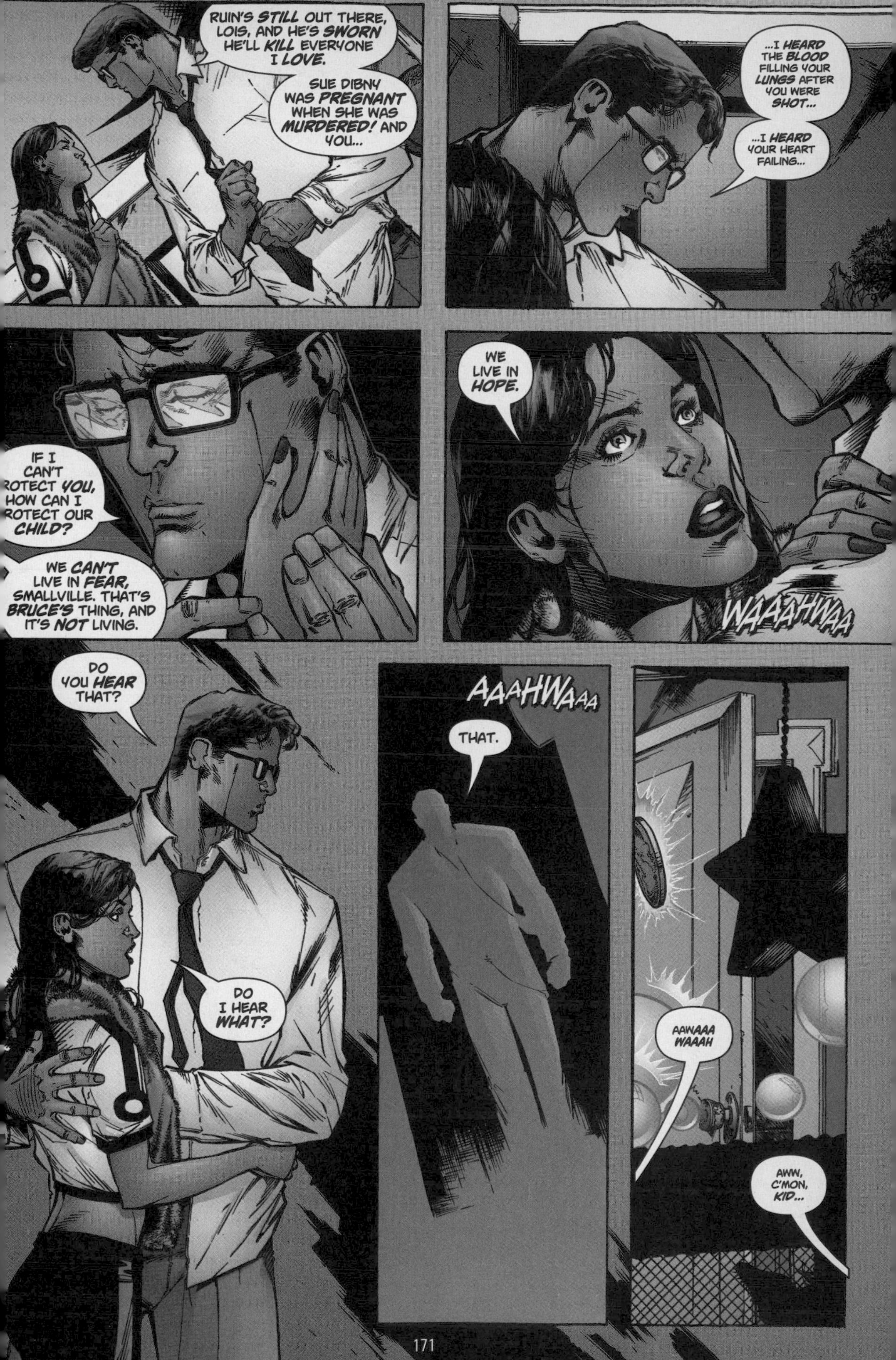

RUIN'S STILL OUT THERE, LOIS, AND HE'S SWORN HE'LL KILL EVERYONE I LOVE.
SUE DIBNY WAS PREGNANT WHEN SHE WAS MURDERED! AND YOU...
...I HEARD THE BLOOD FILLING YOUR LUNGS AFTER YOU WERE SHOT...
...I HEARD YOUR HEART FAILING...
IF I CAN'T PROTECT YOU, HOW CAN I PROTECT OUR CHILD?
WE CAN'T LIVE IN FEAR, SMALLVILLE. THAT'S BRUCE'S THING, AND IT'S NOT LIVING.
WE LIVE IN HOPE.
WAAAHWAA
DO YOU HEAR THAT?
DO I HEAR WHAT?
AAAHWAAA
THAT.
AAWAAA WAAAH
AWW, C'MON, KID...

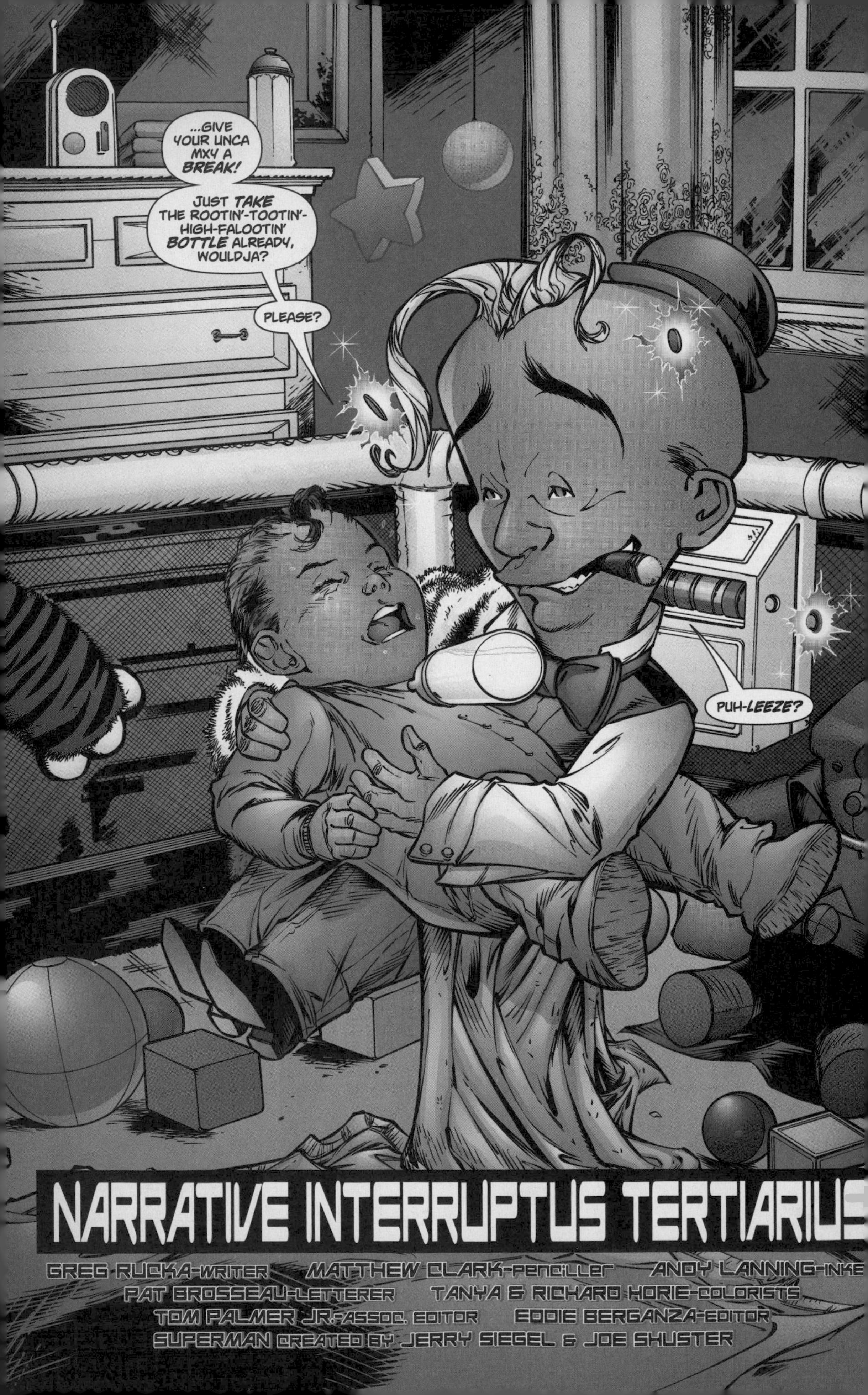
...GIVE YOUR UNCA MXY A BREAK!
JUST TAKE THE ROOTIN'-TOOTIN'-HIGH-FALOOTIN' BOTTLE ALREADY, WOULDJA?
PLEASE?
PUH-LEEZE?
NARRATIVE INTERRUPTUS TERTIARIUS
GREG RUCKA-WRITER MATTHEW CLARK-PENCILLER ANDY LANNING-INKER
PAT BROSSEAU-LETTERER TANYA & RICHARD HORIE-COLORISTS
TOM PALMER JR.-ASSOC. EDITOR EDDIE BERGANZA-EDITOR
SUPERMAN CREATED BY JERRY SIEGEL & JOE SHUSTER

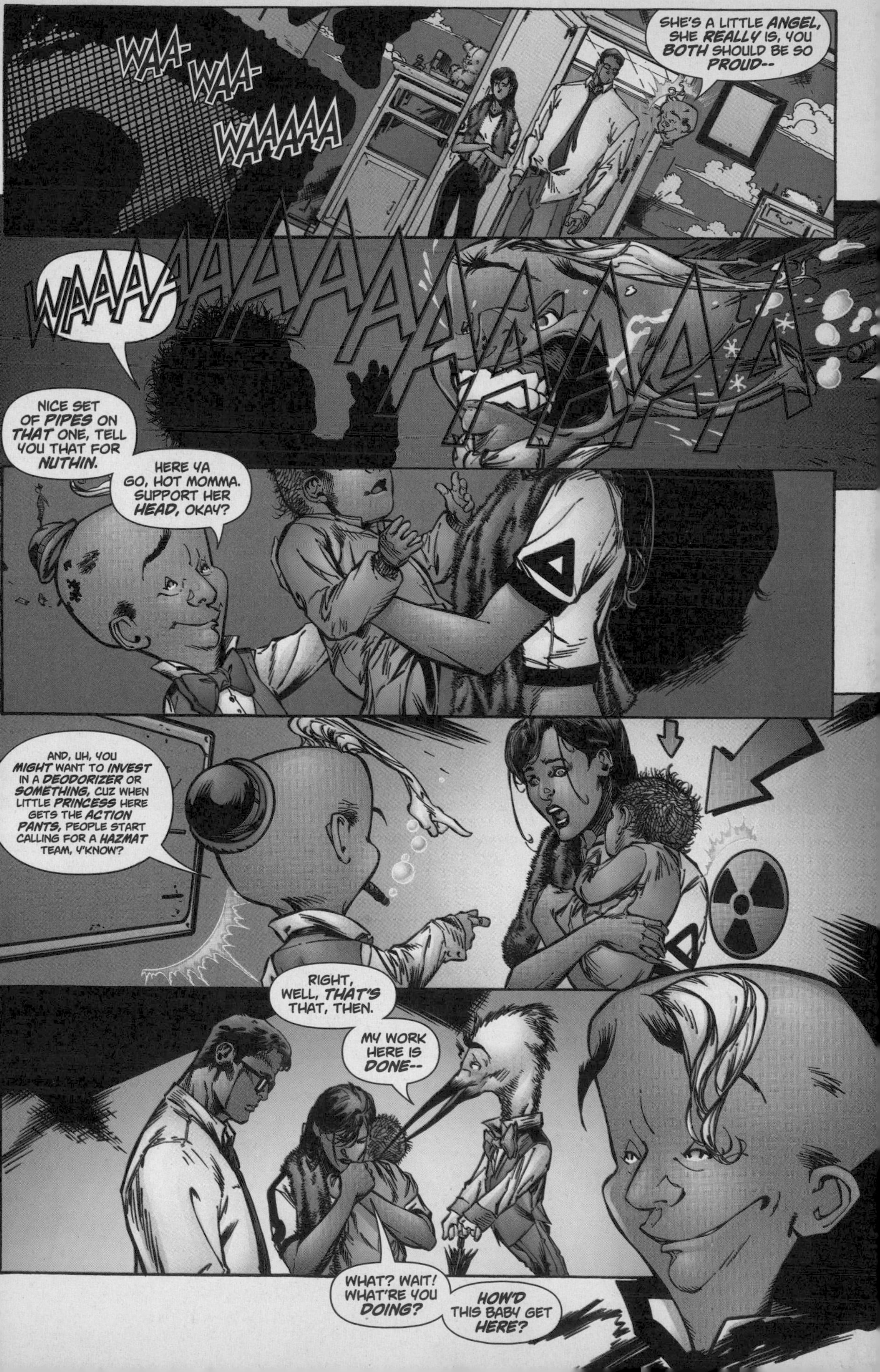
WAA-
WAA-
WAAAA
SHE'S A LITTLE ANGEL, SHE REALLY IS, YOU BOTH SHOULD BE SO PROUD--
WAAAAAAAAAAAAAAA
NICE SET OF PIPES ON THAT ONE, TELL YOU THAT FOR NUTHIN.
HERE YA GO, HOT MOMMA. SUPPORT HER HEAD, OKAY?
AND, UH, YOU MIGHT WANT TO INVEST IN A DEODORIZER OR SOMETHING, CUZ WHEN LITTLE PRINCESS HERE GETS THE ACTION PANTS, PEOPLE START CALLING FOR A HAZMAT TEAM, Y'KNOW?
RIGHT, WELL, THAT'S THAT, THEN.
MY WORK HERE IS DONE--
WHAT? WAIT! WHAT'RE YOU DOING?
HOW'D THIS BABY GET HERE?

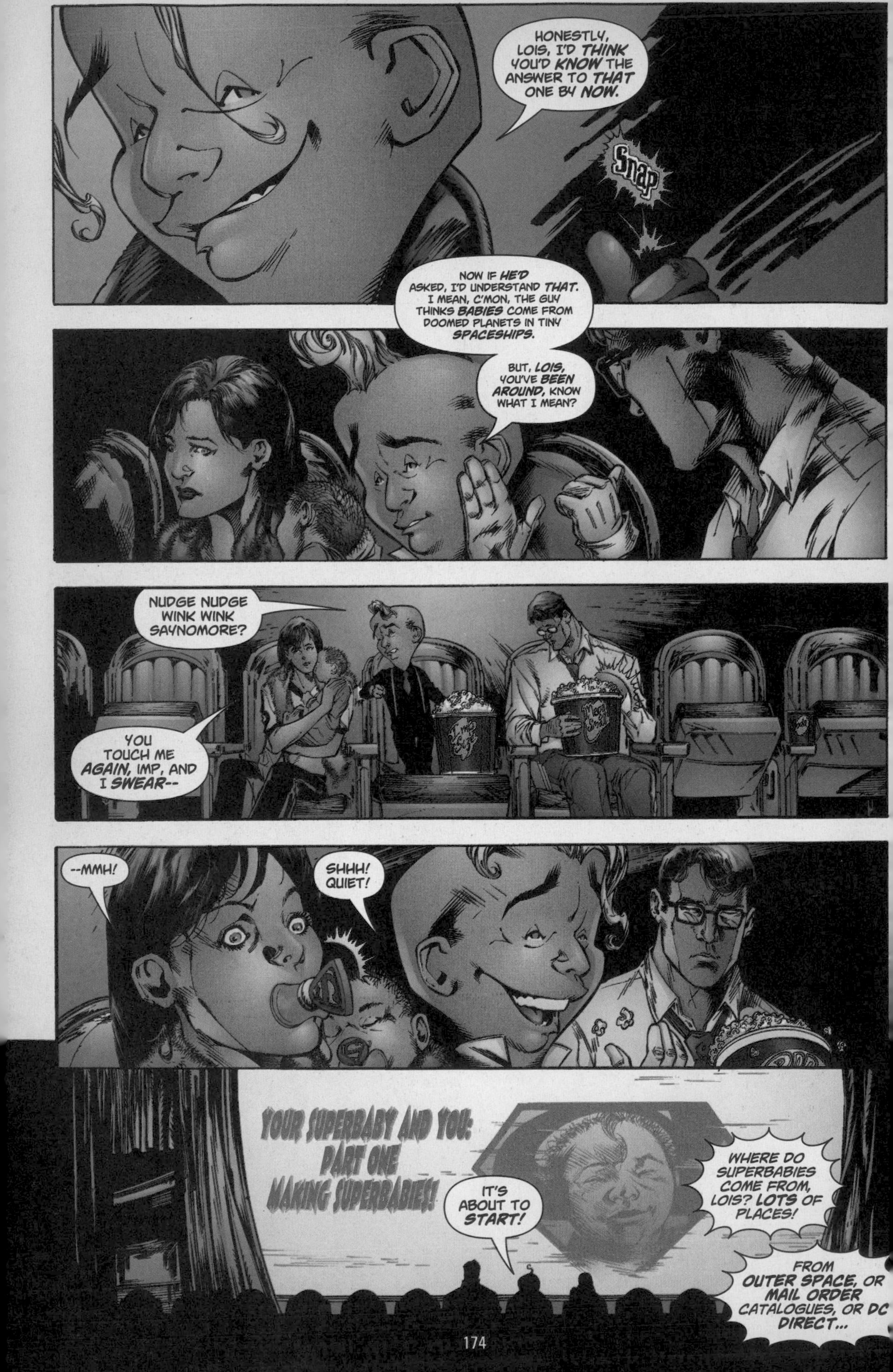
HONESTLY, LOIS, I'D THINK YOU'D KNOW THE ANSWER TO THAT ONE BY NOW.
Snap
NOW IF HE'D ASKED, I'D UNDERSTAND THAT. I MEAN, C'MON, THE GUY THINKS BABIES COME FROM DOOMED PLANETS IN TINY SPACESHIPS.
BUT, LOIS, YOU'VE BEEN AROUND, KNOW WHAT I MEAN?
NUDGE NUDGE WINK WINK SAYNOMORE?
YOU TOUCH ME AGAIN, IMP, AND I SWEAR--
--MMH!
SHHH! QUIET!
YOUR SUPERBABY AND YOU: PART ONE MAKING SUPERBABIES!
IT'S ABOUT TO START!
WHERE DO SUPERBABIES COME FROM, LOIS? LOTS OF PLACES!
FROM OUTER SPACE, OR MAIL ORDER CATALOGUES, OR DC DIRECT...

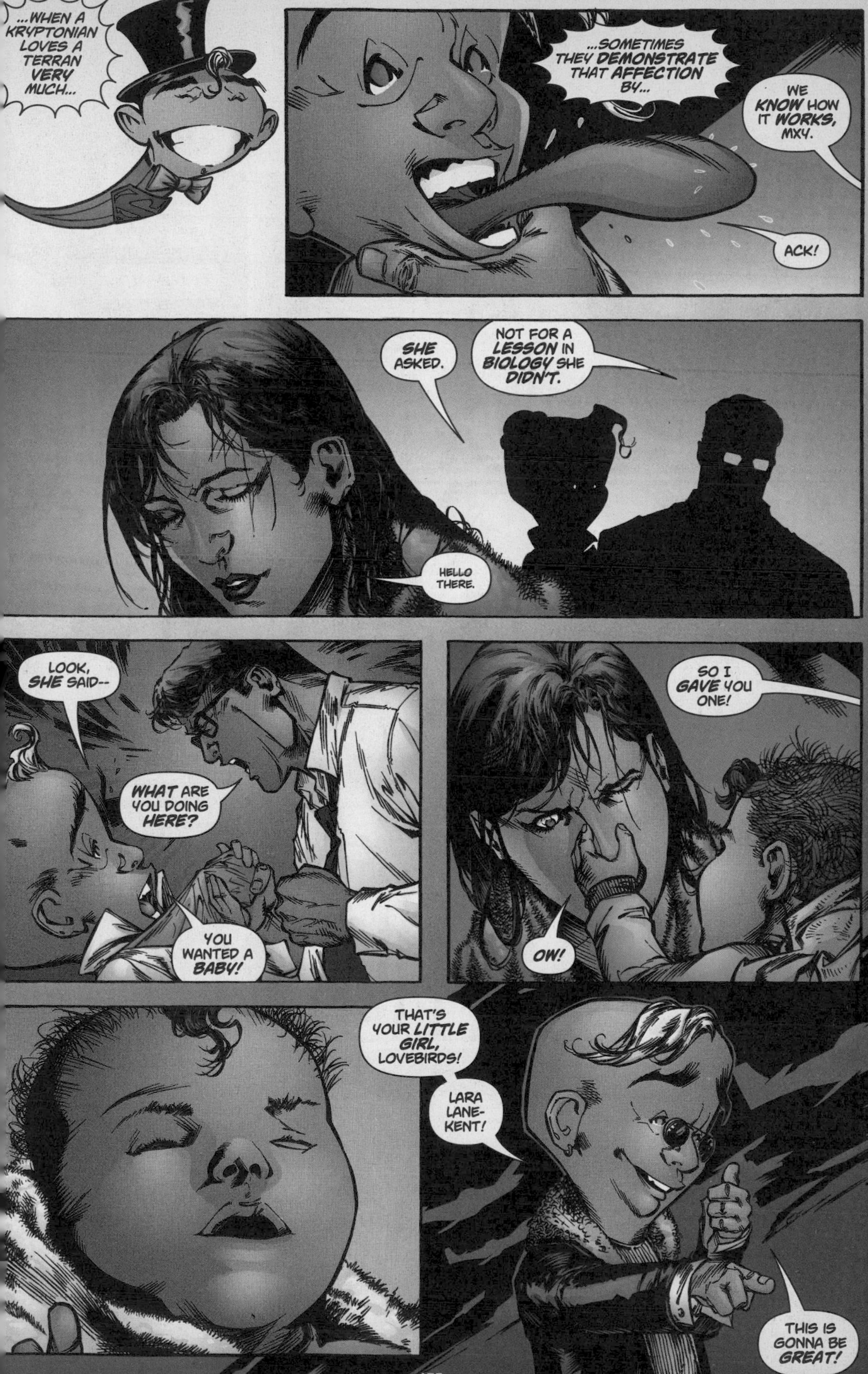
...WHEN A KRYPTONIAN LOVES A TERRAN VERY MUCH...
...SOMETIMES THEY DEMONSTRATE THAT AFFECTION BY...
WE KNOW HOW IT WORKS, MXY.
ACK!
SHE ASKED.
NOT FOR A LESSON IN BIOLOGY SHE DIDN'T.
HELLO THERE.
LOOK, SHE SAID--
WHAT ARE YOU DOING HERE?
YOU WANTED A BABY!
SO I GAVE YOU ONE!
OW!
THAT'S YOUR LITTLE GIRL, LOVEBIRDS!
LARA LANE-KENT!
THIS IS GONNA BE GREAT!

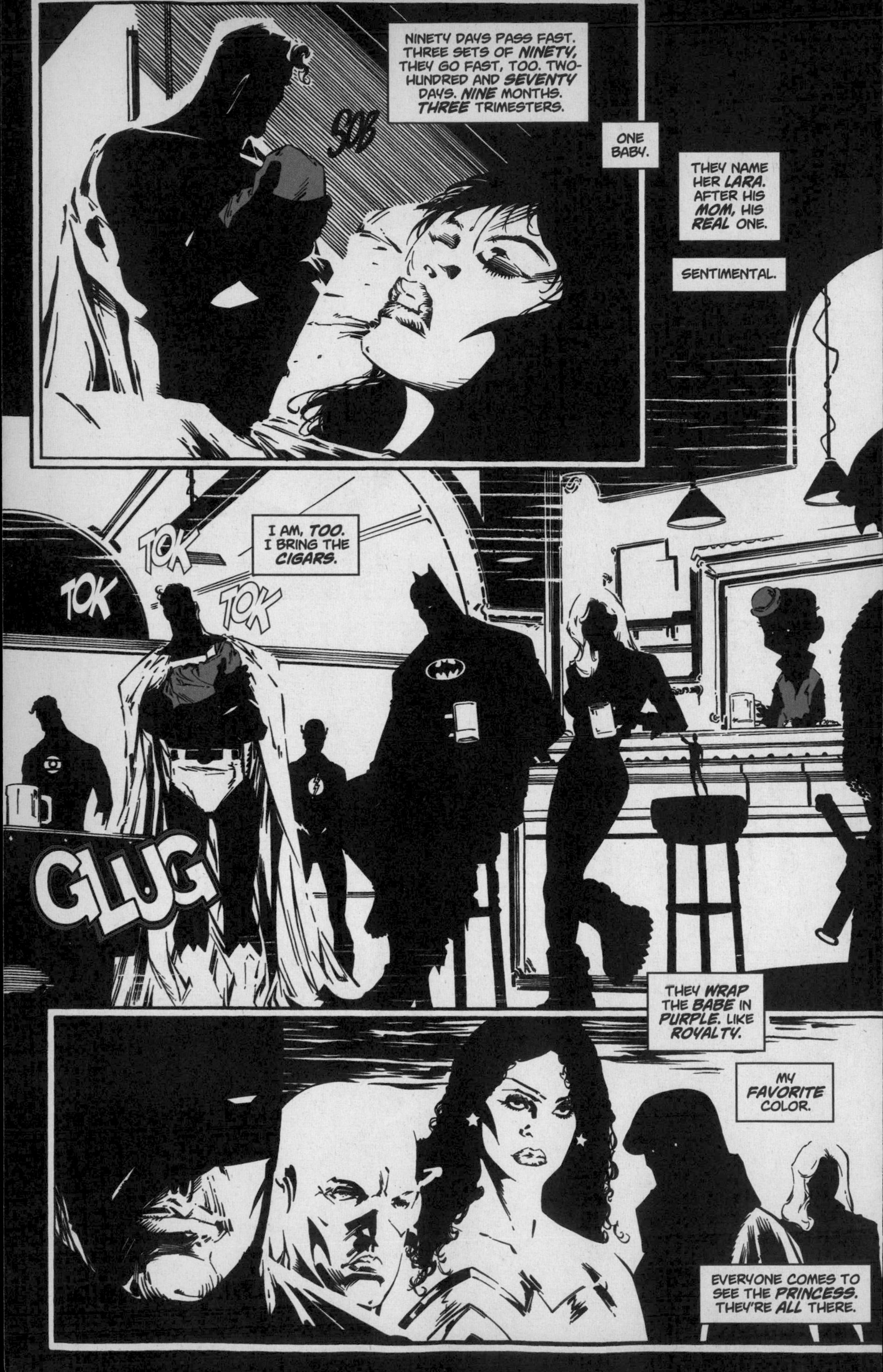
NINETY DAYS PASS FAST. THREE SETS OF NINETY, THEY GO FAST, TOO. TWO-HUNDRED AND SEVENTY DAYS. NINE MONTHS. THREE TRIMESTERS.
SOB
ONE BABY.
THEY NAME HER LARA. AFTER HIS MOM, HIS REAL ONE.
SENTIMENTAL.
I AM, TOO. I BRING THE CIGARS.
TOK
TOK
TOK
GLUG
THEY WRAP THE BABE IN PURPLE. LIKE ROYALTY.
MY FAVORITE COLOR.
EVERYONE COMES TO SEE THE PRINCESS. THEY'RE ALL THERE.

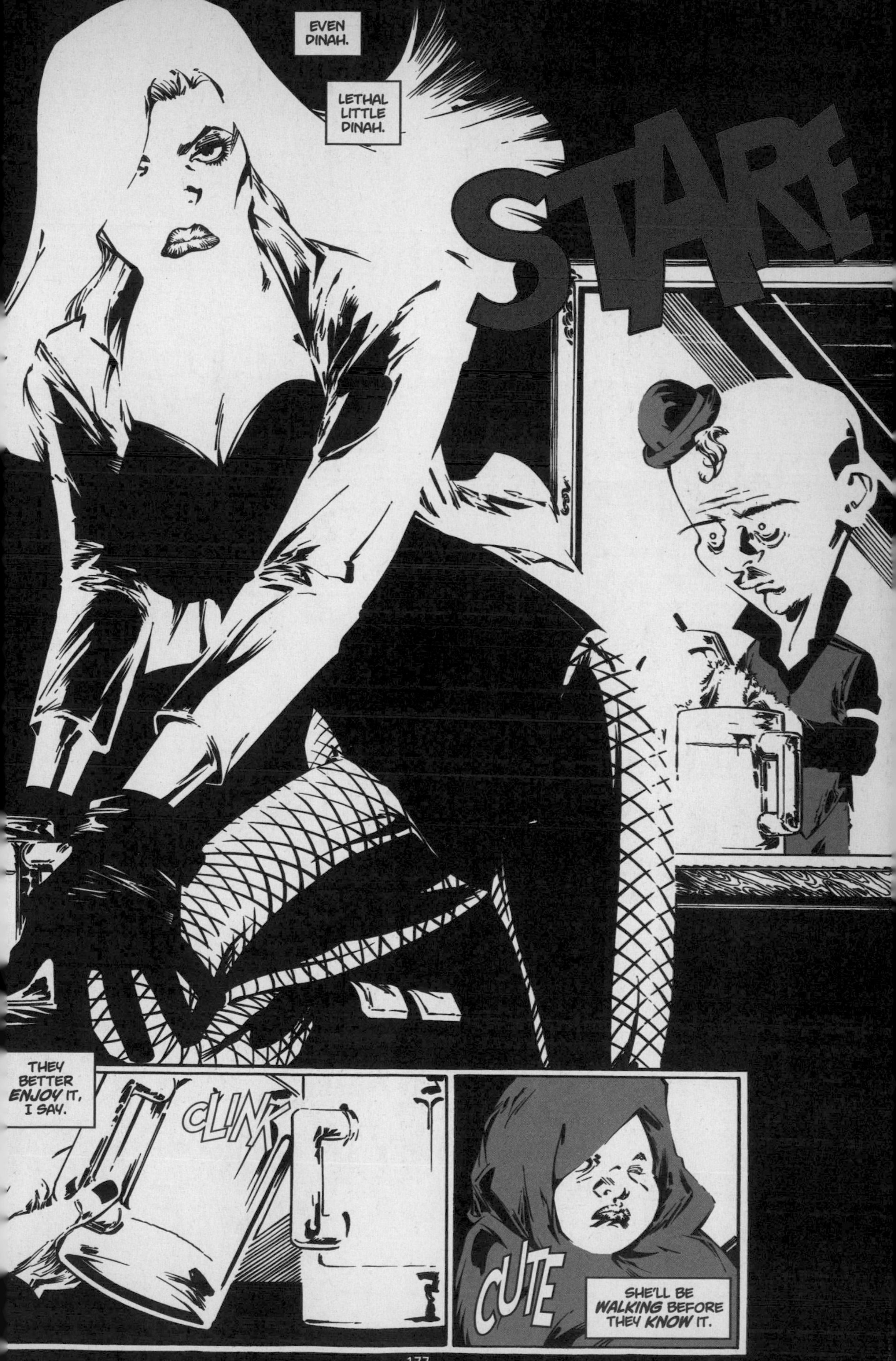
EVEN DINAH.
LETHAL LITTLE DINAH.
STARE
THEY BETTER ENJOY IT, I SAY.
CLINK
CUTE
SHE'LL BE WALKING BEFORE THEY KNOW IT.

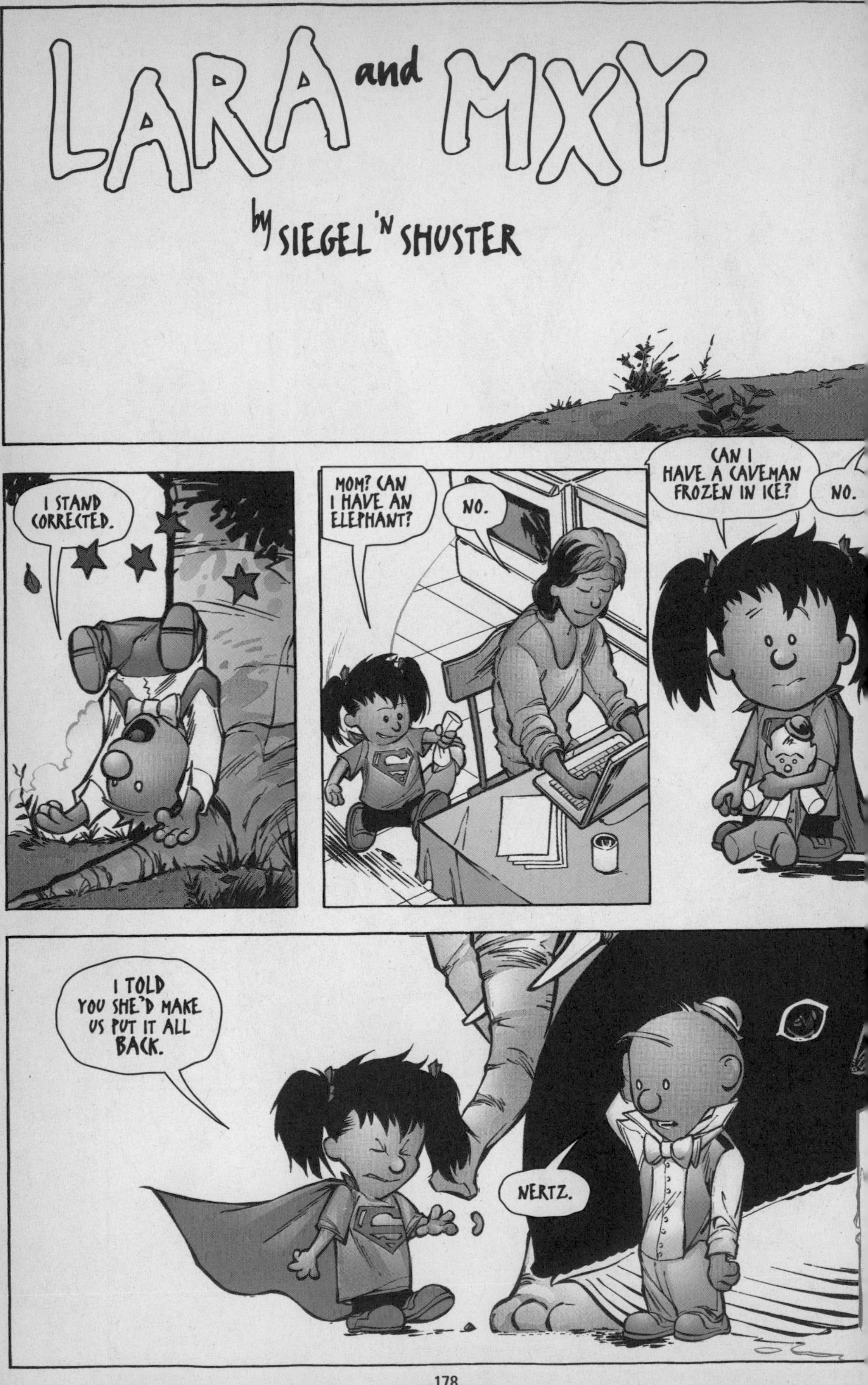
LARA and MXY
by SIEGEL 'N SHUSTER
I STAND CORRECTED.
MOM? CAN I HAVE AN ELEPHANT?
NO.
CAN I HAVE A CAVEMAN FROZEN IN ICE?
NO.
I TOLD YOU SHE'D MAKE US PUT IT ALL BACK.
NERTZ.

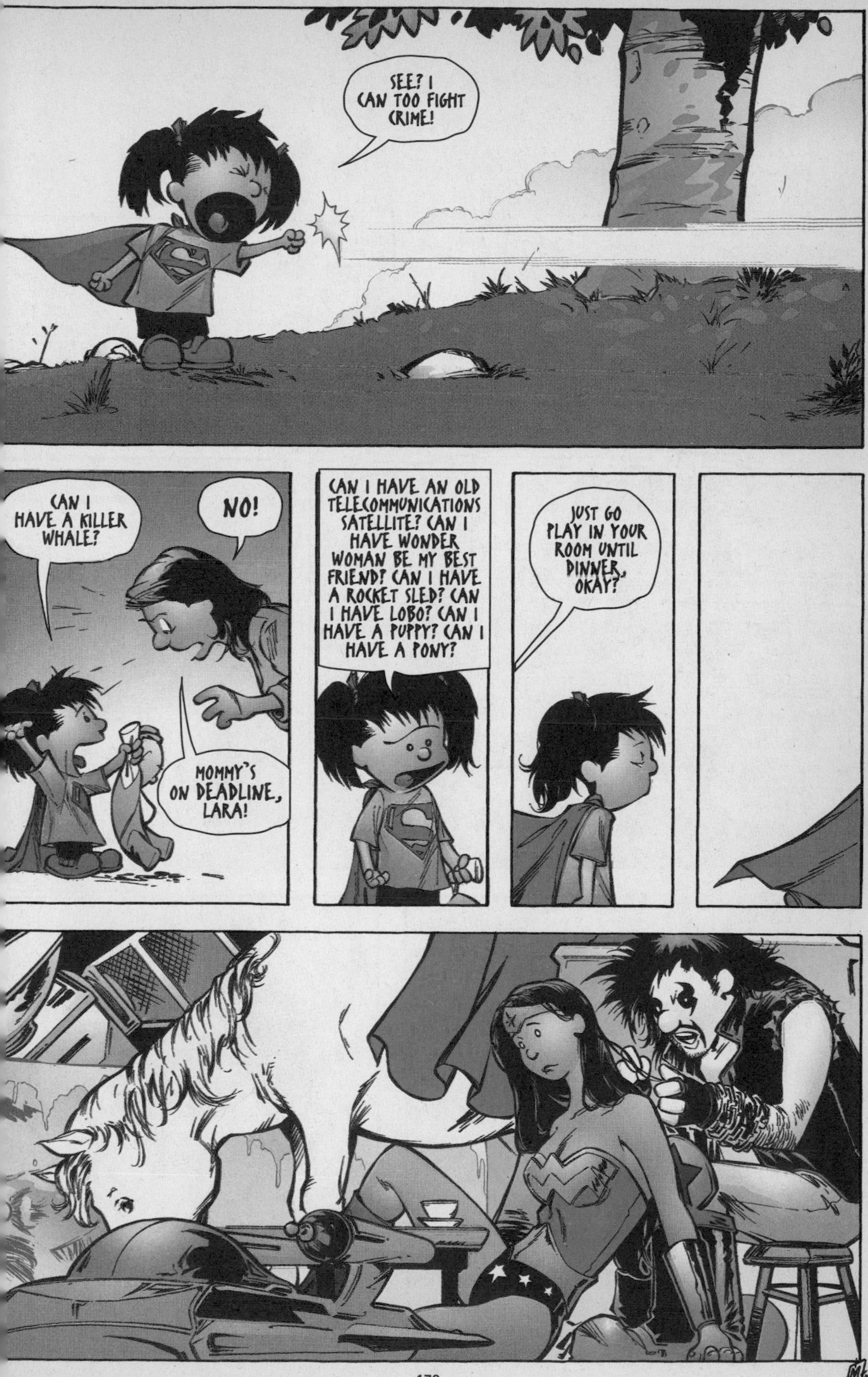
SEE? I CAN TOO FIGHT CRIME!
CAN I HAVE A KILLER WHALE?
NO!
MOMMY'S ON DEADLINE, LARA!
CAN I HAVE AN OLD TELECOMMUNICATIONS SATELLITE? CAN I HAVE WONDER WOMAN BE MY BEST FRIEND? CAN I HAVE A ROCKET SLED? CAN I HAVE LOBO? CAN I HAVE A PUPPY? CAN I HAVE A PONY?
JUST GO PLAY IN YOUR ROOM UNTIL DINNER, OKAY?

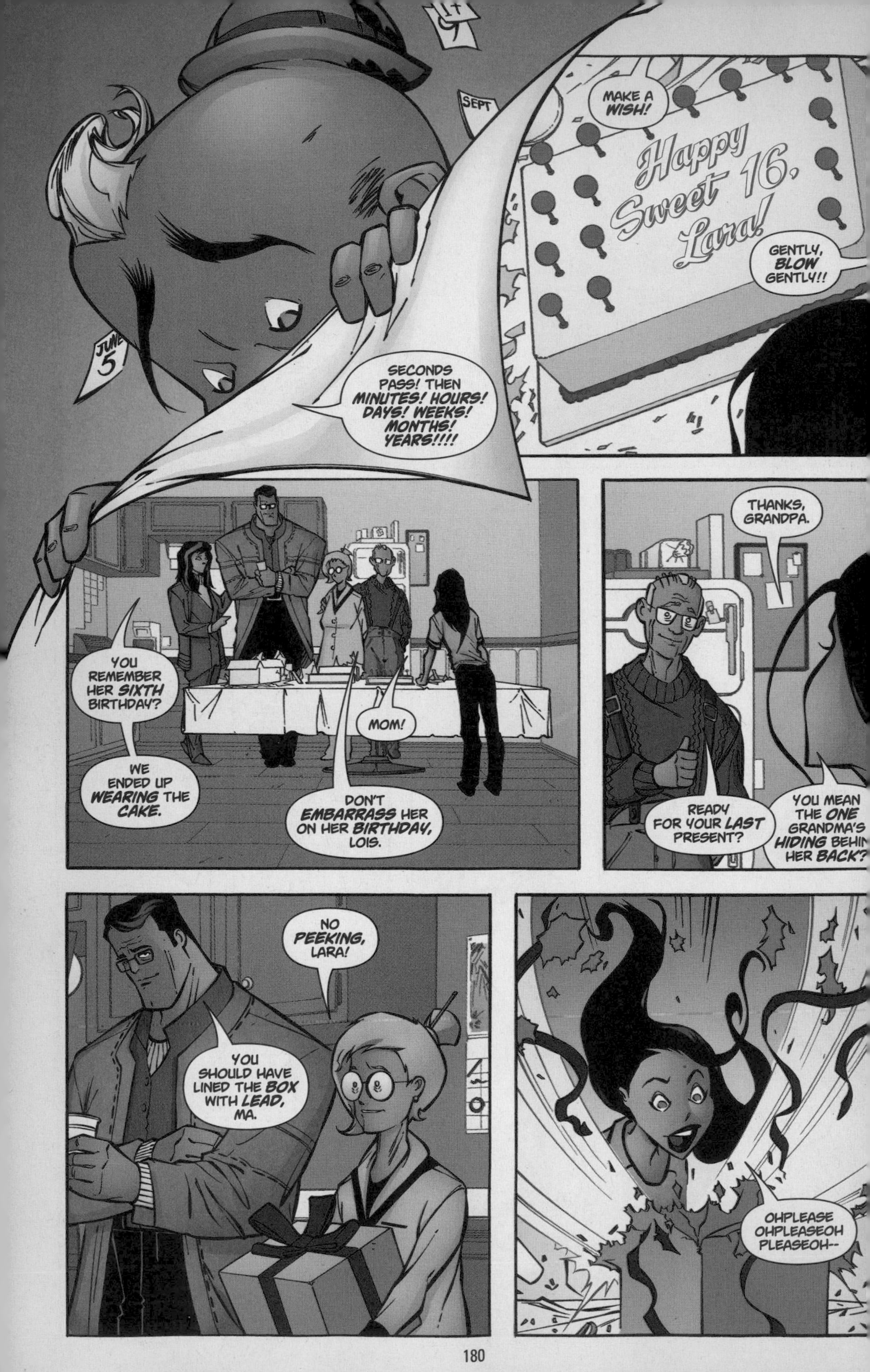
1ST
SEPT
JUNE 5
MAKE A WISH!
Happy Sweet 16, Lara!
GENTLY, BLOW GENTLY!!
SECONDS PASS! THEN MINUTES! HOURS! DAYS! WEEKS! MONTHS! YEARS!!!!
YOU REMEMBER HER SIXTH BIRTHDAY?
WE ENDED UP WEARING THE CAKE.
MOM!
DON'T EMBARRASS HER ON HER BIRTHDAY, LOIS.
THANKS, GRANDPA.
READY FOR YOUR LAST PRESENT?
YOU MEAN THE ONE GRANDMA'S HIDING BEHIN HER BACK?
NO PEEKING, LARA!
YOU SHOULD HAVE LINED THE BOX WITH LEAD, MA.
OHPLEASE OHPLEASEOH PLEASEOH--

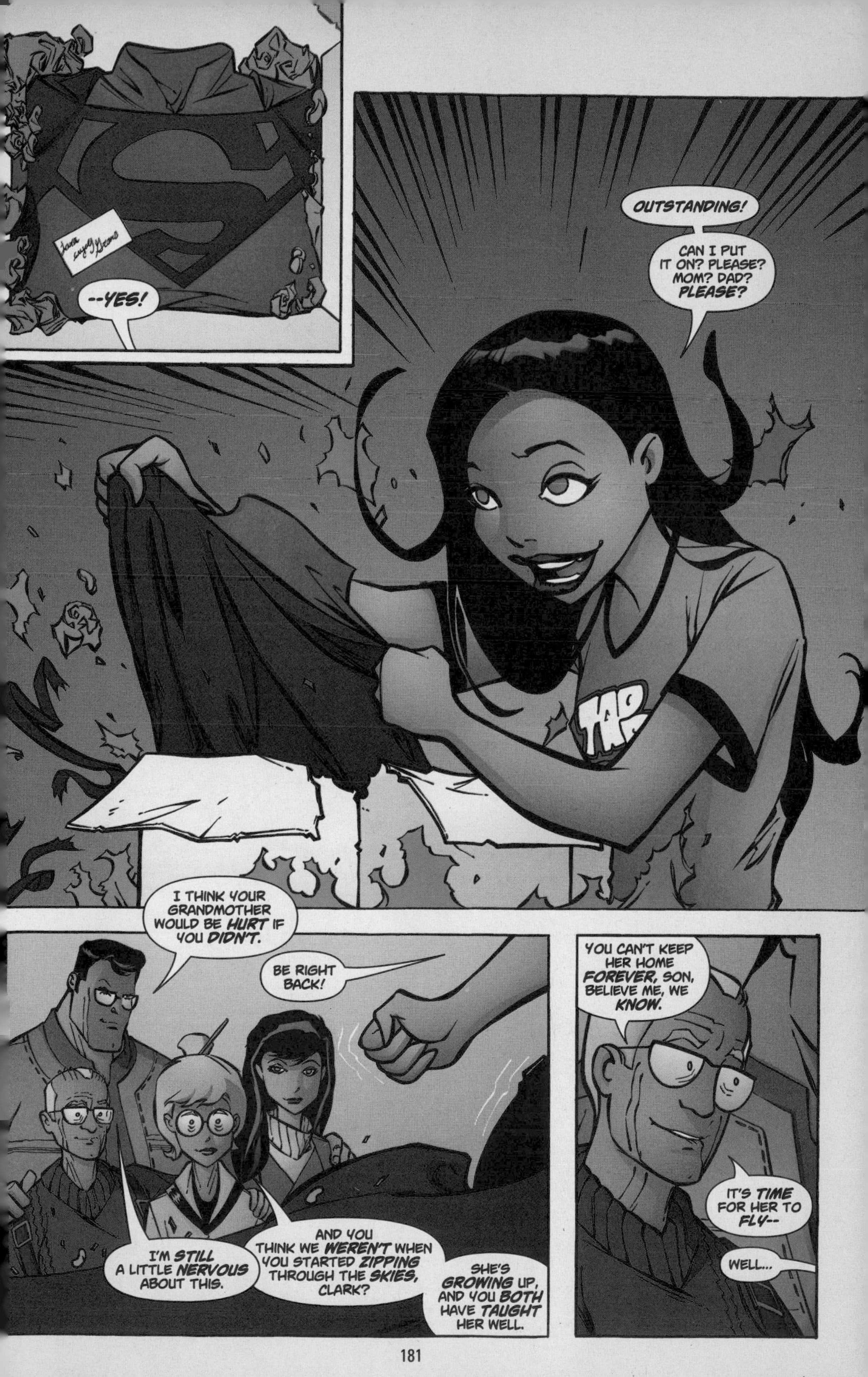
--YES!
OUTSTANDING!
CAN I PUT IT ON? PLEASE? MOM? DAD? PLEASE?
I THINK YOUR GRANDMOTHER WOULD BE HURT IF YOU DIDN'T.
BE RIGHT BACK!
I'M STILL A LITTLE NERVOUS ABOUT THIS.
AND YOU THINK WE WEREN'T WHEN YOU STARTED ZIPPING THROUGH THE SKIES, CLARK?
SHE'S GROWING UP, AND YOU BOTH HAVE TAUGHT HER WELL.
YOU CAN'T KEEP HER HOME FOREVER, SON, BELIEVE ME, WE KNOW.
IT'S TIME FOR HER TO FLY--
WELL...

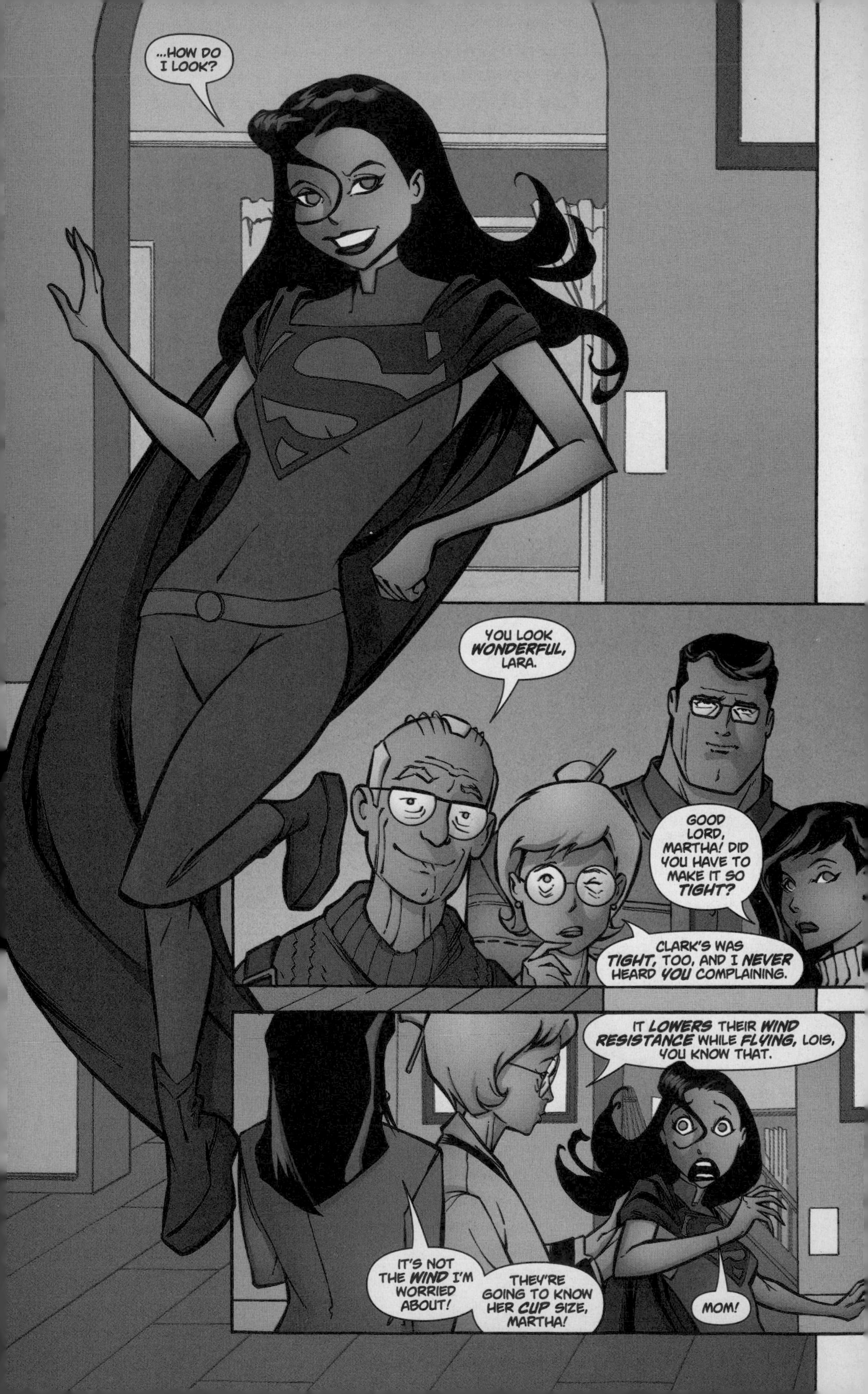
...HOW DO I LOOK?
YOU LOOK WONDERFUL, LARA.
GOOD LORD, MARTHA! DID YOU HAVE TO MAKE IT SO TIGHT?
CLARK'S WAS TIGHT, TOO, AND I NEVER HEARD YOU COMPLAINING.
IT LOWERS THEIR WIND RESISTANCE WHILE FLYING, LOIS, YOU KNOW THAT.
IT'S NOT THE WIND I'M WORRIED ABOUT!
THEY'RE GOING TO KNOW HER CUP SIZE, MARTHA!
MOM!

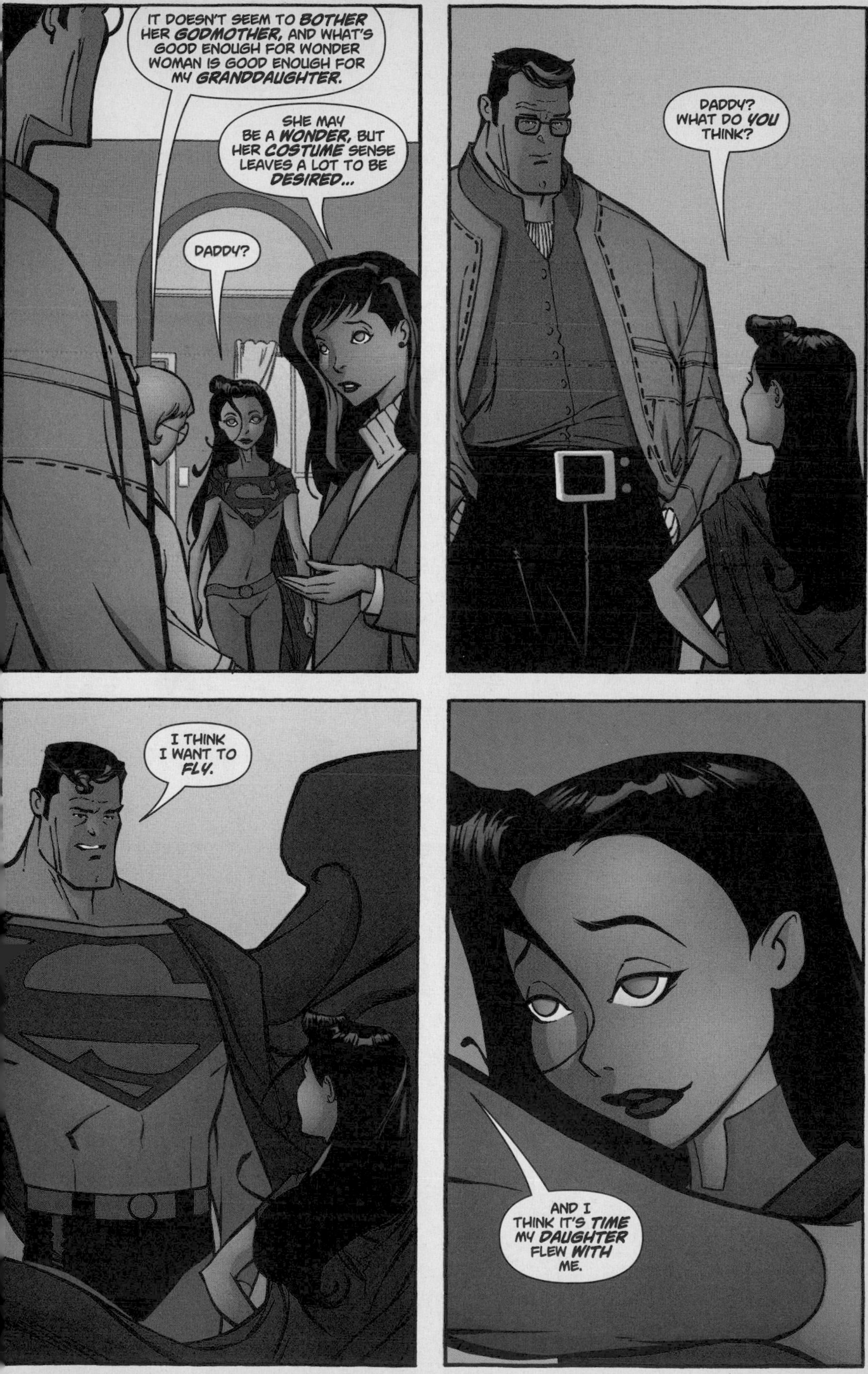
IT DOESN'T SEEM TO BOTHER HER GODMOTHER, AND WHAT'S GOOD ENOUGH FOR WONDER WOMAN IS GOOD ENOUGH FOR MY GRANDDAUGHTER.
SHE MAY BE A WONDER, BUT HER COSTUME SENSE LEAVES A LOT TO BE DESIRED...
DADDY?
DADDY? WHAT DO YOU THINK?
I THINK I WANT TO FLY.
AND I THINK IT'S TIME MY DAUGHTER FLEW WITH ME.

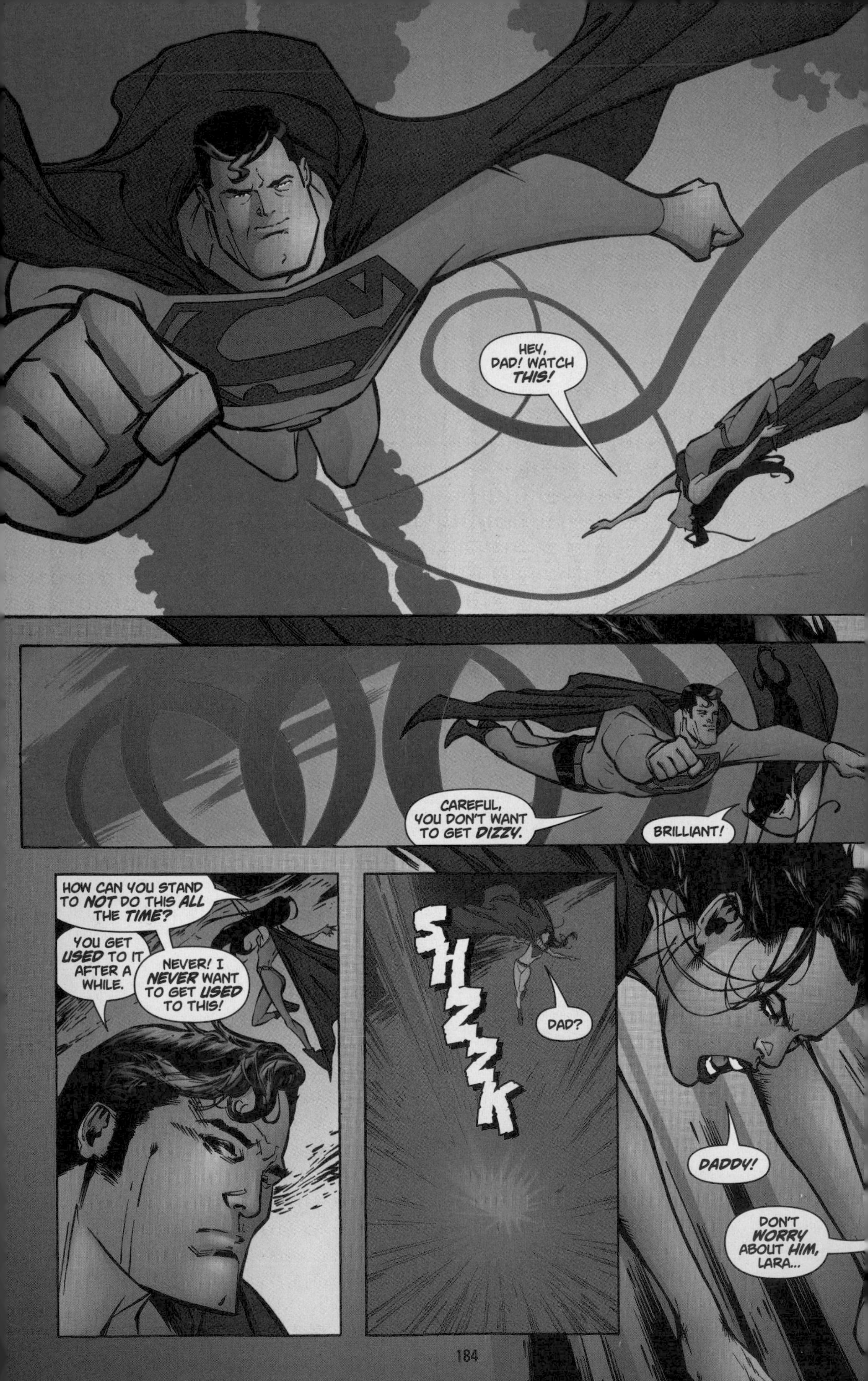
HEY, DAD! WATCH THIS!
CAREFUL, YOU DON'T WANT TO GET DIZZY.
BRILLIANT!
HOW CAN YOU STAND TO NOT DO THIS ALL THE TIME?
YOU GET USED TO IT AFTER A WHILE.
NEVER! I NEVER WANT TO GET USED TO THIS!
SHZZK
DAD?
DADDY!
DON'T WORRY ABOUT HIM, LARA...

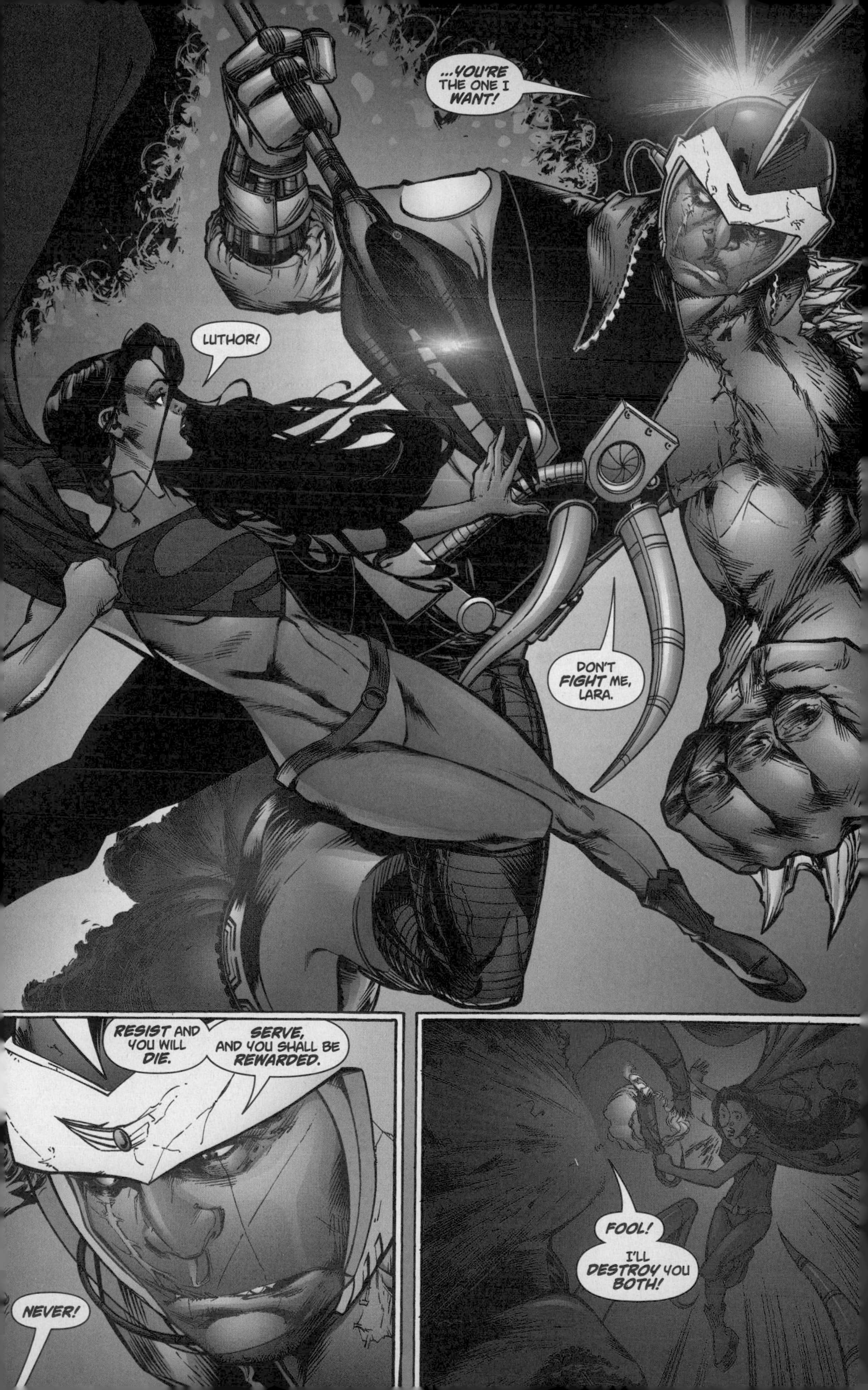
...YOU'RE THE ONE I WANT!
LUTHOR!
DON'T FIGHT ME, LARA.
RESIST AND YOU WILL DIE.
SERVE, AND YOU SHALL BE REWARDED.
NEVER!
FOOL! I'LL DESTROY YOU BOTH!

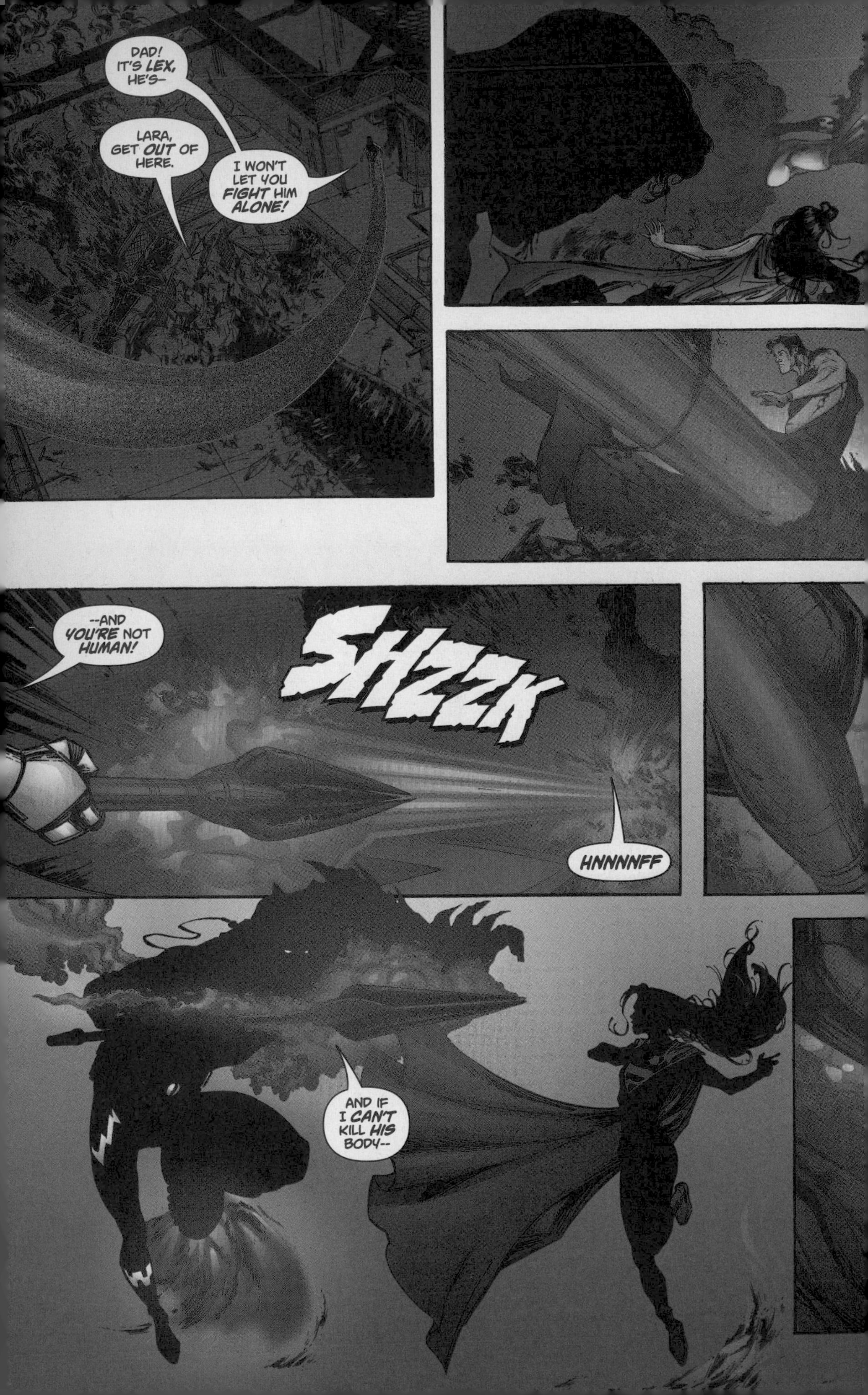
DAD! IT'S LEX, HE'S--
LARA, GET OUT OF HERE.
I WON'T LET YOU FIGHT HIM ALONE!
--AND YOU'RE NOT HUMAN!
SHZZK
HNNNNFF
AND IF I CAN'T KILL HIS BODY--

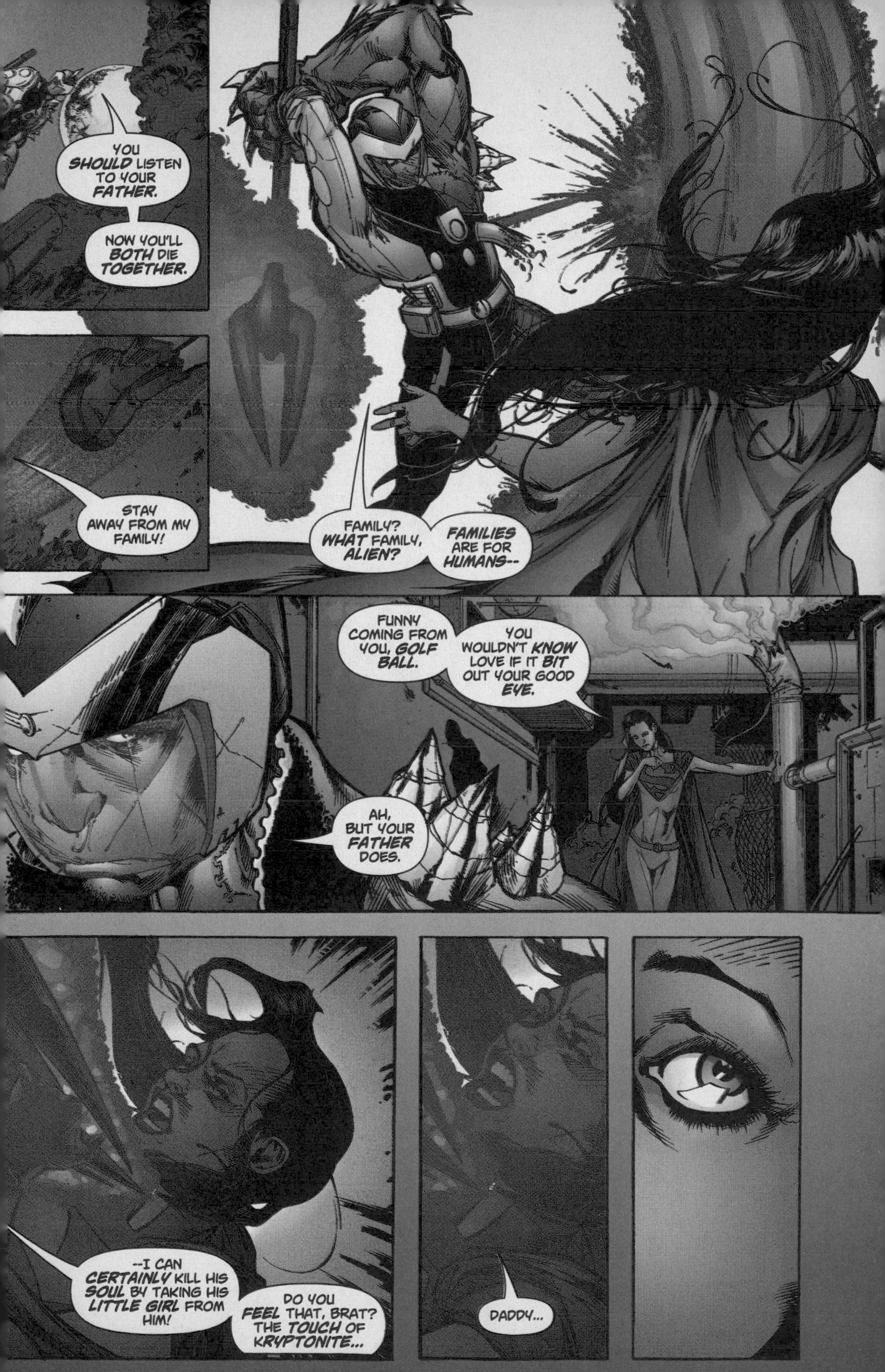
YOU SHOULD LISTEN TO YOUR FATHER.
NOW YOU'LL BOTH DIE TOGETHER.
STAY AWAY FROM MY FAMILY!
FAMILY? WHAT FAMILY, ALIEN?
FAMILIES ARE FOR HUMANS--
FUNNY COMING FROM YOU, GOLF BALL.
YOU WOULDN'T KNOW LOVE IF IT BIT OUT YOUR GOOD EYE.
AH, BUT YOUR FATHER DOES.
--I CAN CERTAINLY KILL HIS SOUL BY TAKING HIS LITTLE GIRL FROM HIM!
DO YOU FEEL THAT, BRAT? THE TOUCH OF KRYPTONITE...
DADDY...

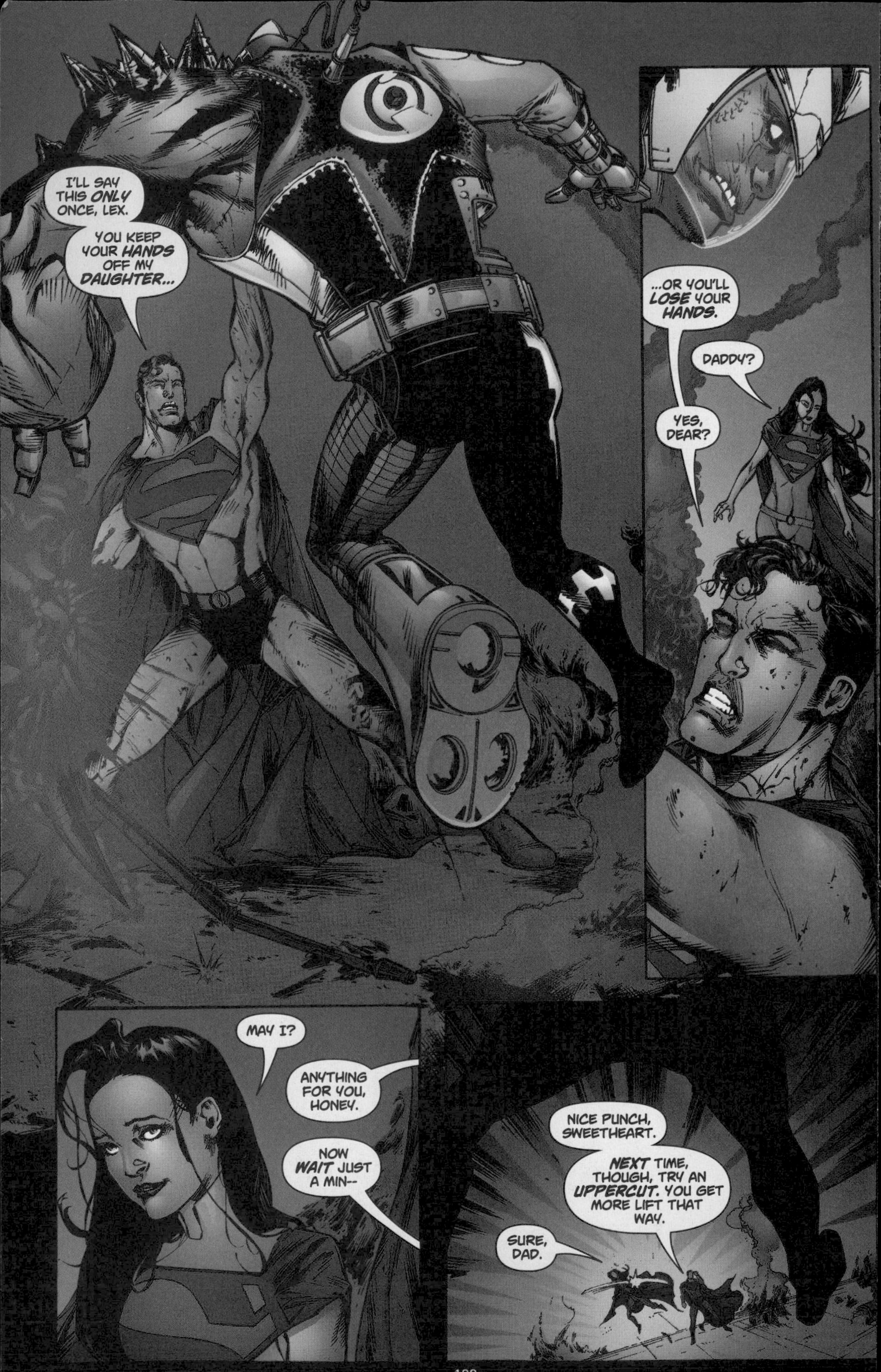

I'LL SAY THIS ONLY ONCE, LEX.
YOU KEEP YOUR HANDS OFF MY DAUGHTER...
...OR YOU'LL LOSE YOUR HANDS.
DADDY?
YES, DEAR?
MAY I?
ANYTHING FOR YOU, HONEY.
NOW WAIT JUST A MIN--
NICE PUNCH, SWEETHEART.
NEXT TIME, THOUGH, TRY AN UPPERCUT. YOU GET MORE LIFT THAT WAY.
SURE, DAD.

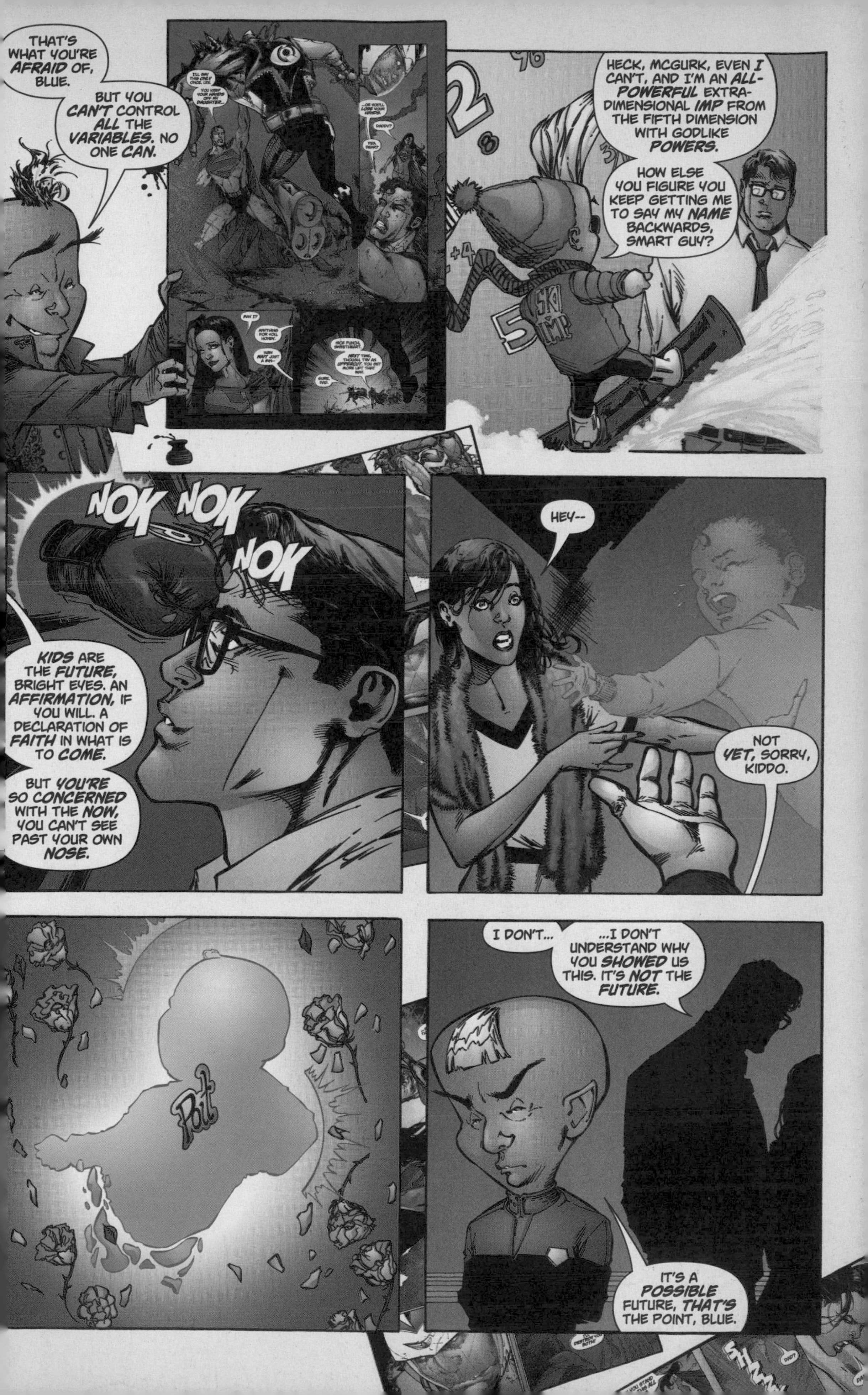
THAT'S WHAT YOU'RE AFRAID OF, BLUE.
BUT YOU CAN'T CONTROL ALL THE VARIABLES. NO ONE CAN.
HECK, MCGURK, EVEN I CAN'T, AND I'M AN ALL-POWERFUL EXTRA-DIMENSIONAL IMP FROM THE FIFTH DIMENSION WITH GODLIKE POWERS.
HOW ELSE YOU FIGURE YOU KEEP GETTING ME TO SAY MY NAME BACKWARDS, SMART GUY?
SKI IMP
NOK NOK NOK
KIDS ARE THE FUTURE, BRIGHT EYES. AN AFFIRMATION, IF YOU WILL. A DECLARATION OF FAITH IN WHAT IS TO COME.
BUT YOU'RE SO CONCERNED WITH THE NOW, YOU CAN'T SEE PAST YOUR OWN NOSE.
HEY--
NOT YET, SORRY, KIDDO.
Pot
I DON'T...
...I DON'T UNDERSTAND WHY YOU SHOWED US THIS. IT'S NOT THE FUTURE.
IT'S A POSSIBLE FUTURE, THAT'S THE POINT, BLUE.

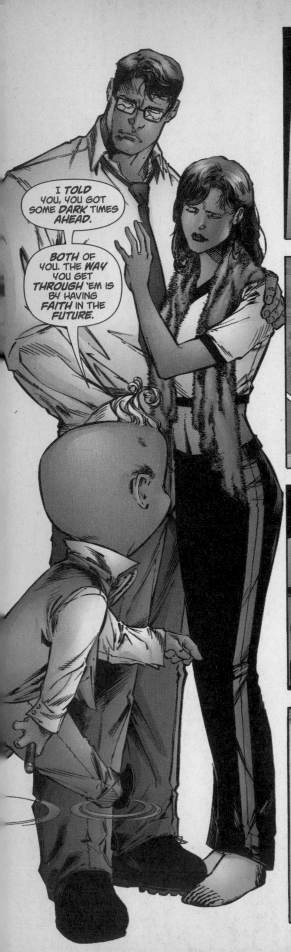

I *TOLD* YOU, YOU GOT SOME *DARK* TIMES AHEAD.

BOTH OF YOU. THE *WAY* YOU GET *THROUGH* 'EM IS BY HAVING *FAITH* IN THE FUTURE.

SHEESH. SUPERMAN *AND* WIFE.

EVERYTHING THAT HAPPENS, IT HAPPENS BECAUSE OF THE *TWO* OF YOU, Y'KNOW THAT?

LOVE, BABY. IT'S THE *MOST* POWERFUL THING IN *ANY* UNIVERSE.

WE LIVE IN HOPE.

SEE YA IN 90.

WE LIVE IN HOPE.

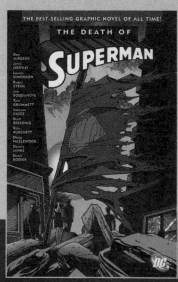